D1256171

THE CASE OF VALENTINE SHORTIS

Detention before Trial
Double Jeopardy
Courts and Trials: A Multi-Disciplinary Approach
Access to the Law
Cases and Materials on Criminal Law and Procedure
National Security: The Legal Dimensions
The Trials of Israel Lipski
A Century of Criminal Justice

MARTIN L. FRIEDLAND

THE CASE OF
VALENTINE
SHORTIS

A True Story of
Crime and Politics in Canada

UNIVERSITY OF TORONTO PRESS
Toronto Buffalo London

© University of Toronto Press 1986
Toronto   Buffalo   London
Printed in Canada
ISBN 0-8020-2606-0

Canadian Cataloguing in Publication Data

Friedland, M.L. (Martin Lawrence), 1932-
The case of Valentine Shortis

Includes index.
ISBN 0-8020-2606-0

1. Shortis, Valentine Francis Cuthbert, b. 1875? –
Trials, litigation, etc.   2. Trials (Murder) –
Canada – History.   3. Canada – Politics and
government – 1867-1896.*   I. Title.

KE228.S56F75 1986   345.71'02523   C86-093988-X

PICTURE CREDITS

Photographs were obtained from the following sources: Public Archives
Canada: Shortis on boat (Capital Case File, RG13, C-1, vol. 1486-7), Tupper
(PA25888), the Aberdeens (PA28026), Cabinet Room (PA8388), Bowell
(PA25851), Parliament Buildings (C36613), Laurier (C16741), St Vincent de Paul
Penitentiary (PA46233), King (C75053); Notman Photographic Archives, Mc-
Cord Museum, McGill University: Valleyfield, Macmaster, Greenshields, St
Pierre, Mathieu; Ontario Archives: Nursey; Liaison Magazine, Solicitor
General, Canada: Kingston Penitentiary; J.M. Neelands: Neelands and family;
C.R. Brown: Beall and friends.

Publication of this book has been assisted by the Canada Council and the
Ontario Arts Council under their block grant programs.

To Glanville Williams

Contents

Preface

THE 1895 TRIAL of Valentine Shortis for murder in Valleyfield, Quebec, was described at the time by the Montreal *Gazette* as 'the most remarkable that has ever taken place in Canada.' This book is about that trial – the longest then on record in Canada – and its aftermath. The case unfolded during some of the most dramatic events in Canadian political history: the Manitoba schools question; the cabinet revolt by the so-called 'nest of traitors'; and the 1896 election in which Sir Wilfrid Laurier swept Quebec and became the prime minister of Canada. The Shortis case played a role in that crucial election.

Like my earlier study, *The Trials of Israel Lipski*, this book relies heavily on archival material and newspaper reports. Unlike the Lipski case, however, which I came upon by accident, this manuscript was the result of deliberate and careful combing of the records in the Public Archives of Canada to find an interesting Canadian murder case with political ramifications that would again permit me to play the role of detective in reconstructing a case and placing it in its social, cultural, and political context. The Shortis case, I believe, provides a good vehicle for achieving that objective. Moreover, it allowed me to explore a number of aspects of the history of psychiatry and corrections in Canada. Like the Lipski study, nothing has been made up; all the facts, including conversations, have been derived from the extensive documentary materials available.

I was fortunate to have had excellent research assistance. Tim McCourt, now in his third year in the Faculty of Law, and Kent Roach, now in his second year, each spent a full summer working with me on the case. Gordon Cameron, Martin Hicks, and Steven Rosenhek, all recent law graduates, and Richard Owens, now in his second year, assisted me in collecting material in Canada and Britain. Expert secretarial assistance was provided by Joyce Kawano and Gerry Naunheimer. The research was supported by the Law School's Legal Theory and Public Policy Program, funded by the Connaught Fund of the University of Toronto, as well as by a grant from the Osgoode Society. Throughout my research, Dean Robert Prichard and his predecessors, Acting Dean Stanley Makuch and Dean Frank Iacobucci, encouraged my work and, more importantly, helped to create a stimulating environment for research activity at the Law School.

Many persons generously provided their valuable expertise in a number of the areas explored in the book, in some cases reading part or all of the manuscript. I am greatly indebted to the following historians for their advice – a who's who of many of the leading historians in Canada: John Beattie, Craig Brown, and Paul Rutherford of the University of Toronto; Father Paul Crunican of the Toronto School of Theology; John English of the University of Waterloo; Douglas Hay, Peter Oliver, and John Saywell of York University; and Peter Waite of Dalhousie University.

I am similarly indebted to Fred Lowy, the dean of the Faculty of Medicine at the University of Toronto; Vivian Rakoff, chairman of the Department of Psychiatry and head of the Clarke Institute of Psychiatry, University of Toronto; and Ronald Stokes, medical director, Mental Health Centre, Penetanguishene, for their help with the psychiatric aspects of the case; to Robert Clark and Douglas Collins of the Canadian Broadcasting Corporation, who generously gave me access to material they had collected on the case over fifteen years ago in preparation for a possible documentary film; to Cyril Greenland, now of the Centre of Criminology at the University of Toronto, who published an article on the psychiatric aspects of the case over twenty years ago and made available to me the important collection of materials on the history of psychiatry assembled by him and J.D. Griffin, and kept at the Queen Street Mental Health Centre; to Jack Robson, Department of English, University of Toronto, for his incisive comments; to Edward L. Greenspan, Brendan O'Brien, and Clayton Ruby for their expert insights into the case; to my colleagues at the Law School for their valuable comments on the manuscript, in particular Professors Bernard Dickens, R.C.B. Risk, Robert Sharpe, Stephen Waddams; and to Gerry Hallowell, a skilled editor at the University of Toronto Press.

A very large number of archivists and librarians assisted me in obtaining material. I am particularly grateful to the always helpful staff of the following institutions: the Public Archives of Canada, Ottawa; the Ontario Archives, Toronto; Archives Nationales du Québec, Ste-Foy, Quebec; Palais de Justice, Valleyfield; the Public Record Office, London; the Robarts Library, University of Toronto, including the Government Documents, Inter-Library Loan, Microfilm, and Reference sections; the Thomas Fisher Rare Book Library; the Faculty of Law Library; the Centre of Criminology Library; the Clarke Institute of Psychiatry Library; the Great Library, Osgoode Hall; the Lionel Groulx Institute, Montreal; the Metropolitan Toronto Reference Library; the Osler Medical Library, Toronto; the Queen Street Mental Health Centre Library; the Solicitor-General's Library, Ottawa; the University of British Columbia Library; the University of Saskatchewan Law Library; the University of Western Ontario Library; the Valleyfield Public Library; and the Notman Photographic Archives, McCord Museum, Montreal. The Notman Archives contains a marvellous storehouse of pictures and I am indebted to its curator, Stanley G. Triggs, for his kind assistance in helping me obtain photographs.

An early version of the story was presented in March 1984 as the first Culliton Lecture at the University of Saskatchewan Law School. That stimulating visit helped me to formulate ideas on how to present the case. I also benefited from the discussion following the presentation of the case at the seventy-fifth anniversary meeting of the Parole Board in Ontario.

To all of the above persons and institutions I offer my sincere thanks. Finally, I would like to express my gratitude to my family for their valuable comments on the manuscript and for their constant encouragement and support.

MARTIN L. FRIEDLAND
Faculty of Law
University of Toronto

Valentine Shortis (marked with an 'X') on board the *S.S. Laurentian*, coming to
Canada, September 1893

THE CASE OF VALENTINE SHORTIS

Valleyfield, Quebec, c. 1900, showing the Beauharnois Canal and the Montreal Cotton Company

1

Tragedy at Valleyfield

FRANCIS VALENTINE CUTHBERT SHORTIS was born in Waterford, Ireland, on St Valentine's Day 1875.

Valentine, as he was called by his family, was the only child of exceptionally wealthy parents. His father was one of the leading cattle dealers in the south of Ireland, exporting to the British mainland a million dollars worth of livestock each year. His mother had had a number of miscarriages before her son was born and was extremely devoted to him. Valentine had difficulty at school and later in learning his father's business. Many thought his mother was spoiling him with too much care and attention. Against her wishes, Francis Shortis decided that his son would have to learn to stand on his own two feet abroad. Letters of introduction were obtained, from the Roman Catholic bishop of Waterford and from a major importer in Liverpool, among others.

In September 1893, at the age of eighteen, Valentine sailed alone to Montreal. His mother, Mary Shortis, had accompanied him to Liverpool to see him on his way. Passengers on the *S.S. Laurentian* observed that the young man wept bitterly and was depressed for days.

On arriving in Montreal, Shortis rented a room in the commercial district and attempted to develop an agency for bicycles. People later said that he was always talking about bicycles – and guns. He wrote away for catalogues, but did little else, drifting from one scheme to another. A little under a year after he arrived, his mother came over for about a month to help him get established. She arranged a job for him without pay at the Globe Woollen Mills, and then returned to Ireland. Friends in Montreal advised her to take her son back home, but she knew it was out of the question, for her husband wanted him to remain in Canada.

Louis Simpson, the general manager of the Montreal Cotton Company in Valleyfield, had been looking for a private secretary and he hired Shortis for a two-month trial period.

Valleyfield is an island in the St Lawrence River about thirty miles west of Montreal. The Montreal Cotton Company was then, and still is now (under the name Domtex), the island's main industry; it is located in Salaberry de Valleyfield, usually simply referred to as Valleyfield, a town with a population in the 1890s of about ten thousand.[1] The plant owed its success to a number of factors: abundant water power, good transportation through the Beauharnois Canal, a large supply of labour, and a very favourable tariff policy. Sir John A. Macdonald's Conservative government had introduced the so-called 'National Policy' in 1879, a scheme that protected industries such as the Montreal Cotton Company from American competition.[2] The import duty on finished cotton was about 30 per cent, and there was no duty on raw cotton or on the machines that produced finished cotton. (In the summer of 1985 the company announced it would be closing its Valleyfield plant because of what it described as the 'continuing deterioration of business conditions in Canada' and the 'nearly unprecedented' high level of cheap imported garments;[3] whether the government will step in to prevent the closure remains to be seen.) Valleyfield supported the protective policy of the Conservative administration rather than the 'free trade' ideas of the Liberal opposition under Wilfrid Laurier. Though the town was mainly French, there were large pockets of English-speaking residents in nearby areas such as Huntingdon.[4]

The plant manager, Louis Simpson, did not keep Shortis as his assistant longer than the trial two months. He was not impressed with his work and, moreover, wanted someone who could take shorthand. Shortis was allowed to remain in the plant, however, without pay, in order to learn the cotton business. But this privilege was terminated at the end of December 1894.

Simpson had been unhappy about Shortis' association with Miss Millie Anderson and he had warned him that he should break off relations with her. Millie was the daughter of the late Alexandre Anderson, an industrialist and former mayor of Valleyfield. Her mother, who had subsequently remarried, was not on good terms with Simpson over some business dealings relating to the Anderson foundry; it seems the manager had taken the cotton mill's business away from the Anderson family. Shortis had refused to stop seeing Millie or her younger brother, Jack. On Friday, 1 March 1895, he spent the evening at the

Anderson home, leaving at about ten o'clock. Shortly thereafter, he knocked on the door of the cotton mill office.

On Saturday, 2 March 1895, Mr and Mrs Shortis received a cable at their home in Waterford, Ireland, from A.F. Gault, the president of the Montreal Cotton Company. 'Your son,' he said, 'must be crazy. He has badly wounded three men, and perhaps fatally too.' The Shortises had not heard from Valentine for almost two months, although previously he had been a good correspondent. His twentieth birthday had passed on 14 February without a note from him. Anxiety was mixed with guilt for having abandoned him to make his own way in the New World. In early January he had asked for more money and his mother had deliberately lied to him: 'My boy, we are on our last legs financially and you must look out for yourself.' In fact, Francis Shortis was worth well over a quarter of a million dollars.

There was no 'perhaps' about the tragedy. At the time the cable was sent, two men were dead and a third was dying. The crime had taken place on Friday evening in the business offices of the Montreal Cotton Company. It was headlined in the Saturday morning papers. 'Never in the world's annals of crime,' declared the Montreal *Herald*, 'has a more cold-blooded and evidently premeditated double murder been perpetrated than that which startled the people of [Valleyfield] this morning.'

Every other Friday the cotton company received a large shipment of money from Montreal for distribution to the employees the next Monday. On Friday evening, 1 March, four employees were placing the $12,000 into pay packets, when at about ten o'clock Valentine Shortis knocked on the office door. They all knew him; he was let in and sat chatting and eating an apple. A loaded revolver was kept in a drawer. Shortis asked to look at it. John Lowe, the man in charge, said no. Shortis insisted; he wanted to check the serial number, he said. Lowe took the shells out and handed him the gun; he cleaned it and gave it back. The shells were replaced by Lowe. The men continued talking and sorting the money.

As the men started to move the money into the safe, Shortis grabbed the gun from the drawer and fired point-blank at Hugh Wilson. Young John Loy ran for the telephone to call the doctor. Shortis fired at him: a bullet entered his brain and he fell dead. More shots were fired.

Lowe, the paymaster, scooped up the money and with the fourth man, Arthur Leboeuf, ran into the vault, closing the door behind them. They held it shut by hand. 'For God's sake, come out, John,' shouted Shortis, 'Hughie Wilson is dying.' Lowe yelled back: 'I can't get out; the door is fast. Turn the combination knob and let us out.' Shortis did so, but instead of opening the vault, it locked – as Lowe knew it would.

Wilson, badly wounded, crawled out of the office into the dark factory. Shortis followed him, striking matches to trace the trail of blood on the cement floor. He found him at the far end of the factory and shot him in the head.

Shortis returned to the two men in the vault. He lit a fire and tried to smoke them out. Around midnight the night watchman, Maxime Leboeuf, whose brother was in the vault, came on his normal rounds. He was shot and killed.

Wilson, in the darkness of the factory, was not in fact dead. Miraculously, he was able to crawl to the engine room to raise the alarm. Dr Walter Sutherland was called; he attended to Wilson, then armed with an iron bar and in the company of another workman he confronted Shortis, who immediately surrendered: 'I will give up; here's the revolver.' He was tied up and a constable was called. In searching him they found a large chisel and a loaded .22 calibre revolver inside his shirt. The secretary-treasurer of the company, the only one with the combination to the vault, arrived. 'So you are the thing that did that,' he said to Shortis. 'I'm the man, shoot me.' 'Oh no, we will do better than that for you,' the official snapped back. Shortis was taken to the Valleyfield police station, lodged in a cell, and charged with two murders.

Some of these details were cabled to the Shortises by a business friend in Montreal, George Bury. Mr Shortis instructed Bury to do the best he could for his son, and then cabled Valentine: 'May the pardon and mercy of God be given my poor boy. I am coming.'

Insanity could be the only possible defence. A cable sent from Liverpool to another Montreal businessman was widely quoted in all the Quebec papers: 'Insanity both sides of the Shortis family. Object could not be robbery; family independent and kept him supplied with money.'

The townspeople, however, were certain that the motive had been robbery. Shortis, they thought, was eccentric, but not insane. His clothes attracted attention – he wore a red sash aroung his waist – but such dress was often seen on stylish English travellers. They knew he carried guns and would occasionally use them: three months earlier he had been fined five dollars by a justice of the peace for firing at two millworkers he thought were talking too loudly – revolvers in each hand, Western style, had been fired simultaneously. Many people also thought that Millie Anderson and her young brother, Jack, may well have been accomplices, intending to provide an alibi after the robbery. A month earlier, Shortis and Jack Anderson had apparently conspired to kill Louis Simpson, the manager of the mill; but the Andersons' stepfather, Bob McGuiness, had intervened and warned Simpson, who told Shortis that if he did not leave Valleyfield he would be charged with conspiracy to murder. Shortis, it was thought, had waited to get even with Simpson for refusing to provide him with a reference and for accusing him of plotting against Simpson. 'Every dog has its day; it will be my turn next,' had been Shortis' final words to the plant manager. The money, people in the town thought, would be used by Shortis to go west with his girlfriend, Millie Anderson.

The morning after the murders Shortis sent the following letter to Millie: 'Telephone home, anticere. Do not fret. If Bob [McGuiness, the stepfather] gives any dirty talk you tell him to mind his own business, or I will make it bad for him. Send Jack to me immediately. I remain, yours lovingly, B. Shortis.' She answered: 'My dear Bertie. Keep up heart. All will come right soon. I will always be true. Your own Millie.'

Shortis told the press reporters that he would always love Millie Anderson.

This was the first murder charge brought in Valleyfield since 1872, when a strike leader had been killed during the construction of the cotton mill. The man then charged had been acquitted.[5] Compared to the United States, where the murder rate was over ten times as high, there were very few murders in Canada. There were then only a couple of dozen murder charges each year and relatively few convictions. In 1894, for example, only eight persons across Canada had been convicted of murder, and none was from Quebec. There had not been a hanging in the province since 1890.[6]

On Saturday morning the coroner, J.A. Demers, wired the attorney-general of Quebec in Quebec City: 'Murder at Valleyfield. Three men shot at. Two dead. One dying. Will I get advocate?'

Attorney-General T.C. Casgrain, an experienced trial lawyer who had been one of the Crown prosecutors in the Louis Riel case in 1885, wired Donald Macmaster, QC, one of the leading lawyers in Montreal: 'Reported Murder at Valleyfield. Please attend inquest held by Coroner Demers.' Macmaster replied immediately: 'Telegram received. Leaving by 5 o'clock train for Coteau [on the north shore of the St Lawrence River] and will there cross river for Valleyfield tonight.' At that time it took at least three hours to travel from Montreal to Valleyfield; within a year, the New York Central system would reduce the travel time to forty-five minutes.

Macmaster was a brilliant lawyer. A gold medallist at McGill University in 1871, he had gone on to prosecute or defend in some of the major cases of the past two decades. Moreover, he was a well-known Conservative, having been a member of the Ontario legislature in the early 1880s and then a member of the House of Commons in Ottawa until he was defeated in 1887. (Many years later, from 1910 to 1921, he was elected as a Conservative member of the British House of Commons.) A number of ridings wanted him to run in the pending Dominion election; indeed, some wanted him to become leader of the party.[7] The Conservative government in Quebec had often used Macmaster as a special prosecutor and therefore it is not surprising that Casgrain turned to him on this occasion.

Macmaster arrived in Valleyfield Saturday evening at eight o'clock. The coroner and the seventeen-man coroner's jury were waiting for him in the town hall. The inquest had started at noon and was adjourned to permit the doctors to examine the bodies, which were then taken by hearse, followed by hundreds of fellow workers, to their family homes. The doctors reported that Loy and Leboeuf had died from bullet wounds, that the single bullet in Loy's body had come from the cotton mill's gun, and that the three bullets in Leboeuf (two in the head and one in the body) matched Shortis' concealed gun.

John Lowe and the other employee who had escaped into the vault gave full accounts of what had taken place. The doctors repeated their evidence. Shortis was asked if he had any questions to put or anything to say. 'I have got a telegram from a friend of mine in Montreal, and he advises me not to say anything till I again hear from him,' he replied, adding: 'If you don't mind gentlemen, it would perhaps make no difference if I was handcuffed in front. The way my hands are now fastened behind my back hurts me considerably.'

The change was made. The newspapers noted Shortis' lack of concern. The Montreal *Herald* stated that he 'went through the evening with a coolness that was simply remarkable. He showed no signs whatever of any fear of the result of his crime or sorrow that he had committed it.' The paper also noted that he sat with a surly expression on his face, his fur collar turned up around his ears, and his face tucked well into it; over and over again he murmured, 'all damned fools.' He was, however, happy to talk to reporters. The man from the *Herald* asked:

'Did you try to make your escape after the murders?'
    'No. I did not. I did not care about escaping. I was waiting for the police.'
    'Did you realize your position?'
    'I did not. Neither do I realize it now. It seems to me like a horrible nightmare, from which I never expect to wake. I can absolutely realize nothing.'
    'Have you a defence? What are you going to do?'
    'I've done too much already, as for my defence that will be left in the hands of my solicitor. I would rather not say anything about that just now. I hope you will not think me discourteous, because anything in the world I can do for you I shall be only too happy. By the way, you might send me the papers. I would be glad to get them, and you can't buy any in this town.'

The papers all commented on Shortis' fine appearance. 'He stands about six feet in height, has a budding moustache and a lot of yellow hair, and looks for all the world like a typical young Englishman,' reported the Montreal *Gazette*. 'He was dressed in tourist style, Scotch tweed suit, knickerbockers and heavy ribbed stockings. His overcoat was a handsome dark beaver.'

Just before the coroner's jury retired at 11:30 in the evening, Shortis complained that he did not have a lawyer: 'You have been very courteous and very kind to me, all of you gentlemen, in fact; but still the fact remains that I have no one to speak for me.' Macmaster assured him there would be plenty of opportunity for him to be defended by counsel at the preliminary inquiry. At five minutes before midnight, the jury returned with their verdict. It was a foregone conclusion: 'that Maxime Leboeuf and John Loy came to their death at Valleyfield on the night of March 1st at the hands of Bertie F.V. Shortis.' The accused was taken to his cell by two constables with an eight-man body-guard.

The preliminary inquiry was to start Monday. Macmaster went with the witnesses to the scene of the crime, and in the early hours of Sunday morning went over their evidence in detail. He was appalled by the scene, which he described in a letter to the attorney-general: 'It was the most shocking sight I ever saw, and I have never heard or read anything that equalled the brutality and disregard of life exhibited by the accused.' This initial impression remained with Macmaster throughout the subsequent proceedings.

George Bury, the Montreal businessman who was a friend of the Shortis family, engaged Henri St Pierre to attend the preliminary hearing. Shortis had expressed a preference for a particular Beauharnois lawyer, but Bury had cabled him: 'You must leave the matter in our hands.' St Pierre later wrote that he had been at home reading about the case in the Saturday evening papers, sympathizing with the victims, when the message arrived from Bury asking him to take on the case.

The fifty-year-old St Pierre was an outstanding criminal lawyer, 'probably the leading criminal lawyer of the Province,' said the Toronto *Mail*; 'few equals and no superior in his native province,' said a contemporary biographical sketch.[8] He had defended dozens of murderers and to this point had lost no client to the gallows. He had a fascinating background. His father had been a 'Patriote' in the 1837 rebellion and his mother traced her origins back to French settlements in the 1600s. St Pierre had been a classical student and classmate of Louis Riel's at the Collège de Montréal. When the American Civil War broke out, he sought his parents' permission to join the Northern forces but this was refused, and he dutifully went to study law at Kingston in Ontario, where he would also improve his English. On his first trip to Toronto for his preliminary examination at Osgoode Hall, he continued on to New York and enlisted in the New York Volunteers. At the Battle of Mine Run, near Fredericksburg, Virginia, he was wounded and taken prisoner, but was eventually released in the spring of 1865. He had been thought dead – indeed, funeral services had been held for him in Quebec – so his reappearance was considered miraculous. Needless to say, his English was now excellent, though some detected a slight Southern accent.

Bury and St Pierre arrived in Valleyfield early Monday morning. The preliminary hearing had been formally opened by Magistrate J. Madden at the mill office; it had then quickly been adjourned till later in the day at the town hall, because the funerals of the two victims were about to take place.

St Pierre met for an hour with Shortis and announced to the waiting press that the accused 'isn't morally responsible.'

Maxime Leboeuf left a widow and five young children, who would now have to survive on the $1,000 insurance policy paid on his death. The funeral, which was paid for by the Montreal Cotton Company, was conducted by the well-known Bishop J.M. Emard at nine o'clock in the morning. By eight o'clock, four thousand persons had filled the Valleyfield cathedral. Two thousand later accompanied the procession in a blinding snowstorm to the Roman Catholic cemetery a mile away.

John Loy's funeral – 'one of the largest ever known in this part of the country,' reported the *Herald* – took place in the early afternoon in the Presbyterian church. The Loys were prominent citizens. John Loy's grandfather, who was Portuguese, was a doctor in the district and his father was the mayor of Valleyfield. The deceased had been very popular: the English-language Huntingdon *Gleaner* called him 'the most exemplary English speaking young man in Valleyfield'; 'had you searched the country over,' said the French-language *Progrès de Valleyfield*, 'one could not have met with anyone nicer.' The townspeople were united in their grief. 'The dead were beloved by all,' noted the Montreal *Star*; 'French and English, Catholics and Protestants all joined in the common grief. Race or religious distinctions were forgotten in the common mourning.'

These distinctions, however, were not forgotten in other parts of Canada. While the Shortis affair was unfolding, the larger political drama known as the Manitoba schools question was coming to a head. That very morning – and this would perhaps explain why no cabinet ministers attended the funerals – Prime Minister Mackenzie Bowell's cabinet was meeting in public session in the Railway Committee Room of the House of Commons to hear representations on whether the Dominion government should pass what was referred to as 'remedial legislation' to force Manitoba to revoke its 1890 legislation limiting the rights of Roman Catholics to have their own schools. Several months earlier the Privy Council had ruled that although the provincial legislation was not contrary to the British North America Act the Dominion could legislate to force Manitoba once again to provide public funding for separate schools. John Ewart, the Winnipeg lawyer, was appearing for the Catholic minority that Monday morning in Ottawa, pleading 'That justice be done though the Heavens fall.'[9]

The preliminary hearing on the charges against Shortis recommenced at three o'clock in the afternoon and was over by 6:30. St Pierre took little part in the proceedings, one paper describing him as an 'interested but unobtrusive spectator.' Once again the paymaster, John

Lowe, was the principal witness. He looked the accused in the face for half a minute before giving his evidence, but Shortis continued to gaze at the ceiling with a look of utter disgust. At one point the magistrate was concerned about Shortis' indifference: 'The prisoner does not seem to pay the slightest attention to the charges. He had better be reminded.' Shortis was asked if he had anything to say, but St Pierre quickly interjected: 'Enter a plea of not guilty.' 'Do you want to call any witnesses?' asked Macmaster. 'Not at this examination,' replied St Pierre. The magistrate committed Shortis for trial at the Beauharnois assizes on two counts of murder and one of attempted murder. The crowd in the town hall began to shout 'Lynch him!' 'Kill him!' but fortunately the disturbance was quelled: Macmaster appealed to the crowd to respect the law and Magistrate Madden ordered the courtroom to be cleared. Shortis shook his manacled hands: 'Damned mobs. There isn't one of them dare touch me. I'm not afraid of them.'

Outside in the square there were over a thousand men and women – Macmaster estimated a crowd of fifteen hundred. A piercing wind blew the snow into high drifts. As Shortis and his guards started across the square there were cries of 'Tuez, Tuez!' 'Kill him!' 'Hang him!' Someone pointed to a gateway with a high cross beam: 'Hang him there!' 'There was a great deal of pent up indignation and all the crowd needed was a leader to strike the first blow or to commence the lynching,' Macmaster later reported to the attorney-general. 'If the first step had been taken nothing would have saved the prisoner.' The first blow was not struck and Shortis was lodged safely in his cell. A practising Catholic, he asked for Father Santoire, the parish priest, who spent an hour with him, though what they talked about could not, of course, be revealed by the priest. Sometime late that evening, while St Pierre was with the accused, Mayor Loy sent a message that a very serious movement was under way to lynch Shortis. Earlier in the evening he had advised a crowd to disband. 'Surely,' he told them, 'if I can be content with the law's action, you can.' Towards midnight, however, a more determined group had reassembled. Macmaster instructed the jailor to find a team of horses and a covered sleigh, and at midnight Shortis was driven off through a snowstorm, arriving at Beauharnois, fifteen miles away, about three o'clock in the morning.

Macmaster was worried about the security of the jail in Beauharnois, a small town of about two thousand people, and wrote the attorney-general: 'There is great danger of Shortis making his escape from Beauharnois jail ... It is stated that the jail is very insecure. Shortis is a powerful man, a very plausible talker and a desperate character.' Later that week Attorney-General Casgrain instructed the sheriff to transfer Shortis to Montreal, an order-in-council having been in effect for several years deeming the Montreal jail (solidly built in 1837 and used that year to confine some of those involved in the rebellion[10]) to be within the jurisdiction of the Beauharnois district. A large crowd had assembled at Montreal's Bonaventure Station to observe the infamous prisoner, with the red sash around his waist. His hands were free and he was smoking a cigarette. Some of the bystanders, the press noted, complained that he was being allowed too much liberty. At the Montreal jail, Shortis was taken to a cell in 'murderers' row.'

Macmaster had no doubt that Shortis was sane. 'I believe,' he wrote Casgrain, 'he is just as sane as men ordinarily are and that the crimes committed by him were committed in cold blood and with the object of getting possession of a large sum of money.' St Pierre, on the other hand, returned to Montreal convinced that Shortis was not sane and not responsible for his actions.

This would be the central, and indeed the only, issue in the trial: Was Shortis responsible for his actions? The defence released to the press a letter from Shortis' father declaring he 'must have been mad to commit such a fearful act ... We now see when it is too late that many things which we looked upon as wildness will go to show that this poor boy has inherited this dreadful malady.' He offered to send 'certificates of the insanity of my poor father, uncle, brother and aunt.'

Could Shortis get a fair trial in Beauharnois, the place where he would normally be tried if a change of venue were not requested? St Pierre announced that he would apply to have the trial moved to Montreal, and the press announced that Macmaster had recommended, and that the attorney-general had consented to, having the trial there. No such recommendation or consent had in fact been given. Macmaster wrote Casgrain: 'I see something in the newspapers about suggesting a change of venue, and some opinions on that subject attributed to myself. I can only assure you that I have expressed no opinion whatever on the subject, and if an application of that kind is made, it will be at once referred to yourself.' The people of the area did not want a change of venue. The local member of the provincial assembly told the press that Shortis could get 'justice in Beauharnois just the same as in Montreal' and he wrote to the attorney-general insisting that a change of venue be resisted.

The local papers continued to build the case against Shortis. A story appeared quoting a Cornwall man who had earlier worked in Valley-field and had spent time with Shortis. 'Say, Mike, how would you like to make $1,000?' Shortis was reported to have asked, and then explained how they could steal the money that was brought in to pay the wages. 'I don't want to do it alone,' Shortis was supposed to have said, 'but with the assistance of a friend who would act with me the matter could be very easily arranged.' The Huntingdon *Gleaner* editorialized that this story would 'remove any doubt but that Shortis was after money and that his action was premeditated.' The *Gleaner* also reported a musical concert under the patronage of Bishop Emard 'to assist the widow of the watchman who met death at the hands of the assassin.'

Strong feelings were not restricted to the Valleyfield area. The Montreal *Herald* declared that the 'gallows is a safer place than any asylum for a man whose sanity is first suspected after he has slaughtered two inoffensive fellow beings.'

In mid-March J.N. Greenshields, QC, one of the most prominent lawyers in Quebec,[11] was added to the defence team, joining St Pierre and a solicitor, George Foster. Greenshields, who had initially been engaged independently by Captain George Matthews, the owner of a shipping line and friend of the Shortis family, had been one of Riel's counsel in Regina in 1885 and had defended the Quebec Liberal leader, Honoré Mercier, on corruption charges in the early 1890s.

He was also Donald Macmaster's chief rival as the leading English-speaking lawyer in Quebec. Like Macmaster, he had graduated from McGill with the Torrance Gold Medal. Upon graduation he went into partnership with Macmaster, who had graduated five years earlier. They later split up and in 1885 Greenshields and his younger brother, who had just graduated (and who later became the chief justice of Quebec), became partners. Greenshields was as solidly a Liberal as Macmaster was a Conservative: he had run unsuccessfully for the federal Liberals in 1887 and in the very week of the killings had been asked to run in the Sherbrooke area in the coming election, which many expected would be announced in the next few weeks. Greenshields had been the favourite prosecutor when the Mercier Liberals were in power in Quebec in the late 1880s, just as Macmaster was often chosen by Taillon's Conservatives in the 1890s. He was also a director of the Montreal *Herald*, a Liberal party organ,[12] and he was able to use it effectively to support his client's cause: no longer would the *Herald* argue that 'the gallows is a safer place than any asylum.'

From the beginning, both Greenshields and Macmaster devoted enormous time and energy to the Shortis case, perhaps in part explainable by the extreme rivalry often engaged in by former partners. The pre-trial manoeuvres employed in the Shortis case had seldom, if ever, been seen in a criminal case in Canada, and they are rare even today.

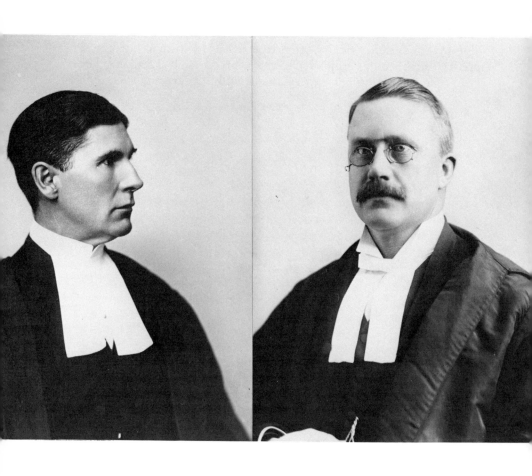

LEFT: Donald Macmaster, QC, Crown counsel, portrait by William Notman & Son, February 1895

RIGHT: J.N. Greenshields, QC, defence counsel, portrait by William Notman & Son, December 1894

2

Pre-trial Manoeuvres

A CHANGE OF VENUE was crucial to the defence. Greenshields told the press: 'He won't be tried in Beauharnois if we can help it.' His first approach was to Macmaster, who in turn reported to the attorney-general: 'I stated to him that I would have to await your instructions; that on general principles the system of jury trial was an educational factor in the community, that it made the people of the localities in which crime was committed responsible for the just administration of the law, and that punishment for violation of the law becomes a potent object lesson to the people and a stimulus to the preservation of peace, order, and good government in the country.' Macmaster went on to say: 'Yesterday I met Mr. A.F. Gault, President of the Montreal Cotton Company [and, he might have added, a prominent Conservative], and he assured me that no doubt a fair trial could be obtained for the accused in the District of Beauharnois, and that it was better from the standpoint of justice that the accused should be tried there. You know Mr. A.F. Gault personally of course. I have no doubt that he reflects the general view of the people in the district.'

The defence team decided to approach Casgrain, the attorney-general, directly. George Foster, the defence solicitor – also a leading Conservative (president of the Eastern Townships Conservative Association and many years later appointed to the Senate by the Conservatives) – was assigned the task of seeing the attorney-general personally in Quebec City. His letter of 28 March to Casgrain, marked 'personal,' suggests – sadly – that he improperly put politics ahead of his duty to his client:

Dear Attorney General

I fear I shall not be able to see you today, and I am sorry as I promised to speak to you about the Shortis case being tried in Montreal and not in Beau-harnois.

There is much to say why it should be changed, and I fear there are more reasons why it should not be changed and I do not see how you can interfere or let it take other than the regular course.

Will you if you look at it in this light write me tomorrow 'referring to our conversation' for I do not like to appear not to have seen and talked it over. I should wait over tomorrow but I *must* be in Montreal. We will then make the usual application ...

The attorney-general saw it in the same light and wrote the next day: 'Referring to our conversation of yesterday re: Shortis, after having considered this matter, I beg to state that in the matter of the proposed change of venue, the only thing I can do is to allow the law to take its course.'

An application would therefore have to be made to the court. But which court? If an application were brought in Beauharnois the local judge, resident in the locality, might have difficulty in saying that the accused could not receive a fair trial there. It would therefore be better for the accused to have the decision made by a judge in Montreal.

As a first step, a writ of habeas corpus was brought before Judge J.S.C. Wurtele in Montreal. Accused's counsel argued that the case was 'brought up so that the Court would know officially that he was detained in Montreal Jail.' Shortis was therefore personally brought before the court – 'crowded to its very doors' – to test the legality of his detention. 'He bowed to his counsel,' reported the *Herald*, 'smilingly and coolly folding his arms on the railing in front, he tried to look unconcerned. He was dressed in a gray suit with low collar and clean shaven face, except for a slight moustache. His dark eyes wandered curiously over the room taking in every particular.' Of course the court found he was properly detained and the writ was discharged. It was a tactic, as Macmaster wrote the attorney-general, to 'try to lay the foundation for creating some jurisdiction in the Montreal Courts.'

Rather than apply immediately to Judge Wurtele for a change of venue, the defence applied the following week to the judge for permission to have Shortis examined by psychiatrists, or as they were then called, 'alienists.' Macmaster questioned the jurisdiction of the Montreal court to grant such an order and then, when the matter was adjourned, wrote to the attorney-general: 'Will you kindly instruct me whether it is your desire, and if so, under what conditions medical men acting on behalf of the Defence should confer with the prisoner with a view to ascertaining whether he is responsible for his acts or not?' Meanwhile, the defence gave notice that they would appear at the Montreal jail with a Dr Anglin to examine Shortis. Neither Macmaster nor the attorney-general knew of a precedent for such an examination, and Macmaster was worried. 'It may be,' he wrote, 'that the defence are really only inviting a refusal, and it may not be wise to comply with such invitation. It would be quite a handle with them at the trial to say that they were not allowed to have a doctor examine the prisoner, to ascertain his mental condition.' The attorney-general, however, felt that he did not have authority to permit such an examination. 'The proper course,' he wrote, 'would be for the defence to apply to the competent Judge.'

Dr J.V. Anglin, who from 1891 was the assistant medical superintendent at the Protestant Verdun Hospital for the Insane in Montreal and, according to the Montreal *Star*, 'one of the best known experts on insanity' in Quebec, had twice been refused permission to visit the prisoner by the Montreal jailor and the sheriff. Judge Wurtele gave his decision: he agreed with Macmaster that 'all legal proceedings must originate in the district of Beauharnois.' This, of course, included the crucial application to change the venue. The judge observed that the permission applied for 'was only reasonable and should be granted by the proper court.' He was referring to the examination of Shortis by psychiatrists and not, as some papers thought, the issue of a change of venue. An application for a change of venue would therefore be made in Beauharnois.

Shortis continued to be held in his small, lime-covered stone cell at the Montreal jail. On Saturday morning, 20 April, his mother arrived in Montreal; Mr Shortis remained for the time being in Ireland. She was described as 'a tall, well built, matronly looking lady of about forty-six years of age ... distinguished in appearance.' She met for an hour with her son. The meeting between mother and son was described by the *Star* as 'truly pathetic, and before it ended, the latter showed signs for the first time since the terrible tragedy, of being visibly affected.' She was permitted to visit him once a day. In early May, he became ill with inflammation of the lungs and his mother was permitted to nurse him through one critical night in his cell.

At an earlier point, Shortis had received visits from George Matthews and George Bury, both friends of the family. He had been given full letter-writing privileges, his communications being scrutinized, however, by the jail staff. Macmaster discovered that he had written a letter containing threats against some people in Valleyfield, and, moreover, had requested that an answer be sent not to the jail but to George Bury. Macmaster urged the attorney-general to instruct the officials to be careful: 'The prisoner is a desperate character. He has proved that. If he is sane, he is a desperado of the worst possible character. If he is insane, the reasons are more forceful that he should be closely guarded.'

Shortis had not yet seen Millie Anderson, although he had corresponded with her. In late May, she had had a lengthy visit with Mary Shortis in Montreal, but there is no record of their conversation. Around this time the press reported the complaint of another prisoner that for two hours early one morning Shortis had roared 'like a lion' and shouted that 'two detectives were hounding him down to give false evidence against him.' The *Progrès de Valleyfield* noted this conduct and observed that Shortis was simulating insanity.

A motion for a change of venue was brought before Judge Louis Bélanger in Beauharnois. Now almost seventy years old, he had been a Superior Court judge in Beauharnois since 1873. The petition was presented by the solicitor, George Foster, who, it will be recalled, had advised the attorney-general not to agree to a change of venue. The petition argued that 'feeling ran so high at the time the offence was committed that the life of the prisoner was threatened, and that an effort was made to form an organization for taking the prisoner's life.' It also argued that 'the public mind was prejudiced and public opinion formed among those from whom the jury would be drawn in the District.' The hearing took place on 7 June. It had been scheduled for 6 June, but was rescheduled because Macmaster and his wife were platform guests at the unveiling of the statue of the 'Old Chieftain,' Sir John A. Macdonald, in Montreal. An even earlier date had been changed because Macmaster's eldest son had pneumonia. 'Matters were so serious at home,' Macmaster wrote Casgrain, 'that the two doctors in attendance advised me that it would not be safe for me to go out of town, even for ten hours.' His son recovered.

The Criminal Code gave – and still gives – a judge discretion to change the venue from the county or district where the crime took place – from earliest times the place where the trial would be held – 'whenever it appears to the satisfaction of the court or judge ... that it is expedient to the ends of justice that the trial ... should be held in some district, county or place other than that in which the offence is supposed to have been committed.'[1] St Pierre told the court about his own experience at the preliminary inquiry, where an attempt had been made to lynch Shortis, and also about information he had received about the potential lynching at Beauharnois. 'We find ourselves,' he argued, 'with the declared enmity of the two largest centres of population in the district of Beauharnois.' Moreover, he argued, medical experts could more easily be obtained in Montreal. Finally, he added an argument that would surely not impress the local judge, that 'he and his confreres did not want to spend weeks and weeks in the district trying the case.' Perhaps the judge was equally unimpressed with the argument presented by the *Progrès de Valleyfield* that it would be unfair to deprive the Beauharnois innkeepers of the business if the trial was moved. Greenshields followed, pointing out that the *Progrès*, as we have already seen, had told its readers that Shortis was faking insanity (the paper also later said that 'an acquittal because of insanity would be a crime'). Twenty-four affidavits were prepared for the defence by local citizens and a commercial traveller who had once been a detective stating they were satisfied that a fair trial could not be obtained for Shortis in Beauharnois.

Macmaster countered that the threats against Shortis at the time showed 'nothing more than a condemnation of the commission of crime, which is a very proper feeling in any well ordered community.' In any event, he said, it should have 'no weight when sufficient time has expired to allow such feelings to subside and disappear.' The great Lord Mansfield, he observed, had expressed the view over a hundred years earlier that before the venue is changed 'there must be a clear and solid foundation' that 'there could not be a fair and impartial trial had by jury' in the county.[2] Finally, he reiterated the traditional view that 'the trial for crime is an object lesson to the community, a wholesome civilizing influence, and it is fitting that justice should be vindicated near to the scene where it was outraged.' The Crown filed sixty-five affidavits to the effect that a fair trial could be obtained in Beauharnois: nearly all the parliamentary representatives in the surrounding area swore such affidavits, as did seven notaries, eight practising physicians, and twenty merchants.

As it turned out, one of the affidavits filed by the defence helped the Crown. A Mr Kellert, a commercial traveller and former detective, had claimed that for two years he had been superintendent of the Pinkerton Agency in Chicago. Macmaster then filed an affidavit from William A.

Pinkerton of Pinkerton's National Detective Agency in Chicago, stating that the company had never employed Kellert. Greenshields responded, weakly, that the agency referred to was not the same Pinkerton concern that Kellert had been superintendent of in Chicago. The impression was left with the court that the defence affidavits were suspect.

Judge Bélanger reserved his judgment and a week later announced that the venue would not be changed. 'There was,' he said, 'no widespread or deep-seated prejudice against Shortis, such as would prevent a jury selected from among the yeomen of the District of Beauharnois from doing even-handed justice to the prisoner, as well as to the Crown.'

Would a change of venue be granted if the case arose today? Most of the same arguments would be presented and the outcome would by no means be certain, but it is very likely that a change of venue would be granted in similar circumstances.[3] Indeed, it would be shocking if it were not.

The defence immediately moved before Judge Bélanger for authority for doctors to examine Shortis in the Montreal jail and for a commission to go to Ireland to collect evidence regarding insanity in the Shortis family and Shortis' conduct there.

There was little difficulty in obtaining an order to examine the prisoner. Judge Wurtele, it will be recalled, had been sympathetic to this request if the proper application was made in Beauharnois. Dr Anglin swore that 'it is essential to determine whether at the time of the commission of the offence the prisoner was insane or not.' 'Therefore,' he said, 'physicians should have every opportunity to examine and converse with him, and to note his language, acts, and conduct while in gaol during the time that will elapse between now and the trial.' An order was made to permit Dr Anglin; Dr C.K. Clarke, superintendent of the Rockwood hospital for the insane in Kingston, Ontario; Dr R.M. Bucke, superintendent of the asylum in London, Ontario; and a French-Canadian physician to be named, to examine Shortis. The only issue was whether a Crown representative had the right to be present, as Macmaster suggested. Bélanger, who reserved his decision on this question, later decided that the defence psychiatrists could see Shortis without representatives of the Crown being present.

Anglin visited Shortis on a number of occasions over the next six weeks and prepared a report stating that 'there is not the least doubt as to the prisoner's insanity.' C.K. Clarke, who had been Anglin's professor at Queen's and was later to become the superintendent of the Toronto asylum and dean of the Faculty of Medicine at the University of Toronto – and after whom the Clarke Institute of Psychiatry is named – arrived in Montreal towards the end of July to begin his examination. There is no evidence that Shortis was examined by psychiatrists for the Crown. Shortly after the murders Dr Georges Villeneuve, superintendent of the Catholic asylum at Longue Pointe, had written to the attorney-general suggesting that Dr T.J.W. Burgess, the superintendent of the Protestant Verdun hospital, should look at Shortis, but the records do not indicate whether any such examination was made.

Judge Bélanger also permitted the defence, at their own expense, to obtain commission evidence about Shortis' prior history in Ireland. An affidavit from Dr Anglin had been filed, stating that 'from his experience and study of mental diseases, he found that it was essential and necessary to get a complete history of the person from childhood, in order to determine the insanity of a person.' Further, he said, from what Mrs Shortis had told him with regard to her son's acts and conduct while in Ireland, it was absolutely necessary to a fair trial that the evidence of persons residing there should be heard and put before the jury. Mrs Shortis swore to insanity in her husband's family and her son's conduct in Ireland. Judge C.A. Dugas, a judge of the sessions in Montreal, was named as the commissioner to gather the evidence. The Crown had put forward the name of a counsel who would be in England to appear in a Privy Council case – 'with the sole purpose of curtailing expenses' – but the defence argued that, as they were paying the bills, they should have the choice of commissioner. The evidence, signed by the witnesses, was to be filed with the Beauharnois court in a sealed package on or before 15 August.

Macmaster was worried about this evidence. Long before the application he had written Casgrain: 'It is now absolutely certain that the friends of the accused are going to make a great fight for his life, and that unless the evidence taken abroad, if it can be taken abroad, is carefully watched, enough may be elicited to cast a doubt upon his sanity.' The Crown did not join in the application, Macmaster wrote, because 'it would be extremely dangerous for the Crown to recognize the conduct or ancestry of Mr. Shortis, as a test for relieving him from guilt.' Indeed, Macmaster opposed the application on the ground that 'the trial of the case was about to be conducted in Ireland, instead of in the

Province of Quebec'; and such examinations in Ireland were unnecessary, he argued, because it would be possible to produce witnesses from Ireland at the trial.

Once the Irish evidence was allowed, Macmaster insisted on going to Ireland to cross-examine the witnesses. As he wrote the attorney-general: 'I imagine that an attempt will be made to put in a good deal of more or less bogus evidence, to support the Shortis plea, and it is important that this should be knocked out. I take very firm ground with regard to this, as having seen Shortis on the day after the murders, and conversed with him, I am perfectly satisfied that he was as sane then as you are or as I am now.' This letter was followed the next day by a telegram: 'I cannot impress too strongly upon you that the scene of conflict in Shortis' case is now transferred to Ireland and as Judge has intimated that evidence taken there will be receivable on plea of insanity such evidence must be carefully sifted on the spot. It is easy to find people who for a consideration will give bogus evidence and the Crown should carefully guard itself against this contingency.'

Casgrain agreed to Macmaster receiving a $500 fee for the trip to Ireland plus an additional $50 a day and expenses. This arrangement, with the low daily fee, would ensure that Macmaster would not waste time dragging out the proceedings in Ireland. Towards the end of June, Greenshields, his wife and daughter, and Judge Dugas, the commissioner, sailed on the *S.S. Mongolian* for England. Macmaster had left the previous week.

Mrs Shortis also sailed with the Greenshields. Before leaving, she had, accompanied by Millie Anderson, spent three hours with her son. He was now said to be in good health. His mother had been arranging his meals and he had gained considerable weight. 'Every afternoon,' said the *Star*, 'he makes out a list of the delicacies he intends to have the following day. This order is taken to the Gaoler's office and then is sent to a St. James Street purveyor, who fills the order.'

This was Millie's first visit. 'Although Shortis has exhibited a certain amount of love and affection for his mother during her daily visits to him for the past seven weeks,' the *Star* reported, 'he has never fully demonstrated how deep that love was until the hour for parting came yesterday evening. He had very little to say to Miss Anderson, devoting the whole time to his mother.'

Greenshields and Macmaster met in London at the Constitution Club, Macmaster's London club, to make final arrangements. The sittings in Ireland started on 18 July in the grand jury room at the Waterford Court House, around an immense table thirty feet in diameter. More than sixty witnesses were examined over the next five days.

Reports about the commission began to appear in the Montreal papers. Macmaster was not surprised. Earlier in the year he had told the attorney-general: 'I see little interviews and suggestions in the papers every few days, evidently manufactured and put forth in order to prepare the public mind for the plea of insanity.'

Greenshields went further. He sent a private telegram to the *Herald*: 'There can be no doubt as to Shortis' mental condition. We have secured sufficient evidence to convince a jury that he is beyond doubt insane.' A special cablegram to the *Star* from an unnamed source – the *Progrès de Valleyfield* was sure it was from Shortis' counsel – stated that witnesses so far heard have all agreed that Shortis, who some referred to as 'cracked Shortis,' was insane. Later cables to the *Star* referred to 'rash and eccentric acts done by the prisoner while residing in Waterford.'

When Greenshields returned to Quebec – after a delightful visit with his wife and daughter to the lakes of Killarney – he gave a lengthy interview to a *Herald* reporter on the vine-clad verandah of his summer residence near Danville in the Eastern Townships. The evidence, he said, showed extreme cruelty to animals. Witnesses had testified that Shortis stabbed one of his father's dogs, 'all the time shouting and laughing with the fiendishness of a maniac'; stuck 'a pitch fork into his father's cows until they bellowed with pain'; shot at a cat tied to the foot of a machine 'and on being interrogated as to his cruel deed said he wanted to see how many bullets the cat could stand before it succumbed.' Shortis had also shot at the open portholes of a passing steamer and at the town clock opposite the family residence. Another witness testified that he had shot at a young girl, grazing her arm, and still another that he had tried to trample on a child with his pony. These incidents were kept from his parents. Macmaster would ask each witness why the parents had not been told and the witnesses, Greenshields said, would reply: 'Begorra, and is it an informer you're after takin' me for?'

While in London, Greenshields met his fellow Liberal, Edward Blake, who had led the Liberal party before Laurier and was now a champion of home rule for Ireland in the British Parliament. Of course, they discussed the Manitoba schools question. Blake had been the counsel for the Catholic minority in the Privy Council, and he expressed the view, later published in the *Herald* interview with Greenshields, that the government had made a mistake and should have drafted a law along the lines of the Ontario system, which provided partial public support for separate schools. No doubt both men agreed that Mackenzie Bowell could not survive for long as leader of the Conservatives, particularly now that all three French-Canadian members of his cabinet had resigned because they did not think the government was committed to remedial legislation. Two men – Adolphe Caron and J.-A. Ouimet – later returned, but Bowell was unable to replace the third, A.-R. Angers, a problem that will appear later in this story.

The commission evidence was properly filed with the Beauharnois court and the defence then applied to have it opened and available to its experts. Macmaster was not yet back from England and Casgrain cabled Macmaster's partner, F.S. Maclennan, to oppose the application: 'If opened, evidence will be published to influence public opinion. Make strongest opposition.' This the Crown did, but Judge Bélanger reserved his decision.

The attorney-general then improperly tried to influence Bélanger's decision. He wired Maclennan: 'Can't you intimate to Judge Bélanger that I would consider it very detrimental to the due administration of Justice if Commission were opened now. Call his attention to all reports actually published in this case by Press.' Maclennan's reply, marked 'private,' is worth quoting at length because it shows the subtle ways in which justice can be swayed:

> I went out to Beauharnois yesterday afternoon. I had some hesitation about calling on Judge Bélanger but I saw Laurendeau [who had been assisting Macmaster] and arranged with him that he should see the judge today and show him your telegrams to me and a number of the newspapers in which the lawyers of the prisoner have been giving their version of the evidence taken in Ireland. Laurendeau had an appointment with the Judge for this morning on another matter and could call the Judge's attention to your views without making it appear that he called on him specially for that purpose ... I am in hope now that he will come to our view of the matter and refuse to open the Commission before the trial takes place.

Judge Bélanger eventually decided in the Crown's favour and the evidence was not opened until the trial.

Macmaster reported to the attorney-general on his return that he still believed Shortis was sane:

> That he did many eccentric, rash and even reckless acts in Ireland, there is no doubt, but he never was arrested there or confined in a Lunatic Asylum. Now, a great attempt is made to magnify these eccentricities into such acts of folly as would go to establish insanity, and I believe that some of the evidence given with regard to shooting, is perjured – and that it bears the stamp of perjury on its face ...
>
> As I wrote to you before, I have simply to repeat that, notwithstanding the fact that insanity existed in his grandfather, my own opinion is, from what I have seen and heard, that he was perfectly sane at the time of the commission of the crime, that he had no reason or motive for the commission, except the acquisition of money, and that he had no ill-will or grudge towards any of the parties against whom he raised his hand.

The Crown hired Detective Carpenter (his firm advertised 'Detectives of the most reliable character furnished by the Canadian Secret Service') to trace Shortis' movements from the time he came to Canada until he went to Valleyfield. Steps were also taken to trace the young man, Gleason, who had disappeared after saying that Shortis had earlier proposed that they rob the mill.

On Sunday evening, 22 September, Mr and Mrs Shortis, bringing with them an Irish setter for their son, sailed into Montreal harbour on the *S.S. Laurentian*, the very ship Valentine had sailed on two years earlier, passing the Montreal jail as they approached. Mrs Shortis was, of course, well known to the reporters, who described her again as 'a motherly, good-looking woman of about 45,' with a broad Irish accent. This was the first glimpse the press had of Francis Shortis, who was described as 'tall and every inch an Irish gentleman.' The *Herald* reporter had a brief conversation with him:

> 'Do you bring any further news, sir?'
>
> 'No. There is very little to say. We have come, as you may know, to look after the interests of our poor boy, and there is very little to be added to what has already been said. I want to say to you, however, that I think the English papers have treated us well, and have fairly put the sad story, but, unfortunately, I cannot say the same for the French papers. I am sure our poor son knew not what he did.'

'It has been suggested here, Mr. Shortis, that in view of the many acts which look like insanity, he should not have been allowed to come alone to this country.' To this Mr. Shortis replied:

'I assure you we did not know of his remarkable actions. Why! when I sat in the court room and listened to the evidence of his strange behaviour I was dumbfounded. Mr. Greenshields and Mr. Macmaster brought from the witnesses stories which seemed impossible to believe, but which I fear were only too true. At home, as Mrs. Shortis has just told you, he was kind and lovable, a good boy, and never had we reason to suspect his madness.'

'We have not yet been allowed to publish the results of the commission, but an interview with Mr. Greenshields tells us that the evidence of his insanity is startling.'

'It is. It leaves no room for doubt.'

'The news of your kindness in sending the Leboeuf family a thousand dollars has been published. I presume you knew of their want.'

'Yes, I heard of it. Poor people, how much they must have suffered.'

'You will visit your son here?'

'Yes.'

Mrs Leboeuf denied she had received any money, and wrote the *Herald*: 'Sir – You published that the Shortis family had given me a large sum because their son had killed my husband. I declare to you that I never received a cent, and I ask you to say so.' Mr Shortis explained that he had, in fact, sent $1,000 to Greenshields, who thought it best not to hand over the money until after the trial. He conceded that 'it was not, perhaps, wise to make such a present just before the trial,' but now that it was known, he had asked Greenshields to send a cheque to Father Santoire for Mrs Leboeuf.

Mrs Shortis was asked about her son: 'He is well in health, but, poor boy, knows and cares as little about what is going on in connection with the terrible affair as he does about the romping of the dog we brought him.' 'I was telling him,' she added, 'that last evening there was a meeting of his counsel, Mr. Greenshields, Mr. St. Pierre and Mr. Foster and that they – here he broke in,' continued the mother, 'by clasping my wrist and asking me if my bracelet was solid gold. I replied "yes" and he said: "Sometimes they're not, you know." He seems to have less and less idea of his position and there remains no doubt of his insanity.'

The trial would start on Tuesday, 1 October. Both the Crown and the defence had rented houses in Beauharnois. The Great Northwestern

Telegraph Company had installed an extra seventeen miles of wire for the newspaper dispatches. It would be, said the *Herald*, 'the greatest legal battle that the criminal courts of this province have ever known.'

3

The Crown's Case

JUDGE BÉLANGER would not be trying the case. The *Progrès de Valleyfield* expressed surprise at this decision and claimed it was insulting to Bélanger and to the people of the district. Instead, Judge Michel Mathieu of the Quebec Superior Court was assigned the task. A highly respected senior jurist, Mathieu had been appointed a judge in 1881 by Sir John A. Macdonald, and had sat in the Quebec legislature, having previously been a Conservative MP in Ottawa in the early 1870s. Sir John A. had declared that if his friend Mathieu had not chosen a judicial career he would have become a cabinet minister. The Ross-Taillon government in Quebec (1884-7) had unsuccessfully tried to induce him to leave the bench to join its cabinet. He was a noted scholar and had earlier been the publisher of the *Lower Canada Jurist* and the *Revue Légale*. While a judge, he was also a professor of civil law at Laval University, later becoming the dean of the faculty. He was said to be 'the idol of his students, and as an after-dinner speaker he was without a rival, being quick at repartee and possessing a fund of anecdotes.'[1]

Mathieu was perhaps best known to the public as the chairman of the royal commission appointed in 1892 to look into improprieties in the Liberal Mercier government (Greenshields had been counsel for Mercier and Macmaster a commissioner). Coincidentally, he had been the defence counsel in the last and only murder case in the Valleyfield district which, as previously mentioned, also involved the Montreal Cotton Company. His client was acquitted. Before becoming a judge, he had often acted as a Crown prosecutor.

Judge Mathieu arrived in Beauharnois Tuesday morning, 1 October, on the Grand Trunk train from Montreal. He was about to preside at the longest murder trial ever held in Canada up till then, and possibly

Valentine Shortis, sketch from the Montreal *Daily Star*, 30 March 1895 the longest in the British Empire. It was to last twenty-nine days, not including the holidays on which the court did not sit. In England, by contrast, few murder cases then ever lasted more than ten days.[2]

There was a vast crowd waiting to meet the train, whose whistle, the press reported with their typical quest for detail, was heard approaching the station at precisely 8:50. The people were there, of course, to catch a glimpse of Shortis, not the judge. Shortis was transferred into the charge of Sheriff Philemon Laberge and eight special constables. This time, there were no threatening gestures. Shortis, in the words of the press, 'will be dealt out British fairplay.'

The prisoner, wearing a dark business suit with a black Derby hat, was a little stouter than when he had left. His hands were shackled in front, covered over by a plaid shawl, but this had not prevented him from giving a cigar to a policeman at Bonaventure Station in Montreal. Shortis himself constantly smoked cigarettes – 'coffin nails,' he told a reporter, using an expression one would have assumed was of a more recent vintage. His parents, both dressed in black, were on the same train but in a different car. Many had expected that Shortis would leave Montreal on Monday evening and some were sure that the large crate of legal documents accompanying Macmaster that evening, marked 'The Queen v. Shortis,' contained Shortis himself. Greenshields arrived Monday evening from his country home in the Eastern Townships. Shortis was taken to the same cell in the Beauharnois jail he had occupied before.

The judge entered the large courtroom with its multicoloured ceiling at 10:25 in the morning. Macmaster and Charles Laurendeau, a Beauharnois lawyer, were there representing the Crown. Greenshields and Foster represented the defence. St Pierre had not yet arrived: he was in Montreal continuing to research some points on the insanity defence. Mr and Mrs Shortis were seated beside the defence counsel. The prisoner remained in his cell.

This was the opening of the assizes and the first stage was to empanel a grand jury – an ancient institution now no longer used in England or Canada[3] – to investigate whether there was sufficient evidence to warrant a trial. Twenty-three grand jurymen were selected to hear evidence on the charges; a majority of twelve was needed to find a 'true bill' of indictment on which the accused would stand trial before a petty jury. Judge Mathieu charged the grand jury in French and then in English:

Your district, as a rule, so peaceable and law-abiding, was struck with terror on the second day of March last, when it was reported that during the night of the first day of the same month, an awful murder had been committed in the thriving little town of Salaberry of Valleyfield. Two respectable citizens, John Loy and Maxime Leboeuf, were reported as having been murdered, and Hugh A. Wilson as having been seriously wounded. A bill of indictment will be submitted to you concerning the murder of John Loy and Maxime Leboeuf. ... You are only to enquire upon your oath whether there be sufficient case to call upon the party accused to answer the accusation. If you consider that a prima facie case is made against the accused, you will return the indictment into Court as a true bill, which then becomes the foundation of the process before the petty jury.

The grand jury retired to their chamber and, as was the practice, commenced hearing witnesses in the absence of the accused or his counsel. As the judge had told them, their task was 'comparatively easy,' and at noon the foreman, François Chrétien, announced that they had found true bills against Shortis for murder and attempted murder (as well as a true bill against another person in an unrelated case who would be tried at that assize for rape). The court was adjourned.

At two o'clock Shortis, dressed in black with a red and green silk handkerchief in his breast pocket and with his flowing hair artificially bleached almost blonde, first appeared in court. He approached the circular prisoner's dock with a quick springy step, his head erect and his chest out, smiled and bowed to the counsel. 'How do you do?' he said graciously to Macmaster. The judge entered the courtroom and the clerk read the two murder charges. Twirling his moustache and with his eyes fixed intently on the judge, Shortis said: 'I am not guilty.'

Greenshields rose, adjusted his glasses, and submitted the following additional plea:

That at the time of the commission of the act alleged in the indictment the prisoner was labouring under natural imbecility and disease of the mind to such an extent that rendered him incapable of appreciating the nature and quality of the act and of knowing that such an act was wrong; and was at the time suffering from unconsciousness and disease of mind by which a predetermination of his will was excluded; that he was in a state of madness and was insane.

(Signed)   J.N. GREENSHIELDS,
H.C. ST. PIERRE,
G.G. FOSTER.
Counsel for the Defence.

Macmaster at once objected. There was no precedent, he argued, for such a plea; and a special plea was not needed for the defence of insanity. In any event, he said, the latter part of the plea should be struck out because this would not provide a defence to the charge. The first part, he said, repeated section 11 of the Criminal Code and could do no harm: 'No person shall be convicted of an offence by reason of an act done or omitted by him when labouring under natural imbecility, or disease of the mind, to such an extent as to render him incapable of appreciating the nature and quality of the act or omission, and of knowing that such act or omission was wrong.' The latter part, however, introduced two foreign concepts:

> Now, if Your Honour please, that portion lets in what is popularly known as 'uncontrollable impulse' and possibly under the head of madness it might let in what is known as 'moral insanity' and by law both these are excluded from the legal definition ... as would exempt from responsibility. Now, I have no doubt that if these words are allowed to stand as part of this plea that under it, it might be competent for the accused to offer evidence of 'uncontrollable impulse' and possibly of 'moral insanity' by the doctors. I state that does not constitute a defence ... The effect of this addition to the plea is to enlarge the terms of the statute ...'

Judge Mathieu was not sympathetic to Macmaster's argument: 'I think that this plea ... is a notice of what [counsel] intends to prove. I do not think it amounts to anything else.' Macmaster then made a formal application to have the latter part of the plea struck out – 'I cannot, as Crown Prosecutor, let a plea of that kind go without objection' – which was reserved by the judge.

Throughout this exchange not a muscle of Shortis' face or neck moved: 'il pose,' remarked the *Progrès de Valleyfield*. There were two more items of business before the trial was adjourned. Greenshields again moved to have the Irish evidence opened, but once more was unsuccessful. Finally, the names of the list of possible petty jurors who would hear the case were called. All were there, except one French-speaking juror who was fined $10 by the judge. Although it was not yet three o'clock, the defence did not wish to proceed further because St Pierre had not yet arrived. The real reason for the adjournment may have been to permit the defence counsel, aided by a former Crown prosecutor who had twenty-five years of experience in the district, to find out as much as they could about the potential jurors.

Hundreds fought for admission to the courtroom the next morning. A large press contingent was there, and part of the centre of the courtroom was reserved for special guests, which that morning included Mrs Macmaster and the local MP, Joseph Bergeron, the deputy speaker of the House of Commons, who will reappear later in our story. Shortis was brought in, having been trimmed and shaved by a town barber earlier that morning. His nails were carefully manicured and his shoes were said to be 'like mirrors.' Again the press noted his 'remarkable sang froid.'

Judge Mathieu, as expected, allowed the special plea of insanity to stand. He also allowed Greenshields' request for a mixed jury (still possible in Quebec today) which ensured that half the jurymen would speak French and half English.[4] The jury in Canada then, as now, had to be unanimous to bring in a verdict, and the defence wanted some English-speaking persons on the jury, persons who might not have appeared by a random selection because of the predominantly French-speaking population in the district. The right to a mixed jury is granted, said Judge Wurtele in another case around the same time, 'in order that there may be in the jury which is empanelled to try him six jurymen at least whose thoughts are communicated, and whose opinions are formed in the language spoken by the accused person.'[5] In the Riel case ten years earlier, Greenshields had wanted the trial to be held in Manitoba where a mixed jury was then also possible; but Riel was tried in Regina before an entirely English-speaking – and possibly less sympathetic – jury.[6] Having a mixed jury meant that all the English evidence had to be translated into French and the French into English. Similarly, there had to be French and English addresses to the jury by counsel and the judge. This, of course, substantially added to the length of the trial.

St Pierre objected to both counts of murder being tried at the same time. To do so, he said, would deprive the accused of his full right to challenge peremptorily the jurors. Then, as now, an accused charged with murder was entitled to challenge 'peremptorily' – that is, without assigning any reason for the challenge – twenty jurors. If the charges were combined, St Pierre argued, he would, in effect, have only ten peremptory challenges on each murder charge. Once again, Judge Mathieu agreed – even before Macmaster could say that he was sorry His Honour had made his ruling before hearing from the Crown. 'Score two' was heard from the defence table. The judge was bending over backwards in favour of the defence, perhaps not wanting to give any ground for a successful appeal. Macmaster said he would not object, thinking no doubt that it might in the long run be an advantage to have another murder count up his sleeve. The Crown would proceed with the charge respecting John Loy, whose name appeared first on the indictment. Loy had been killed while trying to telephone the doctor.

The panel of forty jurors was summoned. As each name was called, counsel for the accused would challenge the juror for cause. The law provided that the last two jurors chosen were the persons to decide in each case whether the challenge should be upheld; the decision whether the first jurors chosen were impartial was made by two persons selected by the judge for that purpose, in this case the clerk of the court and the local member of the legislative assembly, E.H. Brisson, who had earlier taken the position that an impartial jury could be found in Beauharnois. Robert Brooks, an English-speaking juror from Huntingdon County, was the first juror called. He had, he said, read about the case and had formed the opinion that Shortis was guilty. Was it not true, Greenshields asked, that he had said to a neighbour that Shortis should be shot and not hanged, whether he was crazy or not? The juror had no such recollection. Brooks was declared impartial by the trier of fact, but was then peremptorily challenged by Greenshields. The next juror, Georges Sauvé from St-Louis-de-Gonzague, admitted to St Pierre that it made no difference whether Shortis was insane or not, he should hang. The Crown conceded that he was biased and he was asked to step down. And so it went. Not one juror was selected from the first eight called. By the lunch break, after some remarks by the judge to the jury panel about the law of insanity, six jurors had been selected and by the end of the day eleven had been chosen and the jury panel had been exhausted. The jury was short one English-speaking member.

The court suggested that the additional potential jurors simply be selected from those in the courtroom, but the defence objected. Consequently, the court ordered the sheriff to secure a panel of fifteen men

(called talesmen) from the district to choose from the following morning. By midnight, Sheriff Laberge had secured only seven names. By
three in the morning he had the requested fifteen.

Shortis continued to seem indifferent to the proceedings. He had a
brief conversation with the *Herald* reporter, who had asked him how
he was being treated: 'Splendid; but what a damn farce this is. I want
some Pears soap. The soap I get here is all right for washing clothes,
but not fit for a Christian.' 'They're getting along slow, aren't they,'
added the reporter. 'Some one seems to enjoy it,' said Shortis, 'but as it
doesn't concern me, why let them alone. By the way, will you send the
Herald, and tell Mother, if you can get a word with her, to send me
some more soap.'

Seven of the talesmen were examined by Greenshields and rejected.
'If he was insane or sane I'd swing him anyway,' said the first juror
called. Shortis twitched nervously, reported the *Star*, adding that it
was the first time he appeared aware of his position. Mrs Shortis began
to cry. Finally, just before noon, the defence withdrew its challenge to
John Cunningham of Howick, who swore he could disabuse his mind
of any preconceived opinion. The jury was now complete. A day and a
half had been taken, longer than many complete murder trials at the
time.[7]

The clerk of the court charged the jury: 'Gentlemen – Hearken to the
charge against the prisoner: That Francis Valentine Cuthbert Shortis
murdered John Loy on the first day of March, one thousand, eight hundred and ninety-five. Upon this indictment, gentlemen, the prisoner
was arraigned, he pleaded that he was not guilty, and for his trial has
put himself upon God and his country, which country you represent.
Your duty, therefore, is to enquire whether he is guilty or not guilty of
this felony. You will remain together and hear evidence.'

St Pierre requested all the witnesses to leave the court, with the exception of the psychiatric experts and the parents of the accused. Macmaster objected to having the witnesses leave until after he gave his
opening address, but the court once again agreed with the defence sub-
mission.

Macmaster spoke for exactly one hour, first lucidly setting out the
facts he would be proving and then outlining the law of insanity:

> In the first place the law presumes that everyone who does any act is sane at
> the time of doing it until the contrary is proved; that is, until the doer is

proved to be insane, and this proof must be such as will satisfy you to a moral certainty that he was insane at the time the act was committed; and when you decide that a prisoner is insane it must be insanity within the meaning of the law.

In the next place the law leaves no doubt as to the standard or test which you are bound to apply in determining whether an accused person is responsible or exempt from responsibility. That standard or test is put down in the statutes and in the Criminal Code. It governs you and me and every man who walks before the law. That law provides [s. 11] that the criminal shall answer for the crime unless he can clearly prove that at the time of the killing he was labouring under natural imbecility or disease of the mind to such an extent, mark you, as to render him incapable of appreciating the nature and quality of the act he was doing and of knowing that such act was wrong.

That is the test of the law and you can take no other. Quacks and cranks may tell you that there should be another and different test. Learned doctors may tell you that this test is not sufficient and that the law should be amended. Philosophers may tell you that the doctors know nothing about it and that philosophy and science should say when a man is of sane mind and when he is not. The thoughtless or the prejudiced or the interested may set up a standard of their own as to when a man is crazy or mad or insane.

If we had to accept opinion of each of these, or even the most learned of them, we would have no uniform standard of responsibility. The law has intervened, and on the experience of ages has constituted this trial enquiry: 'Did the man know what he was about, and did he know that what he was doing was wrong?'

He then warned the jury of the consequence of a finding of insanity: 'There is one thing I wish you specially to remember ... It may be said he will be confined in the asylum for life. This is not so. If you excuse him on the ground of insanity and find a special verdict to that effect he will be confined during the lieutenant-governor's pleasure. It may be one year, two years or whatever is his pleasure, but there is no law that he will be confined for life.' Macmaster concluded by telling them: 'Do your duty like men and leave the rest to the laws of your country and to the powers beyond.' Laurendeau then went over the same ground in French.

Section 16 of the Canadian Criminal Code today is similar to section 11 of the 1892 Code – Canada's first Criminal Code – but there are some important differences. The onus is still on the accused to prove insanity, but it can now be proved by a 'mere preponderance of probability,' not as Macmaster stated 'clearly' proved.[8] Moreover, recent Supreme Court of Canada cases have interpreted the word 'appreciate' in a wider sense than the word 'know.' As Mr Justice Brian Dickson, as he then was, stated in 1980, the word 'appreciate' was deliberately used 'to broaden the legal and medical considerations bearing upon the mental state of the accused and to make it clear that cognition was not to be the sole criterion. Emotional, as well as intellectual, awareness of the significance of the conduct, is in issue.'[9] The words 'appreciate' and 'know' were, however, used interchangeably in 1895.

The really important difference between the law then and today is the use of the word 'and' in the definition of insanity in the 1892 Code and the substitution of the word 'or' for 'and' in the latest version of the Code. The difference is crucial because if the conjunctive 'and' is used the accused must prove that he did not appreciate the 'nature and quality of the act' *and also* that he did not know 'that such an act was wrong.' On the other hand, if the disjunctive 'or' is used, then an insanity defence would succeed if the accused could prove *either* that he did not appreciate the 'nature and quality of the act' *or* that he did not know 'that such act was wrong.'

The 1892 Code had codified the 1843 M'Naghten test.[10] When it was pointed out in the House that the insanity section 'is simply embodying the report of the judges in the M'Naghten case,' Sir John Thompson, the minister of justice, replied: 'I always understood the rule laid down in the M'Naghten case to be accepted without question.'[11] Macmaster told the jury the same thing: 'Now, gentlemen, you must remember that the law as I have given it to you is the supreme law of the land. It was laid down so in England by the judges [in M'Naghten's case], on an application of the House of Lords ... That law governs us, it is our code, it governs you.'

M'Naghten's case had clearly intended that the accused could succeed under either head of the test: 'to establish a defence on the ground of insanity, it must be clearly proved that, at the time of the committing of the act, the party accused was labouring under such a defect of reason, from disease of the mind, as not to know the nature and quality of the act he was doing; or, if he did know it, that he did not know he was doing what was wrong.' English courts have consistently used the word 'or' rather than 'and.'[12]

In fact, the word 'and' would seem to have been introduced into the

Criminal Code by error. The English predecessors of the Canadian Code, James Fitzjames Stephen's draft Code of 1878 and the Royal Commissioners' Code of 1879, had both properly used the word 'or,' but the draughtsman of a Bill introduced into the British Parliament in 1880 had by mistake changed the 'or' to an 'and.' The Bill died on the order paper and therefore was not given the close scrutiny by Parliament that would have corrected the error. Canada based its 1892 Code on this uncorrected 1880 draft. [13]

Whatever the reason for the introduction of the word 'and,' the significance of the difference was never discussed in the Shortis case, in any of the background documents or in any of the subsequent discussions. Everyone – counsel, psychiatrists, and the judge – assumed that the 'and' meant 'and.' This is quite remarkable because Greenshields was thoroughly acquainted with the law of insanity through his involvement in the Riel case (a few weeks before the Shortis trial he had come across and donated to the Montreal Antiquarian Society Riel's original petition as well as the hat he had worn at the Battle of Batoche and when sentenced to death [14]). Insanity was, of course, also the issue in the Riel case and the trial judge had properly used the word 'or' in giving the insanity test to the jury. [15] But this was in 1885, before the enactment of the 1892 Code.

What is even more remarkable is that no one is reported to have challenged the restrictive interpretation of the test for insanity until a five-member Ontario Court of Appeal in 1931 in the case of *Cracknell* [16] raised the issue itself (counsel had not argued the point) and through its eighty-nine-year-old chief justice, Sir William Mulock (who had been a Liberal member of the House of Commons when the section was discussed in 1892, but did not then comment on the insanity provision), stated: 'That this change was a mistake on the part of the draughtsman appears to me obvious ... Thus, in order to establish his defence it was not necessary to prove both incapacity to appreciate the nature and quality of his act and also absence of guilty intent. In my opinion in the present case the word ''and'' should not be construed literally.' In *Cracknell*, the trial judge, Mr Justice W.E. Raney, had told the jury: 'You see the section reads that the defence must not only prove that the accused did not appreciate the nature and quality of the act, but in addition must prove that he did not know that the act was wrong.' After the *Cracknell* decision, there was uncertainty on the issue. The deputy attorney-general of Ontario, E. Bayley, wrote to the federal deputy minister of justice, W. Stuart Edwards, disagreeing with the ruling. 'In my opinion,' he wrote, 'it was all obiter and not very satisfactory.'[17] The matter was raised at the annual meeting of the Canadian Bar Association that year.[18] A resolution was introduced to have the statute amended to conform with *Cracknell*, but was deferred until the following year after an Ontario judge, Mr Justice J.F. Orde, disagreed with that decision, stating that there are 'other judges who disagree.' 'He must prove both and not one or the other,' he said. A Quebec lawyer observed that he thought the Quebec courts would not follow *Cracknell*. But the case was followed in 1932 by the Saskatchewan Court of Appeal,[19] and when the issue again came before the Canadian Bar Association that year it was recommended that the statute be changed. The recommendation was repeated in subsequent years, but the statute was not changed until the revisions of 1955,[20] although *Cracknell* seems to have been followed by other courts.[21]

So, for almost forty years – between 1892 and 1931 – accused persons in Canada who raised the defence of insanity would have had to satisfy both heads of the insanity test. In some cases, of course, they would have been convicted even if the right test had been given. Cracknell, for example, was convicted on his second trial. But many who raised an insanity defence were unsuccessful and were hanged. A few months before the Shortis case, an accused, Amedée Chatelle, whose story will come up later, was hanged in Ontario after the trial judge and later the Department of Justice had used the narrow 'and' test for insanity.[22] A few years after the Shortis case, Thomas Nulty was hanged in Quebec, in spite of an insanity plea, where the conjunctive 'and' was used in the test.[23] How many more in Canada may have been improperly hanged because of, to use Chief Justice Mulock's words, 'a mistake on the part of the draughtsman'? Would Shortis be one of them?

John Lowe, the cashier at the cotton mill, was the first witness. Unfortunately, announced the sheriff, all the jurors had disappeared. They had gone for a walk and appeared a half an hour later in the charge of a constable, strolling leisurely up the lawn leading to the courthouse. In the meantime, St Pierre renewed his request to have the Irish evidence opened and this time Judge Mathieu acceded to the request, on the condition that the evidence be seen only by the lawyers for the defence and Crown until it was read in court.

As Lowe entered the witness box, he and Shortis stared at each other. After several minutes Lowe lowered his eyes. His evidence contained nothing new. It had all been given at the inquest and at the preliminary hearing and had been set out in full in all the papers. Nevertheless, as the *Star* observed, his evidence 'created a sensation in

Court, and the listening crowd eagerly bent forward so as not to lose one word of the narrative.'

Shortis, said Lowe in English and then in French, was familiar with the layout of the mill and the office and knew that a package of money arrived on the three o'clock train from Montreal every second Friday. 'In fact,' said Lowe, 'the prisoner visited the office the previous fortnight as we were about to depart, having completed our labours earlier than usual ... After being admitted, the prisoner walked up to the counter and began talking and laughing in his usual manner. We were all great friends.'

A map was tacked on the wall beside the judge to assist Lowe in describing the scene. He had been giving evidence for about eight minutes when John Cunningham, the last juror chosen, took sick. Dr Adrien Ouimet, from Valleyfield, who happened to be a spectator in the courtroom, examined him and declared that Cunningham would not be able to proceed for several hours. At that time a trial could not go on with fewer than twelve jurors (today it could proceed with only ten jurors[24]). The problem, said Macmaster, was that there was no air circulation in the room and for the third time he applied to have the storm windows, which apparently had been nailed shut before Confederation, removed. Greenshields added his support and Judge Mathieu ordered the sheriff to remove the windows. Court was adjourned. Defence counsel spent the evening reading and analysing the Irish evidence.

By the next morning the storm windows had gone. Drs Anglin, C.K. Clarke from Kingston, and Daniel Clark from the Toronto asylum, who was well known in Quebec as the leading psychiatrist for the defence in the Riel case, were all in court observing the proceedings. All three had visited Shortis in his cell that morning. The fourth defence psychiatrist, R.M. Bucke from London, Ontario, had not yet arrived. Dr Georges Villeneuve of the Longue Pointe asylum in Montreal was in court assisting the Crown.

Virtually all the newspapers noted the large number of 'morbidly curious females' who were anxious to gain admission. They were said to be sympathetic to Shortis. If women were permitted on the jury, said the *Herald*, 'Shortis would escape altogether.' They had apparently been excluded from the courtroom, but the previous day a group of about seventy-five had surged into the room during the noon break and refused to move. 'One pretty Miss took Mr. Macmaster's chair, and seemed quite upset when she was told to get up,' reported the

Herald. The *Star* wondered whether Judge Mathieu would not follow Judge Wurtele's recent ruling in the Demers murder case, then taking place in Montreal, and exclude all women.

Lowe described Shortis' request to see the gun and his own removal of the cartridges. His evidence was interrupted to have Detective E. Poirier describe some specific articles, including the two guns, both fully loaded, showing that Shortis had reloaded them; three bullets that had been taken from Leboeuf's body and another bullet from Loy's head; a broken walking stick, part of which had been used by Shortis to light a fire to smoke Lowe and his companion out of the vault; and a chisel found on the prisoner.

The examination of Lowe was resumed. He described Shortis' request to reload the gun, which was refused, and his request to look again at the serial number, which Lowe showed him while holding the gun himself. The loaded gun was placed in the drawer.

When emerging from the vault, Lowe said, he saw Shortis suddenly swing round, level the weapon at Hugh Wilson, and fire. 'Shortis was only three feet from Wilson,' he testified, 'when he fired the first shot. After being shot, Wilson threw up his hands and started to yell. I ran over, and Loy went to the telephone box. Shortis, turning to me, said: "If you move I will shoot you." I took Wilson in my arms. Loy just then had his hand on the telephone, when Shortis pointed the revolver at him and fired. Loy fell in a heap at the foot of the telephone. The prisoner was five feet from Loy when he fired. Turning quickly, Shortis again levelled the weapon and fired at Wilson and me.'

Lowe described his scooping up of the money and going into the vault, Shortis' attempts to get him out, watchman Leboeuf's entrance making his rounds, and then hearing a shot and the noise of a falling body. He was eventually released from the vault after Shortis had been captured by Dr Sutherland and others. When the constable arrived, Shortis was searched. He asked the man who was holding him to let go for a moment so that he could fix his collar which was choking him. This request was refused and they eventually found a large chisel in his pocket and a loaded revolver concealed under his left arm, attached to a large pocket handkerchief that was suspended around his neck.

Greenshields had very few questions in his cross-examination. He established that the clerks sometimes passed an evening in the office when there was nothing to do and Shortis would often join them there.

There was even greater interest shown by the spectators in the next witness, Hugh Wilson, the first person to be shot. This was the first time he had given evidence. At the time of the inquest and the preliminary hearing he had been close to death. This was also the first time he and his former friend, Shortis, had seen each other since the night of the tragedy. Shortis would not look him in the eye. Wilson told of being shot through the left cheek, the bullet dislodging three teeth and embedding itself in his tongue; the bullet could not be extracted, but worked its way out two months later. Two more shots were fired at him, but both missed. Wilson rushed to the manager's office. Shortis kicked one of the panels out and fired his revolver at close range, which fortunately was out of bullets.

He then escaped to the darkened mill. Shortis pursued him. Wilson fell from exhaustion and loss of blood. Another shot was fired into the darkness. A little later Shortis approached with the dead watchman's lantern, found Wilson and fired another shot into his body. The bullet entered the collar bone and came out below the front of the right lung. Shortis left, thinking him dead. Wilson was able to move to another part of the mill. Shortis came back without the lantern, which he had used to try to smoke out the persons in the vault. He could not find Wilson and struck matches to trace the blood on the floor, shouting 'Wilson, Wilson, for God's sake, where are you?' He could not find him and returned to the mill office. Wilson was able to drag himself to the pump room to summon help. Defence counsel had the good sense not to cross-examine him.

Other Crown witnesses established additional facts, but Lowe and Wilson were the main witnesses. Dr Sutherland was called to describe Wilson's wounds and the arrest of Shortis: he and a fireman had approached the accused, each carrying gas pipes. The doctor shouted 'hands up' and Shortis said: 'I want to give myself up. I do not know why I killed these men.' The doctor was not cross-examined; indeed, few of the Crown witnesses were.

David Smith, the secretary-treasurer of the mill, had opened the vault to release Lowe and his companion. Shortis, he testified, said 'Shoot me, or lend me your revolver and I'll shoot myself.' Smith had replied: 'Oh no, we will do better than that for you; shooting is too good for you.' The press noted that Smith was deeply moved while giving his evidence and that tears welled up in his eyes several times. Mrs Shortis was also moved, particularly when he had said 'shooting is too good for you.'

The prisoner's mother was even more deeply affected when the Valleyfield chief of police, Léon Leduc, produced the clothes Shortis had been wearing when he was placed in the cells. She sobbed bitterly when Leduc showed the court Shortis' wrinkled blue guernsey. Eventually she was led from the court by George Foster, and her husband left shortly afterwards.

A curious phenomenon was occurring. The more heinous Shortis' crime appeared, the more sympathetic the crowds were to the suffering of his mother. 'Mrs. Shortis has changed sadly,' wrote the *Star*; 'the cheeks ... are furrowed with lines, and drawn in a deathly pallor of unutterable pain. Large black circles surround the once bright eyes, now dimmed with incessant weeping.' The *Herald* observed: 'Even the men who mentally hang the son for his deed united in an expression of sympathy for the mother, and more than one who before now has declared in favour of the rope would relent.' As the parents left the jail that evening, the *Star* reported, there were 'expressions of compassion passed from one to another of the onlookers.' Perhaps the jailors were showing greater compassion as well; that evening Shortis was permitted for the first time a walk in the field at the back of the jail.

The court sat on Saturday. The Shortises were accompanied by Father Robert Dunne, a Roman Catholic priest who had come from Ireland specifically to give evidence on their behalf. The Crown still had several more witnesses. Ernest McVicar, an employee at the mill, was called to show premeditation: Shortis had spoken to him on several occasions about robbing the mill and the train carrying the money, but since he did not take the incidents seriously he did not tell anyone about them until after the killings. The *Herald* reporter gave evidence that when he interviewed Shortis, and he was the first to do so, the prisoner had declined to say anything until he had spoken to his lawyer, thus helping to establish that Shortis was aware of the circumstances. Similarly, and for the same reason, the Crown introduced evidence concerning the letter Shortis had dictated to Millie Anderson the morning after the murder: 'Telephone home, anticere. Do not fret. If Bob gives any dirty talk you tell him to mind his own business, or I will make it bad for him. Send Jack to me immediately. I remain, yours lovingly, B. Shortis.' No explanation was given of the meaning of the word 'anticere.' The Crown's case was closed at eleven o'clock Saturday morning. The press speculated – wrongly – that the case would be concluded towards the middle of the next week.

4

The Defence

THE DEFENCE was called on to present its case within minutes of the closing of the case for the Crown. There were no opening statements by defence counsel. The first evidence would be that of the Irish commission, consisting of 575 handwritten pages of statements made by the forty-eight witnesses. Macmaster told the court that he objected now, as he had done in Ireland, to most of the evidence as irrelevant. He wanted his protest to form part of the record.

The official translator, Alexandre Cotté, commenced reading the evidence in English. By noon the testimony of only two of the forty-eight people had been heard.

The first witness, Robert Dobbin, the father's elderly solicitor in Waterford, said that he had known young Shortis for eight or nine years. He once saw the accused put out a large fire that he had surreptitiously started himself. As deputy chairman of the Waterford Railway Company, he knew of incidents where Shortis 'galloped down the line like a madman' in front of approaching trains. He outlined a number of similar incidents to show that Shortis was 'foolhardy' and of a 'freaky' disposition.

John Ryan, the second witness, had been a classmate of Shortis' and considered him a 'hot-tempered fool.' Once, when driving back from the races, he saw him gallop through the streets like a madman, striking a worker on the head with a heavy stick when he did not get out of the way. Shortis, he said, often had headaches and had a great fondness for firearms.

After the lunch break the first evidence read was that of Patrick Sullivan, a cattle dealer, who had known the accused from early childhood. 'Shortis,' he said, 'was wrong in his head.' He once saw him fire

Henri St Pierre, QC, defence counsel, portrait by William Notman & Son, February 1894 his revolver into a crowd at the races, and related other incidents that occurred when they were on their way to the Kilkenny fair: Shortis lit some special powder under a seat in the railway car, frightening everyone; later that day he set fire to the newspaper a man was reading and set still another fire in the train; finally, he struck Sullivan on the head with a stick. 'After that,' said Sullivan, 'I'd go a mile to get out of his road.'

Witness after witness gave similar evidence. William Shallow, one of his father's workers, always considered Shortis crazy, saying that he had fired at him in a field. 'And I suppose when that shot was fired you thought you were killed?' asked Greenshields. 'Faith and I'd have had better reason to think I was if that tree hadn't been in the way,' was the reply. Richard Malone, another of the father's workers, told of Shortis' treatment of animals: 'The accused was cruel to the cattle and took a delight in sticking the pitchfork into their haunches. While the wounded animals were being attended to, Shortis Jr. would stand by and fairly scream with delight over what he had done.' Thomas Kearney, a farmer, testified that he had seen Shortis fire his pistol at a young girl, grazing her arm, and then laughed loudly, clapping his hands.

And so it went, incident after incident involving 'Val, the fool,' 'mad Shortis,' and 'cracked Shortis' in irresponsible acts. Why were the parents not told, Macmaster would ask? The 'holy terror' of being labelled an informer was the answer of most, though one said: 'I did not wish to bring trouble to his mother and father who are highly respected by everyone in Waterford.'

The court rose at three o'clock Saturday afternoon. The reading of the evidence would continue on Monday morning. The judge, Macmaster, and St Pierre caught the five o'clock Grand Trunk train to Montreal and spent Sunday with their families. Life, they no doubt thought, would have been easier if the location of the trial had been changed to Montreal. They had already missed the city's first major cultural event of the season, Nellie Melba's gala concert on Friday night at the Montreal Academy of Music. Greenshields remained in Beauharnois, studying the case, and Foster went to Valleyfield to talk to some witnesses, probably Mrs McGuiness and her daughter, Millie Anderson, whose evidence was eagerly awaited. It was not clear, however, whether Miss Anderson would be called by the defence.

On Monday morning Francis Shortis entered the courtroom with Father Dunne. Mrs Shortis was too ill to appear. As the *Star* reported, she 'lies sick in bed at the convent here, her system completely broken down.'

Much of the testimony read on Monday had been given by doctors and psychiatrists in Ireland. Dr James Shea, the governor of the Clonmel lunatic asylum, gave evidence of the death of a number of Shortis' relatives in his institution. His grandfather, Thomas Shortis, had died in 1891, at the age of sixty-five, of 'softening of the brain'; his uncle, John Shortis, had died there at the age of thirty-nine of 'cerebro spinal disease and epilepsy.' Relatives of Shortis' mother had also been in the asylum, including her sister, one of her uncles, and her nephew. Dr Thomas Cream testified that the grandfather had suffered from mania and hallucinations, imagining that he was going to be hanged. Dr William Garner, the medical superintendent at Clonmel, said that John Shortis, Valentine's uncle, had been admitted at least four times, 'subject to great maniacal excitement, arising from epilepsy, and was very violent and had no control over himself.' Macmaster had closely cross-examined Dr Garner. Shortis' father, Garner said, was not insane. One could, he admitted, be insane and still know right from wrong: out of 670 patients in the asylum, perhaps 600 would know right from wrong. Moreover, 'if there were a sum of money concerned, that would be a sufficient motive for the crime.'

Other witnesses gave further evidence of Shortis' alleged deeds: savagely beating his horse, kicking his dog, stabbing another dog, putting the tail of a cat in turpentine and setting fire to it, shooting a cat, striking children in the street, firing at people, shooting at the town clock and at steamboats, setting fires, and riding his pony through a butcher's shop and into private homes. Father Dunne, who would give evidence in person later, testified in Ireland that he had been the head of the Christian Brothers school in Waterford and that Shortis had been a great problem: he took guns to school and seemed unable to control himself. Dunne had told his fellow brothers that 'if any boy in Ireland would be arrested on a capital charge it would undoubtedly be Valentine Shortis.'

The reading of the evidence in English was finished on Monday, shortly before seven o'clock. Judge Mathieu suggested an evening session, but the French-speaking jurors refused unless they were paid extra for it. This was not possible, said the judge.

Defence counsel seemed pleased with the effect of the Irish evidence. 'The lawyers for the defence make no effort to conceal their evident satisfaction at the manner in which the evidence taken by the commission has been received,' the *Star* reported, 'and state that they regard that alone as an excellent case for them to go to the jury on, quite apart from the testimony of the medical experts ...' The *Star* itself noted 'the unanimous sentiment not only of sympathy, but also of high respect and esteem expressed by the various witnesses towards Mr. & Mrs. Shortis' and went on to observe that 'If any slight feeling in favour of the young man has been aroused, it must have been caused by the testimony of those who speak of the relations existing between him and his afflicted mother.'

On Tuesday morning, 8 October, Cotté started translating by sight the Irish evidence into French. It was a slow process and obviously boring for the English-speaking jurors, several of whom fell asleep – as did the clerk of the court. The reading of the translation continued all day Wednesday.

Mrs Shortis was still sick in bed at the Grey Nuns' hospital, attended by Dr Anglin. Anglin, along with the other three defence psychiatrists (Bucke arrived over the weekend), had visited Shortis early Tuesday morning at the Beauharnois jail: he was at the time reading the life of Napoleon and had been overheard singing *La Marseillaise* in crude French, *La Presse* reported – suspiciously. They had then gone back to their hotel to study the evidence.

The courtroom was still crowded, 'crowded to suffocation' said the *Star*, which also noted that there were over a hundred women in attendance. Macmaster and Greenshields were not there during the reading of the evidence in French; understandably, they were preparing for the days ahead. It was known that Millie Anderson and her mother had arrived in town on Tuesday, but they did not visit the courtroom or the jail.

On Wednesday evening, Laurendeau, the Beauharnois lawyer assisting Macmaster, gave a sumptuous dinner for all the counsel and some of the officials. Judge Mathieu did not attend. He remained aloof throughout the trial, eating his meals in his own room in the Beauharnois Hotel.

It is not difficult to imagine the lively conversation that evening. By convention, it was probably not about Shortis, even though, as the

Herald declared, the trial was 'the one topic of conversation through-out the county.' The talk would no doubt have centred on three important events, two of them political. After several weeks hearing, the Demers murder trial in Montreal, before Judge Wurtele, had ended that day with a hung jury, and Demers was to be retried. Counsel no doubt wondered if that would be the result in the Valleyfield case. Shortis, who knew Demers from the Montreal jail, had expressed pleasure earlier in the day on hearing that he had not been convicted. St Pierre was surprised it was not an acquittal. Another topic that would no doubt have been discussed was the possibility that the lieutenant-governor of Quebec, Joseph Adolphe Chapleau, would join the Bowell cabinet, taking Angers' vacant position. Chapleau had been to Ottawa the day before to see the prime minister. If he were to join the government – a former premier of Quebec and cabinet minister under Mac-donald and Abbott – the Conservatives' chances in the election now expected in the spring would be boosted.[1]

Most importantly, Wilfrid Laurier's famous Morrisburg speech, de-livered not far away along the river from Valleyfield the day before, could not fail to have been a topic of conversation. Leader of the Lib-eral opposition since Edward Blake had retired in 1887, Laurier had first entered Parliament in 1874 – he had graduated in law from McGill ten years earlier – and had been a cabinet minister in Alexander Mackenzie's government in 1877-8. This was the fifty-three-year-old Laurier's most important speech to date on the Manitoba schools ques-tion, sometimes referred to as the 'Torres Vedras' speech and some-times as 'sunny ways.'[2] 'Gentlemen,' he had said to the Liberal crowd, 'I am within the lines of Torres Vedras. I will get out of them when it suits me and not before.' He was, as the audience knew, referring to the Duke of Wellington's strategy in Portugal during the Napoleonic Wars, when he stayed within the Torres Vedras lines and simply watched the frustrated French. Laurier would do the same with the Conservatives on the Manitoba schools issue. But he gave a strong hint of the direction he would take by telling the fable of the wind and the sun trying to get a man to remove his coat: no matter how hard the wind (Bowell and the Conservatives) blew, the coat stayed on, but in the warmth of the sun the man removed his coat. 'I would try the sunny way,' said Laurier to the cheering crowd, meaning he would not impose a solution through remedial legislation. He would repeat this speech in Prescott that very evening and in Brockville the following night.

The translation of the Irish evidence into French was finally completed Thursday afternoon at four o'clock. It had taken ten hours to read the evidence in English and twenty-one hours to translate it into French. Just before the translation was complete, Mrs Shortis came into court on her husband's arm. The journalists observed that an unprecedented number of women were in court, expecting Millie Anderson to be one of the first witnesses.

The first defence witness called, out of a dozen subpoenaed, was James Mulcahey, the caretaker at the building on Commissioners Street in Montreal where Shortis had lived and kept an office for several months from about November 1893 to June 1894, when because of other tenants' complaints about him he was asked to leave. Mulcahey's evidence broke the tedium of the translation of the Irish evidence. Shortis, he said, would bound up the stairs two or three at a time and come down four at a time, shaking the whole building. The caretaker was worried about his reliability and would not allow him to lock the front door at night. He collected books and pamphlets on guns and bicycles, which were now in bags in the basement. Shortis smiled, as did others, when the witness said that Shortis would throw kisses at Mrs Mulcahey and he grinned broadly when the witness added that his wife 'has been me wife for thirty-five years and is old enough to be his mother.' The courtroom became still again, however, when Mulcahey told of Mrs Shortis' requests to him: 'The lady told me to take good care of her only son. And I can tell you gentlemen she loves him passionately; her whole heart and soul is in her boy.'

Each witness seemed to confirm the Irish evidence that Shortis was an eccentric, strange boy who had, in the words of one witness, 'a slate off.' On the other hand, some of the evidence just made him seem playful and mischievous. When Mulcahey came into Shortis' room on one occasion he saw him putting matches into an envelope; Shortis told him he was going to send them to the old country. Was he serious? George Matthews, the owner of the building, on two occasions saw him in the building without shoes or stockings. 'It was good for his head,' Shortis told him. Was he joking? Had not the witness seen sailors with bare feet, asked Macmaster. Yes, but he 'never saw judges, lawyers or businessmen going around in their bare feet.' The manageress of the hotel where Shortis first stayed said that the 'crazy loon' would order his food from the bottom of the menu up, starting with blackberry pie and ice cream and then moving on to the main course. Another witness from the same hotel described him throwing peanuts at a 'large negro' passing by the hotel and, taking the stance of a boxer, saying 'come on and have a fight.' Edgar Bury, who at his father's insistence saw a great deal of Shortis in Montreal, described him coming to a 'full dress soiree' at the Bury house wearing buckskin moccasins and trousers tied up with a rope. Shortis had once suggested they go west and 'hunt buffaloes and shoot Indians.' During walks the accused spat on people and jostled them. An employee of the Queen's Hotel, where Shortis stayed before coming to Valleyfield, said he had seen him in a public washroom, washing his feet in the basin with his socks on and then putting on his boots without his socks. When he asked Shortis about this conduct the accused flourished a gun, which the employee took from him. Were these incidents of insanity or simply irresponsible and eccentric behaviour?

Father Dunne, who had taught Shortis for a year at the Christian Brothers school in Waterford, also confirmed his commission evidence of his irresponsibility: he was 'childish and eccentric'; he took pistols and knives to school and broke windows; he was 'very vain, in fact, it was a monomania.' The only subject he took any interest in, said Dunne, was chemistry, although he did not understand it. Shortis' mind would at times seem utterly vacant and he appeared to suffer from headaches; sometimes he underwent a physical change. In cross-examining Father Dunne, Macmaster established that there were three doctors in Waterford. But none of these, the jury knew, gave evidence at the Waterford commission.

Other defence evidence was directed at Shortis' conduct after his arrest. The defence tried to show that he had immediately fallen asleep, thus showing a lack of grief or regret for what he had done, but the constable would not say that Shortis had actually been asleep. The witness who wrote Shortis' note to Millie Anderson said he just wrote it down phonetically and did not know what the word 'anticere' meant, suggesting that Shortis may not have been coherent at the time. The note itself had been found by the police in an old porcelain pot at Millie's home.

Many of these witnesses were subjected to severe cross-examination by Macmaster, who wanted to show that Shortis' conduct was not as extreme as the defence made it out to be. There were vigorous clashes between counsel: 'I do not propose to take any instuctions from my learned friend,' 'You can give me no lessons in propriety,' and so on.

On Monday morning (the trial was now in its twelfth day), the crowd at the courthouse was the largest it had ever been. Millie Anderson and the Shortises had still not given evidence.

Millie was called to testify. The papers described her appearance in great detail: 'bright pretty girl,' said the *Herald*; 'Graceful though petite figure,' observed the *Star*; 'small featured with a mass of blonde hair, which she wears somewhat loosely low down over the ears,' declared the *Gazette*, adding that her 'eyebrows are long and dark, and the eyes are also of the same deep hue.' Her clothes were also described in detail: 'She was fashionably attired in deep black, with the exception of brown kid gloves and a salmon coloured ribbon that encircled the small crown of a wide-brimmed felt hat, with two ostrich plumes and a quantity of black ribbon behind.' The day after giving her evidence she looked through all the papers and was said to be upset that there was no picture of her. Throughout her testimony she looked at Shortis only once, when asked by Greenshields, 'Do you know the prisoner?' Shortis never looked at her.

She gave her evidence 'in a clear, straightforward manner.' Shortis, she said, was a frequent visitor at her house (in a remote part of the village not far from the mill) for the two or three months she had known him. Her mother and stepfather objected to him, but in spite of this she and her younger brother continued to see him. Shortis often carried firearms, she said, telling the Andersons that he had been big-game hunting in Africa. He did odd things like climb the pole opposite their house and break the electric lights or scratch his arm until it bled. He was fond of notoriety and kept a scrapbook of his name in print.

On the day of the tragedy, Shortis had been with her in the afternoon. They had been invited to a birthday party near Beauharnois that evening and Valentine was anxious to go, but she declined because of a cold. He came over again about seven. Throughout the evening, until he left at ten o'clock, he acted particularly strangely. He was sure people were watching him and insisted on the curtains being closed. He complained of violent headaches and held his head continuously. He had shown her two unopened letters from his mother that afternoon and brought a further unopened letter that evening, and Millie had urged him to write. Greenshields asked her about her relationship with Shortis:

'Was Shortis engaged to be married to you?'
'No,' she replied with a deep blush.

'Did he propose to you?'

'No.'

'Did he propose to elope?'

'No, he never mentioned such a thing.'

'If this thing had not happened,' she said, 'in a few weeks more our friendship would have ceased, because the more I saw of him, the more I became convinced that he was crazy.'

Macmaster cross-examined her forcefully. Why did she write 'I will always be true' if she was going to break off the relationship? 'I changed my mind,' she replied. In any event, she said, she wanted to cheer him up. Had she corresponded with him in prison? She had not written to him, but had received a number of letters which she showed to Mr Foster, the solicitor. Macmaster asked to see them. 'As they contained nothing of importance,' defence counsel said, 'they had been destroyed.' Macmaster concluded by asking:

'Do you know Miss Leblanc, a dressmaker in Valleyfield, and did you have a conversation with her with regard to the prisoner's crime last week?'

'Yes.'

'Did you say anything to her about the prisoner getting off on the plea of insanity, with the expectation of his being put in an asylum for three months?'

St Pierre objected to the line of questioning on the grounds of irrelevance, and the judge asked Macmaster to reframe the question:

'Did you, Miss Anderson, state to Miss Leblanc that after the prisoner got his liberty through release from the asylum that you would marry him then?'

'No I did not,' she replied.

Once again St Pierre objected and the court upheld him, even though Macmaster persuasively argued that the evidence was meant to show the potential bias of a 'prospective wife.' 'But,' he added, 'I will take the rule of the court.' He knew that his point had been brought home to the jury. When Millie had finished her testimony, Mrs Shortis signalled for her to come sit by her. Macmaster's point was brought home even further. Young Jack Anderson then gave evidence which did not differ significantly from his sister's.

Francis Shortis was now called. When the hour-long examination in chief had concluded, said the *Star*, 'few eyes in the Court room were dry.' He told his own history. Now forty-eight he had had eight brothers and eight sisters, though only one of the sisters was now living, three having died in infancy and four of consumption. Valentine, he said, did not speak until his fourth year and often had violent headaches; he stayed at home with his mother until he was seven and then was placed in school. When his son was sixteen, he had tried to teach him the cattle business (which had a turnover of almost a million dollars a year), but after two years he had concluded it was hopeless: his son could not even count thirty cattle in a field. The only solution, he thought, was to send him abroad so he would learn to stand on his own. When Francis Shortis spoke of his 'only child,' the tears welled in his eyes. He did not know about his son's activities in Ireland: 'I knew the child had been shot at and I heard of him riding down the line and, on my oath, as God is above me today, I never heard of another act.' Macmaster, understandably, asked few questions, and those he asked were put in the gentlest possible manner.

Finally, the last non-expert witness was called, Mary Shortis. As with Millie Anderson, Shortis did not look at his mother during her evidence. She started her testimony with one long look at her son sitting 'sphinx-like', with his chair tilted back in the prisoner's box, his eyes riveted on the royal arms above the judicial seat. The court was silent. She described his boyhood: unable to walk until he was two; incapable of articulation until he was six; unable to count at seven; unable to speak plainly until he was ten. He always had a cough and bronchitis and when young had a large stone fall on his head. Between the ages of twelve and sixteen he began to get violent and was careless and untruthful. Nevertheless, she only knew of a few of the incidents in Ireland. She and her son had corresponded two or three times a week until about seven weeks before the murders, when she received the last letter from him. She had felt certain he was dead. During her regular visits to the prison, Shortis would not talk of the crime and protested against the use of an insanity defence. Greenshields had one final question. 'You devoted your whole lifetime to him,' he asked? 'Yes,' she replied, tears in her eyes, 'and now I would give my life for him.' Macmaster wisely did not cross-examine her.

The four psychiatrists for the defence, sketch from *La Presse*, 9 October 1895; LEFT TO RIGHT: Dr R.M. Bucke, Dr Daniel Clark, Dr James V. Anglin, Dr C.K. Clarke

5

The Psychiatrists

THE PSYCHIATRIC EVIDENCE would be the key to the case.[1] All four defence psychiatrists would of course support the insanity defence, but how strongly would they give their evidence and would they be able to withstand Macmaster's cross-examination? Throughout their testimony, three Crown psychiatrists took notes to assist Macmaster and to be available to give evidence in rebuttal.

James V. Anglin, the most junior of the four, was the first to be called. He had graduated from Queen's medical school at Kingston in 1887, where he had studied under C.K. Clarke, and had then worked with Clarke at Rockwood asylum in Kingston, where his father had been the bursar.[2] He later spent a number of years at the large West Pennsylvania asylum in Pittsburgh and since 1891 had been the assistant medical superintendent of the recently opened Verdun Protestant asylum in Montreal, the only Protestant asylum in Quebec, and today called the Douglas hospital.[3] He remained there until 1905 when he became superintendent of the provincial asylum in New Brunswick. This was the first time he had been called as an expert witness.

Anglin first saw Shortis on 25 June and thereafter he visited him two or three times a week. He concluded, he told Greenshields, that Shortis 'was a lad of unsound mind,' and listed the headings under which he came to this conclusion: 'His utter indifference and callousness in view of the terrible charge against him; he is inordinately vain; his self-importance is not in accordance with his accomplishments; his intense and causeless dislikes for those with whom he comes in contact; his memory is deficient. I found him repeatedly suffering from neuralgia (there is an intimate connection between neuralgia and insanity); his want of affection; he has no proper conception of what is right or wrong.'

Macmaster objected to Anglin's final point: 'I object to that kind of evidence Your Honour. The last answer of witness is only for the jury to decide.' St Pierre and Greenshields, however, cited the famous 1843 M'Naghten case where the English judges had determined that while a medical witness 'cannot in strictness be asked his opinion' on the accused's state of mind at the time of the commission of the offence, 'where the facts are admitted or not disputed, and the question becomes substantially one of science only, it may be convenient to allow the question to be put in that general form, though the same cannot be insisted on as a matter of right.'[4] Judge Mathieu, who had reserved his decision for consideration over the lunch break, announced that he would permit the question, a ruling in accord with present Canadian practice.[5]

Anglin then outlined to the court the behaviour that led him to the conclusion that Shortis was insane: his incoherent speech; odd ideas about dress; preoccupation with subjects such as fatalism and the transmigration of souls; delusions; and hallucinations both of sight and hearing. Moreover, he objected to being thought insane, a view often expressed by insane persons, Anglin said.

The Irish evidence, he argued, supported his opinion, particularly the evidence concerning heredity. Psychiatrists in the 1890s gave greater weight to heredity than they had previously given.[6] There had been a shift in thinking by the 1890s in establishment psychiatric circles – influenced no doubt by writers such as Charles Darwin and Cesare Lombroso – away from free will to determinism. Heredity was the key ingredient in mental disorders. Some authorities, said Anglin, traced 75 per cent of all insanity to heredity. Not only were many of Shortis' relatives mentally ill but many had tuberculosis, or, as it was then called, consumption. There were, said Anglin, double the proportion of consumptives in asylums as there were out of them; this, again, was a common view in the 1890s. Insanity was a physical illness, just as consumption was (later studies would show, however, that it was to a considerable extent the physical conditions in asylums that led to consumption and not the interconnection with insanity itself). Moreover, Shortis himself had symptoms of consumption. Even when he was not agitated, his pulse rate was between 90 and 114, rather than the normal 72, and his temperature was 99 to 100.

Anglin's conclusion was that Shortis had all along suffered from natural or congenital imbecility to which later in life had been added a disease of the mind that might be called 'delusional insanity.' His mental disease, he said, was 'incurable' and at the time of the tragedy he was not capable of knowing that he was doing wrong.

Macmaster then commenced a vigorous cross-examination. Many persons in asylums, Anglin was forced to admit, could distinguish between right and wrong. Was Shortis an imbecile? Macmaster asked him what he thought of the following definition of an imbecile contained in a book that lay on the table before him: 'The idiot has not even the animal intelligence. The imbecile is a step higher in the plane of instinct and knowing, but is little, if any, higher in these than a dog, elephant or chimpanzee, and is held not to be accountable because of mental deprivation.' St Pierre demanded to know the author. When Macmaster would not say, St Pierre told Anglin not to answer the question, but the judge ordered him to reply. The psychiatrist conceded that the definition would not cover Shortis.

'Would you put the prisoner on a higher plane than the dog, for instance?'
'There is no comparison.'
'Then according to that definition he would not be an imbecile,' said Macmaster.
'I don't know,' was Anglin's weak reply.

Greenshields intervened, again demanding to know the author. 'Dr Daniel Clark, one of your own experts,' was Macmaster's triumphant reply, adding 'That is a bombshell.' He offered to let the defence psychiatrists take the book home with them for the night. Court then adjourned for the evening.

The next morning and for most of the day Macmaster continued his cross-examination of Anglin. Clashes between counsel continued. Greenshields accused Macmaster of 'playing for the gallery.' 'My learned friend,' Crown counsel replied, 'is such a good judge of playing for the gallery.' St Pierre objected to Macmaster's coarse language. The *Star* reported – tongue-in-cheek – his concern: 'Mr. St. Pierre was shocked beyond measure to have to remind the Court that Mr. Macmaster had used such vulgar expressions as ''stumper'' and ''bombshell'' and worked himself into a state of righteous indignation as he repeated these terrible words over and over again.' Macmaster clearly made headway in the eyes of the jury as he continued. What precisely were the delusions of persecution? What were the hallucinations? Is it not possible that Shortis pretended to hear voices? Was he simulating insanity in prison? And so on.

Anglin then gave an account of what Shortis had told him about the killings:

'In his imbecile way of pointing pistols as he often did, he pointed it at the lad and it went off by accident, and after that, the thought came over him, "now I am in the hands of Simpson" and then the impulse to shoot the victims. After that he remembers nothing. It is a blank.'

'Shortis said that to you,' interrupted Macmaster.

'Yes, in the Montreal gaol last August.'

'If the shooting of young Wilson was an accident, how do you account for Shortis turning to shoot the very man who was going to the telephone?'

'There is no accounting for an insane man's actions.'

'Do you think it was the act of a fool, after he had shot and wounded Wilson, for him to say to Lowe and Wilson standing together, "Don't you move or I will shoot you" and then exercise his intelligence and turn around and shoot the man going to the telephone?'

'It is quite possible in an insane man.'

'Would you say that was the act of a fool?'

'It was the act of a lunatic.'

'You think that is more in keeping with the foolishness of a lunatic than with the good judgment of a trained criminal?'

Greenshields intervened: 'we are not dealing with a trained criminal here.'

'Well, we will say criminal,' answered Macmaster, smiling.

Anglin had been on the stand for more than ten hours over a period of three days. Macmaster's clever attack had clearly diminished the value of his testimony before the jury. The next psychiatrist, Dr C.K. Clarke, the defence counsel thought, would be able to withstand the onslaught.

C.K. Clarke was a remarkable man.[7] As he stood in the witness box he covered his right hand with his left in order to conceal the fact that his two middle fingers were missing – having been amputated following a hunting accident when he was fifteen. The loss of two fingers, however, had not prevented him from winning the Canadian doubles tennis championship in 1890 or later being a member of the violin section of the Toronto Symphony Orchestra when it was first established. He was also at one time the head of the Society for the Protection of Birds.

Although only thirty-eight, Clarke had been medical superintendent of the 600-bed Rockwood asylum for the past ten years. As mentioned, he had been Anglin's professor of mental disorders at Queen's University. He would remain at Rockwood for twenty-six years, returning to Toronto in 1905 to take over from Daniel Clark as head of the Toronto lunatic asylum and then in 1908 become dean of the Faculty of Medicine at the University of Toronto.

He had been working in asylums, he told Greenshields, for over twenty years, having started working at the age of seventeen for his sister's father-in-law, Dr Joseph Workman, then the pre-eminent Canadian psychiatrist, at the Toronto asylum. After graduating from the medical school at the University of Toronto and a brief period at the Hamilton asylum, he had moved to Kingston to become the assistant medical superintendent under Dr William Metcalf, who had married another of his sisters. How it came about that both his older sisters married psychiatrists is not clear. His father was not a doctor: he was a Liberal politician who had been speaker of the provincial legislature. There is little doubt that his brothers-in-law helped influence his choice of career.

Rockwood, like most of the Ontario asylums at the time, had a good international reputation. The eminent British psychiatrist, Dr D. Hack Tuke, visited the institution in 1884 and referred to its 'kind and skilful' management. [8] The following year Dr Metcalf was killed by a patient, and Dr Clarke, who narrowly escaped death himself, was at the age of twenty-eight made medical superintendent.

He was especially qualified to discuss criminal insanity, he said, because Rockwood, although a provincial institution, was responsible for housing persons who had been declared insane while in the nearby Kingston Penitentiary and were still certifiably insane when their sentences expired; until their sentences ended, they were kept in the 'insane ward' of the penitentiary. Persons acquitted on account of insanity did not go to the penitentiary but were held in provincial asylums at the 'pleasure of the lieutenant-governor.' Clarke had given evidence in numerous criminal cases, including that involving the murder of his brother-in-law, where his testimony had resulted in the killer's being acquitted because of insanity and returned to Rockwood.

Clarke had first visited Shortis at the Montreal jail on 24 July, spending over three hours with him. He was convinced he was insane and later wrote: 'I went into the case most reluctantly and only because, after examining the boy, it seemed a duty, if possible, to endeavour to save such an irresponsible and diseased youth from the gallows.' His

subsequent report to Greenshields stated that Shortis' 'whole de-
meanor was similar to that of the various moral imbeciles I have had
under care.' He concluded 'That Shortis is an imbecile and suffers from
homicidal mania': it is likely 'that the prisoner made his attack in an
impulsive manner, without a single thought of the future.' Clarke subsequently saw him a number of times at the Beauharnois jail. Shortis,
he testified at trial, was a 'moral imbecile,' totally indifferent to his
situation. 'His egotism and personal vanity,' he said, 'were inordinate,
and although I led the conversation to the tragedy, he turned it off and
talked on questions suited to a school boy. I discovered evidence of his
delusions as to a persecution. His whole bearing convinced me that he
was what is commonly called a moral imbecile. He told me of his cruelty to a cat in the most matter of fact way and in reply to a question
laughed that they were deucedly unlucky and he hated the beggars.'

The concept of 'moral imbecility' or, as it was usually referred to,
'moral insanity' was at that time accepted by many distinguished psychiatrists, although contested by others. The great English psychiatrist, Henry Maudsley, had written in his 1874 text, *Responsibility and
Mental Disease*, that 'the actual existence of such a form of disease no
one who has made a practical study of insanity entertains a doubt.'[9] He
described the typical symptoms: 'The affective life of the individual is
profoundly deranged, and his derangement shows itself in what he
feels, desires, and does. He has no capacity of true moral feelings; all
his impulses and desires, to which he yields without check, are
egoistic; his conduct appears to be governed by immoral motives,
which are cherished and obeyed without any evident desire to resist
them.' This 'disease,' first described by Dr James Prichard, one of the
pioneers of English psychiatry, was accepted by many other psychiatrists in the 1880s and 1890s.[10] Dr Hack Tuke accepted the concept in
his 1892 *Dictionary of Psychological Medicine*, as he had in earlier
papers. Indeed, in 1885 he used as a model for moral insanity one of
Clarke's Rockwood patients who had interested him during a visit to
Canada the previous year. Like Shortis, the patient had been involved
in acts of cruelty to individuals and animals. 'Such a man as this,'
Tuke wrote, 'is a reversion to an old savage type, and is born by accident in the wrong century ... Are we to punish him for his involuntary
anachronism?' Such a person 'has so far passed beyond the influence of
deterrent motives that he is morally irresponsible for the act.' An 1895
English medical-legal text, *The Insane and the Law*, accepted moral
insanity and hoped a bold court in England would do so as well. An
'irresistible impulse,' said the authors, 'is sometimes the offspring of

''moral insanity.'' ' There had been a change in the thinking of 'establishment' psychiatrists over the past decade. 'Moral insanity' and the
importance of heredity had now become the accepted wisdom. In contrast, the American asylum superintendents who gave evidence for the
prosecution in the trial of Charles Guiteau, charged with the assassination of President James Garfield in 1881, had resisted the concepts and
stressed instead free will.[11] Similarly, Dr Workman had not accepted
'moral insanity.' But thinking had changed, and it is not surprising,
therefore, that Clarke used the concept of moral insanity to describe
Shortis.

The year 1895 was the end of a psychiatric era. Language more familiar to present-day psychiatrists had not yet been adopted. It was not
until the following year that the German psychiatrist, Emil Kraepelin,
brought out his classification of mental conditions and used the term
'dementia praecox' (literally 'early madness'), which in turn gave way
to the designation 'schizophrenia' (literally 'split in mind or personality'), developed by the Swiss psychiatrist, Eugen Bleuler, in 1911.[12]
Had the Shortis trial been conducted several years later, there is no
doubt that Clarke would have called the condition 'dementia praecox'
and not 'moral insanity.' Many years later he wrote that the 'evidence
in the Shortis case today, if published in full, would rank as *the* classical description of paranoid dementia praecox' (his emphasis). And in
an amateurish unpublished novel entitled 'The Amiable Morons,'
written over twenty years later and loosely based on the Shortis case,
he wrote that the psychiatrists 'at once, and independently arrived
at the same opinion – high grade defective plus dementia praecox of
the paranoid form.'[13] Moreover, the year 1895 was just before the
emergence of Freudian analysis: Freud analysed his first dream on the
night of 23-4 July in 1895 and the term 'psychoanalysis' was not used
until the following year.[14]

Clarke's evidence was not dissimilar to Anglin's. He referred to
Shortis' delusions of persecution by Simpson, indications of consumption, and auditory hallucinations. The history of the case, he said, contained in the mass of details put before the court, was probably one of
the most complete on record. 'I consider that the case of the accused is
absolutely hopeless and that he cannot possibly recover.' 'Was he faking?' Greenshields asked.

> 'I have watched his demeanour very carefully throughout this trial,' said
> Clarke, 'and I have come to the conclusion that he could not have so acted
> had he been sane.'

'Do you think that a sane man could have gone through this trial and in the presence of his father and mother with that demeanour displayed by the prisoner?'

'I do not think he could have kept up his action so consistently as he has done.'

So far as he was aware, he told Greenshields, he had never diagnosed a patient as insane who was afterwards found to be sane.

Shortis' case, he said, was one of 'uncontrollable impulse': 'More than once I have nearly lost my life at the hands of patients so afflicted. This impulse is impossible to describe. It comes over these men and they are utterly unable to control themselves. Dr. Metcalf was killed at my side by such a man, and on another occasion a man caught me by the throat and threw me into the lake, falling in with me ... I am of the opinion that the man who tried to drown me did not know that he was doing wrong. He knew, however, what he was doing, but could not control his impulse.' Finally, he was asked his opinion in terms of the test, including the fateful conjunctive 'and,' set out in the Criminal Code: 'Assuming the evidence to be true, and judging by your examinations, do you consider him capable of distinguishing the nature and quality of the act, and able to judge between right and wrong?' Dr Clarke replied: 'The prisoner at the time of the crime was not capable of knowing the nature and quality of the act and that it was wrong.'

Macmaster's cross-examination was similar to that used with Dr Anglin:

Q. Do you think when the prisoner at the bar said to Lowe and Wilson, 'Don't move, or I will shoot you' that he was controlled by his mind or the devil?

A. It was a condition of the mind, of which he was unconscious.

Q. In the ordinary walks of life, if a man turns and shoots another you would call that murder?

A. Most decidedly.

Q. Don't you think it was a clever piece of manoeuvring to keep two men standing still, kill a man and cut off communication by telephone?

A. Matter of opinion.

Q. What do you say to Shortis pleading to the man in the vault to come out; was it not what a thief would have done?

A. Well, I suppose so.

Q. Would the presence of a large sum of money have been an incentive for the crime?

A. I regard it as an unfortunate coincidence.

Some of Clarke's own writings were put to him. Did he still hold the view that the law in its treatment of moral imbeciles was crude and absurd, as he had previously written? Yes, said Clarke, stating that in the present case the law had an excellent chance of vindicating itself.

Daniel Clark, medical superintendent of the 700-bed Toronto lunatic asylum for the past twenty years and who would continue in that position for another ten years (to be replaced by C.K. Clarke), was at the age of sixty the most senior of the defence psychiatrists.[15] He had arrived in Canada from Scotland at the age of twelve, and three years later, in 1850, had left for California, where gold had recently been discovered. He returned to Canada the following year after making a considerable amount of money on placer mining, and graduated from the Victoria medical school, then in Cobourg, Ontario. Like St Pierre, he volunteered for the North in the American Civil War, serving as a volunteer surgeon in General Grant's army of the Potomac.

The new construction at the Toronto asylum on Queen Street was completed in 1870. In 1875 Clark had replaced Dr Workman as superintendent. When Dr Tuke visited the institution in 1884 he was impressed, particularly in contrast to the findings of his brother forty years earlier, who had reported on conditions in the converted jail that was used to hold the insane: 'I left the place sickened with disgust, and could hardly sleep at night, as the images of the suffering patients kept floating before my mind's eye in all the horrors of the revolting scenes I had witnessed.'[16]

Dr Clark was best known to the public as the principal defence psychiatrist in the Riel case of 1885. As in that case and others, his psychiatric evidence was not always accepted by the jury. In Guelph in 1889, for example, Drs Clark, Clarke, and Bucke had all given evidence of insanity, but the accused was found guilty and was hanged. Clark did not think much of the law on insanity. In the very year of the Shortis case he wrote in the *American Medico-Psychological Journal*: 'There is nothing more farcical in jurisprudence than leaving a decision of sanity or insanity in the hands or minds of many who may never have seen a case of insanity in their lives, especially one of the delusional type.' His writings on insanity included a book published just before the trial, entitled *Mental Diseases*. Like C.K. Clarke he had written a novel (concerning the rebellion of 1837), and he had edited a book of poetry and published books of 'photographs of celebrated men and noted places.'[17]

The examination and cross-examination of Clark was relatively brief, both being completed in about three hours. His opinion did not differ materially from the other psychiatrists: 'I have visited the prisoner twice since I arrived in Beauharnois, ten days ago. From what I have heard given in evidence here, assuming it to be true, in conjunction with my own observations, I consider the prisoner a natural congenitive imbecile, on which has been implanted insanity.' Like the other witnesses, he referred to delusions and hallucinations and the prisoner's present health. He, Bucke, and Dr Villeneuve for the Crown had examined Shortis that very morning and found his pulse to be 124, higher than it had so far been. Shortis, he said, had a child's mind in a man's body. He knew of 'no parallel case.' 'There was no chance whatever of his recovery.' Shortis was not capable of appreciating his act or knowing that it was wrong. Would he have acted as he did, asked Macmaster, if a policeman had been present? 'Yes,' was the reply, 'I believe that the prisoner would have fired at Loy just the same if three or four policemen had been present. ... The killing was done from impulse alone to kill. A man when acting under an impulse cannot tell when shooting another that he is breaking the law.' Clark's evidence added little except the weight of his authority, though he added one diagnosis not mentioned so far: that Shortis' periodic headaches accompanied by excitement were most likely caused by what Clark called 'nocturnal epilepsy.'

The most remarkable of all the defence psychiatrists was undoubtedly R.M. Bucke, described by Clarke as 'one of the most striking personalities' in psychiatry.[18] For over eighteen years he had been the superintendent of the 900-bed London lunatic asylum, the largest in Ontario, and he was professor of mental diseases at the University of Western Ontario, whose medical school he had helped establish. He had built a significant reputation in the world of psychiatry, later becoming president of the American Medico-Psychological Association (the predecessor of the American Psychiatric Association) as well as president of the psychology section of the British Medical Association.

Bucke was the first superintendent in Canada and, it appears, the first in all of North America to adopt the policy of *absolute* no restraint, an important part of what was called 'moral treatment,' which had been used in Europe in the previous century by Philippe Pinel in France and William Tuke (an ancestor of D. Hack Tuke) in England. 'It is restraint that makes restraint necessary,' Bucke wrote. When Tuke visited the asylum in 1884 he reported that 'there was no patient in restraint and none in seclusion.'[19] The system Bucke had introduced in the early 1880s, which was quickly followed by Clark in Toronto and by Clarke and Metcalf in Kingston, was combined with schemes for providing farm work and other employment for patients. Tuke had generous comments on all the public Ontario institutions, particularly when compared to the private Quebec institutions. Dr Villeneuve's hospital, Longue Pointe, near Montreal, run by the Sisters of Providence, was described as a 'chamber of horrors': 'The astonishment which I experienced in witnessing this relic of barbarism in the Province of Quebec is still further increased when I see such excellent institutions as the Lunatic Asylums of the adjoining Province of Ontario.' In fairness, it should be noted that the well-run Protestant hospital in Verdun was established after Tuke's visit and steps had been taken to improve conditions at Longue Pointe by providing a measure of provincial control. Bucke had even grander plans for Ontario. He tried to convince the government to build a large community of perhaps four or five thousand mental patients on 'wild government land,'[20] possibly in Muskoka, north of Toronto, where Bucke spent his summers. This project, however, was never undertaken.

Bucke entered the witness box on Friday morning, 18 October, the sixteenth day of the trial. His appearance revealed much about his fascinating background. Obvious to all was a decided limp, the result of the amputation of one foot and part of another when, many years earlier, he and a prospecting companion (the discoverer of the legendary Comstock lode, who died from exposure) had been lost in a blizzard in the American West. His father, a direct descendant of Robert Walpole, the English prime minister, was a Cambridge-educated minister who had brought his family, and an immense library, to London when his son was very young. Bucke had left home at the age of sixteen after both his parents had died, spending five years in the United States plying the Mississippi, working in the Louisiana swamps and searching for gold and silver in the West. He had fought Indians, starvation, and blizzards.

Also apparent to everyone was the remarkable physical resemblance and similarity in dress between Bucke, then fifty-eight, and the recently deceased American poet, Walt Whitman. The head of the Verdun institute described Bucke's Whitman-like appearance a few years later: 'His commanding presence, his massive head, his keen, searching eyes and prominent nose, his face, every line of which carried the stamp of intellectual force, his flowing beard covering the negligée woolen shirt, his silvery locks showing below the broad-brimmed, gray, slouch hat, and his gray tweeds make him a strikingly conspicuous and original figure.'[21]

It was no coincidence that he looked like Whitman. In fact, he deliberately imitated him, and the single most important aspect of his life was his devotion to the man. Bucke had read *Leaves of Grass* in 1868 and had met the poet ten years later. Whitman's writings had transformed his life. He identified Whitman with the Messiah, and *Leaves of Grass* as the Bible of the future for the next thousand years. The two men became friends, spending four months together in 1880 on a trip up the St Lawrence, where they visited C.K. Clarke at Kingston and perhaps went through Valleyfield.[22] Bucke wrote a biography of Whitman and became his literary executor. In his own will, drafted in 1894, he described Whitman as the 'greatest man of my day.'

Bucke had strange – even, it could be said, 'crackpot' – views on the development of the mind. In a paper the year before the Shortis trial to the annual American Medico-Psychological Association meeting in Philadelphia he presented his ideas on what he called 'cosmic consciousness.'[23] In brief, his theory was that mankind was approaching a higher form of consciousness, experienced up to the present by only a select few, including Christ, Mohammed, Bacon, Blake, and of course Walt Whitman. These individuals had gone through a form of transcendental transformation similar to Bucke's own upon his discovery of Whitman. In the years to come, this level of consciousness would become more prevalent in society. Bucke's theory perhaps seemed far less strange in the age of Darwin than it does to most of us today. Man, according to him, would have gone from the earliest stage of 'simple consciousness' to 'self-consciousness' and finally to 'cosmic consciousness.' A recent biographer of Whitman refers to Bucke's 'preposterous inferences from his data.'[24] In 1901 he published a massive book, *Cosmic Consciousness*, which, whatever its defects, has run through more then twenty editions and is still in print. He died one winter evening in 1902 on the verandah of his home in London, having cracked his head after slipping on some ice.

In a letter to his daughter a few days before he gave evidence, Bucke revealed his sympathy for and identification with Shortis' parents:

Sunday night

Sweet Birdie

Your dear mother, sweet Johnie and your darling self will think 'the old man' is never coming back again – but he *is* after a while if he has any kind of luck. This Shortis case is the biggest fight I have ever seen in a court. Mr. Shortis is going to spend in the neighbourhood of from $30,000 to $50,000 to try to prevent the wretched boy being hanged – not so much for the boy's sake (for he cares nothing about it and it really matters nothing at all *to him* whether he is hanged or not) but to avert the disgrace of having a murderer in the family. Just think if one of our boys had killed two men *by accident* (it really comes to that for Val Shortis knew nothing of what he was doing) and was likely to be hanged for it – think what we would all do to save him. Of course, the thing is not the same for Val S. is a hopeless imbecile and a lunatic – still our feeling in the matter would be very much the same as the feeling of Mr. & Mrs. Shortis now. I have become very much interested in the trial and while (of course) I shall not say a word beyond what the facts warrant I am *very* anxious that the poor wretch should not be convicted if it can be prevented by legitimate means ...

I am, sweet birdie,

Your loving father

R.M. Bucke

Bucke had visited Shortis three times in his cell. His evidence was consistent with the letter to his daughter. Like the other defence psychiatrists, he asserted that Shortis' case was hopeless and recovery entirely out of the question. He had no doubt about it. 'I am perfectly certain,' he told Greenshields, 'that he is absolutely incurable.' It was impossible, he said, for the prisoner to feign the hallucinations and his present condition. He viewed heredity as enormously important, stating that 80 or 90 per cent of cases of insanity could be traced back to heredity. 'I say,' he testified, 'that the prisoner is a natural or congenital imbecile, both morally and intellectually, and I also say he is a lunatic.' Then, borrowing the language he used in his *Cosmic Consciousness,* he declared: 'This man committed these homicides in an unconscious or rather in a simple conscious condition, without the possession at the time of self-consciousness.' 'Simple consciousness' was not what the defence wanted to establish; lack of consciousness would have been more helpful. Unfortunately for the defence, Bucke added: 'I attribute the killing only in a limited sense to impulse.' He emphasized imbecility and told Macmaster that he did not concur in a number of his confrère's opinions and conclusions regarding the accused.

Although his evidence was given with great authority, it was far less useful to the defence than that of the other psychiatrists. Macmaster trapped him into conceding that there was premeditation, a position obviously inconsistent with the defence of irresistible impulse. In stressing Shortis' delusion of persecution by Simpson, Bucke stated:

'I think Shortis would have liked to kill Mr. Simpson and also anyone he thought under Simpson's influence.'
'Then there was premeditation?' interposed Macmaster.
'Undoubtedly there would have been,' was the reply.

The psychiatrist also conceded that if it could be shown that Shortis really loved his mother he would not be a 'moral imbecile.' But, said Bucke, Shortis showed no such affection: 'When I saw his mother in the witness box, her whole soul going out to her boy, her heart breaking for him; the father watching his child, his eyes bathed in tears and that boy paying absolutely no attention to them and seeming to care less, then I say he could have no love for his parents.' The jury may not have been as convinced as Dr Bucke that Shortis did not love his mother.

Two dramatic events occurred while Bucke was giving his evidence, the first shortly after he began and the other late in the day. Fifteen minutes after the proceedings commenced, Mr and Mrs Shortis entered the courtroom accompanied by a distinguished high official of the Roman Catholic church, Monsignor Henry O'Bryen, the head of the Papal College in Rome. [25] Judge Mathieu rose and bowed to the prelate, saying 'My Lord, will you honour us by taking a seat on my right.' The sixty-five-year-old churchman, looking, according to *La Presse*, like Wilfrid Laurier, but dressed of course in his clerical robes, sat beside the judge throughout the morning, occasionally conversing with him. In the afternoon he sat in the body of the court in front of the jury box, in a large plush chair placed between the Shortises. O'Bryen had known them in Ireland many years before. Indeed, he had officiated at their marriage. His visit to Beauharnois – he had arrived the night before and had visited them at the Convent of Jesus and Mary where they were staying – was specifically to support his friends, a fact which must surely have made a strong impression on the French-speaking and Catholic members of the jury. Monsignor O'Bryen, who was fluently bilingual, had visited Canada and the United States on many occasions, and it was thought by many, although denied by O'Bryen, that this visit to Canada was to be the eyes and ears of the Pope on the crucial Manitoba schools question.

The second incident occurred in the late afternoon. A fierce argument took place between Francis Shortis and David Smith, secretary-treasurer of the Montreal Cotton Company. Smith, sitting behind the Shortises (and O'Bryen), was heard to say 'there is not a man on the jury insane enough to bring in any other verdict than guilty.' Turning, Mr Shortis said, 'I think a little manners would be a good thing.' 'I think it would,' replied Smith. 'Your honour,' said Mr Shortis, making menacing gestures towards Smith, 'I'd like to call your attention to this man who sits here day after day passing remarks and laughing with his friends. I don't mind for myself, but it's for my poor wife who sits here breaking her heart.' Judge Mathieu, who had overheard similar comments, pointed to Smith and said sternly, 'Put that man out.' After further vigorous exchanges by the participants and by counsel, it was agreed that Smith would move to another part of the room. The judge warned those in the courtroom that 'when a witness is speaking, no one may laugh, nor even make motions of approval or disapproval.' The press noted Shortis' lack of reaction to these proceedings, the *Herald* reporting: 'Throughout all this Mrs. Shortis wept bitterly, but the son remained unmoved. Like a wax figure, its glossy fair hair neatly combed, its moustache waxed, its eyes riveted upon the coat of arms over the judge's seat, and its head set erect by its shoulder, Bertie Shortis stood, as he has during the greater portion of the trial, which means life or death.'

6

Rebuttal

THE DEFENCE CASE was closed late Friday afternoon, 18 October, on the sixteenth day of the trial. Shortis could have been, but was not, called as a witness (the 1892 Code had changed the previous law which had prevented an accused from giving sworn testimony). Then, as now, however, it would have been very unusual for the accused to give evidence when the defence was one of insanity. After a short adjournment, Andrew Robertson, the first of the Crown's many rebuttal witnesses, was called by Macmaster. Robertson, the secretary-treasurer of the Globe Woollen Mills, testified that he first met Shortis in June 1894 when he appeared at the Globe offices accompanied by his mother, with a letter of recommendation from A.F. Gault, the president of the company. Shortis, he said, worked at the mill for three weeks, without pay. Macmaster asked the witness a number of questions, as he did of other rebuttal witnesses, designed to show that there was nothing remarkable in Shortis' manner to suggest insanity. He was no different from other young men, Robertson said; 'He made a few clerical errors, but nothing more than a young man would make who was commencing business.' Greenshields' cross-examination showed, however, that it took Shortis sixteen days to copy out forty-five pages of foolscap, where an ordinary man could have done the same work in two days. Moreover, within the three-week period, Shortis was absent half a day because of a headache.

On Saturday, Louis Simpson, the manager of the Montreal Cotton Company, was called by the Crown, an event eagerly awaited by all those following the case. Seats were once again in great demand. Earlier in the week the Montreal *Star* had asked: 'How would Shortis act were he to find himself once more face to face with this man whose

Mr and Mrs Shortis in court, sketch from Montreal *Daily Star*, 3 October 1895 figure is constantly before him during his waking hours and whose image even visits him in his dreams?' All eyes were on Shortis when Simpson appeared, but, as the *Herald* reported, 'There was not a move, not a sign of care whether Simpson was there or not.' The prisoner gave two or three twirls to his moustache, stared vacantly in front of him, and, according to the *Gazette*, 'rivetted his gaze upon the Royal arms above the judicial seat, which he contemplates for many hours each day.' Simpson's evidence made a strong impression on the spectators and the jury.

Simpson, a forty-two-year-old Englishman, who had learned the cotton business at his brother's mill in Lancashire[1] and had been in Valleyfield for seven years, had first met Shortis in July 1894 in Montreal. He had been looking for a private secretary and Shortis came well recommended. He was given a two-month trial – at a dollar a day – writing letters, copying, filing, and other similar tasks. As a rule, he said, the young man discharged his duties correctly, although there were some understandable mistakes, such as sending a letter to Manchester, England, instead of Manchester, New Hampshire. Shortis stayed five weeks: 'Eventually I got a secretary who was a stenographer. I thereupon informed Shortis that as he could not write shorthand, his services would terminate at the end of the month. We parted good friends. He asked me for a recommendation, and I informed him that if anyone came to me I would give him a good character.' Shortis was permitted to remain in the carding section of the mill, without pay, to learn the cotton business. After reading in a Montreal paper that he was out hunting, when he should have been in the plant, Simpson gave him a warning, but allowed him to return.

A second incident occurred in December, when Shortis was arrested and brought before Simpson, in his capacity as a justice of the peace, for shooting at and frightening two mill workers in Valleyfield Shortis apparently thought were talking too loudly. 'He conducted his own case in a very intelligent manner,' Simpson testified, 'and called one witness on his behalf. He was fined $5, however, as it was found from the evidence adduced that he was guilty. The next day I warned him again at the cotton mill office.' He then referred to the Andersons:

I, at the same time, told him that, although I told him not to go to McGuiness', he continued to do so. Shortis replied that he did not remember having been so warned. At the same time he said: 'Mr. Simpson, I have been told that you always give a man three chances. You have given me only two chances: are you going to be harder on me than any other person?' I replied that I was not harder on him, but I wanted to be obeyed. He promised to do as requested in future. I then allowed him to go back to work. Previous to this, however, I advised him that he had better return to Montreal.

Simpson then – apparently without objection by the defence to the hearsay nature of the evidence – told of a meeting he had with Bob McGuiness, Millie Anderson's stepfather, on 23 January 1895, at which McGuiness related a plot by Shortis to kill him. McGuiness had placed four loaded revolvers on Simpson's table, declaring that one was his own; one belonged to Shortis, who had left it on the piano at the house; one had been taken from under the pillow of his stepdaughter; and the fourth from under the pillow of his stepson, Jack. Shortis had approached McGuiness with an offer to shoot Simpson: if McGuiness, who liked the plant manager as little as he did, would say he had spent the night there, Jack Anderson would swear he had slept with him, thus providing an alibi. Shortis was to get out by the window, do the deed, then return to the house. Simpson testified that he believed, from what McGuiness had said, that both Millie and Jack were in on the conspiracy. Their stepfather had felt it his duty to warn Simpson, who had turned the revolvers over to the police and instructed Detective Poirier to warn Shortis to leave Valleyfield. (The easy availability of handguns in Canada at the time is apparent. A permit system had first been introduced in 1892, but only a minor penalty – from $5 to $25 – was provided for its breach. The legislation was not tightened until just before the First World War.[2])

Several weeks later, Simpson said, 'Shortis came to the office and asked for a character reference. I refused, stating that circumstances altered cases. He then told me that I was "no gentleman." I ordered him out, and he went. In the outside office he kept shouting: "You are no gentleman, every dog has his day, and mine will come yet." ' From that time to the present he had not seen the man. When the tragedy occurred, he was vacationing with his family in Savannah, Georgia.

Macmaster concluded his examination early Saturday afternoon in time for the lawyers and the judge to catch the 3:20 train to Montreal. Francis and Mary Shortis went to the station to say good-bye to their friend, Monsignor O'Bryen, and then returned to the convent. They knew, as did the defence counsel, that Simpson's evidence had made a powerful impact. The *Star* did not exaggerate in stating that his evidence 'was the turning of the tide, which ... has recently flowed strongly against the Crown.'

'Don't be so anxious to hang this man,' were Greenshields' opening words to Simpson, who denied that this was his intention. The cross-examination in no way diminished the impact of the testimony. As Simpson left the box he offered his hand in sympathy to Francis Shortis, who refused to accept it.

For the entire week the Crown called rebuttal evidence. Shortis' banker said that the accused had been in his shop between three and four on the afternoon of the killing, acting quite normally. David Smith, the secretary-treasurer of the cotton company, who had had the exchange with Francis Shortis the previous week, found Shortis to be a normal person: 'I was impressed with his behaviour, and considered him very gentlemanly in his manner.' Witnesses from the plant told of his intelligence in his understanding of the operation of the machinery and in making suggestions for its improvement. 'He spoke like an average businessman,' said a Montreal sporting goods dealer with whom Shortis had tried to do business. The druggist in Valleyfield noticed nothing strange about his conversations. A Montreal druggist, who had befriended Shortis, remembered a Christmas dinner at his house in 1893 when he had intelligently discussed English literature and Irish politics, sympathizing with the home rulers. John Lowe testified that Shortis had always talked reasonably; Hugh Wilson, one of the victims of the tragedy and a former friend, had never heard Shortis say he heard voices. Guests at the Windsor Hotel, where Shortis had stayed in Valleyfield, and at the Queen's Hotel in Montreal, where Shortis often ate with his mother, found nothing strange in his eating manners or his intelligence.

Two Valleyfield doctors gave evidence for the Crown, not as expert witnesses but simply as persons who knew the accused. Dr Adrien Ouimet, who had studied medicine in Paris and like Shortis boarded at the Windsor Hotel, met him at least twice a day: he always conversed rationally and conducted himself like other young men, and went through the menu properly, never starting at the bottom and going to the top. Dr Walter Sutherland, the mill doctor, had treated Shortis on at least four occasions, but he had never complained of headaches. They often talked, and Sutherland considered him of more than average intelligence. On one occasion Shortis had loaned him a copy of

Robert Louis Stevenson's then popular short novel, *The Strange Case of Dr Jekyll and Mr Hyde*, a story of a man with two distinct personalities; Shortis had said there were just such people nowadays. St Pierre asked if he might take the book back to his hotel room to see if it shed any light on the case.

Macmaster called witnesses from the post office in Montreal to show that a year before the killings Shortis had tried to defraud the institution by claiming he had not received full payment of a money order his mother had sent him. He even swore a declaration to this effect, which he later acknowledged to be false, and arranged for a family friend to guarantee the debt without telling the guarantor the true circumstances. No charges had been brought, however. Greenshields objected to this evidence, saying that it was put in 'for the purpose of proving malice or premeditation' and so should have been introduced as part of the Crown's original case and not as reply evidence. No, asserted Macmaster, 'the object of putting in this evidence is simply this: it is to show that the prisoner came in contact with the post office authorities and disclosed a certain amount of mind and memory and understanding, which are the essential ingredients of sanity.' Of course it also showed that Shortis was eager to have more money. 'I will allow the question,' ruled the judge, 'for I do not think I can stop the Crown when offering to prove a fact, to establish the sanity of the accused.'

The court adjourned early on Tuesday at Macmaster's request to permit him to obtain commission evidence in Huntingdon from Bob McGuiness, who was too ill to attend the trial. On Wednesday this evidence was read to the court, and it supported Simpson's testimony with regard to the conspiracy, though there were some discrepancies in detail:

> I had a talk with Shortis in the presence of young Jack about the proposed shooting of Simpson. Shortis asked me how it would be if he were to give Simpson a thrashing. I said it would be all right I supposed. I did not care. Then he asked me how would it be to fill him full of cold lead and asked me if I would swear an alibi. I said, 'No, I guess not,' that I did not want to have anything to do with it. He said he knew right where to find him. This was in January last. When I refused to comply with his request he said your conscience is not elastic enough I suppose ... Afterwards I called on Simpson and took three revolvers. One was found in Jack's bed and one in Millie's room. I told Simpson Shortis was not all there and he might do some harm, and Mr.

Simpson said the same himself, that there was a screw loose in him. The family and Mrs. McGuiness were not on friendly terms with Mr. Simpson. He had been running them down and had taken their foundry business from them. He tried to ruin them in every way he could. The foundry was built to do the factory's business and Simpson, instead of giving it to them, took it somewhere else. The foundry was closed up. In connection with the proposed shooting of Simpson I think Shortis thought he could do anything. That was about his style. I always called the man a fool from the moment I met him. He thought it great fun to go to my house and tell them I was coming home full and would raise the devil ... He was eccentric and queer acting ... I told Mrs. McGuiness that her daughter should not run the streets with a madman or something to that effect.

Macmaster asked McGuiness: 'From what you know of him in connection with the tragedy, do you think it was the money he was after?' The judge sustained Greenshields' objection that this was a matter that should have been put in as part of the Crown's original case, not in reply. In cross-examination, McGuiness supported the defence evidence of the reckless use of firearms: 'The first time I met him he and Jack and I went out duck shooting and a fellow fired a shot at a duck. The shot struck the boat and scattered all over it. Shortis jumped up and swore he would blow his brains out. He carried on so that I got home as soon as I could and told him I did not want to have anything more to do with him. He used to shoot at doors through which I had to pass and I did not think I was safe.'

McGuiness' evidence cut both ways. One statement, however, clearly harmed Shortis' case: 'I saw him at nine o'clock on the night of the murder. He never complained to me of headaches.' He also added, to Shortis' detriment: 'He knew the difference between right and wrong, but I always thought he was not level.'

Ernest McVicar, a friend of Shortis', who had earlier given evidence for the Crown about the possibility of robbing the mill, was recalled by the Crown. Had he received a letter from Shortis about two weeks after the murder, asked Macmaster, in which the accused had stated that he should be careful about what he (McVicar) said, as silence was golden? Greenshields at once objected, but of course the jury had already heard the question. The practice of holding a *voir dire* (that is, a trial within a trial) to determine admissibility in the absence of the jury was not well established in the nineteenth century.[3] A complicated legal discussion then ensued on the admissibility of the evidence.

Greenshields argued that the Crown was improperly trying to prove motive through reply evidence. Macmaster said he was simply trying to show that the accused was a 'trickster' who had 'absolutely and successfully deceived the medical men into giving evidence that he was an idiot.' St Pierre cited authorities, such as the well-known case of the American Guiteau,[4] to the effect that evidence of sanity *after* the event is not relevant. The judge reserved his decision and later in the day, citing the then current English texts, Taylor, Roscoe, and Archbold,[5] ruled that the Crown was limited to evidence contemporaneous with or prior to the event. To some extent, the defence victory backfired, however, because it also meant that the defence psychiatrists were not entitled to give evidence of Shortis' mental condition after the event – and the jury were in theory not entitled to rely on such evidence they had already heard. All the newspapers printed the following letter to McVicar, but whether the sequestered jury ever knew its details is not known:

MONTREAL, Que., March 27, 1895

TO MY DEAR ERNY, I have not received my laundry, please try and see about it as soon as possible and send it along to me, per express. I have no news to tell you, but want you to make up for my lack of news by telling me in all the various would be authentic stories set afloat about me or others. Do not withhold any of the nasty things for fear of hurting my feelings. I despise all in Valleyfield, with a few exceptions (need I say you and yours included). They (the majority) hate and fear me. At least whilst I was free they feared me. They shall yet do so again, and with reason. I have a good memory. How are J. and M. Tell me all you know. I lent a pair of skates to McD. of McD. and R.'s. Get them from him and keep them. There is an old saying 'Silence is golden' – sometimes even more. Old man I want you for your own sake to give up even beer and _____. The people in the English village K.B.A.S. and B. lego etc. You understand, do you not? Ask Jack what two things I said, play the deuce with a fellow, particularly in a hot country, where in some cases a fellow, if he goes there, would have to govern more than himself. Then the best thing is to begin by governing himself. Put no reliance in anything you read in the papers, till I tell you 'cest vrai.' I have retained the three best criminal lawyers in Canada for my defence.

The venue has not been changed from Beauharnois to Montreal yet. I thought it had, but my counsel said they had not yet asked to have it shifted. Do you remember when Wattie had the trouble? How some of us were near being made to come forward as witnesses? Well, it was our own talk; if we said nothing people would not have known we knew anything. How is W?

You know how much I like him. My plans for 1896, that I had, will probably in a modified form be carried out in the autumn of '95 or first of '96, subject to the approval of a certain party. I shall ('if all goes well.' 'God is good.' I don't think my time has come yet) go to the west coast of Ireland. As Mahomet said, 'God holds in his hand the fate of the morrow.' What is the name of the grocer that has the shop below Parker's? Register your reply. I enclose an envelope to prevent the possibility of a mistake. I hope you and my other friends M. and F. continue to remember my defence has yet to be made. There are two sides to every story. Think of how that low cur Simpson would talk about me. Then remember the facts of the case.

Ask M. to send me S.'s letter of December 28th, his first shot, to same address. I want it soon as possible. Ask her to register. You know who runs the post office at V. Please spare me the short few minutes to have laundry sent and reply soon as you possibly can. Remember my advice, if the game is worth the candle you ought to do as I tell. You know best. People might say what game – why, health, etc., of course; that's the only one I could mean. Thank God my friends have up to now stuck to me as I did and would do to them. Oh, 'tis sweet to live' when a fellow sees none of his friends are deserters in his hour of trouble.

With kindest regards to you, your father, mother, sister and younger brother and my friends join, I remain, my dear Erny, as heretofore,

Very faithfully, your friend,

BERTIE

Please tear up all my letters. I do not want them to get lost or mislaid. Burning or tearing them up will be the safest. I trust you on your honor to do so. Please don't join the A.O.F.

Address all letters to George Bury, Esq., Montreal.

McVicar was recalled later in the proceedings to state that for two months prior to the tragedy he often went with Shortis in the evening to the Anderson home. Shortis, he said, never spoke in his presence of seeing people come to the window or of hearing noises or voices, and on no occasion did he ever mention anything of the kind to him.

The judge's ruling on the admissibility of evidence would, however, permit evidence of *prior* correspondence, and the Crown received the court's permission to obtain a letter from Shortis to A.F. Gault, who was ill in Montreal. This letter was put before the jury:

PRIVATE

Wednesday Morning, January 30th, 1895

DEAR MR. GAULT, It was with the greatest horror and indignation that I heard last evening what kind of stories Mr. Simpson has been circulating about me in Montreal, viz., about a conspiracy being on foot to kill him. Certainly I was told that he would use every method in his power to put me out of this town; but I never for a moment thought that he would resort to a ridiculous, improbable story about my entering into a conspiracy to kill him. Poirier, who was the chief of the police here formerly but owing to habits of intemperance lost his position, told me this evening that Mr. Simpson told him to tell me 'that if I did not leave the town he would have me put in jail for conspiring to take his life.' The reason Mr. S. is so anxious to get me to leave is, he hates Miss M.G. Anderson and her brother, because their mother, now Mrs. McGinnis, and him are very bad friends and on the 24th or thereabouts of last month, he told me I should not speak to Miss Anderson or her brother in future, because he made up his mind that none of his friends or any person in the mill should have anything to do with them. Is not that as great a piece of high handed boycotting as ever you heard about? Certainly, by such conduct Mr. S. displayed an awful amount of petty spite to say the least of it. I would not insult any friend of mine by behaving in such an un-mannerly way, and notice the result. First I am told I must leave the mill, and then a trumped up charge is brought against me. In Canada such a story cannot fail to be ridiculous. Are you not astonished, Mr. Gault, at any man doing such things as Mr. S. to vex a person who he dislikes. Rather hard on the person that he selects to use as the punishing medium. Will you please tell me what to do? Here I am all alone without one to advise me. I shall see this morning Mr. S. and will tell him that he shall have my answer within a week. Such nonsensical thoughts as my 'prowling around the mill waiting to kill' any person. I am too young to right away decide my conduct, but pray to our good God that you will tell me what you think best for me to do and in the meantime tell Mr. S. to stay proceedings for a week. You have been formerly so kind to me that I feel that you advise me in my hour of trouble. If I will be permitted to stay here I expect to get a position in the office of one of the lumber mills here. Should I be forced to go away what am I to do goodness only knows. Should you like to hear an impartial account of my conduct whilst here I feel confident that you will receive a good report about me if you write to any one who knows me. There are more ways than one, you know, to tell every story. Won't you, please, try and get an impartial one before you judge me? Thanking you from the bottom of my heart in anticipation for your advice and former kindness, also hoping you will forgive my giving you such a lot of trouble.

I remain, dear Mr. Gault,

Very gratefully your friend,

F.V.C. SHORTIS.

No doubt the jury agreed with the *Star*'s headline, 'Another Shrewd Letter Written by Shortis.'

A.F. Gault's evidence, read Friday morning, completed the Crown's reply. Immediately before this, the Crown had called Charles Vallée, the governor of the Montreal jail where Shortis had stayed. He testified that Dr Georges Villeneuve, medical superintendent of the Longue Pointe asylum, had gone to see Shortis on Macmaster's instruction a week before the trial started, but that Shortis had refused to be examined: 'I don't want you to think it discourteous, do not be surprised at my sudden silence, but I have been advised to speak to no one by my doctors.' Defence counsel strenuously objected to this evidence, declaring that it was put in to prejudice the jury and that, while the eyes of the whole scientific world were on Beauharnois, the Crown did not *dare* to put its medical witnesses in the box for fear of what they might say. The line of questioning was, however, permitted by Judge Mathieu. Greenshields established in cross-examination that Dr Villeneuve was the only Crown doctor to attempt to examine Shortis, that he had only gone there once, and that he had given up after a couple of questions. The Crown, it was suggested, was not really interested in having a medical examination.

It was now the defence's turn to rebut the reply evidence – an unusual procedure. Each of the defence counsel in turn went into the witness box – an even more unusual procedure – and swore they had never instructed Shortis to refuse examination by Crown psychiatrists. They did not know, each said, that Dr Villeneuve had been refused permission. Indeed, if an application to examine Shortis had been made, they would not have opposed it.

The final witness of the trial – the 133rd witness in the twenty-second day of the trial – was again Dr R.M. Bucke. Nothing that he had heard in rebuttal, he said, had caused him to change his opinion of Shortis' insanity. Once again, however, Macmaster would be able to cross-examine, with great effect on the jury.

Q. 'Assuming that Mr. McGuiness' evidence be true that the prisoner intended to shoot Simpson, and that he asked McGuiness to help him prove an alibi, what does it indicate to your mind?'

A. 'It exhibits a certain amount of cunning,' replied Dr. Bucke.

Q. 'Do you think that it indicates that the prisoner wanted to escape punishment for that crime?'

A. 'Yes, in case he committed the crime.'

Q. 'Assuming the statement by Mr. Brophy to be true, that Shortis asked Brophy not to tell Mr. Hachette [the guarantor] the real character of the post office money order transaction, what inference would you draw from that circumstance?'

A. 'I consider that he saw it might have an unpleasant consequence, not necessarily that he knew it was wrong.'

Q. 'Would not the natural inference be that he knew he was doing wrong?'

A. 'Yes, if the man was fully equipped mentally, it could only bear that construction.'

Q. 'Do you think that when Shortis proposed to fill Simpson full of cold lead and asked McGuiness to swear an alibi that he knew that the killing of Simpson was murder?'

A. 'He probably had some suspicion of that kind.'

Macmaster then turned to the definition of imbecility, set out earlier, given in the article written by Dr Daniel Clark: 'An imbecile is little better intellectually or morally than a dog, an elephant or chimpanzee.' What did Dr Bucke think of that definition?

A. 'In the first place, I do not know whether those are Dr. Clark's words. In the second place, I have been given to understand in that lecture there is a lot of other stuff which modifies that definition.'

Q. 'Did you hear me reading that definition when examining Dr. Anglin?'

A. 'Yes.'

Q. 'You heard counsel for defence ask Dr. Clark if he disavowed that definition and he did not?'

A. 'Yes.'

Q. 'Is there anything in the article which modifies your definition of an idiot and an imbecile?'

A. 'No, I don't think that is a good definition.'

Q. 'How did you arrive at your conclusion that prisoner is an imbecile?'

A. 'I discovered it by examinations of prisoner.'

The Crown had thus thrown into doubt the defence's reliance on the concept of imbecility. The Criminal Code, it will be recalled, required an initial finding that the accused was 'labouring under natural imbecility, or disease of the mind.' Macmaster now turned to 'disease of the mind':

> Q. 'What disease of the mind was the prisoner suffering from on March 1st?'
> A. 'I can only tell that from inference. It could not be discovered by superficial examination. I believe him insane by his delusions and his history.'

Re-examined by Greenshields, Bucke testified that many of his insane patients were capable of doing ordinary tasks. 'Of the 1,000 patients in the London Asylum today,' he said, 'fully 100 are able to write as sensible a letter as that sent to Mr. Gault. They are also able to converse freely; 300 or 400 among them can copy letters and a good many can keep a systematic letter file.'

> Q. 'Is a doctor or layman who has not studied insanity qualified to detect insanity?' Greenshields asked.
> A. 'It would be very difficult for them to do so.'
> Q. 'Does the ordinary education of a physician qualify him?'
> A. 'Oh, dear, no.'

Macmaster had the final questions of the trial, and the result was devastating:

> Q. 'Who files your letters?'
> A. 'A clerk or a medical assistant.'
> Q. 'Do you employ lunatics to file your letters?'
> A. 'Not generally.'
> Q. 'Tell me the name of one lunatic who has been employed by you to file letters?'
> A. 'I cannot recall one. Such occupation is not a specific part of the institution.'

During a break in the cross-examination Mrs Shortis appeared in court for the first time in several days. She had remained in bed at the convent, the press reported, with a bad cold and neuralgia. The weather had turned cold and raw. She was also depressed by Simpson's evidence and by the news that her friend, Monsignor O'Bryen, had collapsed on Sunday morning while celebrating mass at St Patrick's Church in Montreal. He had been taken to the church presbytery, where last rites were given at his request. He died on Thursday afternoon, but the news had been kept from Mrs Shortis. Told shortly after she entered court on Friday afternoon, she was, in the words of the *Star*, 'violently affected, sobbing hysterically.'

The funeral was held in St Patrick's on Saturday morning, with burial under the high dome of St James' Cathedral later that day. Only two others had previously been so honoured. O'Bryen, 'famous all over the civilized world,' it was reported, was 'one of the most distinguished English-speaking members of the Roman Catholic Church that ever visited Canada.' His position was just to the right of the Papal throne, thus taking precedence over the Cardinals. The Pope was said to be visibly affected by the news of his death. The Shortises were too distraught to attend the funeral.

The news of O'Bryen's death had come the day after the tragic death of Lord Waterford in Ireland, who had also been taking a keen interest in the case. Two days earlier he had committed suicide by shooting himself in the head.[6]

Judge Mathieu and Macmaster left for Montreal on Friday evening along with Dr Bucke. The defence counsel remained in Beauharnois to prepare their jury addresses. The London asylum records show that Bucke did not arrive there until four o'clock Sunday morning, not having slept for two nights. He would have arrived earlier but his horse had been left unattended at the train station while his luggage was being collected and had run away smashing the buggy. It had been a difficult month. The next day Bucke sent a form letter to his many correspondents around the world telling them that he had not expected to be away 'more than one week at the very outside' and that 'it will be weeks (perhaps many weeks) before I shall be able to give much attention to my private affairs.'

Because the defence had called witnesses, the Crown had the right to address the jury last.[7] In one of the heated exchanges between counsel on Friday, St Pierre had remarked that Macmaster would have the final word. 'I will soon show my learned friend that I am not at all afraid,' said Macmaster hotly, 'for I will follow directly after Mr. Greenshields if he pleases.' 'I shall be pleased to take advantage of the offer,' replied St Pierre. The judge intervened, however, declaring that the speeches would be made in the order usually followed in such cases. Court was adjourned till Monday morning at ten o'clock.

7

Towards the Verdict

T HE LARGEST CROWDS since the beginning of the case showed up at the courthouse on Monday morning, 28 October 1895, hoping to hear the addresses to the jury. Two minutes after the doors were opened the room was filled. Some seats near the counsel table had been reserved for special guests, such as Mrs Greenshields and Mrs St Pierre and a group that had travelled from Montreal that morning on businessman W. Barclay Stephens' steam yacht, *Dama*. Mrs Shortis remained sick in bed at the convent. The accused did not appear in his usual spirits, the *Herald* reporting that 'he looked haggard and his eyes were sunken and marked with black rings.'

Counsel for both the defence and the Crown presented to the court several legal authorities relating to the defence of insanity. There were many difficult issues for the judge to decide. Was 'homicidal mania' a form of legal insanity? Was 'moral insanity' recognized by the law? Was 'irresistible impulse' a defence? To what extent would delusions provide a defence? How does the law define 'imbecility'? What was the burden of proof? St Pierre quoted English, American, French, and German law in support of the defence. The accused, Macmaster said in French, was not being tried under the laws of France, Germany, or any of the American states, but under the Canadian Criminal Code, where 'there is no law for impulsive insanity.' 'I submit, as a proposition of law,' he said, 'that there is no authority in any case in English or Canadian Law Courts recognizing impulsive insanity as a justification for crime.' 'The doctors have set up this disease, in fact. The prisoner has been given more diseases than the law could cover in a thousand years. The general term of the law bears on natural imbecility and insanity only, and the definition of the former by law states that a man suffering from that disease does not know his own father or mother nor the

Mr Justice Michel Mathieu, portrait by William Notman & Son, February 1895 time of day. He cannot count to twenty.' Moral insanity does not exist, Macmaster asserted: 'I cannot find one case, in the whole course of English decisions, where a Judge has charged that moral insanity could be a defence for a man.' He cited one authority from 1863, where Mr Justice Wightman refused to accept moral insanity and uncontrollable impulse: 'This would appear to be a most dangerous doctrine, and fatal to the interests of society and security of life.'[1] Referring to *Roscoe on Evidence*, he argued that the burden of proof was on the accused to prove insanity beyond a reasonable doubt. If Macmaster's interpretation of the law of insanity was accepted by the judge and, more importantly, by the jury, the defence would be in serious trouble.

Greenshields began his address to the jury at three o'clock and ended shortly before six. Fortunately, full transcripts of the jury addresses and the judge's charge to the jury were preserved and later printed for commercial sale.[2] There is no doubt Greenshields' speech made a strong impact on the jury. It was a masterful analysis designed to put powerful pressure on individual jurors.

'Thou shalt not kill,' were his opening words. 'Whoso sheddeth man's blood, by man shall his blood be shed,' has been a precept 'embodied in the penal code of every civilized nation, down to the present day.' He then applied it to the trial: 'if anyone of us should, by any wrongful act, contribute to bring about an unjust verdict, which would deprive the prisoner of his life, we too should have violated that command "Thou shalt not kill." ' He stressed the British sense of justice – he was, of course, addressing the English-speaking jurors – in comparison to the lawlessness in the United States: 'I asked you ... if in the trial, evidence was unfolded before you which disclosed an irresponsible condition of the prisoner's mind, you could give him that fair and impartial trial which he was entitled to in a British country, and you each and all said "yes." We have not here what we too often see across the line in the far distant west, men taken and executed without trial, without reason sometimes, by an enraged public, who have allowed themselves to be carried away by their passions' (that very morning the Montreal press had reported an attempted lynching in Ohio).

It is often said today that counsel should not express a personal belief in the innocence of the accused. Greenshields did not adopt this view: 'If I did not believe that this man came into this world an imbecile, if I thought that he was a responsible being, I would not utter one word in his defence, and my voice would never have resounded through these halls.' There was no comment from the judge.

Throughout his address he attempted to make the jury feel the full responsibility for what he described as the 'terrible consequences' of a guilty verdict:

> In the years to come, when the intense excitement pervading this community and this Court shall have passed away, when the recital of this tragedy shall be spoken of as a story that is often told, when children gathered around the fireside shall speak of this, the greatest trial that has ever taken place in this district, when your names shall be mentioned because of the serious importance of your part in this great trial, when you shall be asked to tell a rising generation of your verdict, I trust you will be able to put your hand upon your heart and say: 'I did right, I acted honestly, and I did no wrong in the verdict which I rendered in the case of the Queen against Valentine Shortis.'

If Shortis' act was committed in an irresponsible moment, he told the jury, 'let us not extend the terrible consequences of that act, by ... perhaps hastening to an early grave the father and mother of this unfortunate boy.' Throughout his address, the jurors' natural sympathy for the accused's parents was underlined.

Heredity was important, he said: 'Now, you have heard the doctors examined, and they have told you that in all their experience of the history of insanity that seventy-five to ninety per cent of the insane who are confined in lunatic asylums trace their insanity back to their heredity.' He called on the jurors to use their own knowledge: 'Every one of you who are sitting in that box, know the affects of heredity. You who are farmers, raising stock and animals, know how the taints and habits of the ancestry of any one of them shows itself in the next generation, and sometimes down to two or three generations.'

Greenshields carefully reviewed Shortis' background to show 'homicidal mania.' 'From his early childhood he develops this homicidal mania, this desire to shoot, this desire to kill, because insanity is of many forms and many types, and one prominent among them all is the insanity of homicide.' Shortis, he said, was a 'slumbering volcano.' The jury were reminded of Shortis' hallucinations:

> He comes to this country with his moral nature undeveloped from his early childhood, or in a rudimentary condition, with hallucinations, and delusions developed from the time that he reaches the age of fourteen or fifteen years, so that we have him at that time a natural imbecile, and implanted upon his natural imbecility is the insanity as evidenced by the delusions which existed up to the time that he came to this country. When he came

here, had these delusions disappeared? We find, from the evidence of Miss Anderson and Jack Anderson, that he, at their house, has visual and aural hallucinations, that is to say, he hears imaginary sounds, he hears imaginary voices, imagines people are looking at him, that people are walking on the verandah and asks Jack Anderson to come out on the verandah and to close the blinds or shutters, to see whether these people are there or not. You cannot attach too much importance, you cannot attach too much importance to the existence of these hallucinations; they are the most dangerous in the disease of insanity; a man who has aural or visual hallucinations, is the most dangerous class of lunatic, and they often lead to homicidal results.

Now, on the night of the first of March, we find this boy with this heredity, as I have pointed out to you, with his history as it has been stated to you under the Irish Commission, with his history as it was continued in this country, with his hallucinations and delusions; on that very night, with a severe attack of this neuralgic headache, which headaches are the premonitions of an attack of insanity, from which he was suffering. This is the condition of the boy, and I desire to consider with you the evidence of the tragedy. Was it premeditated? Was it for the purpose of robbery? of murder? or was it the act of an insane man, without premeditation and without malice?

The theory of the defence, Greenshields told the jury, was that the first shot was an accident: 'The prisoner at the bar tells you through the doctors, and the statement is, that it was accidental.' He conceded that the trial judge could tell them that Shortis' 'self-serving' statement made to the doctors was not proper evidence, but no doubt he privately hoped they would give it some weight.

All those there, considered that first shot an accident, that that revolver went off and struck Wilson without intention, without the purpose of robbery, without the purpose of killing. The prisoner says it was so, the actions of every man who was present in that room bear out that theory in its entirety, and their actions are not compatible with any other theory whatsoever, but that they considered that the first shot fired was an accident. After that, then comes in the disease of the mind, then comes in that lapse of self-consciousness, then comes in the effect of this insanity, then strikes him the taint of his ancestry in his blood, his insanity takes full possession of him, and he becomes utterly irresponsible and thoroughly indifferent to what then takes place. That is his story. That is what he says. That is the history that is compatible with the theory and the knowledge of the insanity such as he is afflicted with.

He then turned to the psychiatrists' evidence, stressing their expertise and the fact that they all said the insanity is incurable. It was important to the defence for the jury to believe that Shortis would never be released:

Four men have been brought before you, and have given their evidence as to their opinion as to his mental condition, based on the evidence adduced before you in this Court, as also upon interviews with the prisoner. This evidence, I deem of the most vital importance, and I ask your kind and close attention to me for a few minutes, while I deal with that part of this case. The men who were examined are men who stand in the front rank of their profession in this country. Dr. Anglin made a study of this case, covering a long period of time, from the 25th of June or July, up to the present time; he had a large number of interviews with the prisoner, as stated, and considered the matter, and with his experience in Verdun Asylum, with his experience in Kingston Asylum, with his experience in Pennsylvania, he comes before you and takes his reputation in his hands and tells you that this man is a natural imbecile, is diseased in his mind, and is irresponsible and knows not the difference between right and wrong. I do not propose at this late hour, because I wish to finish my address to-night, to discuss in detail the evidence as given by these men. You have it before you. Dr. Daniel Clark, of Toronto; Dr. Charles Clarke, of Kingston; Dr. Bucke, of London; men who, with their experience with the insane represent altogether an aggregate of some seventy years. These men are men well known in the profession; they are men who have made a study during their whole life of mental diseases; they are men who, of all the men that have come before this Court and have given evidence before you, are the most competent to speak upon this question, and they tell you, after having sat from day to day in this Court, and heard unfolded from that witness box the testimony of all the witnesses regarding this young man, and from their own examination of him, they tell you that he is insane, they tell you that the case is one of the strongest cases of insanity that has been brought before the courts of justice within their recollection; they tell you that in their asylums where there are hundreds, and in Dr. Bucke's case a thousand poor afflicted humanity, that there are many of them there not so insane as the prisoner at the bar; they tell you more, they tell you, with his poor father and mother sitting in front of you; that the affliction which God has put upon their son is incurable, and that his mental disease and imbecility has so attacked his constitution that never can he be cured, there is no hope of a cure, that the only hope, that the only thing possible for these two poor parents who sat in front of that jury box, was that their son, their only child, in the event of your saying that he was insane, should be confined in a lunatic asylum for the rest of his lifetime. It is a dismal out-look for them at best. These four doctors, men of science, men who have written upon the subject, men who have made the subject of mental diseases the study of their lives, they, who, of all others, are most competent to speak of it, come before you, and they tell you that he is insane, and on the night of that fateful tragedy, he knew not what he was doing, he did not know the responsibility of his act, that he was unable to distinguish right from wrong.

In contrast, he said, the Crown doctors did not give evidence: 'the other doctors sat in this Court, took notes of this trial, and listened to every word of the evidence, and then they would not go into the box as medical men and express their opinion as to whether he was insane or not ... If there is any one incident in this whole trial, if there is one thing which ought to convince you as honest men that this man is insane, it is the fact that we have called our four experts and that the Crown brought their physicians and had them here throughout this whole trial, and they did not dare – they did not dare, to put them in the box, because their answers would have killed the case for the Crown.'

The three-hour address, which examined the evidence in detail, concluded by again highlighting the position of Mr and Mrs Shortis and by making the jurors feel the full responsibility for their decision. The *Herald* reported that as Greenshields was approaching the end of his oration 'the scene became deeply impressive as dusk began to fall and the room was lit dimly by a few lamps.'

The father with the mother crossed again to this country, come here and stand here day by day before you in a community that knows them not. They come here because they say you are human, because they say that you are men, because they say you are prompted by all the actions which govern good and honest men, because they know that you believe in the principle and the doctrine of Christ, 'Do unto others as you wish that they should do to you,' and I ask you as *men*, I ask you, if you have any question or doubt, if there is any doubt upon your minds that this man is insane, give the benefit of the doubt, not to the prisoner at the bar, because to him it makes little difference whether he is locked up in a lunatic asylum for the rest of his life, or whether you take him to-morrow forth from this door and execute him upon a scaffold which you may erect behind this Court House; he is indifferent to it all; but I ask you, if you have any doubt, give the benefit of that doubt to the aged father and mother, that mother who at this moment is lying on a bed of sickness in the hospital of the nuns, suffering with heart disease which ere morning may carry her off; but, oh God! if you have any doubt, send these people back across the Atlantic, let them think that we are good people here, let them think that we have good hearts, and do not, do not, God forbid! by your verdict open three graves at the same time.

Oh, gentlemen, I have but one more request to make of you. I will soon have ceased speaking. The last words on behalf of that unfortunate father and mother will have been said, and to-day I feel strongly that there is perhaps no position in which a man could be placed so responsible, to my mind, as the lawyer who stands before a jury and pleads for the life of a fellow-being.

All that I wish to ask of you is simply to follow the just dictates of your conscience and your heart, give us justice; and in the event of your coming to the decision that the prisoner is sane, then I invite you to come with me, when the dread sentence which you will pronounce shall have been carried out, and stand around that grave in the potters field, see the prisoner lying there, each one of you put a sod of earth over his grave and say in good faith, putting your hands on your heart, 'This is my work, it is well done, it is well done.'

Let your verdict be such, that it will be to you an immortal Crown of Justice and of Right. Let it be such, that when you are passing through the valley of the shadow of death, it will be possible for you, on looking back over your life's history, to feel no remorse and no regret for the verdict which you are to render in this case. Rise above all personal feeling, rise above all local prejudice. Do naught but justice, and if you give that justice which we expect from you, the only verdict that you can render is one in favour of insanity, which consigns the prisoner for his life to the darkness of a lunatic asylum. Strange, strange demand it is, for a man to ask twelve of his countrymen on behalf of another, to consign that other for life to a lunatic asylum, but such is the only request which can be made for a man like the prisoner, afflicted of God and deprived of his reason.

This is all his father and mother ask of you, and they feel that their request will not be in vain.

Gentlemen, I have finished.

The next morning St Pierre commenced his address in French.[3] His reputation was such that at one point over a thousand people lined up in front of the courthouse. When the doors were opened, reported the

Star, they 'went up the stairs like McGill students on a college theatre night.' Half the audience were women. In contrast to Greenshields' crisp, carefully constructed style, St Pierre rambled on for twenty-one hours – over a three-day period, from Tuesday to Thursday inclusive. Tactically, this was a serious mistake. Friday was to be a holiday, All Saints' Day, on which the court would not sit. It would have been better for the defence if the jury had started their deliberations before Friday; not to do so would mean either that the jury would have Friday to themselves in seclusion with Macmaster's words the last they had heard or if he did not conclude his address on Thursday he would address the jury on Saturday before the judge charged the jury. In either case, Greenshields' powerful speech would have lost much of its impact.

It was not entirely St Pierre's fault that his address covered three days. Like many in the courthouse he was suffering from the flu. At five o'clock on Tuesday, after speaking since ten o'clock in the morning, he announced to the court that it was physically impossible for him to go on any longer. When he was prepared to continue Wednesday morning – hoping to conclude his address at noon – the sheriff announced that two of the jurors, John Cunningham, who had been ill earlier, and Théophile Doré, the last two jurors chosen, were too ill to appear. Judge Mathieu asked Dr A.N. Brossoit, the prison doctor, for his opinion. Doré, looking pale, quietly took his seat in the jury box, but Cunningham, said the doctor, had a severe cold and tonsillitis and had fainted while getting dressed that morning; he would not be able to appear before two o'clock. The alternating stuffiness and blasts of cold air when the window was open behind the jury box was said to be the cause of the illnesses. There was no power at that time[4] to proceed with fewer than twelve jurors, and so there was no option but to adjourn.

At two o'clock, Cunningham appeared with a broad bandage around his neck, and St Pierre, who also had an inflamed throat, continued with his address. At three o'clock, Doré had a severe nosebleed and the court again adjourned, until Dr Brossoit was able to stop the flow of blood. Once again, St Pierre commenced his address, but shortly before five o'clock he again announced that he could not go on. The jury suggested an evening sitting, for they were anxious to return to their homes before the weekend, but the judge said that under the circumstances he could not ask St Pierre to continue. St Pierre reminded the court that in the American *Guiteau* case the senior defence counsel had spoken for nine days!

The following day, Thursday, St Pierre concluded his address at 12:30. The worst had happened: Laurendeau would speak for the rest of the day, the jury would be free on Friday, and Macmaster and the judge would speak on Saturday.

St Pierre's address, in French, naturally covered much of the same ground as Greenshields'. For instance, he stressed the position of the parents: 'Ah! Gentlemen, after the moving scenes that you have witnessed; in the presence of this father overwhelmed by the weight of the pain, of this mother whose heart is broken, both of whom come to you to beg for their only child, is it indeed to the side of hatred and vengeance that the scales of justice should tilt? Is it not rather on the side of pity and commiseration?'[5] He also drew the attention of the jury to Monsignor O'Bryen's visit during the trial:

This justice, gentlemen, I have the right to expect it from you. You are the judges today; who knows if tomorrow you will not be judged in your turn? Have we not, during the investigation of this trial, received from Providence the most solemn of warnings? You have all seen that holy Prelate Monsignor O'Bryen. Upon learning of the immense pain into which this distressed father and mother had been immersed, he rushed from afar to pour into their hearts a little of this balm of consolation, which the priest, more than any other, knows the secret. Who of you, on seeing him so full of health and vigour, would have imagined that four days after his visit he would be outstretched without life in a funeral parlour? Who would have ever guessed, when we saw him sit on the judge's bench, that this honour would be the last that he received on earth, and that eight days later, he would be in his grave, sleeping the sleep from which we never awake.

One main difference between the addresses was that St Pierre went over the evidence in much greater detail. In particular, he concentrated on the evidence obtained in Ireland, reading long excerpts from the testimony, about a third of the four hundred printed pages of his address; in contrast, Greenshields devoted only about ten printed pages out of fifty to the Irish evidence. Surely this long repetition was a mistake. It took up most of Tuesday. Although the Tuesday afternoon *Star* reported that St Pierre's address up to that point 'was a powerful one, and seemed to carry weight and effect,' no such comment was contained in the Wednesday or Thursday report of the proceedings. Indeed, the headline in the Thursday *Star* was: 'Mr. St. Pierre still talking.' The speech was long and tedious. After the trial, the Huntingdon *Gleaner* expressed the view of many: 'Mr. St. Pierre overdid it when he claimed the attention of the jury on three successive days.'

Another major difference in the addresses was the surprising extent to which St Pierre referred to authorities and cases from France. This is odd in view of the fact that the criminal law in Canada was English and had had no connection with French law since 1763.[6] He obviously thought that the use of French cases would have a positive impact on the French-Canadian half of the jury. Whether this case was unique or whether other French-Canadian counsel at the time cited cases from France is not known.

The great French psychiatrist Philippe Pinel was quoted at length – though at first the source of the quotations was not identified – to show that many persons in asylums are as coherent as Shortis appeared to be.

> Gentlemen, the scholar who wrote those lines deserved the label 'the benefactor of humanity'; he is the famous mental specialist, Doctor Pinel, to whom France, his native land, in recognition of his works on mental health, has erected statues.
>
> Do you doubt his experience and his knowledge? Would his knowledge, that has revolutionized the systems used up until now in lunatic asylums, in all of the civilized nations, be treated with contempt and indifference in Canada? This would expose us to the ridicule and contempt of all the nations of the civilized world.

Three murder cases from France were then explored at length: Henriette Cornier, who killed a child in Paris in 1825; Adrienne Lecouvreur, who killed a young man in Lyons in 1851; and Dominique Miller, who killed a fellow Corsican in Marseilles in 1852. All three, said St Pierre, escaped the guillotine and were confined in a mental asylum. He asked the jury to apply these cases to Valentine Shortis:

> The three cases that I have just cited (and if I had the time, I could cite several others) were, as I have mentioned, investigated and tried in France.
>
> A madman, whether he resides in England or whether he lives in France is nevertheless a madman, and if he is judged irresponsible in France, because

of his madness, I don't see how we could in England or Canada ... treat this madman as we would treat a sane man. I can only assume that in France, and on the entire European continent, they send to the asylum the madman who committed homicide, whereas they send them to the scaffold in England and here. If a man is insane, he becomes by this very fact irresponsible; simple good sense tells you that he cannot be criminal.

St Pierre's closing words, like Greenshields', invited the jurors to accompany Shortis to the scaffold on the day of the execution. They brought tears to the eyes of many in the courtroom:

Come here the day of his execution, come see Valentine Shortis climb the scaffold. If, that day, you find him as indifferent to his fate as he has been before this court to his father's spectacle of desperation and his mother's tears, if, after having seen him die without emotion, without love and without hate, you are finally convinced that you have condemned an insane man, maybe then regret and remorse will lodge in the depth of your conscience, and for a long time this remorse will poison your days and trouble your sleep.

But no, let me remove this distressing and sombre picture. No, no, never will you have such regrets, no such bitter memories. Faithful to your oath, you will declare, based on the crushing evidence that was put before you, that Valentine Shortis, on the first of March, was irresponsible, insane, and that the awful tragedy that he was author of in Valleyfield was the act of a lunatic.

Your verdict will not set free ... a raving maniac ... dangerous to society. This unfortunate young man will go to an asylum, joining those like himself who are insane.

Your verdict will revive a little happiness in the broken hearts of his father and his mother, who have come from afar, in their mourning clothes, to solicit, not your pity, but your justice. At least they could return to their country with the knowledge that they will go without the stigma, embarrassment and infamy that the death of their son on the scaffold would imprint upon them.

You will return to your families and on your arrival while hugging your children you will think that soon another father will hug his son, perhaps for the last time; but in leaving his son he will not leave a dishonoured name. You will think that over there in Ireland, in the city of Waterford, where so many sympathetic hearts beat in unison with those of these unhappy parents, more than one Irish mother, before rocking her child on her knees, will join his little hands together and make him stutter a prayer of gratitude and love for the men who, by an act of justice, will have brought a ray of sunshine to the hearts of this father and this mother ...

Gentlemen, I end. They will ask you for the death of Valentine Shortis. I ask you for his life, with hope.

Laurendeau, Macmaster's associate, commenced his address in French after the lunch break on Thursday. It was his maiden speech in a criminal case. The press reported that it was a 'strong one and to the point, the counsel confining himself strictly to facts so as to bring the trial to a speedy termination,' no doubt silently contrasting his speech with St Pierre's. 'Every word that fell from the speaker's lips,' said the *Star*, 'was attentively listened to, and the address was followed throughout its delivery with marked interest.' His five-hour speech, with a break from six to eight for dinner, ended shortly before nine. He closed by attempting to shift the jury's sympathy away from the accused's parents to the families of the victims:

I leave the case in your hands and I entreat you to render a verdict according to your conscience leaving aside any misplaced sympathy. The prisoner's parents have nothing to do with this case. You have to render your verdict as if they did not exist. You are bound to place yourselves above these considerations.

They appeal to you for sympathy gentlemen. Did the prisoner at the bar show any sympathy when he turned in the direction of poor John Loy and with a single shot launched his soul into eternity, without a moment of preparation, and sent this young man, aged only 24 years, to render an account of his conduct before his Maker? Did he show any sympathy when he broke the heart of that poor father and mother of young Loy by taking away from them their son, their mainstay, the pride of their family, when he robbed society of a young man who gave promise to become a useful member of the community? Did Shortis show any sympathy, gentlemen, when young Wilson, after lying wounded, begged of him for God's sake not to fire any more?

Did he show any sympathy when he heard Maxime Leboeuf coming in, and cried out: 'Come here, come here, Maxime'? 'You're the father of a family, but what care I? Come here that I can kill you. What do I care whether I make your wife a widow and your children orphans?' 'Come here,' and turning to Maxime, and with a well-aimed bullet sends his second victim's soul to his Maker. Now, gentlemen, instead of receiving a loving embrace from her husband the dead body is brought to her on a stretcher.

At the conclusion of his speech Laurendeau was warmly congratulated by his many friends in the courtroom. The court was then adjourned till Saturday morning.

Macmaster's address took a little over four hours to deliver. Throughout, Shortis showed the same apparent indifference he had maintained during the entire trial. 'Soon after he had taken his seat in the dock,' observed the *Gazette*, 'he tilted his chair well back, placed his feet against the front of the dock and admired his patent leather shoes, the tips of which just appeared above the top of the dock. When tired of this pastime he resumed his old occupation of contemplating the Royal arms above the judicial seat.'

Before starting his formal address, Macmaster cited legal authorities to the judge relating to insanity. This was done in the presence of the jury – today the jury would not hear such arguments – and was undoubtedly directed more at them than at Mathieu. The procedure was designed to undermine the authority of the defence psychiatrists. He cited a case from 1840 where Lord Chief Justice Denman had stated: 'as for moral insanity, I, for my own part, do not consider that a medical man is better able to judge than a person acquainted with the ordinary affairs of life, and bringing to the subject a wide experience.'[7] The leading evidence text of the time, *Taylor on Evidence*, was also cited: 'Perhaps the testimony which least deserves credit with a jury is that of skilled witnesses ... It is often quite surprising to see with what facility, and to what an extent, their views can be made to correspond with the wishes or the interests of the parties who call them.'[8] Finally, an oft-cited quotation from Lord Campbell was called in aid. 'Scientific witnesses,' he had quite unfairly stated in 1843, 'come with [such] a bias on their minds to support the cause in which they are embarked ... that hardly any weight is to be given to the evidence.'[9]

Macmaster's jury address skilfully wove a net of responsibility around Shortis. The Crown, he said, had no obligation to call psychiatrists. It was up to the defence to prove insanity, 'to your complete and perfect satisfaction.' There was nothing to stop the defence from calling the Crown experts, he argued: 'if they felt so inclined, they could have put Dr. Villeneuve, who was in court, in the box, they

could have put Dr. Lussier in the box, they could have put Dr. Gird-
wood in the box. There was nothing to prevent them.'

The Irish episodes were minimized. 'I have very grave doubts,' he
told the jury, 'as to whether many of them ever occurred.' Other incidents showed that Shortis was a criminal, not a lunatic. Still others
were made to seem unimportant:

> What do you think of the attempt to prove the prisoner insane because he
> rode backwards on a horse? Have not many of you, when little boys, been put
> on a horse, looking backwards? Have not some of you ridden at times stand-
> ing on a horse when you were boys? I was brought up in the country myself,
> and it was not surprising to see a boy put by his father sitting backwards on a
> horse, as a joke, or even to see a boy attempt to imitate the circus people, and
> ride standing. And yet it is solemnly sworn to by a witness, that he had lived
> forty years in Ireland, had been in the United States, and that he never saw a
> person sit backwards on a horse, except the prisoner. Why, so far from that
> being a remarkable fact, some of the best trained Russian and French regi-
> ments are taught to sit on a horse backwards, so that they can defend the
> army when moving in retreat. It is an historical fact, and I have seen it my-
> self, and my learned friend Mr. St. Pierre, who is a soldier as well as a lawyer,
> knows it is a fact. Then, it is mentioned as a mad prank, that he tried to
> upset a boat by rocking it from side to side whilst on the water. I asked the
> witness if he was brought up by the river side, and he said no. That accounts
> for it. Because, sitting in this town where you now are, is there one citizen of
> Beauharnois that has not often seen boys rocking boats from side to side?

Why was Shortis sent from Ireland, he asked the jury:

> If he was an imbecile and idiot, and could not tell right from wrong, why did
> the parents turn him out on the cold world of the western continent, alone
> and friendless? Can you conceive of such inhumanity? Can you conceive that
> this loving mother and this father, with his fine business capacities, would
> have sent their son, if an idiot, bereft of his reason, without moral principle,
> lacking the moral ballast which is the first essential to a man fighting the
> battle of life, away from his own home, among strangers – there to fight the
> battle of life?

How is it that the bishop of Waterford gave a letter of reference?

> And again, gentlemen, what do you say to His Grace the Bishop of Water-
> ford, the Roman Catholic Bishop, giving a letter of introduction and recom-

mendation to this young man coming to this country? Do you imagine that a high dignitary in the Roman Catholic Church, a Church whose dignitaries have such a knowledge of the world and its affairs, who are not merely strict in morals as ecclesiastics, but are politicians in their shrewdness, do you imagine that a high dignitary in the Roman Catholic Church such as His Grace the Bishop of Waterford, would have given a letter of introduction and recommendation to Valentine Shortis to bring to this country, if he were an imbecile and a fool?

Great weight should be attached, he said, to Millie Anderson's reply to Shortis the morning after the murders when she said: 'My dear Bertie. Keep up heart. All will come right soon. I will always be true. Your own Millie.' Her evidence, and that of her brother Jack, Macmaster argued, was suspect:

> Now, gentlemen, when we come to consider the evidence of young Jack Anderson and of Miss Anderson, we must remember that they stand close to the prisoner; Jack Anderson was a co-conspirator with him before the law on the proposal to take Simpson's life, and Jack Anderson and the prisoner are open to an indictment for a conspiracy to murder on that proposition. What weight are you going to give that young man's evidence in this case? What weight can you give to the evidence of a young woman who was ready to say 'I will always be true,' and 'I am your own Millie,' after she knew that he proposed to kill Simpson, and after she had the news brought to her that he had killed two men?

Who is to say, he went on, that Shortis did not have accomplices, implicitly suggesting the Andersons:

> How do you know, gentlemen, that the prisoner at the bar had not an accomplice? How do you know that he did not suggest the scheme to somebody else, who would take the bait a little more readily than McVicar? ... How do you know that he had not some place arranged in which to put the money, or if he did not have accomplices on the spot, that he had not them where he could find them, and where the money could be hid, and that he had not people who were ready to swear to an alibi, whose conscience would be 'sufficiently elastic,' as he expressed it, to swear an alibi? But, gentlemen, when Miss Anderson came into the box, she swore that this young man heard noises and voices, and thought he saw faces at the windows. By the proof, he never saw these at any other place except the Anderson house – not one word of proof that he saw these at the hotel, or at any place where he ever lived –

all at the Anderson house. Are you going to believe that story from these people?

At a later part of his charge he was more explicit: 'What more natural than that Jack Anderson, who was his accomplice in the other crime, should be his accomplice in this? I go no further than that, though perhaps I might.' Millie Anderson, he submitted, was engaged to Shortis:

Now, there is just one more thing with regard to Miss Anderson's evidence. Can any reasonable man doubt that this young woman was engaged to the prisoner? Her letters show it. His letter to her shows deep affection, 'Yours lovingly,' and her letter to him shows the extreme of affection, 'I will always be true. Your own Millie.' It is impossible, gentlemen, for any girl of self-respect to have written that letter unless she was engaged to the prisoner, and felt she was actually his; and that being so, gentlemen, you must take her evidence with that bias by which it is affected, and you must, in taking her story, consider how far she is not merely making the case out for the prisoner, but how far she may be making out a case for herself.

Macmaster's strongest attacks were reserved for the four psychiatrists called by the defence: 'In the first place, gentlemen, you remember with regard to the doctors, that, as Lord Campbell said, they are experts, and extremely little weight is to be given to their opinions; they come so biased on the side that they are called for, that they become practically partisans, and you could see it yourselves when some of these doctors were in the box here.' Indeed he went even further, arguing that it was the doctors who were insane:

There is a certain class of doctors that have been brought so much in contact with the insane that actually they become more or less insane themselves, so that it has passed into a proverb now that these doctors have been so tinged with insanity, that if you even mention insanity, they are ready to pick it out of everybody that comes in their way. These men are now universally called, 'mad doctors' – or extremists. Now, you are not bound to take their opinions, you are not bound to take them, on the high authority of Lord Campbell, of Mr. Taylor, and Lord Chief Justice Denman, one of the greatest Judges that ever sat on the English bench, whose opinion I handed up to His Lordship this morning.

The writings of the defence psychiatrists were skilfully used to neutralize their evidence. Was Shortis a moral imbecile? Macmaster used Dr Bucke's own writings to argue he was not:

> In the first place, gentlemen, you know that Dr. Clarke, of Kingston, said that this man was a moral imbecile, and he described what a moral imbecile is. Dr. Bucke came into the box and said the same thing, that a moral imbecile had no morals, and he could not distinguish with regard to morals, and he put the prisoner down as a moral imbecile. But what did I do? I picked up the lecture that he had delivered at McGill College in Montreal and I showed him where he had put down a man of the same description, and with the same characteristics as he ascribed to the prisoner, as a criminal, and I read this passage from his own lecture: 'A criminal (speaking broadly and roughly), is simply a person who was born with a defective moral nature' ... Gentlemen, when a doctor comes down from London and delivers a lecture, an inaugural address before the learned men of McGill College in Montreal, and says that a man lacking in the moral sense is a criminal, not an imbecile, how can he come into this Court and say he is an imbecile?

'So much for Dr. Clarke, of Kingston, and Dr. Bucke, of London,' he told the jury.

> Now what was the next stage? Dr. Anglin told us that the prisoner was an imbecile. I read a definition to him of an imbecile – I read a definition out of a book, you all heard that definition read, and I asked him if it was correct.
>
> 'The idiot has not even the animal intelligence; the imbecile is a step higher in the plane of instinct and knowing, but is *little, if any, higher than the dog, elephant and chimpanzee, and is held not to be accountable because of mental deprivations.*' I asked him if the prisoner at the bar would come within that definition of an imbecile, and he said, 'No.' ... According to that definition of Dr. Clark, of Toronto, the prisoner at the bar is not an imbecile unless you put him down with the dog, elephant, and chimpanzee. Can you do it? If you cannot class him with the dog, elephant, and chimpanzee, he is not an imbecile, and Dr. Clark's own book rules the prisoner out of the imbecile class, just as Dr. Bucke's book rules him into the criminal class.

'Irresistible impulse' and 'moral insanity' were similarly disposed of:

> Dr. Clark, of Toronto, says it was impulse that did this, and Dr. Clarke, of Kingston, says it was impulse, and Dr. Anglin, of Montreal, says it was im-

pulse, and then I picked up a book containing the lectures delivered by Dr. Clark, of Toronto, as a university professor to his students, and I read him his own statements out of the book, ridiculing the idea of impulse being the ground for committing murder, and ridiculing the idea of moral insanity being set up in justification. I will read you the sentences: –

'It was a common thing years ago for a guilty man to escape under the plea of impulsive insanity. No man becomes insane for a few moments to accomplish a specific act.'

And, again, speaking of impulsive insanity, he states in this same book, page 45: 'This is sometimes called temporary insanity. It has been used in the United States Courts of Justice for many years to shield criminals from receiving the just desserts of their crime ... The plea for there being such a form of insanity is absurd in the highest degree.'

Again, in the same course of lectures, he says (page 59) this in regard to moral insanity: –

'Prichard calls this moral insanity – The insanity of morality is a better name. The term as used in the Courts of Justice has allowed many criminals to go unwhipped of justice.' So the very cause designated by three doctors for the homicide forms a subject of the fiercest condemnation by one of the trio.

The concepts were dangerous ones to accept, he urged:

You and your families, and everybody connected with you, may be the victims of any villain who will put up a scheme to murder, if the prisoner is to be let off on a plea of impulsive insanity and moral insanity, if he can say that sudden impulse drove him to murder, or that the 'devil drove him to do it, or that he got an order to do it.' What sort of an excuse is that for trampling on the laws of the country? As Mr. Justice Stephen said in one case, 'If a man tells me that he should be excused for committing murder because he got an order from Heaven to do it, I would not excuse him. I would hang him, unless I got another order from Heaven not to carry out the sentence.' And as for moral insanity and moral imbecility, what does all that mean? Does that mean that you are to excuse him because he had not morality enough to obey the law? The law takes no cognizance of such a defence.

Shortis' letter to Gault a month before the murders was, said Macmaster, 'one of the strongest evidences of the sanity of the prisoner that could be produced':

I do not wish to offend you, but I ask you, gentlemen, of the twelve of you, now, how many could write a better letter than that young man wrote to Mr.

Gault? A more intelligent letter, or a better statement of the case? Put it to yourselves. See how he makes his points. See how he even used craft to make his points. Note the expressions in the letter, the adroitness and the skill. Do you imagine, gentlemen, that that letter could have been written by a fool – by an imbecile? Far from it.

The night of the killings was reviewed in great detail. Shortis, Macmaster argued, wanted to get the money without any witnesses:

If he killed these men, there was not a single witness. Look how nearly he succeeded; Wilson was as good as dead – two men were dead within two or three minutes of each other. If he could have killed these two men in the safe, he could have filled the pockets of his big overcoat; he had this chisel to open the drawers if necessary, and could have put this money in the enormous coat he had ... He was safe – Jack Anderson and he had surveyed the country well over, when they went out. He was safe. If he, in the depth of the night, at two, three, or four o'clock in the morning, had got out of that office with that money, and fired the building, who ever would have suspected Valentine Shortis? No one. Well, now, gentlemen, we have him just on the morning of the homicide. He gives his pistol to Dr. Sutherland; that was a piece of deceit, he had the other pistol then under his clothes. Still the criminal; still the criminal. If he did not know why he had killed these men, if he had done it in a fit of frenzy or anything of that kind, and had come to consciousness, why didn't he deliver up both pistols? Then Smith comes to him, and asks him if it was he who did this, and he looks up defiantly, and says: 'Yes, it was; shoot me, shoot me.' What does this mean? Is not that conscience's recognition of wrong doing? Did not he feel that he had offended the law?

The robbery, he told the jury, was premeditated:

There is evidence that he meditated the robbery. There is evidence that he had a double motive, revenge on Simpson, and desire to get the money. There is evidence that the tragedy was executed with that motive and design, and these go to repel the idea that it was a mere sudden outbreak of temper or frenzy. There is evidence that he was in desperate circumstances, because he was four months in arrears for his board at his hotel. He had some little bills that he owed, but he did not commit the murder for them alone. There is evidence that he was getting small pittances from home, as for instance, the one pound, and three pounds ten shillings post-office orders. There is evidence that he was in love with Miss Anderson. It is a fair inference from the correspondence between them and the evidence, that they contemplated marriage, and this may be another illustration of the desperate lengths to which a man will go for a woman. The French have a proverb, 'In difficulties that seem insolvable, *cherchez la femme.'* You may have to do it here, gentlemen. It may be that to accomplish the desires that were near and dear to his heart, he resolved to enrich himself in this way.

A verdict of insanity might be less than incarceration for life, he warned: 'imprisonment during the Lieutenant-Governor's pleasure does not necessarily mean for life. It means during the pleasure of the Lieutenant-Governor, and if his Counsel chose to advise him at any time that the prisoner should be released, then the custody would be for a shorter period than life.' Moreover, the question of hanging was not their responsibility: 'My learned friend invited you to go to the scaffold of this unfortunate man if you found the fact of murder against him, and to attend the funeral obsequies. Let me tell you, gentlemen, that you are not bound to accept that invitation. You have nothing to do with the scaffold. You are not erecting his scaffold. If he is condemned, he has erected his own scaffold. You are only performing your part of duty, if you condemn him for sufficient cause.'

Finally, as had Laurendeau, Macmaster attempted to shift the jury's sympathy from the parents to the families of the victims:

You are not there to consider the terrible grief that has come over Mr. and Mrs. Shortis. You are there to do your duty as men, bound and sworn to bring in a verdict according to the evidence, without regard to the feelings of anyone. For, gentlemen, if you allow sympathy to sway you from the path of duty, how would you distribute your sympathy? You must feel for this unfortunate gentleman and his unfortunate wife, the grief-stricken parents of the prisoner, whose hearts must bleed for their son's unhappy condition. Everyone in this Court House, everyone in this country and in Ireland, must feel sympathy for them; but, gentlemen, do not you see that if your hearts are carried away, and if your heads are unmanned, and if you are asked to go aside from the straight path of duty – the sworn path of duty – for the sake of Mr. and Mrs. Shortis, you might equally be asked to think of those who are dead and gone, never to return, and to extend your sympathy to the father and mother of that bright boy, who was their great hope and joy, who was stricken down on the threshold of manhood, without one moment to make his reckoning with his God? ... Think not of them. And think not of the sorrowing widow and fatherless children in that humble Valleyfield home, of her who has lost for ever the support and succour of her husband, or of the children who can never know how great their loss is. No more will the orphan children of Maxime Leboeuf feel the gentle caress of their father's strong hand. Think not of the sadness in that humble home. Put that aside, gentlemen – you have nothing to do with it. Put the case of Mr. and Mrs. Shortis aside – you have nothing to do with that. Let the law be truly and honestly administered above every consideration. Be firm. Be strong. Be just ... Therefore, gentlemen, whatever your verdict may be, let it be a verdict according to justice, a verdict according to your consciences, and a verdict in accord with the evidence. Perform that duty honestly and faithfully as men, and you can leave those who mourn in Valleyfield, and those who mourn in Ireland, out of your present consideration. Leave them to the succour and comfort of another Power, leave them to the God of infinite justice, of infinite mercy, and infinite truth – to that God 'who bindeth up the broken hearted, and comforteth those that mourn.'

Macmaster's powerful address was concluded. It was now for the judge to address the jury.

Judge Mathieu commenced his charge to the jury, first in English and then in French, concluding at seven o'clock Saturday evening. Each charge took about two hours to deliver. Shortis appeared restless and for part of the time stood erect with his arms folded in front of him. Mrs Shortis was not in court; she was still ill at the convent.

A trial judge in Canada has great latitude in analysing the evidence as long as he leaves the ultimate decision to the jury. How far would Mathieu go in signalling his personal view of the facts? And how far would he go in recognizing an expanded version of the defence of insanity?

Mathieu's charge did leave the issue of insanity to the jury, but, as the Montreal *Gazette* noted, 'Taken on the whole it might be said to be somewhat against the prisoner.' Indeed, the charge was strongly against the accused.

Insanity as a defence, Mathieu said, was confined to the law set out in the Criminal Code: 'No person should be convicted of murder, if the killing was done by him when labouring under natural imbecility, or disease of the mind, to such an extent as to render him incapable of appreciating the nature and quality of the act, *and* of knowing that such act was wrong. A person labouring under specific delusions, but in other respects sane, should not be acquitted on the ground of insanity, unless the delusions caused him to believe in the existence of some state of things which, if it existed, would justify or excuse his act.'

Note the word 'and,' which has been italicized. As mentioned, the Canadian Criminal Code, unlike the English law at the time, required the accused to satisfy both branches of the test. Throughout his charge, Judge Mathieu almost always used the word 'and,' thus making it more difficult for the accused than if the word 'or,' as contained in the present Criminal Code, had been used.

It will be recalled that the judge had not struck out the defence's opening plea which had added the words: 'And was, at the time, in a state of unconsciousness and disease of the mind, by which a free determination of his will was excluded, was in a state of madness, and was insane.' He explained to the jury that he did not strike it out because he considered the plea 'more in the nature of a notice to the Court' and 'was reluctant to impede the defence in the evidence which they intended to make as to the exact condition of the prisoner's mind at the time of the killing.' The plea, he told the jury, could not expand the insanity defence: 'If that means, that, at the time, he was labouring under natural imbecility and disease of the mind to such an extent as rendered him incapable of appreciating the nature and quality of his act, and of knowing that such act was wrong, his excuse, if proved, is legal; but if that means something else, then it is not legal, as the law does not recognize it. We are not here to make the law; we cannot make the law; we have no power to make the law. That law has been made by the competent authority, and we must follow that law.'

The issue was for the jury: 'Whether the prisoner was sane or insane at the time of the murder is a question of fact triable by the jury, and dependent upon the previous and contemporaneous acts of the accused.' Specific delusions, he said, would not be a defence. They are only a defence if they would justify or excuse the act if true: 'It is now pretended that at the time of the killing the prisoner was labouring under the specific delusion that he was persecuted by Simpson and that he was in his hands to a certain extent. If the prisoner was sane in certain respects, but labouring, at the time of the killing under the delusion of the persecution of Simpson, I must tell you now that that delusion would not justify him, because, if the facts which form the object of the delusion really existed, that would not justify the murder of Loy by the prisoner.'

The Irish evidence was carefully examined. Heredity was accepted by the court as a cause of insanity: 'It is proved, and I think it cannot be denied, that hereditary influence is undoubtedly a great factor in the production of insanity. Insanity, being the result of a disorder of the brain, may be transmitted like any other disease.' But, he added, 'insanity, like any other disease, is not necessarily transmitted by heredity.' The Irish evidence should not be taken at face value: 'it seems to be exaggerated.'

> As I have told you before, perhaps you will find that evidence exaggerated through the great sympathy of the people there for the family of the accused. However, there is no doubt that it establishes very extraordinary dispositions. You will probably consider that that evidence shows that this unfortunate young man is not like all the other young men.
>
> But does that evidence show conclusively that, at the time the prisoner did those acts in Ireland, he did not know what he was doing and that he did not know the difference between right and wrong? That is the question which you will have to consider in passing on his plea of insanity.

Shortis' conduct in Montreal was examined. Again, it revealed that the accused was 'always peculiar, boisterous and very eccentric in his ways,' but did it show insanity? Shortis' run-in with the postal authorities was highlighted by the judge as being inconsistent with insanity: 'The Crown relies on that fact as establishing that the prisoner was not then an insane or an imbecile; and perhaps you will consider that if this transaction is not evidence of perfect honesty, it is evidence of a certain amount of intelligence, and perhaps you will find in his request to the Post Office employee not to mention that affair to his friend, a circumstance indicating a certain amount of knowledge of right and wrong. Otherwise, why would he be afraid that that affair should be known to his people.'

Doubt was thrown on the alleged hallucinations in Valleyfield: 'Now, the two Andersons are the only persons who speak of those hallucinations of the prisoner before the murder. Do you believe that they tell the truth? You must consider that Miss Anderson was in love with him; that she and her brother Jack knew of his plans to kill Mr. Simpson, and remained his friends; that he wrote to Millie immediately after the murder, telling her not to fret and asking her to send Jack to him at once, and that Millie wrote to him after that, that she would always be true to him. All these are circumstances which will help you to weigh their evidence.'

And the letter by Shortis to A.F. Gault at the end of January 1895, complaining about Simpson's conduct, was quoted in full, the judge adding: 'It is for you to consider and say whether this letter, written on the 30th of January last, one month before the murder, is the letter of a natural imbecile or of an insane; whether that letter was written by a man who did not know the difference between right and wrong.'

Was there a motive, he asked the jury? 'The prisoner was under the impression that it was an easy thing to rob the office,' he told them: 'He said that twice to young McVicar.' The judge certainly left the impression with the jury that robbery may well have been the motive:

> You will also remember that two weeks before the murder, on the Friday evening, he went to the office when the money had just been locked up in the safe, and the clerks were going out, and that he knew that the clerks of the Company were in that evening, of the first of March, preparing the money to pay the men.
>
> You will also remember that he began to fire on those men, just when the money was being put in the vault, and before it was locked in out of his reach.
>
> Are all those circumstances, which tend to show that the prisoner was aiming at the money, purely accidental? He did not want that money for his support. He must have known that his mother would have sent him enough for that. Did he want that money to marry Millie Anderson? They were in love, but there is no evidence that they intended to be married. However, it is for you to say whether he had a motive and whether that motive, if he had any, was that sum of money ...
>
> You will, gentlemen, consider whether when the prisoner killed Loy he had the intention of stealing that sum of fourteen thousand dollars which was lying there, and if you find in your conscience that it was his object, that opinion will undoubtedly help you to decide the question of insanity.
>
> The prisoner went armed to the office. He had a four-chamber revolver loaded. It is true that he used to carry revolvers in Ireland, and that he used to do so here, but he had also a big strong chisel under his coat. That chisel was found on him after the murder. It did not belong to the mill, so you may assume, I suppose, that he took it with him. If the revolver is to be credited to his habit to carry revolvers, the chisel is not. But it is said that you cannot suppose that he went there to kill, because he had only a small revolver of four chambers, and with that he could not kill five persons. That has to be considered; but it is not sure that he expected to find five persons in the office. If he had not found a better revolver there, which he had oiled and prepared, perhaps he would not have attacked those men that evening. When he

attacked those men he had in his hands and on him revolvers and cartridges enough to kill twenty men.

On coming to the office he saw Lowe's revolver on the table, and he asked permission to oil it and put it in order. If he was a sane man, we would ask him, 'Why were you so kind as to oil and put in order Lowe's revolver? Was it to be sure that the revolver would fire well when you would use it against those very parties who received you so friendly and so kindly?'

Turning again to the psychiatric evidence, he told the jury, in part, that they should consider the evidence of the doctors, but the decision was for them to make: 'Their opinion is worthy of your consideration, but it is only an opinion which you must consider and weigh with the facts proved, according to the dictates of common sense and of your conscience.' Judge Mathieu put the burden of proof at a high level, far higher than is used today in Canada, where insanity can be proved by the accused on a 'balance of probability.' 'In order to support a defence of insanity,' he said, 'it ought to be proved by the most distinct and unquestionable evidence that the prisoner was incapable of distinguishing between right and wrong. In fact, it must be proved beyond all doubts ...' The judge did not even add the word 'reasonable.' Thus the onus on the defence was even higher than that placed on the Crown to prove the act.

Finally, the judge turned to the question of Shortis' parents:

Gentlemen, it has been represented to you, with a great deal of force and ability, that the prisoner at the bar is the only son of most respectable people, occupying a most enviable position in their country, and that both the father and the mother, and specially the mother, have done all they could for his moral and intellectual education, and it has been hinted that, taking into consideration the inappreciable sorrow and grief of the prisoner's good mother, you would lean to clemency. On the other side it has been said that you must not lose sight of those that have been killed, and that the hearts of those near to them have also been broken by this horrible crime ...

Gentlemen, I appreciate the difficulty of your position. You would be happy – we would all be happy – to return this unhappy boy to the good-will of the Lieutenant-Governor and to the love of his mother, if before God, who sees the secrets of your hearts, you believe that he did not know what he was doing, and that he was doing wrong; but you must not do it if you believe that he is guilty of a wilful and conscious murder.

The judge's charge certainly indicated that he believed that Shortis was 'guilty of a wilful and conscious murder.' Three specific questions were then put to the jury:

1st. Did the accused, Francis Valentine Cuthbert Shortis, murder John Loy on the first day of March last (1895)?

2nd. Was the accused, at the time of the murder, labouring under natural imbecility or disease of the mind, to such an extent as to render him incapable of appreciating the nature and quality of his act, the said murder, and of knowing that such act or murder was wrong?

3rd. Is the accused guilty or not guilty?

It was, Judge Mathieu said, for the jury to determine these issues:

Gentlemen, before leaving the case into your hands, I must tell you that you are bound to follow the direction of the Court on the questions of law, but that, on the question of fact as to the murder and as to the insanity, you are the absolute and the only judges. On the question of culpability, you are bound to follow no other opinion than your own. In fact, you are bound to decide according to your own conscience and not according to the conscience of anybody else, not even the President of the Court, whether the prisoner at the Bar is guilty or not guilty.

Gentlemen, I now leave the case in your hands, convinced that you are honest men, and that you will decide and render a true verdict between Our Sovereign Lady the Queen and the prisoner at the Bar.

At seven o'clock the jury retired to have dinner and then to consider their verdict.

Sunday morning, 3 November, at nine o'clock, while the church bells were ringing outside, the jury filed back into court. It was a beautiful warm autumn day: the papers noted that rays of sunshine fell on Shortis in the prisoner's dock; he was dressed ominously in a black suit and black tie, and carelessly curled his moustache. His father studied the jurors' faces, fearing the verdict. His mother was not in court. She was kneeling before the altar of St Clements' Church.

All were now assembled, waiting for the judge to appear. Four hundred persons were in court. St Pierre sat drumming the table in front of him. Greenshields rapidly rolled and unrolled one of the bands of his gown. Judge Mathieu entered. All rose.

The clerk of the court addressed the jury:

'Gentlemen of the jury, how say you? Do you find the prisoner at the Bar guilty or not guilty?'

'Guilty,' said the foreman.

The judge glanced over at the prisoner who was staring at the coat of arms, showing no visible emotion.

St Pierre asked the court to put each question to each of the jurors. They were put in English and then in French and each juror in turn announced either 'guilty' or 'coupable.' Macmaster moved that the sentence be imposed, but Judge Mathieu declined to pronounce the death sentence on Sunday. Court was adjourned until Monday morning at ten.

The press later reported that the members of the jury had more or less made up their minds at the early stages of the trial after Lowe and Wilson had given evidence. They had substantially agreed amongst themselves that insanity had not been sustained at the end of the re-examination of Dr Bucke. On their retirement on Saturday evening the French jurors very quickly arrived at a verdict of guilty. The English jurors took slightly longer because, it was said, juryman Finney suggested they consider a recommendation for mercy. He was talked out of it and the ballot of guilty was taken within an hour from the start of their deliberations.

As Shortis was about to be led to his cell, he leaned over the front of the dock and touched Dr Anglin on the shoulder. Had Anglin, Shortis asked, heard from the publishers about the music Anglin had ordered for him?

Millie Anderson had arrived in Beauharnois that morning from Valleyfield and was having breakfast in the Hotel Kelley when she was told of the verdict. She left the dining room in tears for her own room. Mrs Shortis was not informed until later in the afternoon. On hearing the news she collapsed. Dr Anglin was called to attend her.

Shortly after ten on Monday morning, Shortis, again dressed in black, was brought into court. He nodded to the press and then, smiling pleasantly, fixed his gaze on the judge. Mrs Shortis again was not in court, and for the first time since the proceedings started her husband was not there either.

Macmaster asked the judge to impose the mandatory sentence: 'I now beg to move for sentence of the Court on the prisoner at the Bar.' The clerk of the court turned to Shortis:

Prisoner, you are indicted, tried, and convicted, for the murder of John Loy on the 1st day of March, 1895. Have you anything to offer why sentence of death should not be pronounced against you according to law? If you have, you must offer it now, and you shall be heard.

In a clear, steady voice Shortis said, 'No, thank you.'
Judge Mathieu then addressed the prisoner:

Francis Valentine Cuthbert Shortis, you have been accused of having murdered John Loy on the 1st day of March last; to that accusation you have pleaded that you were not guilty: your ground of defence was that at the time you murdered Loy you were labouring under natural imbecility and disease of the mind to such an extent as to render you incapable of appreciating the nature and quality of that act, and of knowing that such act was wrong. Twelve honest men have been sworn to try your case, and after a month's close attention and reflection, and after you have been most ably defended by able, eminent and learned Counsel, they have returned a verdict of 'guilty,' declaring thereby that your plea of insanity has not been proven.

It is now over eight months since you have killed Loy. It has taken eight months for the justice of the country to declare in your case that he who commits murder shall be punished. Still, the jurors have paused and reflected a long time before bringing to you the just reward of your most atrocious crime. The law says that he who commits murder shall, after conviction, be sentenced to death. It is with deepest sorrow that I am obliged to-day to pronounce the sentence of the law. A father will easily understand the blow that this sentence will give to your father, and a son who had also a good mother will share to a certain extent the grief that cannot be expressed of your good mother, even when he is bound to be the instrument of the inexorable justice that must punish and cannot forgive. I am bound to-day to pronounce the sentence which the law pronounces in your case.

At this point Judge Mathieu placed the traditional black cap on his head. This was to be the first time in a long career on the bench that he would impose a sentence of death. His voice was choked with emotion:

The sentence of the Court of Our Sovereign Lady the Queen, sitting now here, is, that you, Francis Valentine Cuthbert Shortis, be taken to the common jail of this district of Beauharnois, and there kept in custody until the third day of January next, at eight o'clock in the morning, when you will be taken from the said common jail and conducted to the place of execution, and there you shall be hanged by the neck until you are dead, and may God have mercy on your soul.

In a mock English cockney accent Shortis responded: 'I wish to thank you, my Lord, for the kindness and consideration you have shown to me, and all the people connected with this honourable Court have given me whilst I have been here.' With a broad smile on his face, he walked 'calmly and indifferently' to his cell. The judge thanked counsel and, taking off the black cap, left the courtroom.

8

After the Trial

S/ HORTIS WAS TO BE HANGED at the Beauharnois jail on Friday, 3 January 1896. Counsel and the judge returned to Montreal. The next day Greenshields was asked if any further proceedings would be taken on behalf of Shortis. 'The only thing we now intend doing,' he replied, 'is to petition the Minister of Justice for commutation of sentence from the death penalty to imprisonment for life.' An appeal to the Quebec Court of Appeal on a point of law would have been possible, but it required the consent of the attorney-general of Quebec.[1] Even if consent had been granted, an appeal would not likely have been successful, as Judge Mathieu had, in most cases, made rulings in the accused's favour. Today there is no question that a new trial would be ordered because of the improper use of the word 'and' in the test for insanity, the limited meaning given to the word 'appreciate,' and the unduly high burden of proof that was placed on the accused. At that time, however, these rulings were considered proper ones. It is also likely that an appeal today would succeed because of the failure of the court to order a change of venue and the consequent prejudice to the accused.

Even if an appeal were successful, the best result the defence could have hoped for would have been the ordering of a new trial and another long, expensive ordeal. It is not known what the defence lawyers' fees were, but it is likely they were at least as large as the $200 a day, plus an initial retaining fee, that Macmaster sometimes received when acting for the defence. This fact is known because Macmaster had pointed out his rates when he submitted his final bill to the attorney-general ($7,500 for the inquest, preliminary hearing, and trial), stating that 'under all the circumstances, and particularly considering the vindica-

Sir Charles Hibbert Tupper, March 1895

tion of public justice obtained by the result of the trial, we think you will probably find the amount charged, reasonable.' In fact, Attorney-General Casgrain was concerned, and wanted the trial fee reduced to $100 a day: 'As you know, an order of the House has been voted for the production of all your accounts in this matter and they will be the object of close scrutiny at the next session. I think that it would be better for the both of us if you allowed me to make this reduction.' Macmaster agreed.

'Shortis will not hang,' St Pierre told the press: 'Judge, jury and everybody else who was at Beauharnois agrees that the boy is insane, that he is a monster, an individual without moral sense.'

'Why did the jury convict him then?' a reporter asked.

'Because,' said St Pierre, 'the law left them no alternative. The way the law is now it would almost hang a dog for murder. But the judge and jury and everybody else who was at Beauharnois will sign a petition to the Minister of Justice asking for a commutation.'

Macmaster, when asked about a possible petition, remarked that it would be undignified for him to give his opinion on such a subject unless authorized by the federal minister of justice; 'but I think,' he added, 'the decisions of our courts and the verdicts of our juries should be respected, otherwise what was the use of holding trials.'

Editorial comment agreed with Macmaster's view. The Montreal *Gazette* stated: 'the jury have decided that the prisoner was criminally responsible, and the decision must be accepted as final. Shortis had had every advantage that justice could grant or money could buy.' The Huntingdon *Gleaner* found it 'inconceivable that the executive will intervene to defeat the righteous judgment that has been rendered and pronounced.' The Toronto *Globe* reminded its readers that 'we must not lose sight of the other homes which were plunged in sorrow by the destructive passions of the accused.' The French papers took an equally strong view. 'Let the law take its course,' said *L'Evénement*; 'a commutation would be iniquitous.' *La Patrie* declared that 'the verdict satisfied public opinion,' and *La Minerve* maintained that 'the hanging was necessary to prevent such atrocities in the future.'

Shortly after the capital sentence was imposed, Mr and Mrs Shortis visited their son in jail. According to observers, he seemed totally oblivious to the fate that was facing him. The following day, 5 November, his parents spent considerable time with him to say good-bye – his father perhaps for the last time – before leaving by the afternoon train for Montreal. On Wednesday morning they consulted with Greenshields and that evening Francis Shortis took the train to New York, from where he would sail for Ireland. There he would gather petitions and statements to assist the case for commutation. Mrs Shortis said she would remain in Canada to the very end.

Attention then focused on the Dominion cabinet. Unlike England, where the home secretary himself made the decision as to whether the sentence should be commuted, in Canada the decision was made by the cabinet. Technically, the governor-general exercised the official power of commutation on the advice of the cabinet, just as in England the Queen was advised by the home secretary, but in fact neither of them acted on their own authority at that time. In Canada this was made clear by special instructions to the governor-general, issued by Great Britain at Canada's request in 1878, after Lord Dufferin had, against the cabinet's advice, commuted the death sentence to two years' imprisonment and then banishment of Ambroise Lépine, one of Louis Riel's confederates in the 1869 Red River Rebellion.[2]

The instructions stated, in part: 'And We do hereby direct and enjoin Our said Governor-General shall not pardon or reprieve any such offender without first receiving in capital cases the advice of the Privy Council for Our said Dominion, and in other cases the advice of one, at least, of his Ministers.'[3] Of course, the minister of justice had the responsibility of advising the cabinet. Commutations were not uncommon. In 1894, three of the eight persons sentenced to death in Canada had had their sentences commuted; in 1893, five out of seven had been commuted.[4]

A petition addressed to the Governor-General-in-Council, that is, the cabinet, was prepared and signed by the three defence counsel and by Mr and Mrs Shortis. It asked that 'royal clemency ... be exercised and the sentence commuted to imprisonment for life,' and alleged that Shortis was not responsible for the killings: 'That the evidence adduced before the court at the said trial shows that the prisoner was from his birth a moral and intellectual imbecile, on which imbecility was implanted later in life, insanity or disease of the mind, from both of which he suffered to such an extent as rendered him incapable of distinguishing the nature and quality of the act with which he is charged and knowing that such act was wrong; or at least, to raise grave and serious questions as to his responsibility for his acts.' Affidavits from all four psychiatrists called by the defence, setting out the substance of their previous testimony, were attached to the petition.

It was also alleged that the members of the jury were prejudiced against the accused:

That there existed a strong prejudice in the minds of the community in the district where the said trial took place, and each and every of the jurors in said trial so sworn to try the said prisoner admitted that they had formed a previous opinion as to his guilt, but that they thought upon sufficient proof of insanity being brought before them that they could do justice and render an impartial verdict and were thus accepted on such statements by the tryers sworn to determine the question as to whether or not each of the said jurors stood impartial, but the said jurors were unable to relieve their minds of the preconceived idea of guilt which they had attaching the prisoner, and thereby were unable to give due and proper weight to the evidence.

George Foster, as the solicitor – but perhaps of equal importance as an important member of the Conservative party – was assigned the task of personally presenting the petition to the minister of justice in Ottawa.

On Monday, 11 November, one week after the death sentence had been pronounced, Foster and Mrs Shortis left Montreal for the capital. Mary Shortis had spent the weekend – as she would every weekend – in Beauharnois, staying for long periods with her son in his large double cell at the jail. On Sunday morning she had attended high mass at the parish church, where the priest asked his congregation to pray for the parents and for Shortis that he might die like a Christian. Shortis continued to seem unconcerned. The *Star* reported: 'Valentine Shortis acts as though his stay at the Beauharnois gaol is but a mere holiday ... He reads much, chats pleasantly with the guards and often sings.'

At ten o'clock on Tuesday morning, Foster and Mrs Shortis left the Russell Hotel (then at the corner of Sparks and Elgin streets and therefore close to the Parliament Buildings) for the East Block, which at that time contained not only the prime minister's office but also the offices of other ministers of the Crown and many civil servants, including all of the approximately fifteen officials of the Department of Justice.[5] Mrs Shortis waited on the lawn outside, while Foster met with Sir Charles Hibbert Tupper, the minister of justice, and Augustus Power, QC, the acting deputy minister (E.L. Newcombe, the deputy, was away on a hunting trip).

Power might have been present in any event because he was the departmental official responsible for preparing the reports to the minister of justice on all capital cases. A McGill graduate, he had practised law in Montreal until joining the Department of Justice in 1874, rising to chief clerk. He might have become the deputy minister in 1887 when

G.W. Burbidge, the deputy, was elevated to the Exchequer Court, but his drinking, it seems, put him out of the running.[6] Foster no doubt hoped to receive a good reception from Power who, like the Shortises, was an Irish Catholic, his late father, a former Superior Court judge in Quebec, having come from Waterford. Power's mother was French Canadian.

Tupper had already received a letter from Joseph Bergeron, the member of Parliament from Beauharnois, then visiting Chicago, warning him of the danger of a commutation. Bergeron, a lawyer and the deputy speaker of the House of Commons – who had, part affectionately and part mockingly, been dubbed the 'Beauharnois Boy' by Laurier because of his identification with the English (his wife was Irish) – was worried about the political consequences of a commutation, particularly in Beauharnois:[7]

Chicago, 9th November, 1895

My dear friend

Although far away in the land of Uncle Sam, I see by our Canadian papers that it is intended to present you with a petition to commute Shortis's sentence to imprisonment for life on the plea of insanity. I do not need to tell you the bad effect such a commutation would have in our district after the fair trial he had. Also, after your judgment in Chatelle and their own pleading in favour of Riel in 1885 on the plea of insanity.

Shortis deserves to be hanged ten times – he is purely a monster.

I hope you will not be annoyed with this letter. Do unto others, etc. Wishing you lots of good things, I remain,

Your Friend,
J.G.H. Bergeron.

P.S. Please remember my wife and I to Lady Tupper.

Tupper replied on 12 November, the day he had met Foster:

My dear Bergeron,

I beg to acknowledge receipt of your letter of the 9th instant, respecting Shortis. You may rely on my looking into this case in the most careful possible manner. Reciprocating all your good wishes, and with kindest regards to Mrs. Bergeron and yourself, in which my wife would join did she know I was writing, believe me,

Always sincerely yours,
Charles Hibbert Tupper.

Bergeron followed up several weeks later with another letter:

My dear friend

As I see by the papers that great efforts are made to have Shortis's sentence commuted to imprisonment for life, I again wish you to remember my letter to you from Chicago, asking that the law be carried out.

The commutation of the sentence could have a most terrible effect, and the more so as the prisoner's parents are rich.

Hoping that the law will be carried out according to the verdict of the jury and the sentence of the judge, I remain,

Yours very sincerely,
J.G.H. Bergeron

Sir Charles Hibbert Tupper,[8] the minister of justice in Mackenzie Bowell's administration, was the second son of one of the Fathers of Confederation, Sir Charles Tupper. Sir Charles, Sr, who would later become the prime minister of Canada, had been a federal cabinet minister in the 1870s and 1880s and since 1888 had been the Canadian high commissioner in London. His son, Charles Hibbert – who, for convenience, as others have done,[9] will be called Sir Hibbert – grew up in Nova Scotia, graduated with the governor-general's scholarship from McGill, and then, after obtaining an LL B from Harvard Law School, practised law in Halifax with the firm that included Sir John Thompson and Robert Borden, both of whom would later become prime ministers.

He was elected to Parliament in 1882 and then in 1888, after his father left Sir John A. Macdonald's cabinet to become high commissioner, he became, at the age of thirty-three, the minister of marine and fisheries, the youngest person to hold a portfolio in the Dominion cabinet up to that time. Sir Hibbert had served in the cabinets of Sir John A. Macdonald, Sir John Abbott, and Sir John Thompson. He was described by a political opponent as 'a handsome man' and a 'splendid speaker,' and contemporaries spoke of his 'fine speaking voice and his power to hold an audience.'

When Mackenzie Bowell – one of the so-called 'unknown' Conservative prime ministers after Macdonald – became leader of the government in December 1894, following Thompson's untimely death in England while at Windsor Castle, Sir Hibbert was asked to become the minister of justice. As a first-rate lawyer, he was delighted with the elevation: it was no exaggeration for Macmaster's partner to write him that 'your appointment will be hailed with satisfaction and approval from one end of the country to the other'; nor was it an exaggeration for the governor-general, Lord Aberdeen, to state that the new position is 'no small tribute to the manner in which you have discharged the onerous duties of the public positions which you have already occupied.'

One such position was as the British government's agent at the famous Bering Sea Arbitration in Paris in 1893, for which Tupper was knighted on his return to Canada. Publicly the arbitration was a great success for Canada. In fact, it was not, because the regulations drawn up by the arbitrators effectively excluded Canadian sealing vessels, during all but a short season, from a large area of the Bering Sea. Coincidentally, Donald Macmaster had at the age of forty-eight written a doctoral dissertation for McGill University on the arbitration.[10] Britain's actions, Macmaster wrote Sir John Thompson, then prime minister, who had been one of the arbitrators, was 'one of the most scandalous and disgraceful surrenders of modern times.' 'If we were the meanest little republic of South or Central America, we could have made as good – and probably better – terms than Great Britain did with Uncle Sam.'[11] Sir Hibbert privately agreed with this sentiment.

Sir Charles Hibbert Tupper, like most others in Canada, had of course been following the Shortis case. Lady Aberdeen had written to him about it in the spring and had forwarded a letter from a Miss Sullivan, an internationally acclaimed harpist and daughter of the lord mayor of Dublin, whom the Aberdeens had known when Lord Aberdeen had been lord lieutenant of Ireland in 1886. The letter conveyed 'an earnest request from the father of the prisoner for consideration on the plea of insanity'; and in May Lady Aberdeen had sent Sir Hibbert medical and death certificates from Ireland, as well as an affidavit from Mr Shortis, all of which had been collected by Miss Sullivan. Lady Aberdeen simply added at the end of her own letter: 'I forward all these to you so that they may be dealt with as they should.' Because the relationship between Sir Hibbert and the Aberdeens will become increasingly important in the story, more needs to be said about the Aberdeens at this point.[12]

Lord Aberdeen had been appointed as governor-general of Canada by Prime Minister William Gladstone in April 1893. This was not, in fact, the Aberdeens first extended stay in the country. In 1890 they had spent a year in Hamilton, because Lady Aberdeen had had a nervous breakdown and the city was thought to be an ideal place for her recovery. Both were great admirers of Gladstone. Like him, Lord Aberdeen had prowled the streets of London searching for prostitutes to be rescued.[13] Many Conservatives in Canada were not entirely happy that Gladstonian Liberals were occupying the vice-regal residence. Their suspicions about the Aberdeens' sympathies would have been confirmed if they had read Lady Aberdeen's letter to Gladstone in March 1895: 'Although we must have no politics yet we cannot help personally hoping that the Liberals under Mr. Laurier may come in at the election ... they seem to have a stronger set of men as leaders.'[14]

Lady Aberdeen, born Ishbel Maria Marjoribanks, came from an old Scottish family on her father's side and an Irish family on her mother's. She had married Lord Aberdeen (the 7th earl) in 1877 when she was twenty, he ten years older. He had succeeded to the title unexpectedly some years earlier, when his eldest brother had died at sea and the next eldest had shot himself in his rooms at Cambridge.

Their period in Ireland in 1886 was terminated when Gladstone lost the election that year, though they continued an active interest in Irish affairs. At the time Gladstone asked Lord Aberdeen to assume the position as the Queen's representative in Canada, they were at the Chicago World's Fair on behalf of Irish Industries. Many years later, they had the chance to return to Ireland: from 1905 to 1915 Lord Aberdeen was again lord lieutenant.

Lady Aberdeen had a strong personality and was undoubtedly the dominant partner in the marriage, referring to her husband as 'Gentle Johnny.'[15] She took a keen interest in politics, as her diaries and letters show, and was also active in organizing a number of voluntary organizations in Canada, in particular the National Council of Women of Canada and the Victorian Order of Nurses. Though not interested in giving women the vote, she wanted them – like herself – to have influence.

By the fall of 1895, Sir Charles Hibbert Tupper and the Aberdeens had become very close. It had not started out that way. Sir Hibbert had not thought much of their style. In a letter to a friend in early 1895 he had complained: 'Lord Aberdeen is making the office of Governor General very cheap. He presides at all kinds of meetings, and knocks about in such a democratic way that the people will soon begin to think that the office is not so high or important.' Moreover, he was no doubt disappointed that Aberdeen had called on Bowell to form the government when Sir John Thompson died, rather than on his father, for whom the Aberdeens did not have a high regard. The Aberdeens, influenced by Thompson's widow's strong views, did not want the elder Tupper to lead the government. Lady Aberdeen had assured Lady Thompson that 'Never if [Lord Aberdeen] could help it should Sir Charles be again in Canadian politics.'[16] There was no clear choice of leader, and members of the cabinet decided to support Bowell when it was thought that the governor-general might call on Laurier, the leader of the opposition, to form the government.

The relationship between Sir Hibbert and the Aberdeens developed, however, over time. They admired his ability and took a particular interest in him. He 'is clearly the man of the future in the Conservative party,' Lady Aberdeen noted in her diary during the summer, adding 'if he learns to have self-control and to realize that it is possible for him to make a mistake.' She was referring in particular to his sudden resignation from the cabinet in March 1895; at the time she had written to her friend Gladstone in England: 'We are in the midst of a crisis now, for young Sir Charles Tupper the Minister of Justice has sent in his resignation, practically because although an Order in Council was passed promising that remedial legislation should be given for the Roman Catholics in Manitoba, yet he understands his colleagues not to mean to carry it out. He is the strongest man they have and we do not know what will be the outcome.' The outcome was that the Aberdeens, along with his father and others, talked him out of resigning, and Lady Aberdeen later noted in her diary: 'Our relations with him personally have been very cordial since the time of his threatened resignation, when His Excellency and I talked to him and Lady Tupper ... and advised him not to throw it up both on public and private grounds. He very much appreciated His Excellency's action and seems to remember it.'

Sir Hibbert's resignation had been occasioned by Bowell's decision to have another parliamentary session before calling an election. Tupper wanted an election then on the issue of the Manitoba schools question, which would mean, he wrote a fellow cabinet minister who had been trying to talk him out of resigning, that 'Canada would be saved a racial-religious conflict.' Bowell's position of waiting, he wrote, was 'an old man's folly and tyranny' and would mean that agitation against remedial legislation would grow, and result in no legislation and 'possibly rebellion in Quebec.' No other issue dominated Canadian politics at the time as did the matter of separate schools.

In July, the Aberdeens left for an extended stay in British Columbia, where they owned a large tract of land near Vernon. Sir Hibbert had been asked by Lady Aberdeen, she wrote in her diary, to 'give us warning during our absence West, if he thought it would be wise for us to return here and be at the seat of war.' The warring parties were primarily in Mackenzie Bowell's own cabinet. The following day, after hearing that another minister, Arthur Dickey, might resign, Lady Aberdeen noted in a letter to Sir Hibbert: 'It is indeed an anxious time and the course of events during the next few months must mean much in the future of this country.' The Aberdeens could not rely on Bowell to keep them informed. Lady Aberdeen wrote in her diary of 'the uncomfortable feeling which has been growing in [Lord Aberdeen's] mind as to the weakness and consequent shiftiness of Sir Mackenzie Bowell.' Moreover, Bowell, apparently because he had been a printer in his younger days, had difficulty in writing letters, which made written communication with the governor-general difficult.

The Aberdeens clearly recognized Bowell's weakness. Lady Aberdeen noted in her diary before leaving for the west 'the awkward things that might happen with a weak Premier, and more especially one whom his colleagues do not trust, and who having no notion of the relations which should exist between a Premier and the Governor General, and no conception of the loyalty which must at all hazards, protect the actions of the representative of the Crown, might well be willing to shelter himself, if need be behind the Governor General and throw the responsibility of his acts on him if it seemed advantageous for party purposes.' Prophetic words, as we shall see.

Throughout their stay out west the Aberdeens kept in touch with Sir Hibbert. Lady Aberdeen, for example, asked if he thought there was 'any opening where His Excellency may intervene with advantage about Manitoba say in summoning any sort of Round Table Conference or suggesting it.' Another letter described a fancy dress ball that they were planning upon their return: 'Immediately on arrival, I want to try to arrange a fancy ball, respecting various periods in Canadian history, and trust I may look to Judy Tupper for assistance.' 'For reasons you will quite understand when you see Lady T.,' answered Sir Hibbert, referring of course to his wife's pregnancy, 'she will not be able to join in the merry throng this winter but we both think the idea of a costume ball delightful.'

On 4 November, the day of the sentence of death in the Shortis case, Tupper described political events in Ottawa:

> Efforts are being made to reorganize the Government, and it is not improbable that Mr. Chapleau [the lieutenant-governor of Quebec and a potential replacement for Angers], and Chief Justice Meredith may be with us.
>
> This is of course very confidential – the delay in all these things is heartbreaking. Our party is terribly handicapped, and it looks as if we must continue the fight under a leader who does not lead!

Sir Hibbert advised the Aberdeens to return to Ottawa: 'I do think your Excellencies ought to be here. A crisis may be upon us in the discussion of the [Manitoba] schools – trouble may arise in the new organization [of the cabinet].'

The reorganization anticipated by Sir Hibbert was more drastic than he indicated to Lady Aberdeen. He had hoped that his father would replace Bowell as prime minister; in a letter to the minister of trade and commerce, W.B. Ives, written on the same day as his letter to Lady Aberdeen, he wrote: 'It is utterly impossible for that man [Bowell] to lead our party to victory in the coming struggle ... Now then we have to have a man as Premier of this country who will be able almost instantaneously ... to make the public realize that a change has taken place. I know of no man living who can do it better – and of course I do not know if he can do it – than Sir Charles Tupper the High Commissioner ... Bowell might go to England as High Commissioner. It ought to satisfy his vanity.' A few days earlier Arthur Dickey, the minister of militia and defence, had written to Sir Charles in London that 'the prime minister has shown that the task of governing this Country is too heavy for him ... The only hope of the Country and of the party is in yourself. It is unfortunate that under the weakest premier the Dominion has ever had, the most difficult question in her history (the Manitoba Schools) should come up for settlement.' Perhaps as a follow-up to this letter, or possibly independently, Sir Hibbert wrote his father: 'These be troublesome times indeed ... We lack only a leader! ... I verily believe if you could visit Canada on some excuse the party would rise and form up under you ... You could do a thousand times better than Bowell without any work.' Sir Hibbert offered to resign his seat in Pictou, Nova Scotia, for his father; he would enter private practice in Ottawa, which, he wrote, is 'growing faster than any city in Canada,' and then 'branch out' to Toronto 'when I wish to.'

On 18 November Lady Aberdeen wrote Sir Hibbert from Vancouver, thanking him for his frankness and telling him, 'we have now started on our return journey and plan to arrive at Ottawa about ten days after you receive this.' She expressed her pleasure in learning that 'we are to be near neighbours now,' the Tuppers, with their growing family, having moved to a house close to the governor-general's residence at Rideau Hall. 'I hope,' she added, 'that the compact between us may continue even after our return.'

A later letter, written on Tuesday, 3 December, from Rat Portage, Manitoba, announced that they were 'due to reach our journey's end on Friday' and expressed the hope that Shortis' death sentence would be commuted to life imprisonment:

I hope you will come and see us very soon. Now that you are so close to us we shall look for you dropping in whenever you have time and feel inclined so to do.

I anyway shall be at home all Saturday if you would ask for me at any hour most convenient to yourself and come and have a chat.

Meanwhile may I just say one thing. I know you must be simply burdened with letters, petitions, etc. regarding young Valentine Shortis.

Many friends in Ireland thinking that His Excellency has the same absolute power in Canada regarding pardons and commutations of death sentences as he had in Ireland have written to us personally and several to me begging me to intercede. These letters are mostly from magistrates, people in good positions and not liable to take an over-lenient view of murder cases. But they feel the proof of insanity in the family is so strong as well as borne out by the early life of the young man himself that they conclude that the death sentence means an antipathy to anyone from the old country. This is likely to have a serious effect in giving a feeling against Canada all over the South of Ireland when the parents are so well known and respected.

I cannot help hoping that you will in any case recommend that the sentence be commuted to life imprisonment ...

Au revoir
Yours very sincerely
Ishbel Aberdeen

9

December 1895

SHORTLY AFTER the Aberdeens returned, Mary Shortis and her solicitor, George Foster, arrived in Ottawa. On Thursday morning, 12 December, Mrs Shortis drove from the Russell Hotel to Rideau Hall and had a private interview with Lady Aberdeen, joined later by her husband. Lady Aberdeen was not keeping her journal during this period – she did not take it up again until the new year – and so there is no record of what took place. There is no question, however, that the scene would have been a touching one, with the mother pleading for the life of her only child. Lady Aberdeen's own sons, Lord Haddo and Gordon, only a few years younger than Valentine Shortis, would soon be returning from England to spend the holidays with their parents. Lady Aberdeen no doubt promised to continue to do all she could to save Shortis' life.

For the previous month Mary Shortis had worked unceasingly to build support for a commutation. As Bergeron, the Beauharnois MP, later said: 'Mrs. Shortis went to many people; she went to Ministers of the Crown, she went to the railway magnates and those who were at the head of great corporations, she did everything that ... a mother would do in such a case ...'[1] During the week she saw Lady Aberdeen, she and Foster continued to see Department of Justice officials and ministers of the Crown. At the beginning of the following week, she had a long interview with Arthur Dickey, the minister of militia and defence, and a one-hour meeting with the prime minister, Mackenzie Bowell.

A month earlier she had visited Judge Mathieu in his chambers at the courthouse in Montreal. 'There was a sorrowful scene between herself and the judge, who was most kind and considerate,' the *Herald* reported: 'His Honour told her that, though he sympathized and deeply felt her pain, he could not help her in any way.'

Lord and Lady Aberdeen, 1898

That weekend she had returned as usual to Beauharnois. 'She looked very pale,' reported the *Star*, 'and tears streamed from her eyes when she was met by the Grey Nuns, who had placed their carriage at her disposal. She expressed very little hope of saving her son's life, and she met with very little sympathy for him.' Her pessimism had communicated itself to her son, who, when his mother was called back to Montreal shortly after her arrival, had asked her to 'give up troubling about him and remain constantly with him until the 3rd of January.'

Throughout this period the newspapers circulated, and then scotched, one rumour after another. The popular Montreal *Star* in a one-week period reported false rumours that Shortis had attempted to commit suicide, had escaped, and had had his petition turned down.

Perhaps it was the rumour of a possible escape – although there is nothing in the files to indicate the reason – that caused the Beauharnois jailor suddenly to refuse to let Mrs Shortis visit her son in his cell. Henceforth, she would have to see him through the bars of his cell door. Foster pleaded with the attorney-general of Quebec: 'in the name of common justice, and common humanity, for God's sake do not let it be said that a mother is not permitted in this country to spend perhaps the few remaining hours of her son's life with him, but have to suffer the terrible indignity of looking at him through the bars in his cell.' The attorney-general's department wired back that they could not interfere.

Sir Charles Hibbert Tupper was not in Ottawa when the Aberdeens returned. He and Dickey had left for their constituencies in Nova Scotia and to address public meetings throughout the province, preparing for the coming election. The following weekend he travelled to New York to meet his father, whom he had not seen in several years, and who had now found a good pretext to visit Canada – to consult Bowell and others on the question of a fast Atlantic steamer service, an important issue at the time. Sir Charles, dressed in a mink-lined coat and a mink hat, impressed the waiting reporters with his vigour: 'a robust man, at least sixty years of age,' wrote one New Yorker, although Sir Charles was a dozen years older than that. The Conservative Montreal *Gazette*, as if part of a plot to show him in the most favourable light, declared: 'His many friends in Canada, political and social, will be rejoiced to learn that the High Commissioner, the intimate and long time colleague of Sir John A. Macdonald is in such excellent health, and has such prospect of years of good service to the Dominion.' Perhaps this was stressed to counteract an earlier story in the Liberal

Herald that 'The state of Sir Charles Tupper's health is reported to be not altogether satisfactory.'

'What is the cause of your present visit to Canada?' he was asked by the Gazette reporter. 'I came here at the invitation of the Premier, Sir Mackenzie Bowell, to confer with the Government on the question of the fast Atlantic service.'

'That, then, is your sole object?'

'Of course. I could not decline such a request. It was my duty to consult with the Cabinet and to give them my advice and what information I possess in reference to a matter with which I have been intimately connected during several years in London.'

'But the Liberal papers say that you are coming out to lead the Conservative Party until after the general elections.'

'Then, I cannot be responsible for what newspapers or individuals may report.'

'Then you will make a prolonged stay in Canada?'

'No, I do not expect to stay here long. I will go back very shortly; just as soon as the Canadian government is of opinion that I have discharged the object of my visit, and given them the information necessary to enable them to call for tenders for the building of the fast Atlantic steamers.'

Sir Hibbert and his parents arrived in Ottawa in a special government coach. The Tuppers would stay with their son. Sir Charles met Bowell the next day, 16 December, the day on which Mrs Shortis had pleaded with the prime minister to save her son from the hangman.

This was to be the first hanging ever in Beauharnois. The assistant attorney-general of Quebec wrote to Sheriff Laberge instructing him to obtain the services of J.R. Radclive, the official Canadian hangman, who lived in Toronto and would conduct the hanging within the walls of the Beauharnois prison. Public executions had been abolished shortly after Confederation. Sheriff Laberge wrote to Radclive: 'I received instructions from the Attorney General for the Province of Quebec to retain your services for the execution of Shortis, on the third of January next, at eight o'clock in the morning. Please let me know immediately if you can dispose of your time at that date. I beg also to inform you that we have no apparatus to carry out this execution, Shortis being the first one condemned to death in this district.'

Radclive had been designated the official Canadian hangman by a Dominion order-in-council in 1892. He was paid $700 a year by Ottawa and reasonable travelling expenses by the sheriff or provincial attorney-general. The order-in-council had been requested by Sir Oliver Mowat, then premier of Ontario, and was passed on the recommendation of Sir John Thompson, then minister of justice,[2] 'at the urgent solicitation of the Attorney General of Ontario, he representing in effect that it was highly desirable in order for the due and proper execution of capital sentences that some one individual specially experienced and qualified should be designated as a permanent office for that purpose ... holding himself available for all capital cases that might occur in any part of Canada.'

Radclive had been a British sailor off the coast of China and had had some experience hanging pirates. It seems he had been trained under the official British hangman, William Marwood. He had settled with his wife in Toronto and became the steward of the Sunnyside Boating Club in Parkdale. After hearing of a bungled hanging in 1890 he volunteered his services, and later that year, dressed in a plain black suit without a mask, he successfully hanged the notorious murderer, the Oxford-educated Reginald Birchall, in Woodstock. Two years later he became the official hangman. In the four-year period between the beginning of 1892 and the end of 1895, twelve persons had been hanged in Canada and presumably Radclive had hanged most, if not all, of them. He was known for speed of execution.[3]

Laberge received no reply to his letter and so informed the attorney-general's department; they wired Ottawa and discovered that Radclive had moved from 132 Lisgar Street to 210 Sorauren Avenue, also in the Parkdale area and therefore close to the rowing club. In the meantime, the first letter had been forwarded to Radclive who informed Sheriff Laberge that he now lived at 52 Fern Avenue, still in the Parkdale area. Were these frequent moves because Radclive was able to afford better accommodation with his double salary, or were they because he was asked to move as soon as the owner of the house found out about his occupation? Radclive replied to Laberge:

Dear Sir
In answer to your letter, will be with you few days beforehand to see that everything is ready. Will write you again about the 20th of next month [December] what we shall require.

I am, Sir
Your obedient Servant
J.R. Radclive

Arrangements were made for an Irish Jesuit priest from Montreal, with the wonderful name, Father Devine, to minister to Shortis' spiritual needs. He visited the condemned man on several occasions and celebrated mass with him in an improvised chapel in the prison corridor. It was agreed that Father Devine would come to Beauharnois shortly after Christmas and remain with Shortis till the end.

Most of Shortis' time was spent writing and reading, though only the American newspapers were permitted. Four novels he had ordered from a Chicago firm, including a translation of a work by Alexandre Dumas (whose death had just been reported in the papers), arrived in early December and others were then ordered – to arrive sometime after Christmas. About two dozen postcards, similar to the following, were sent in December:

Messrs The Boston Woven   Beauharnois P.Q.
    Hose and Rubber Co.   Canada
Boston

                                     Dec. 18th 1895

Gentlemen
    Please forward a copy of your book 'Bicycle Advice' to above address soon as possible, also your export price list and terms for 'cash with order.' Have you electros on your tyres.
    I remain, in haste, truly yours

                                  Cuthbert F.V. Shortis

The above card was not in fact sent. Rather, it was forwarded by the sheriff to the attorney-general: 'See for yourself if the coming of the third of January next is of much concern to him.' Shortis seemed wholly indifferent to his fate, the sheriff reported to the press; only once since the sentence was pronounced had he mentioned the 'doom that overhangs him, and then it was more in a jocular style than anything else.'

Sir Charles Hibbert Tupper, Mackenzie Bowell, and the Aberdeens were deluged with letters and petitions concerning the case, for the most part against carrying out the sentence.[4] The documents from Great Britain all favoured a commutation. The colonial secretary, Joseph Chamberlain, forwarded a memorial from 130 influential persons living in or near Liverpool; 'The signatures seem worthy of consideration,' he noted on the Colonial Office file. The Duke of Norfolk, a prominent Catholic nobleman, sent on a letter from the bishop of Lismore. Sir Charles Tupper had earlier forwarded an unsolicited letter from a professor of agriculture at Edinburgh University, saying that he had come over on the boat with Shortis and 'got to know him very well': 'At that time there was no doubt his mental condition was far from right. At certain periods he was an agreeable enough companion and humorous, but on other occasions he was morose and so unlike an ordinary individual that his familiar name amongst ourselves was the mad Irishman. I happen to have a photograph of him in a group which I took on board, in which he exhibits the expression which he assumed during those peculiar turns or moods which he took.' (This photograph is reproduced at the beginning of this book.)

The documents from Ireland, obviously arranged for by Francis Shortis, almost uniformly argued that there was a history of insanity in the family and that there had been a strong feeling against Shortis in the district where he was tried. Petitions were received from the mayor and alderman of Waterford, the Waterford Chamber of Commerce, the Waterford Harbour Commission, and similar groups in other municipalities in southern Ireland. The governors of the lunatic asylum in Waterford declared that they 'from their own observations and from common repute regarding the mental condition of Valentine F.C. Shortis believe that he was not accountable for his actions.' One major petition contained over a thousand signatures, including those of the Protestant and Roman Catholic bishops of Waterford, the Crown solicitor, and twenty-two barristers and solicitors, as well as eighteen members of the medical profession residing in and near Waterford.

In Canada, most letters also favoured a commutation. Certainly the letters from religious leaders did. A Protestant minister from Halifax wrote that 'to execute Shortis would be the commission of a barbarous judicial murder; and this is the general feeling down here.' A Catholic priest from Ontario maintained that 'Every Catholic priest with whom I have met expresses himself like this Protestant minister [from Halifax].' The archbishop of Kingston, James Cleary, whom Monsignor O'Bryen had visited on his way to Valleyfield, wrote a long letter severely criticizing Macmaster's treatment of the medical witnesses as 'mad doctors': 'The common sense of the community has been shocked by Mr. Macmaster's extravagant utterance.'

Some letters in favour of commutation were from less impressive names. A woman from Vermont, a daily reader of the Montreal *Star*, wrote: 'now that I am a mother, and have a mother's feelings, I implore you to have pity on the poor, broken-hearted Mother.' A Montreal woman put the blame on Louis Simpson, the manager of the mill, who she claimed had caused her injury by speeding up the pace of work when she had worked at the mill: 'a more unfeeling brute I never tried to serve. Shortis, going around with his revolver, was never so much of a terror among the people than what Simpson used to be to the poor people who were trying to earn a living on the work he was appointed overseer ... I believe Simpson is to blame. Dear Sir, mercy for the boy and his poor parents.'

A number of private letters were received from influential Conservative politicians, however, urging that the law be allowed to take its course. We have already seen the letters sent by Joseph Bergeron, the Beauharnois MP. Senator G.A. Drummond, a wealthy banker and industrialist, wrote from Montreal that 'the opinion here is that he, Shortis, deserves it if ever a criminal did, and that if he escapes it will be due to his having friends and money.' A similar letter from the editor of the *Gazette*, until recently an MP, argued that 'if the Government interferes it will go far to create the impression that if a man has money enough, he can produce, by the hiring of advocates to importune the Government, such a feeling as to secure him against the extreme penalty of the law.' Other letters came from ordinary citizens: one from Valleyfield urged that the government 'leave things as they are,' and a Montrealer demanded that 'in the case of the double dyed murderer Shortis let Justice be done, though the Heavens should fall.'

In mid-December the three defence lawyers submitted a sworn affidavit and a further petition to the governor-general stating, in part, that 'in all our experience in criminal trials, extending over a great many years, we have never seen a criminal trial heard in this country where the jury in the case were prejudiced to such a degree as were the jury in this case.' They asked Lord Aberdeen, as was done in the Riel case, 'to exercise the royal prerogative and order a medical commission to be appointed to examine and report upon the sanity or insanity of the prisoner.' They also asked the minister of justice and the prime minister to obtain the judge's opinion 'as to whether he considers the extreme penalty should be inflicted.'

Judge Mathieu was asked his opinion and concluded that although 'no other verdict than one of guilty could have been rendered' the evidence of the psychiatrists had given him 'a great deal of anxiety.' He concluded by suggesting that 'perhaps this is a case where the clemency of [the cabinet] might be exercised.' His full report is as follows:

December 9, 1895

To the Honourable Sir CHARLES H. TUPPER,
    Minister of Justice.

SIR, – In answer to the letter of your deputy, Mr. Newcombe, of the 3rd day of December, instant, saying that you would be glad to receive, for the confidential information of His Excellency the Governor General in Council, the evidence and any other matters touching the case of Shortis, which I may desire to advert to, I beg to say that I believe that, under our law, as it stands, no other verdict than one of guilty could have been rendered, because I believe that at the time of the murder Shortis was not labouring under natural imbecility or disease of the mind to such an extent as to render him incapable of appreciating the nature and quality of the murder, and of knowing that such murder was wrong.

I believe he knew what he was doing and that he was doing wrong. The circumstances of the murder and the convict's words to Smith immediately after he was arrested 'Shoot me or lend me your revolver and I will shoot myself,' according to me, establish that he knew he was doing wrong and that he had done wrong. At the same time I am bound to say that the evidence of the convict's acts previous to the murder points to the conclusion that he is not perfectly sane. Those acts seem to show that Shortis was not like other young men of his age and of his education. If he had been perfectly sane, perhaps he would have foreseen the difficulty and the risk of the enterprise. But, although I think that he was not perfectly sane, at the same time, I believe that he was not so insane as not to know that the murder that he was committing was wrong. That is my personal conviction, but I must remark that the evidence of the medical men, all on the side of the defence, has given me a great deal of anxiety. Those men are able and honest men; they are men of first class standing and they all swore positively that Shortis could not appreciate the quality of the murder, and, in fact, that he did not know what he was doing. Taking into consideration the evidence of the acts of Shortis previous to the murder, and especially his acts in Ireland, and also the evidence of the medical men and all the other circumstances, perhaps this is a case where the clemency of His Excellency the Governor General in Council might be exercised, in sending Shortis to the penitentiary for life instead of having him executed.

I have the honour to be, sir,

Your obedient servant,
M. MATHIEU.

Note that Judge Mathieu again used the word 'and.' To him, Shortis'
insanity defence could not succeed: Shortis knew that what he was
doing was wrong.

Dr Georges Villeneuve, the superintendent of the asylum at Longue
Pointe, the principal Crown psychiatrist at the trial, who, it will be recalled, was not asked to give evidence, had been seen after the trial by
Mrs Shortis and by Greenshields in the hope that he would assist in securing a commutation. He sent the following letter to Macmaster,
who forwarded it to the minister of justice:

> The verdict is right according to the law, and one that the Crown was in-duty
> bound to obtain from the jury. And such a verdict only could satisfy public
> opinion. But the law may be wrong in establishing a fixed criterion of in-
> sanity, which does not admit of forms or degrees, and to which all cases
> must frame themselves, whether it suits them or not.
>
> ... It is my opinion that some facts in such cases may be more properly
> taken in consideration by the executive than by the jury, as they warrant cle-
> mency rather than acquittal ...
>
> What strikes me about the mentality of Shortis is that, though the facts of
> the case have not shown to my entire satisfaction that he was or is insane,
> they show a certain amount of *desequilibration mentale*, resulting from
> hereditary degeneracy of the mind, which implies a more or less defective
> judgment and impaired volition. I think this opinion is justified by the
> history of his life. His responsibility may be considered to be diminished
> therefrom, and it might be meted out by a proportional punishment. I may
> say that I am speaking from a medical, and not from a legal point of view ...
>
> I have been seen by Mrs. Shortis, and, at her most urgent request, I had a
> short interview with Mr. Greenshields. I may say that I was deeply moved by
> the tears of the mother who is run to desperation by the thought that her
> only son and child will ascend the gallows.

C.K. Clarke had written to Macmaster on the day the sentence was
pronounced that 'the execution of that boy would be a mistake, in the
interests of common humanity, and I am not mistaken when I say that
no more marked case of insanity exists in the wards of Rockwood today than the same Shortis.'

> I have learned to regard you as a big-hearted man, full of sympathy and gentle
> instincts, and I shall be much mistaken if, now after the victory of a verdict
> has been won, you will not be one of the first to help prevent a judicial mur-
> der that would only add one more horror to the dreadful tragedy already en-

acted. As far as Shortis himself is concerned, it matters not the toss of a copper, as he is a creature devoid of every moral attribute; for his poor father and mother it does matter.

Canada has long ago earned the reputation of being the most heartless country in the world, where the criminal insane are concerned, and she deserves it. We make the boast that the insanity dodge cannot be played upon us, for we hang insane and malingerers alike. It is a boast we should not be proud of.

Clarke ended by stating: 'This letter is of course merely a personal matter, and quite voluntary; in fact known of by no one but my wife, who, by the way, sides with your view of the case altogether.'

A month went by before Macmaster answered. The case had taken a great deal out of him – he was off work for the next seven or eight days, taking a short vacation with his wife at the Waldorf-Astoria in New York. He wrote to Clarke: 'my duty was ended when the verdict was rendered and the sentence pronounced. The whole responsibility after that rested with the Minister of Justice. I represented the provincial authorities ... I could not well volunteer any opinion to the Minister of Justice, and, besides that, the Minister of Justice has not asked me for my opinion.' Macmaster was still convinced that Shortis' actions were premeditated: 'One very serious difficulty confronts me, namely, that I am perfectly convinced that Shortis, on the 1st of March, knew the nature and quality of the act he was doing and that he knew it was wrong and punishable by law; further, that there was premeditation, design and motive for the commission of the act. That being so, how could I very well interfere?'

The minister of justice did, in fact, ask for Macmaster's opinion – at the suggestion of W.B. Ives, the minister of trade and commerce. Macmaster received Sir Hibbert's telegram at four o'clock on Monday, 23 December; a reply was requested by the next morning, the day of the cabinet meeting to discuss the case. Macmaster pointed out that the trial was 'absolutely fair' and the judge's charge 'absolutely impartial.' Was Shortis insane? 'The symptoms given by the doctors were completely pulverized in the course of cross-examination.' Moreover, he maintained again that there was premeditation: 'If it was not for the presence of motive for the commission of the crime, I would be inclined to say that the prisoner's mind must, at all events on the particular occasion, have been unbalanced to an extent sufficient to affect his power of self-control. But a large sum of money being present on the scene and a previous suggestion that the mill could be easily robbed, combined with the design in the execution of the crime, are powerful factors that it is difficult to disregard.'

The letter was uncompromising. Macmaster, however, was obviously worried about his position. The following day he sent a telegram to the minister of justice correcting two minor errors in his letter. The telegram was an excuse to add some second thoughts: 'Though I think the prisoner was rightly convicted, you are the best and most disinterested judge whether the mercy of the Crown should be extended to him.'

The cabinet meeting was scheduled for Tuesday, 24 December. Augustus Power, the chief clerk in the Department of Justice, prepared a report on the case for the minister of justice, as he did in all capital cases. His twenty-five-page report reviewed the evidence and the law and stated that 'the verdict appears to be entirely correct, according to law.' 'I may say,' he pointed out, 'that the evidence offered by the Crown in rebuttal, in my opinion, completely dispels the idea of any lack of intelligence on the part of the prisoner. In fact, much of it points quite clearly in a contrary direction.' On the other hand, the judge 'does not consider that he was perfectly sane and he suggests that the case may be one for the exercise of clemency,' and Dr Villeneuve stated that the facts 'show a certain amount of mental disequilibrium.' Power offered no opinion on the case, concluding his report: 'How far these matters are to be taken into consideration by the Executive, in dealing with the case in the interest of Society is a weighty question upon which I do not, of course, presume to offer an opinion.'

On the morning of 24 December the minister of justice prepared his opinion to the cabinet:

Department of Justice, Ottawa, 24th December, 1895
To His Excellency the Governor General in Council:
The undersigned has the honour to submit the report of Mr. Justice Mathieu upon the case of Valentine Francis Cuthbert Shortis, recently convicted at Beauharnois of the crime of murder and sentenced to be executed on Friday, the third day of January next, together with the record of the proceedings had and the evidence given at the trial; also, several petitions, letters and other communications urging the commutation of the death sentence, and generally all the correspondence touching the case.

Upon careful consideration of the whole, the undersigned has the honour to recommend that the law be allowed to take its course.

> Humbly submitted,
> Charles Hibbert Tupper,
> Minister of Justice.

In the meantime, Sheriff Laberge was becoming increasingly concerned about Radclive's seeming indifference to the hanging scheduled for 3 January. The night before the cabinet meeting he wrote to him again:

> By your last letter I understood you was to write me about the twentieth December instant and I received no news from you since. Please let me know at what date you will be in Beauharnois for the erection of the scaffold in view of the execution in question, on the third of January next. In my last letter, I must have stated that we had no apparatus at that effect and I rely upon you to watch the construction of that apparatus as I never saw any one before.
>
> Please answer immediately.

Francis Shortis had now arrived back in Canada. He and his wife were in Ottawa to await word of the decision of the cabinet.

The Cabinet Room, East Block, Parliament Buildings, sometime after 1886

10

Cabinet Meetings

O N TUESDAY AFTERNOON , 24 December, the cabinet met to discuss the Shortis case. Mackenzie Bowell, the prime minister, presided as usual.

Bowell, it will be recalled, had become prime minister a year earlier. Lady Aberdeen described him in her diary on the day her husband asked him to form the new government: 'Mr. Mackenzie Bowell himself is 75, rather fussy, and decidedly common place, also an Orangeman, at one time the Grand Master of the Orangemen of North America and also presided at one of the tip-top grand Orange affairs at Belfast – but he is a good and straight man and he has ideas about the drawing together of the colonies and the Empire ...'

He had been born in England in 1823, come to Canada with his family ten years later, became a printer's apprentice for the Belleville *Intelligencer* in Upper Canada, and later its editor. First elected in 1867, he served continuously in the House of Commons until made a senator by Sir John Thompson in 1892. He had been brought into Sir John A. Macdonald's cabinet in 1878 and served in successive Conservative governments, most recently as minister of trade and commerce in Thompson's government. History has not been kind to him. 'Sir Mackenzie Bowell is remembered, if at all,' said one biographer of Canadian prime ministers, 'as a stupid, bigoted, conceited and slightly paranoic little man.' Such an assessment is too harsh. Lady Aberdeen's label, 'common place,' is closer to the mark. 'An evident mediocrity' was the way she described him to Gladstone later that summer; 'mediocrity must toil or fail' was the verdict of Bowell's private secretary when he died in 1917 at the age of ninety-four.[1]

'Bigoted' appears to be an unfair charge. Though an Orangeman, he was acceptable to Roman Catholics. Sir John Thompson, a Catholic, had in fact suggested to Lord Aberdeen that Bowell should be chosen as leader rather than himself. Senator Sir Frank Smith, a founder of the Ontario Catholic League, strongly supported Bowell for prime minister, telling Aberdeen that he 'had never offended a Roman Catholic.' It was Bowell's Conservatives, not Laurier's Liberals, who wanted remedial legislation to coerce the Manitoba government into restoring support for Catholic separate schools. Many, however, were not convinced that Bowell had his heart behind the legislation. On the other hand, Father Albert Lacombe, the priest who represented the Catholic bishops on the Manitoba schools question, had close dealings with Bowell, and wrote the archbishop of St Boniface that he was 'my friend, whom I regard as sincere.'[2]

Bowell did not, however, have the qualities of intelligence and leadership to run a government. Sir Joseph Pope, then the assistant secretary of the cabinet, characterized him as 'a worthy, loyal man, but one as little qualified to be Prime Minister of Canada as Lord Aberdeen was to be Governor General.' In his memoirs, Pope described Bowell's administration as 'days which I never recall without a blush, days of weak and incompetent administration by a cabinet presided over by a man whose sudden and unlooked-for elevation had visibly turned his head, a ministry without unity or cohesion of any kind, a prey to internal dissensions until they became a spectacle to the world, to angels, and to men.' The handling of the Shortis case was used by Pope as an example of the incompetence of Bowell's administration.[3]

There was clearly dissension within the cabinet. Sir Charles Hibbert Tupper, Ives, and Dickey were, as we have already seen, unhappy with Bowell and wanted Sir Charles, Sr, to be prime minister. The three Quebec Catholic ministers, J.-A. Ouimet, Adolphe Caron, and A.-R. Angers, had left the government during the summer, the first two later returning. There were festering disputes between Caron and Walter Montague and between Ouimet and John Haggart.

Moreover, the Manitoba schools issue had come to a head on 20 December, when the government there refused to accept the remedial order-in-council for the funding of separate schools and dissolved the legislature in order to hold an election. Bowell had no real choice but to proceed with remedial legislation when Parliament met again on 2 January, for a compromise had been ruled out by the action of the province.

Ten cabinet members attended the meeting on the Shortis case. There were sixteen cabinet positions. Angers' portfolio was still vacant, as

Bowell had not been able to replace him with a strong French Canadian. Another position had recently been given to an MP from Victoria, who would remain out west for some time fighting a by-election. Two further members were senators without ministerial portfolios who were not in Ottawa during this period: Frank Smith, a wealthy financier and prominent Catholic from Toronto, and Donald Ferguson, a cattle dealer from Prince Edward Island. Both might well have been sympathetic to Shortis. The two remaining ministers, John Costigan, a Catholic from New Brunswick, and Ouimet, were in Montreal, involved in campaigning for a by-election in Montreal Centre, one of four by-elections that month that would test the popularity of the government and its policy on Manitoba schools. The first – in Ontario North on 12 December – had resulted in a Conservative victory. On 24 December, the day of the meeting, a crucial by-election was taking place in Cardwell, Ontario: the Conservative seat was being contested by a Liberal and by a McCarthyite Conservative (named after D'Alton McCarthy, who opposed the government's school policy). Two other by-elections were scheduled between Christmas and New Year's: Montreal Centre on 27 December in a predominantly English-speaking riding, and Montreal Jacques Cartier on the 30th in a predominantly French-speaking riding.

At the end of a three-hour session, at which no other official business was conducted, the cabinet was equally divided, five to five. The minister of justice had recommended that the law be allowed to take its course and this position was supported by Mackenzie Bowell, Thomas Daly, John Wood, and George Foster (no relation to George Foster, the solicitor). Opposed, and in favour of life imprisonment, were Adolphe Caron, Arthur Dickey, John Haggart, W.B. Ives, and Walter Montague. Although a record was kept of the actual votes, nothing is known of the various considerations that led to the result. Nevertheless, it is not difficult to imagine the issues that would have been discussed.

The case of Amedée Chatelle, decided earlier that year, would have been on everyone's mind.[4] Chatelle, a French Canadian who had killed a fifteen-year-old girl in Stratford, Ontario, was convicted of murder and sentenced to be hanged on 31 May 1895. There had been petitions for a commutation by Quebec citizens and by Ontario doctors on the grounds of insanity, but the Dominion cabinet had rejected the petitions and decided the law should take its course. As in the Shortis case, ten members of cabinet decided the issue; all but Angers were still in the cabinet, and seven of them were at the meeting to decide Shortis' fate on 24 December.

It is remarkable that Chatelle's life was not saved. He was not defended by his counsel (who failed to represent him at the last minute because of a disagreement) and Chatelle himself called no psychiatric evidence. Indeed, he called no evidence whatsoever. He was certainly in no condition to represent himself, and when asked if he had anything to say in his defence he offered a few incomprehensible sentences: 'As it was said in the first place you know, ''Of such is the Kingdom of Heaven'' and in the second place of course it would be a matter of forming a true, direct, incorruptible church. That is as far as I can go at the present time.' The trial judge did not even put the issue of insanity to the jury, and they of course convicted.

The registrar of the Toronto medical college wrote that Chatelle was insane, his condition being 'a form of insanity known as (Cerebral) Parathesia Sexualis.' Nine other Ontario doctors, including the editor of the *Ontario Medical Journal*, swore affidavits to the same effect. The trial judge, Chief Justice J.D. Armour, was unimpressed with this new evidence when it was sent to him, and Augustus Power stated in his report to the minister of justice that 'there does not appear to be any ground for rejecting the Judge's view that the prisoner was responsible according to the legal test.' If Chatelle, a French-speaking person who appeared to be really crazy, was hanged, then how could Shortis' life be spared? This was the position, it will be recalled, that the local MP, Joseph Bergeron, had urged on the minister of justice.

Of equal importance, of course, was the case of Louis Riel, sentenced to be hanged for treason in Saskatchewan ten years earlier. In spite of a recommendation for mercy by the jury and considerable evidence of insanity, Sir John A. Macdonald's government refused to interfere. Mackenzie Bowell, Adolphe Caron, John Costigan, and George Foster were members of the cabinet when that decision was made. Could they now reprieve an 'Englishman' when there was no recommendation for mercy? The political consequences of doing so, as Bergeron had pointed out, would be disastrous to the Conservative party and therefore to the issues they advocated such as tariff protection and separate schools.

To vote for a commutation would give ammunition to those who suspected the Shortises were trying to buy their son's life. This view had been expressed by the *Progrès de Valleyfield* that week: 'We are persuaded that there are politicians who will get rich if a commutation is arranged and there isn't a sensible man who doesn't share our opinion.'

Still, the evidence of the four defence psychiatrists would have made a strong impression on some members of the cabinet, particularly Walter Montague, who was himself a practising physician. Like Dr Daniel Clark, he was a graduate of Victoria University medical school in Cobourg. He had been at the meeting that had decided to hang Chatelle, but whether he voted for the decision is not known; in either case, he would have been embarrassed by the decision in his later dealings with the medical profession. We do not know whether the defence psychiatrists attempted to lobby for his support in the Shortis case, but he had been with Clark at a medical school dinner in Toronto earlier in the month and it would be unusual if their conversation had not at least touched on Shortis. It is not surprising that he voted for commutation.

There is no way of ascertaining what considerations swayed individuals; one cannot know enough about their psychological and emotional makeup and their relationships with others to say with confidence what influenced them. Adolphe Caron, the post-master general, for example, had conflicting pressures. He had been the minister of militia at the time of the Riel uprising and had supported the government's decision to hang Riel. Moreover, as the chief political organizer for the Conservatives in Quebec he would have been aware of the political consequences of a commutation. On the other hand, he may have been influenced by his brother-in-law, Judge Mathieu, who was of course the trial judge in the case and seemed to be in favour of commutation. Another brother-in-law was Charles Fitzpatrick, who had been one of the defence counsel in the Riel case and a friend of Greenshields and would also likely have supported a commutation. Further, we do not know whether Caron saw Mrs Shortis, whether she offered him election funds, and if so whether he accepted them, as the Liberal papers hinted. All we really know is that he voted for commutation. Similarly, what influenced Dickey, Haggart, and Ives to vote for a commutation is not known. Mrs Shortis had a long personal interview with Dickey, but there is no record of her meeting with Haggart or Ives.

That the other five favoured the law taking its course is not surprising – at least in retrospect. Bowell would have wanted to support the position taken by his minister of justice, particularly when that decision coincided with the political fortunes of the government. George

Foster, the minister of finance, was a 'no nonsense' politician who would not have been swayed by the emotional arguments in Shortis' favour; a former professor of classics at the University of New Brunswick and an ardent teetotaller, he was, in the words of a contemporary, 'inexorably and fervently serious.'[5] Thomas Daly, the member of the cabinet from Manitoba, also voted in favour of hanging: he was a lawyer, later becoming a police magistrate in Winnipeg. Similarly, John Wood, a lawyer from Brockville, who was attending his very first cabinet meeting having been sworn in that morning, also voted with the prime minister and the minister of justice.

At five o'clock, as Christmas eve approached, the cabinet decided not to try to resolve their differences: instead, they would report to the governor-general that they were equally divided and that the decision was therefore up to him. He would have to take full responsibility for the decision to commute, which members of the cabinet apparently assumed he had the constitutional right to do under the circumstances, and which they knew he wanted to do. Whose idea it was to leave the matter in this way is not known. It sounds as though it could well have been Bowell's, being consistent with the indecisive leadership he had demonstrated for the past year. Moreover, he had been a minister in 1888 when consideration of the *Kehoe* murder case resulted in a similarly divided cabinet – the only other recorded case of such a split – and the governor-general, Lord Derby, had commuted the sentence.[6] Joseph Pope, the assistant secretary of the cabinet in 1895, suggested in his autobiography that Bowell had masterminded the plan: 'I myself heard the Prime Minister openly announce, with the air of having done something clever, that the Cabinet were equally divided in the case, and that in the circumstances they had no advice to tender the Governor-General ...' Pope went on to say that the 'whole proceeding had the appearance of being deliberately planned to save the neck of an atrocious criminal ...'[7] Bowell then left for Belleville to join his family for Christmas – and to hear the political news that Cardwell riding had been lost to the McCarthyite candidate.

It was left to Sir Hibbert to communicate the Shortis 'decision' to the governor-general that evening.

Sometime after the meeting, Tupper met with his departmental officials, Newcombe and Power. They did not share his view as to the power of the governor-general to commute the sentence: The instructions that had been issued in 1878 were, they said, clear: the governor-general 'shall not pardon or reprieve ... without first receiving, in capital cases, the advice of the privy council for said dominion.' These instructions, it will be recalled, had been the result of the Canadian government's protest against the exercise of the power of clemency by the governor-general in 1875 in the case of Lépine, one of Riel's associates in 1869; the government had voted to allow the sentence to be carried out, but Lord Dufferin had commuted the hanging to two years' imprisonment and loss of political rights. Tupper accepted the interpretation of his officials, and he thus wrote to Lord Aberdeen:

Tuesday evening

Dear Lord Aberdeen

Council could not agree in the Shortis case and accordingly have no recommendation to make to Your Excellency. We were evenly divided in a meeting of 10.

I have caused the papers to be transmitted to Your Excellency this evening and will call tomorrow to ascertain if I can be of any assistance to Your Excellency further in the case.

I am

Your Excellency's
Obedient servant
Charles Hibbert Tupper

The governor-general replied the same evening:

Dec. 24   10.20 p.m.

Dear Sir Charles

I am very much obliged to you for your note which reached me a few minutes ago.

I shall be glad to have the opportunity of seeing you tomorrow as you kindly suggest, and as I suppose Council will not meet again before Thursday at the earliest, I would propose 3.15 as the time, if that is convenient for you.

All good wishes for Christmas

Yours sincerely
Aberdeen

At twelve midnight, on Christmas eve, the governor-general sent a messenger to the Russell Hotel to inform Mr and Mrs Shortis that no decision had yet been reached.

The two men met on Christmas day. There is no indication that Lady Aberdeen was there, though she likely was. The discussion was undoubtedly intense, as the governor-general did not accept Sir Hibbert's interpretation of his powers.

Later that day Tupper sent a note to Aberdeen referring specifically to the authoritative Todd's *Parliamentary Government in the British Colonies*: 'It seems to me that Your Excellency [cannot] interfere without first receiving the advice of the Government. This Your Excellency cannot get as we are equally divided. May I at least ask that Your Excellency communicate by cable for advice on the subject stating my view which is that Your Excellency under the circumstances ought to allow the Law to take its course.'

Lord Aberdeen replied very late Christmas day that although he saw the force in the paragraph in Todd, still 'it might possibly be argued that though the Governor General must *receive* he need not necessarily *act* upon the advice given. However, I do not think it necessary to dwell upon these aspects of the matter – for, after the vote of yesterday it seems clear that to carry out the extreme sentence would on the whole be inappropriate.' He then added, 'at least I understood that you were prepared to adopt that view.' If that was in fact the position conveyed by Tupper at their meeting, it was obviously no longer his view.

The governor-general was prepared to seek an opinion from England, if requested to do so, 'but I cannot say,' he wrote, 'that I am prepared to do so on my *own* account.' He then added a new dimension to the issue: 'I may add that Mr. Costigan called here this evening to tell me that he did not know that the Shortis case was to be dealt with at Council yesterday until he returned from Montreal too late to attend. Had he been present he would have voted for commutation.'

John Costigan, from New Brunswick, the minister of marine and fisheries, was the Irish Catholic representative in the cabinet. He would obviously have been sympathetic to a commutation: both his parents had been born in Ireland, his father in Waterford. He had been in Parliament since Confederation and a cabinet minister since 1882; P.B. Waite has described him as 'burly, lazy,' having 'a pronounced taste for liquor and rarely seen without a cigar.'[8] Costigan felt he had been deliberately excluded from the meeting and wrote to Bowell: 'I felt very much disappointed that I had not been made aware of [the meeting] in time to be present. On my return here Tuesday night, I wished to see you but found you had gone to Belleville. Yesterday I called on His Excellency to explain my absence and state to him that had I been notified, I could have been present at the meeting of Council and would have voted for commutation ...'

The following day, Boxing Day, Lord Aberdeen cabled the colonial secretary:

> I have been expressly requested by the Minister of Justice to ask your opinion on the following case. Valentine Shortis was sentenced to death for murder: upon consideration of petitions on Tuesday the Cabinet were equally divided (five to five) and therefore no advice to Governor General was forthcoming, without which according to instructions Governor General cannot act. If no intervention – execution would take place January the 3rd. At Cabinet meeting Minister of Justice advocated allowing the sentence to be carried out but in view of the equal Vote passed he now recognizes objection. I may add that the judge's confidential report is on the whole in favour of commutation. I concur in this opinion.

Aberdeen did not, it will be noted, follow Sir Hibbert's request that the Colonial Office be told that under the circumstances the minister of justice felt the law should be allowed to take its course.

Bowell returned from Belleville that morning and later went to see the governor-general. There is no record of their conversation, but it ended with the promise of another cabinet meeting to reconsider the decision. That meeting would take place on Saturday afternoon, 28 December. In the meantime, Aberdeen wrote to Caron, Haggart, and possibly others, asking them to see him. 'While of course the Governor-General acts on the advice of his constitutional advisers,' he said, 'he is at full liberty to ask for the reasons on which such advice is based ... In the present case I propose as far as may be practicable to ask each of the members of Council to give me the benefit of a statement of the grounds on which their action individually has been taken in this matter.'

The cabinet met again on Friday, 27 December, Mackenzie Bowell's seventy-second birthday – a floral offering was given to him by the clerks of the Privy Council office – but the Shortis case was not officially discussed.[9] Nor was it discussed at another meeting on Saturday morning. No doubt some mention was made of the loss to the Liberals of Montreal Centre the day before; the next electoral test would be on 30 December in Jacques Cartier.

Twelve ministers attended the Saturday afternoon meeting, the ten who were at the earlier session plus Costigan and Ouimet. Costigan would, of course, vote for commutation. But at the end of the session the vote was seven to five in favour of hanging. J.-A. Ouimet, the minister of public works, supported Tupper: a Quebec lawyer who had received his LL B from Victoria University in Cobourg, he had previously been speaker of the House and had seen military service both in the Fenian Raids of 1870 and as leader of the 65th Mount Royal Rifles in the rebellion of 1885; more than likely, having just returned from Montreal Centre, he was sensitive to the political consequences of a commutation.

Obviously, one cabinet minister changed his mind. There is no record, however, of who it was. The result was communicated to the governor-general, who was clearly unhappy with the latest development. Over the next two days he summoned individually all the ministers who had taken part in the decision.

Shortis' parents waited in agony at the Russell Hotel, catching whatever rumours were circulating. Cabinet members were extraordinarily cautious in their dealings with the press. 'For some reason,' reported the Toronto *Globe*, 'the utmost secrecy is observed in regard to it by members of the council.'

Shortis himself was in Beauharnois with Father Devine. Twice a day they celebrated mass.

Radclive, the executioner, had still not appeared. On Christmas day he sent a note to a worried Sheriff Laberge saying that he would be there on 30 December:

> Toronto
> Dec. 25, 95
>
> Sir
> In answer to yours, the reason that I have not written you was that I have been expecting to hear from Ottawa every day that the case would be settled, but in case my services are required will be with you on Monday at latest to see to everything.
>
> I am Sir
> Your obedient servant
> J.R. Radclive

On 27 December Laberge had still not heard from him. 'When will you be in Beauharnois? Answer right off,' he wired. 'Will be with you on Monday,' was the telegraphed response.

Rumours of a possible commutation were circulating throughout the country. 'You are obliged to continue preparations for the execution,' the attorney-general instructed Laberge; but Casgrain agreed with Shortis' counsel, George Foster, that 'should a reprieve be granted no time whatever should be lost in removing the prisoner from the Beauharnois District.' No one wanted to risk a possible lynching.

On Monday morning, 30 December, on the 8:30 Grand Trunk train from Montreal, Radclive, wearing his usual black suit, arrived in Beauharnois.

During Sunday and Monday Lord Aberdeen talked individually to nearly all the members of the cabinet. He also met Bowell again, and the issue of bribery was raised. On Saturday the Montreal *Witness* had republished a critical article from the *Progrès de Valleyfield*: 'People ask themselves, with uneasiness, whether money or justice will triumph. So far, the dollars seem to turn the scales which poor Mackenzie Bowell, who deserves more pity than blame, holds in his hands, while blindfolded.' This brought the matter into the open. Bowell passed on to Aberdeen – why he did so is not clear – a memorandum that had been prepared for the minister of justice by Augustus Power:

Confidential   20 December 1895
Dear Sir Charles,
   At your suggestion I put in writing what I told the Deputy Minister respecting an interview Mrs. Shortis had with me some time ago.
   Mrs. Shortis called at my house a little over a couple of weeks ago – I think on the 12th or 13th inst. At the conclusion of a long conversation during which she exhibited the greatest distress, she recurred to the fact, which had already been mentioned by her, that she and her husband were very well off and asked me to advise her if there was nothing they could do by that means to save her son, adding: 'God knows I would give all I have to save his life' or words to that effect. Not exactly understanding her, I asked her what she meant, when she explained that she meant politically, by contributing to election funds. I advised Mrs. Shortis not even to hint at such things – and she excused herself on the grounds of her grief.
   I do not of course pretend to give anything like a verbally accurate report of the conversation, but the above is its purport as I understood it. I did not attach much importance to the matter.
                                                                                         Yours sincerely,
                                                                                         A. Power

In his own note to the governor-general Bowell wrote: 'If Mrs. Shortis would make suggestions to a responsible officer of such an outrageous character, no doubt she has been trying the same in other quarters.' Perhaps Aberdeen had asked Bowell about allegations of bribery and was in some way using this volatile issue to pressure members of the cabinet to change their minds. In any event, he succeeded in convincing the prime minister to place the following memo he had written before a cabinet meeting called for Monday afternoon, 30 December:

> Although Council are not of opinion that the charge of the judge and the verdict of the jury are in any way open to criticism, yet in view of certain circumstances, – for example,
> (1) the equal division of opinion in the council in the first instance;
> (2) the smallness of the majority on the second occasion;
> (3) the communication received from the Secretary of State for the Colonies, considered in its application to these proceedings as a whole;
> (4) the suggestion of the judge's confidential report, which may be considered as being supported by the family medical history and the inherited predispositions of the condemned man;
> (5) also, and specially, in view of the precedent afforded by what occurred in the case of John Kehoe, in 1888, –
> it is suggested that in harmony with the courteous consideration uniformly given by the Dominion Government to a strongly expressed desire on the part of the Governor General, Council might, without in any way going back upon their actual vote, and without any infringement of their constitutional powers, authorize a recommendation to His Excellency to commute the sentence to imprisonment for life.

Lady Aberdeen also tried to change Tupper's mind. She had, she said, some additional information to tell him, sending him the following note early Monday morning:

Confidential   Dec. 30th, 1895
My dear Sir Charles
    In a time when you are so driven with work, it seems unfair to lay an extra burden on you.
    But the more I think over the matter the more I feel that it is only being true to the sort of compact we entered into, to ask you at this juncture to spare me ten minutes.
    I therefore ask you if possible to come here at 9.30 before you go to your office.

Do not think that I am seeking to influence you regarding the decision you have come to. I trust you think you are only doing what you deem to be your duty & I can but respect you for this. But there is an aspect of the matter which I want to lay before you in a very few words & so as friends, I ask you to come & hear this.

Believe me.

Yours sincerely,
Ishbel Aberdeen

No subsequent document reveals the information she conveyed to Sir Hibbert.

It is difficult to say what effect Lady Aberdeen's communication had on Tupper. Formally, it had none; he continued to express the opinion that the governor-general could not interfere and that the *Kehoe* case was not a reliable precedent:

Ottawa, 30th, December, 1895
My dear Lord Aberdeen:

I send again Mr. Newcombe's memo and also a note on Queen v. Kehoe.

I have spoken to Mr. Power who tells me that Sir John told him that he had overlooked the last Imperial Instructions when he informed Lord Derby that council being divided the matter rested with him.

My Department is convinced that Your Excellency cannot interfere with the sentence without the advice of Council to that effect, and since the last instructions there is no record which conflicts with this view.

I am,
My dear Lord Aberdeen,
Yours sincerely,
Charles Hibbert Tupper.

Another drama that was unfolding during this period was the effort being made to fill the vacant cabinet position left by the resignation of A.-R. Angers. The person playing the key role in this quest was Father Albert Lacombe, the priest from the west who was acting on behalf of Archbishop Adélard Langevin of St Boniface, Manitoba.[10] Only the Conservatives, the archbishop thought, would bring in remedial legislation in Manitoba. Laurier would not. On Christmas eve he had given a speech in Montreal Centre denying that the constitution compelled Parliament to coerce Manitoba while it was possible to conciliate. Langevin had written to Laurier: 'We know what our rights are, and we shall have our rights, or die for them.'[11]

Father Lacombe met Bowell, Caron, and Ouimet on Monday, 30 December at two o'clock in the afternoon, just prior to the cabinet meeting, to plan their strategy. Bowell had to fill the position, 'the empty portfolio,' in the words of historian John Saywell, 'remaining the symbol of his incompetence.'[12] The English-speaking members of his cabinet were exasperated and some were threatening to resign. French Canadians, however, were reluctant to join, for they – and the Quebec clergy – were not as convinced as was Father Lacombe of Bowell's sincerity. 'Any French candidate who takes Angers' position,' wrote *Le Moniteur de Lévis*, representing the Quebec clergy, 'would be a Judas.' One after another, Quebec politicians refused: Senator Rodrique Masson pleaded poor health; Louis-Phillippe Pelletier said no. Senator Alphonse Desjardins, the ex-mayor of Montreal and president of the Banque Jacques Cartier, was one of the few remaining possibilities. Lacombe went to Montreal to speak to him, subsequently informing Bowell, Caron, and Ouimet at a meeting on the following day that Desjardins would give his answer on New Year's day.

No decision was reached by the cabinet that afternoon. Lord Aberdeen's memo was before them, as was the Colonial Office's reply to the cable that had been sent to London: 'As Privy-Council tender no advice, you must decide according to your own judgment.' The Colonial Office's confidential file on the matter reveals that Joseph Chamberlain and his officials had no difficulty in coming to this decision.[13] The colonial secretary noted on the file, his officials agreeing with him:

> The instructions enjoin that our said Governor General shall not pardon or reprieve any such offender without first receiving in capital cases the advice of the Privy Council of our said Dominion.
>
> The receipt of such advice is not necessary to the validity of the Governor General's action and the clause is intended to ensure there is a voice in the matter if they choose, and as they refuse to advise him he must simply use his own discretion.

The cabinet decided to meet again later that evening, as Bowell told Aberdeen: 'The Shortis case was considered for a short time today but I shall not be in a position to give you a final answer till tomorrow morning.' This would be the fourth meeting – an incredible amount of cabinet time – devoted almost exclusively to the case. The Liberal Toronto *Globe* reported the next morning that 'the Affair has grown to the proportions of a scandal.'

Again a weary and dejected cabinet met. The result of the Jacques Cartier election that day had been announced: a resounding Liberal victory. Once again, no record is available of the discussions that took place. The meeting, according to the knowledgeable Montreal *Gazette* correspondent, lasted until six in the morning.

In the meantime, Radclive had been assessing the possible location of the gallows within the Beauharnois jail. He and Sheriff Laberge agreed that it would be best to use the second floor of the shed in the prison yard, the rope attached to an upper beam, a trap door cut out of the wooden floor to allow the body to drop to the lower level. The hangman preferred that a condemned man not be forced to climb steps to the gallows. A railway lever, which Radclive had brought with him, would be used to open the trap door. The construction of the gallows had begun. Radclive had also made arrangements, as required by the regulations,[14] for a black flag to be hoisted from a conspicuous part of the prison at the moment of execution and for a church bell to be tolled for fifteen minutes before and after the event. The execution would take place at eight o'clock in the morning.

The solicitor, Foster, wired the attorney-general asking that the body not be buried in the prison yard, but be given to Mrs Shortis: 'Will you give necessary order should sentence of death be carried out in Shortis case to have body delivered to his mother? Please answer.' Casgrain telegraphed back 'Yes certainly' and instructed Sheriff Laberge to 'deliver body to mother without mutilation.'

When the cabinet meeting concluded early in the morning there was once again an equal division, this time six in favour of hanging and six opposed. Once more, someone had switched his vote.

The result was reported to the governor-general, who immediately commuted the sentence to life imprisonment and sent the following message to the prime minister:

Dec 31 1895

Dear Sir Mackenzie Bowell

I have just received your letter of today which informs me that the case of Shortis having been again considered by Council, the opinions of Ministers were equally divided.

In view of the fact that no specific advice can in these circumstances be tendered to me, and in view of the Official opinion which I have received from the Secretary of State for the Colonies, that in such a case it is the duty of the Governor General to act according to his own judgement, I decide that the Sentence of death pronounced upon the prisoner Shortis shall be commuted to imprisonment for life as a criminal lunatic, or otherwise as may be found most fitting; and I hereby ask you to take the necessary steps for instructing the Officers of the Law accordingly.

> I remain
> Yours sincerely
> Aberdeen

Who switched his vote? Nothing in the files provides an answer. Could it have been Tupper because of the information Lady Aberdeen had passed on to him? A letter from Aberdeen sent later in the day suggests, however, that Tupper maintained his earlier position: 'I regret that our views on this subject have not been in accord.' On the other hand, Sir Hibbert's reply hints that he may have changed his mind: 'I need not say that I freely concede that Your Excellency is proceeding in the case prompted by the same sense of duty which brought me to a certain temporary [the word 'extent' had been crossed out and replaced by the word 'temporary'] collision with Your views & wishes, but I am gratified beyond measure to know that our mutual confidence has been confirmed after the end of the difference of opinion.'

It may, however, have been Bowell who switched his vote in order to shift the responsibility to the governor-general and also to avoid the constitutional crisis that might well have developed if Aberdeen had overruled a seven-five decision in favour of hanging. Perhaps no one actually switched votes, but at the end of a long and difficult discussion a consensus emerged to leave the matter unresolved.

Aberdeen's decision to commute the sentence to 'imprisonment for life as a criminal lunatic' created problems, said Department of Justice officials. There was no specific institution for criminal lunatics in Canada outside the penitentiaries. The final Privy Council order, which required considerable negotiation, was therefore changed to 'life imprisonment in the St. Vincent de Paul Penitentiary as a criminal lunatic.'

That afternoon the cabinet met again to work on the speech from the throne, which expressed a determination to introduce remedial legislation. The speech would be delivered by Lord Aberdeen on Thursday, 2 January, when a new parliamentary session would begin.

At 10:45 on 31 December 1895 telegrams were sent to the attorney-general of Quebec and to the Beauharnois prison carrying the news that the sentence had been commuted. The Beauharnois telegram was not, in fact, delivered until eleven o'clock the next morning: Valentine Shortis therefore spent New Year's eve thinking it might be his last. Mr and Mrs Shortis were informed of the decision late that evening at the Russell Hotel. The Aberdeens celebrated the coming of the New Year quietly with their children at a torchlight service in Rideau Hall.

11

Repercussions

WORD REACHED VALLEYFIELD on New Year's eve that the sentence had been commuted. An angry mob of about a hundred and fifty men, who were clearly in the mood for a lynching, seized a train at the deserted Grand Trunk station and attempted to start it and drive to Beauharnois, but without success; the fire to power the engine was lit, but the one person in Valleyfield who could actually drive it refused to do so. Horses and carriages could not be used, for a severe snowstorm that day ('caused by the Liberal supporters in Montreal Centre and Jacques Cartier,' stated the Montreal *Gazette*) had made the roads impassable. The mob would, however, return.

Shortis did not, of course, know of this threat to his life. Indeed, as previously noted, he was unaware that the sentence had been commuted until the sheriff told him the news on New Year's day. His reaction was not recorded by the sheriff, although he himself later said: 'I had made up my mind that I was to die and that my time was come, but of course when the news came I was well pleased.' Any doubts about the accuracy of the telegram were dispelled when his parents arrived from Ottawa. Shortis later asked the jailor to invite the hangman to come up to his cell to 'take a drink and a cigar together,' but the message was not passed on to Radclive.

Francis and Mary Shortis left the following day for Montreal in company with the hangman. Radclive and Mr Shortis apparently 'shook hands and had a very pleasant conversation.' Mr Shortis left for New York the next day to sail back to the old country. His wife remained at the Windsor Hotel in Montreal and would return to Ireland later.

The newspapers on New Year's day did not contain an official announcement of the commutation. Their stories were based on state-

Sir Mackenzie Bowell, prime minister, May 1896

ments Francis Shortis had made to the press the previous evening. The *Gazette*'s short account added that 'Mr. Shortis has said while here that the defence of his son has cost him $60,000.' Shortis later protested in a letter to the editor that he had made no such statement, but he did not in fact deny the figure. The reports of the sum confirmed for many the view that justice had indeed been purchased.

The government prepared a press release, which appeared on 2 January in the so-called 'ministerial press,' that is, the papers loyal to the government. Bowell, Tupper, and a number of other cabinet ministers had worked on the statement on New Year's eve. Sir Hibbert had insisted that it was not proper for Lord Aberdeen to commute the sentence, as he wished to do, to 'life imprisonment in the St. Vincent de Paul Penitentiary as a criminal lunatic.' The warrant of commutation was therefore drawn up commuting the sentence to 'imprisonment in the St. Vincent de Paul Penitentiary for and during the term and period of the natural life of the said V.F.C. Shortis.' Bowell wrote to Aberdeen late on 31 December enclosing a copy of the release: 'Your excellency will note a slight change by which the Reporter is made to say "a Criminal Lunatic Asylum will be his home for the future."' Doctored press releases are obviously not a modern invention. The ministerial press dutifully printed the release: 'It is understood that after a number of meetings of the Council, at which the case of the prisoner Shortis was discussed, the Cabinet, not having recommended any interference with the sentence of the court, His Excellency, the Governor-General ... decided that, under the circumstances, the sentence should be commuted to imprisonment for life. The necessary steps have been taken to carry out the decision of His Excellency. There can be no doubt that a criminal lunatic asylum will be Shortis' future place of confinement.' The government was obviously trying to shift the sole blame onto the governor-general. The Conservative Toronto *Mail and Empire*, for example, quoted above, accepted the government line, stating that 'it is clear that Valentine Shortis escapes the gallows solely through the intervention of Lord Aberdeen on his behalf ...'

Others, however, such as the Huntingdon *Gleaner*, placed the blame squarely on the government: 'For that setting aside of the verdict of the jury the Bowell administration is responsible, and the effort to saddle it upon the Governor-General is as cowardly as it is unjust.' 'The average individual,' wrote the Toronto *Star*, 'will marvel at the Government, which has not the moral courage to decide upon a petition for clemency in the case of a convicted murderer, but has the colossal cheek to coerce a province.' The Liberal *Globe*'s Ottawa correspondent asserted: 'This is the depth of Cabinet debasement, the climax of a course of irresolution and incapacity ... The action of the Cabinet is freely spoken of ... as the most humiliating thing that ever happened to a body of men calling themselves a Government.' 'The responsibility,' alleged the Montreal *Witness*, 'rests solely upon the Cabinet.' 'It had simply to say,' wrote the *Herald*, 'that the law must take its course, or that the sentence must be commuted, and the Governor General would not have been forced to make a choice.'

Although there was a division of opinion on who was responsible for the commutation, there was virtual unanimity that the sentence should not have been commuted. 'With few exceptions,' stated the Ottawa *Free Press*, 'the press of Canada consider the commutation of the death warrant as an outrage and a gross miscarriage of justice.' Many referred to the wealth of his parents. The Toronto *Telegram*, for instance, charged that 'The wealth of his parents saved him from the punishment which his crime had deserved.' 'An insanity plea is a great thing,' agreed the Hamilton *Times*, 'when backed up by a long purse.' And the Huntingdon *Gleaner* noted that 'there is one measure of law for the poor man and another for the rich.'

Many of the papers, particularly in Quebec, linked the affair to the earlier cases of Riel and Chatelle. *La Patrie*, a Liberal paper, immediately made the comparison: 'What is certain is that if a fellow-countryman had struck the blow, his life, in the hands of Mackenzie Bowell and company, would not have been prolonged nor his execution delayed. We are not thirsting for blood, but we want the law to be applied in all its rigour against English as well as against French Canadians, and we do not want a man to be asked before hanging what is his origin and what is his language.' These arguments – using almost the same words – would continue to be pressed by Laurier and his Quebec lieutenant, Israel Tarte, in the coming election.

Early Friday morning, 3 January, Sheriff Laberge was wakened at his home by a telephone call from the jail informing him that a mob of four to five hundred persons was massed around the jail and was attempting to break in. When Laberge arrived, the front gate was already dislodged. He pleaded with the crowd, saying that it was he who would suffer most by their actions and cleverly suggested the discussion be continued at the nearby Brunet's Hotel, where, he said, he would order drinks for everybody. This idea proved attractive, and Laberge managed to subdue the hotheads for the time being. Anxieties were raised again, however, when word reached Beauharnois that another four or five hundred persons were expected to arrive on the afternoon train from Valleyfield.

Laberge pleaded by telegraph with Quebec City for instructions. The attorney-general was of course aware of the danger: he had earlier received warning telegrams from the defence counsel. The day before, Greenshields had wired: 'Consider it most important in the interests of Justice that Shortis be removed today from district of Beauharnois. Lose no time.' The attorney-general's department instructed Laberge to contact Ottawa: 'Wire Minister of Justice for instructions as to removal. State matter very pressing as prisoner may not be in safety.' He did so: 'No order for removal received. Where will I send him. Waiting for orders. In danger of being lynched. Answer immediately.' No reply was received from Ottawa. He could wait no longer to act.

Sheriff Laberge circulated a rumour that he was going to take Shortis to Montreal by the Grand Trunk train. The mob, increased by the fresh arrivals from Valleyfield, went at once to the station. Meanwhile the prisoner was removed to a waiting sleigh at the far end of the farm behind the jail. The party drove along the south shore of the St Lawrence River, crossing the Chateauguay River by rowboat, drove on with a fresh team of horses, and then walked through the drifting snow to Caughnawaga where they crossed the Canadian Pacific Railway bridge over the St Lawrence to Rockcliffe. 'We waited for a train there,' Shortis told a reporter the next day, adding: 'I was wrapped in a big coonskin coat and so arranged that nobody would see I was handcuffed. Sheriff Laberge, Montpetit, Elliot and I stayed there for an hour waiting for the train. No one knew me and I heard the station agent remark: ''Well, I am glad anyhow that Shortis got off. His mother is a splendid woman and the fellow has lots of pluck, too.'' ' 'I thought to myself,' he told the reporter, 'that there was one man in Canada who had a good word for Shortis.' To avoid a crowd that might have been waiting at the Montreal station, they got off at St Henri and drove by carriage to the Montreal jail, the prison in which Shortis had been held pending his trial.

The following morning he was interviewed by several reporters. The *Gazette* related that he 'seemed to take the whole proceedings as a huge joke,' thus underlining its editorial policy that a 'miscarriage of justice' had occurred. Shortis, who was engaged at the time in writing the Lord's Prayer on a piece of paper the size of a ten-cent coin, was described by the reporter: 'His conversation was rational, and his fashionable dress, a brown tweed coat with knickerbockers to match, black stockings and patent leather shoes, together with a light blue regatta shirt and stylish collar, made him have more the look of a diligent student than that of a man undergoing a sentence for foul murder.' The *Herald* also painted a glowing picture of sanity: 'It is not too much to say that Shortis is one of the handsomest specimens of physical manhood there is in Montreal. Standing six feet high, with a mass of yellow hair, worn a la football style, and a delicate blonde moustache carefully waxed at the ends, he was the beau ideal of a well bred young Englishman and seemed far removed from the terrible crime of which he was found guilty ... His appearance belies any idea of insanity, and he talks well, in fine English, and his flow of ideas were equal to that of any other cultured man.' To add insult to injury, Shortis was quoted as referring to the jury as 'the twelve unwashed' and to the English-speaking inhabitants of Valleyfield as 'the low English crowd from Valleyfield,' sentiments that naturally caused much comment in the town and surrounding areas.

The newspaper reports, it should be observed, were not always scrupulously accurate. The *Herald*, for example, described in great detail on Monday Shortis' supposed removal to Kingston Penitentiary on Saturday evening: 'His mother remained with him until the last, and Miss Millie Anderson ... bade him an affecting farewell. Shortis was chipper and gay as usual, and although tears filled his eyes when embraced by his mother for the last time, at least for many months, he did not betray any particular emotion.' No such scene ever took place, although Shortis did see his mother and girlfriend for an hour that Saturday afternoon. He did not leave the Montreal jail that weekend, the *Herald* was obliged to acknowledge the following day, blaming the false report on information supplied by a gatekeeper at the institution.

While Laberge was crossing the bridge over the St Lawrence River on foot with Shortis, he had a conversation with him, and an account was later published in the *Progrès de Valleyfield* and other papers. 'I have never spoken to you,' he said, 'of your famous Valleyfield escapade; but now that your fate is sealed, tell me why did you do it.' Shortis' reply, as told by Laberge, is as follows:

I am quite aware that you will not believe me whether I tell the truth or not; but I shall give you a written authorization addressed to Father Santoire and

Father Devine, absolving them from the obligation of preserving the secrets communicated to them in the confessional by me, when, with the mob outside the prison, I expected every moment to be my last. I am a believer and I do not make a jest of confession. I faithfully related to my confessors an account of what I had done. You can ask them and you will see if I deceive you.

When I left the McGinnis' home in the evening, I left with the fixed intention of answering my mother's letters. I had made a mental calculation that, by writing that night, I would be able to catch the next mail, while, if I waited until the following day I would miss it. I had no stamps, and it was necessary that I should post my letter that same night.

I suddenly remembered that the pay lists were being prepared at the cotton factory, and that some of the clerks would surely be there, so that I could get stamps from them. I went thither accordingly. You know what happened.

Young Leboeuf told the whole truth. Lowe made some serious errors in his deposition; but his account was for the greater part accurate enough.

I knew that Lowe and Wilson were both very nervous, and that the mere sight of a pistol would put them beside themselves, Wilson especially.

Just for fun, I pointed the pistol at Wilson; it went off; I don't know how. I was horror-stricken. Thoughts rushed through my mind of my family disgraced and ruined and of the scaffold.

In a second I knew that all was over and the idea took possession of me that I must kill everybody around me and I killed all I could. I would have killed all who presented themselves. I only regained calmness a long time afterwards. I understood that nothing remained to me but to kill myself, and I was going to do so. But, as I have told you, I am a believer. I reflected upon the frightful consequences of suicide, and I should have liked to have had some one kill me at the time. When I surrendered the next day, I asked them to kill me.

The Valleyfield paper was quick to point out that according to this version he was not an 'idiot' but rather a 'bandit.' The Huntingdon *Gleaner* observed that 'the confession he made adds lying to murder ... He ... never asked for a stamp; ... there was no mail for England on Saturday, and there was no cause for hurry in getting a stamp. The purpose he alleges for which he went to the mill was a lie in every regard. He went to the office of the mill for what he stood in need – money, and, in the effort to obtain it, he committed as foul and wanton murders as there are on record. There is not a redeeming feature in the conduct of this self-indulgent, cruel-hearted young man.'

Over a thousand people attended a rally held in the town hall in Valley-field on Saturday night. Called by Mayor Loy, for whose son's murder Shortis had been convicted, the orderly crowd, spurred on by a speech by plant manager Louis Simpson, unanimously passed resolutions addressed to the governor-general and the prime minister. 'They protest at this miscarriage of justice,' read the document to Mackenzie Bowell; 'They believe that there should be in Canada one law for the rich as for the poor.' The resolution to Lord Aberdeen argued that his action was 'likely to bring discredit upon the administration of justice in the province. By thus commuting a sentence considered just by the public, dangerous reasons are being given to the citizens of this country to take into their own hands the execution of justice.' The *Gazette* pointed out that the resolutions 'probably represent the general sentiment throughout the country.'

The well-conducted protest in Valleyfield could be contrasted with the crowd in nearby Coteau Landing that burned Shortis in effigy, or with the death threats received that very day by the governor-general. Lady Aberdeen passed them on to Sir Hibbert, asking 'if the detective department should be warned.' One of the threatening letters said that Lord Aberdeen would be 'pendu ou assassiné par la bande du Jarret Noir' on Friday, 10 January. Lady Aberdeen had recommenced writing her diary on 2 January, noting in her first entry: 'What has made this Christmas and New Year's time so trying is this wretched murder case of young Shortis ...' On 10 January she expressed relief that no attempted assassination had in fact taken place: 'This is the day of which I have been thankful to see the close, for it was especially mentioned in one of the anonymous threatening letters to His Excellency. The local feeling on the fact of Shortis' sentence having been commuted is still intense. A large public meeting was held at Valleyfield and a formal address sent to H.E. numerously signed, setting forth the injustice of the commutation. However there is no reason to distress ourselves on the subject, as it is clear that most thinking people perfectly agree with the action taken and one specialist medical man [Dr Anglin] has written to H.E. thanking him for saving the country from a judicial murder.'

Many 'thinking people,' however, did not agree with the decision. One person who clearly did not agree, and strongly said so in his Sunday sermon in Montreal, was the former moderator of the Presbyterian church, Rev. James Smith, whose sermon was widely quoted throughout the province: 'The Government was afraid to do its duty. It was a pitiable sight to see the Government Council agreeing to disagree, in order to save their positions. It looked like a secret scheme to throw the responsibility on the Governor General ...' Referring to 'a weakly and cowardly Council,' he asked, 'Is it not time for the righteous people of this grand Dominion to demand that justice shall be properly administered?' He suggested a further prosecution: 'Shortis was guilty of more than one murder, and surely the people of Valleyfield will use yet the righteous laws of our land at their disposal to rid the world of a wretch whose crimes have been without parallel.' Others shared this view. Not surprisingly, the *Progrès de Valleyfield* and the Huntingdon *Gleaner* wanted further action, the latter stating: 'The life of the miserable being who sneered at the honest farmers who sat on the jury as ''the unwashed'' and who talks of ''the low English of Valleyfield'' is of small account; but the principle whether the law shall be enforced is of vital consequence to every decent man. When it is ascertained it can be done, we hope all will unite, either by public meetings or petition, to ask attorney-general Casgrain to have Shortis tried for murdering Maxime Leboeuf.'

The attorney-general told the press, who had asked about a further prosecution, that 'The question you ask is receiving very earnest consideration and cannot be answered yet.' Henri St Pierre declared that 'the idea that Shortis can now be tried on a second charge is absurd. A man cannot be sentenced to death twice. Shortis is now dead in the eyes of the law, or, if he is not dead, he must be considered insane ... The Attorney-General would never offer such an insult to His Excellency as to order another trial of a man whom His Excellency has adjudged to be insane.'

James Crankshaw, the legal authority whose annotated Code is still in use in Canada, offered an unequivocal – and, it should be added, sound – legal opinion that a second prosecution would not be barred:[1] 'As to the question whether Shortis could still be tried for the murder of his other victim, Maxime Leboeuf, I have no hesitation in answering in the affirmative, the murder of which he has been convicted and the indictment found against him in the Leboeuf case being two separate and distinct charges ... he certainly could not plead ''autrefois acquit'' or that he had already been convicted on that indictment.' As a practical matter, however, Crankshaw said: 'His Excellency might find it inconsistent with his former decision to refuse a second commutation upon facts which would be identical.' Macmaster expressed the same legal opinion: 'There is no doubt whatever that he can be tried again.'

Whether he should be, he observed, was up to the attorney-general. 'There is ... no hurry for a decision,' said Casgrain, 'as Shortis is now in the penitentiary for a life term and the Court at Beauharnois does not hold another session for six months. This leaves us time to consider.'

Shortis had been taken from the Montreal jail to the St Vincent de Paul Penitentiary on Monday afternoon, 6 January, the warrant of transfer having finally arrived that morning. In the company of Charles Vallee, governor of the jail, Sheriff Laberge, and three guards, Shortis was taken on the three-hour ride in a covered conveyance to the large federal penitentiary located on the north bank of the back river about ten miles from the centre of the city. The penitentiary was intended to serve the needs of the province of Quebec for offenders sentenced to two years or more. The month before Shortis' arrival, a typhoid epidemic had been raging through the institution, with at least one death.

Shortis was now convict #3134, dressed in the regulation black and grey striped suit and cap; he was given a regulation close haircut and his moustache was shaved off. After a few days in the receiving cell to acclimatize him to the penitentiary, he was moved to a regular cell.

He would remain in St Vincent de Paul Penitentiary for his natural life, an official said, 'unless he should show any signs of insanity in which case we shall be obliged to send him to Kingston.' Like most convicts, he worked during the day: he chose tailoring and was, it was reported, given the bench next to Hooper, another famous criminal who had also been defended by Greenshields and prosecuted by Macmaster in an earlier *cause célèbre*. There were three other murderers in the penitentiary who had had their death sentences commuted to life imprisonment.

Mary Shortis was permitted to visit her son on a number of occasions until she left for New York three weeks later to sail back to Ireland. She planned to return to Canada in the summer. There is no record of whether Millie Anderson saw him in St Vincent de Paul. Probably not, as visiting regulations were strictly confined to members of the family or, in exceptional cases, other persons of the same sex. She would have said her good-bye at the Montreal jail.

Parliament Buildings, Ottawa, 1893

12

Political Turmoil

WHILE SHORTIS was being transferred from the Beauharnois jail to St Vincent de Paul Penitentiary, some of the most dramatic events in Canadian political history were unfolding. On Saturday, 4 January, seven cabinet ministers – the so-called 'nest of traitors' – submitted their resignations to Mackenzie Bowell. Did the Shortis affair have anything to do with this event?

Parliament had opened as scheduled on Thursday, 2 January, at three o'clock in the afternoon. This was the sixth and final session of a parliamentary term that had thus far seen a succession of four Conservative prime ministers, Macdonald, Abbott, Thompson, and Bowell. The Commons members were immediately summoned to the Senate chamber, where Lord Aberdeen read a short speech from the throne. The crucial item in the speech announced, as expected, that there would be remedial legislation to restore public funding for separate schools in Manitoba. 'I regret to say,' Lord Aberdeen recited, first in English and then in French, 'that the advisers of the Lieutenant Governor [of Manitoba] have declined to entertain favourably these suggestions, thereby rendering it necessary for my Government, in pursuance of its declared policy, to introduce legislation in regard to this subject.' The session would see a major fight on the issue. On opening day no business was conducted apart from formal notices of motion. Joseph Bergeron, the Beauharnois MP, served such a notice requesting 'copies of all petitions, and other papers relating to the commutation of the death sentence passed on Valentine Shortis, including the report of Mr. Justice Mathieu.' Parliament then adjourned until Tuesday, 7 January.

Lady Aberdeen sat immediately to the left of her husband in the

Senate in her full court costume, with its elaborate train borne by two pages. Her diary entry that evening notes: 'I wore my blue velvet, made to look very pretty combined with my white and gold embroidered poplin, and the pages were in white and gold and were much admired.' She also recorded in the same entry that political trouble was anticipated: 'there have been other anxieties in connection with the Government other than those connected with [the Shortis] case and these seem likely to come to a head soon.'

There were many rumours circulating about general dissatisfaction with Bowell's leadership. 'Sir Mackenzie,' Lady Aberdeen wrote in her journal, 'was aware that there was some caballing against him and told His Excellency so.' The *Globe* reported that Sir Charles Tupper, Sr, would take over from Bowell with Chief Justice William Meredith and Lieutenant-Governor Adolphe Chapleau as his lieutenants from Ontario and Quebec.

On Saturday, 4 January, in Lady Aberdeen's words, 'the storm burst over the political horizon.'[1] The previous evening Foster and Haggart had gone to see Aberdeen (who was meeting with the prime minister at the time), to say that they could not go on under Bowell's leadership and intended to tell him so. They wanted Tupper to head the government. Other cabinet ministers, friendly ones such as Daly and unfriendly ones like Sir Hibbert, also told Bowell he had to resign.

At noon the prime minister informed his minister of justice that he intended to resign, but later that day Daly revealed that Bowell would not leave until the dissenting ministers had submitted their resignations. For two hours on Saturday evening, Bowell met with Sir Charles Tupper to discuss the crisis. According to the latter's sanitized journal,[2] they were simply discussing Atlantic fast lines and cable service, but clearly they were discussing politics, Tupper offering Bowell a number of options, including a seat in the cabinet, the lieutenant-governorship of Ontario, or Tupper's own high commissioner's position in London.[3] At seven o'clock, while these discussions were going on, the resignations from the seven bolters arrived: Foster, Haggart, Tupper, Montague, Ives, Wood, and Dickey. To everyone's surprise, Bowell did not resign; he wanted time to think things over.

On Sunday afternoon Bowell met Lord and Lady Aberdeen and joined them again after dinner until one in the morning. Lady Aberdeen noted in her journal that Bowell 'feels rather pleased with himself at not having fallen into the trap of resigning at once. One can but admire the pluck of the old man, for this desertion is a most extraordinary exhibition of treachery ...' The Aberdeens urged him not to resign, but rather to try to reconstruct a new cabinet. As we know, they had a low opinion of Tupper, Sr: 'Of course it has all been hatched by the old Sir Charles,' Lady Aberdeen noted, 'who is well known as a dodger.' Moreover, they were afraid that if Tupper came in remedial legislation would be lost: 'we know that the retiring ministers and Sir Charles mean to drop the remedial policy.' On Sunday evening Lady Aberdeen wrote: 'we urged him to make every effort to get men to join him and keep to his pledge of bringing in remedial legislation and putting it to the test – and not to throw the country to the hands of one who would doubtless deal with it only in such a way it would suit himself.' Bowell tried to reconstruct his cabinet, but was unable to do so particularly with respect to the crucial additional French-Canadian representation. The bolters, Costigan later said, 'adopted the tactics of a stevedores' strike and blocked his efforts to fill their places with Ministers by appointing pickets to watch the railroad stations and hotels for arrivals.'[4]

On Monday afternoon Bowell met his supporters. The situation, he concluded, was hopeless and he sent his resignation to the governor-general: 'I ... fear that there is no solution of the present problem than for me to resign.' Lord Aberdeen replied: 'I am not at this moment prepared to accept it. The Speech from the Throne, although delivered to Parliament, has not yet been considered; and it would be unfitting that the head of the administration responsible for the preparation of that Speech should not have full opportunity to review the situation, and, should he so determine, to test the feeling of Parliament thereupon.'[5]

Parliament met the next day. Caron, who had taken over the House leadership from Foster, asked for a two-week adjournment, which Laurier refused. Foster spoke on behalf of the bolters, telling the House that they had left only because Bowell was unable to attract a third French Canadian into the cabinet. 'There is no disagreement between ourselves and the Premier upon any question of public policy ... we found ourselves face to face with Parliament, having a Government with its numbers incomplete and with no assurance that the present premier could satisfactorily complete it.'[6]

Foster's comments angered Bowell, who was listening to the debate from behind Lady Aberdeen sitting near the speaker's chair. When the House adjourned, the prime minister walked over to the opposition bench, shook hands with Laurier and other opposition members, and, in the hearing of Lady Aberdeen, who recorded the event in her diary, said: 'It is such a comfort to shake hands with honest men, after having been in company with traitors for months.' This was Bowell's famous 'nest of traitors' remark, a phrase, according to Lady Aberdeen, he did not actually use. About ten years later, Bowell himself declared in the Senate: 'I may now say I have no recollection of using the words "nest of traitors" ... I may add, however, that if I did use them, I was justified in doing so, and if I did not use them then, I ought to have done so.' At the same time he referred to 'the poisonous fangs of the reptile plunged into his bosom,' 'espionage,' 'nest of conspirators,' and 'treachery.'[7] The desertion was not quickly forgotten.

The next day, and again the day following, Bowell formally tendered his resignation, but on both occasions the governor-general refused to accept it. The House then adjourned until Tuesday, 14 January. On Friday, Lady Aberdeen 'fully expected Sir Mackenzie to appear with his resignation for the third time when its acceptance could not have been avoided.' But Bowell did not appear.

On Wednesday, 15 January, after intense negotiations, all seven bolters were back in Bowell's cabinet. They had agreed to return and, just as important, Bowell had agreed to have them back. What caused this reconciliation was simply fear that Lord Aberdeen was about to call on Laurier, not Tupper or any other Conservative, to form a government. In the early stages of the crisis, Laurier had let Lady Aberdeen know, through a Mrs Cummings, who had frequent contact with her over Council of Women matters, that he would like to try to form a government if Bowell was unsuccessful in reconstructing his cabinet. A similar message was again conveyed later in the week. On Saturday night the Lauriers came to a skating party at the governor-general's residence. Lady Aberdeen introduced the opposition leader to Captain John Sinclair, Lord Aberdeen's secretary (and much later, as Baron Pentland and the husband of the Aberdeens' daughter Marjorie, the Liberal secretary of state for Scotland in the British Parliament). Her journal records the meeting: 'So the two went off for a walk and talked the whole matter over and what would be the course to take if he did come in. Dissolution of course at once. And he says he could form his Cabinet in three days and he is very confident of the country if he is in power at the dissolution – but if Sir Charles were in power, this might be difficult.'

The Aberdeens feared Tupper as leader because they thought he would win the next election: 'if Sir Charles comes into power and dissolves, he will not hesitate to use means fair and foul to bribe the country into returning him. This is not mere supposition – his past record is clear enough on this subject.' Sir Hibbert told Lady Aberdeen that his father would support remedial legislation and he had heard rumours that Lord Aberdeen was thinking only of Laurier as an alternative to Bowell; indeed, she had noted in her journal that 'should Sir Mackenzie now fail, H.E.'s mind is pretty well made up.' But she assured Sir Hibbert that such could not be the case, though it clearly was, and in a later letter to him she declared the rumour that Laurier would be called upon 'has not a shadow of foundation.'

At this juncture Caron told the House that Senator Desjardins, the respected ex-mayor of Montreal, had agreed to enter the cabinet to replace Angers, so there was no reason for the bolters to stay out. The cabinet would be led by Bowell, with Sir Charles Tupper, who would seek a seat in the Commons, as secretary of state and leader of the House (as Bowell was in the Senate). Sir Hibbert would no longer be in cabinet because of his father's new position. Dickey replaced him as minister of justice. It was expected that at the end of the session Sir Charles would take over as prime minister and lead the party into the election.

'They could not stay away from the money bags,' was Laurier's alleged comment.[8] And Sir Richard Cartwright, who had been in the House since Confederation and a Liberal cabinet minister in the 1870s, made a brilliant speech on the afternoon of their return, referring to the cabinet as the 'Royal Ottawa Low Comedy Troupe': they had, he said, an 'undress rehearsal' in July when three ministers went out and two came back; now they had had a 'full dress rehearsal' when seven went out and seven came back, and the 'real performance' will be at the coming election when 'all will go out and none come back.'[9]

The crisis was over. It had been an intense few weeks. In her diary, the Aberdeens' fourteen-year-old daughter, Marjorie, viewed the events in terms of the uncommon activity in Government House: 'First there was Shortis' murder case, and the Ministers were always coming up and discussing about, and then there has been a Ministerial crisis, because seven of the ministers resigned, and since that ministers and ex-ministers have filled the house at all times of day.'[10]

Lady Aberdeen walked home from the Parliament Buildings with Sir Hibbert after the reconstructed cabinet first met Parliament. He no longer held a cabinet position and was simply the member from Pictou. She wrote that evening: 'He walked home with me to-night – he is very anxious about his little boy to-day and also about Lady Tupper who is just expecting her confinement.' She continued to maintain a close relationship with Sir Hibbert, becoming godmother to his son born shortly thereafter.

We do not know if they talked about politics. Neither knew that Sir Hibbert would never again hold a cabinet position. This was effectively the end of a brilliant political career, having sacrificed his future in politics for the sake of his father. Later, writers such as John Willison of the *Globe* and Richard Cartwright speculated – accurately, it would seem – that if Sir Charles Tupper had not come back from England his son would have succeeded Bowell as the leader of the Conservative party.[11]

It seems reasonable to speculate, too, that the Shortis case and the ministerial crisis were linked, at least in a general way. Bowell was considered a weak leader and the Shortis affair was another example – perhaps for some the final straw – demonstrating his indecisiveness. The cabinet had been widely attacked for its lack of action in the case. The influential *Globe* had called the cabinet's refusal to advise the governor-general 'the depth of Cabinet debasement, the climax of a course of irresolution and incapacity.' A prominent, but unidentified, Conservative told reporters that the government's failure to agree in the Shortis case was 'probably one of the strongest indications to establish the oft-repeated charges by our friends that the Government is lacking in capacity to deal with important questions as they arose.'[12] Some Conservatives felt so strongly about the government's inaction in the case that they left the party. Mayor Loy and James Robb, who had been the foremen of the grand jury, were only two of many prominent Conservatives in the Beauharnois riding who joined the Liberal party; both were later elected to Parliament, Robb becoming minister of trade and commerce in Mackenzie King's cabinet.

There is, furthermore, one specific link between the actions of the bolters and Shortis. The stated cause of the revolt was that Bowell had been unable to replace Angers with a strong French Canadian: the dissenters had been telling Bowell – although his recollection was not as clear as theirs – that 'unless a French colleague was obtained they would not go on as members of the Government.'[13] Sir Hibbert later assured John Ewart, who represented the Catholics in Manitoba, that the crisis 'has nothing to do with ''Schools'' except so far as failure to secure a colleague in place of Mr. Angers is concerned.' A replacement was necessary, according to a private letter written by Foster, because 'Ouimet and Caron have actually no influence in Quebec, except an absolutely negative one. Going to elections with them meant a clean sweep against us in Quebec.'[14] The loss of two important Quebec by-elections gave substance to this view.

As we have seen, Bowell desperately tried to add another French Canadian to his cabinet. When Father Lacombe travelled to Montreal on New Year's day to receive an answer from Senator Desjardins, the latter declined to join the government. The Shortis affair may have tipped the balance in his decision. The following day Lacombe wrote to Archbishop Langevin in St Boniface, outlining the government's political blunders during the previous year: 'And then to commute Shortis, something that exasperates our people! that's a deadly blow against us.'[15] Desjardins did join the cabinet two weeks later, so it seems likely he was close to joining on New Year's day. Bowell later wrote to the governor-general: 'I had hopes of being able to fill that position up to the very day when Parliament met.'[16] If the cabinet had not permitted the Shortis sentence to be commuted, Desjardins probably would have joined then, and the revolt might never have taken place. At least it might not have taken place at that time, using the vacancy as a pretext. It is likely, however, that steps would have been taken to replace Bowell, because most agreed with Sir Hibbert's view, expressed in a letter to a friend that month, that 'if Bowell is not out of the way at the General Election we are doomed beyond peradventure.'[17] No doubt Father Paul Crunican is correct in concluding that there was no simple explanation: 'the bolting ministers ... were simply searching for a viable combination which would give them a chance for political survival, with or without remedial legislation.'[18]

One cannot help but think there may be other connections between Shortis and the revolt that we will never discover because of the strange silence on the case by all the cabinet ministers involved. None of their papers refer to it, yet there were four long meetings devoted to the case. Were there, for example, allegations of corruption against ministers that were never made public or recorded even in private correspondence? Certainly the press thought so, and Bowell had investigated at least one incident in which Mrs Shortis had tried to bribe a senior government official. It is odd that an old allegation of corruption against Adolphe Caron was anonymously brought up at this very time.

Caron accused Montague of sending anonymous letters to the prime minister about an incident involving an alleged railroad payoff: Montague threatened to bring charges of criminal libel, and the matter was eventually resolved with the assistance of the governor-general and Donald Macmaster, who travelled to Ottawa on Caron's behalf and interviewed Bowell on the very Sunday the Aberdeens talked him into trying to reconstruct his cabinet. There is nothing to suggest this incident had anything to do with the Shortis case, but one does wonder whether more was going on than we know about from the available documents.

The Shortis case was raised in the Commons at the end of January, when Joseph Bergeron moved that copies of all papers connected to the case be made available. 'I rise to perform a very disagreeable duty,' he said, 'I intend to question why mercy was extended in the case of Valentine Shortis.'[19] No one doubted that the case would be debated in Parliament. The Conservative *Mail and Empire* had said in early January that 'there can be no doubt that the Liberals, or some of them, will not be above trying to turn the affair to political account.' And the Conservative Montreal *Gazette* remarked: 'It is to be feared that the Shortis case is likely doomed to be a serious political factor during the present session and the coming general election, as there appears to be a strong disposition on the part of the Opposition to raise the "race and revenge" cry and endeavour to pass a vote of want of confidence in the Government because Shortis, an Englishman, was not hung, while Riel, a Frenchman, was – one being, it is claimed, the same as the other. It would be a curious thing if the Government should succeed in passing its remedial bill and be defeated on the Shortis case, but more improbable things have happened.'[20]

It was perhaps a surprise to many to find that it was a Conservative who was attacking the government. Bergeron, however, was fighting for his political life. He had to keep as much distance as possible between himself and the supporters of Shortis, particularly because his wife was Irish and would be thought to have influenced him to favour commutation. He had earlier refused an invitation to join the team defending Shortis, and in late December he had even refused to speak at a Montreal election meeting in Jacques Cartier because Foster, Shortis' solicitor, was to be on the same platform. Foster wrote criticizing Bergeron's activities: 'you are acting in the whole of this matter as though you were the paid attorney for the prosecution rather than a prominent member of Parliament ... it does seem strange that you should be making a life and death struggle of it ... I feel bound to add that among some of our friends your attitude is being criticised as over-zealous, and as though you were constituting yourself a public avenger ...'[21]

Bergeron informed Parliament – though really he was informing his constituents – that he had written to the minister of justice on two occasions, asking him not to commute the sentence. He recited the facts of the case in detail, arguing that Shortis had received a fair trial and should have been hanged. Referring to 'old Chatelle ... [who] had no lawyer and no money and no friends,' he asked: 'if Chatelle deserved to be hanged, under the circumstances, why did not Shortis deserve the same fate under similar circumstances?' The case, he said, had done great harm to the administration of justice, and if a similar case arose again in Valleyfield, he warned, 'there would be no trial and no chance for a commutation of sentence – the murderer would be hanged to the first telephone pole.'[22]

Laurier naturally joined the attack: 'the Government refused from first to last to shoulder the responsibility as to what could be done with the prisoner ... They were guilty of gross dereliction of duty towards the Sovereign and towards the people.' Why was the case not handled in the same way as the Riel case? In that case, he pointed out, 'a petition had then been submitted for the commutation of Riel, and the Government came to the conclusion that as the fact of the insanity of Riel had been passed upon by the jury, the Government could not undertake to review the sentence of the jury.' He then read the words of Sir John Thompson as minister of justice in the Riel debate: 'the great patience exercised by the jury in sifting the fact ... show[s] that the jury discharged their duties carefully and conscientiously.' The Shortis jury acted in the same manner, Laurier said; something must have happened in council to cause the minister of justice's view to be rejected. A few other speeches were made and the motion to produce the papers was carried. The member for Huntingdon disagreed with only one aspect of Bergeron's speech: 'I do not think there is the slightest danger under any circumstances, that the people of that district would be disposed to import and to put into practice the vile practices which prevail in another country.'

A week earlier, a Liberal MP, David Mills, had attacked the government's handling of the case in his reply to the speech from the throne.[23] A respected lawyer with a University of Michigan law degree, Mills occupied the chair of constitutional and international law at the

University of Toronto; he had been in the House since Confederation and would later become minister of justice and then a judge of the Supreme Court of Canada.[24] He reviewed the earlier precedents with respect to pardons and commutations and, not surprisingly, concluded that the cabinet was at fault in the Shortis case. Quoting Gladstone that a cabinet 'cannot give a discordant or divided advice,' he went on to say: 'It is a total abnegation of their functions to go to the Sovereign and say: We are divided in our opinion and cannot advise you. I say you are bound to advise the Sovereign or retire from your places.' The legal community seemed to share this view. The Toronto-based *Canadian Law Journal*, for example, took the position that the cabinet 'had no right to leave him unadvised on so important a matter; but being so unadvised, through no fault of his own, it was clearly within his power as a constitutional Governor to exercise his prerogative according to his own deliberate judgment.'[25]

The Shortis papers were presented to Parliament in mid-February. The Montreal *Herald* concluded that they 'contain little of what has not already been published ... beyond the fact that the ex Minister of Justice, Sir Hibbert Tupper, reported to Council in favour of the law being allowed to take its course, instead of commutation, as he was reported to have done.' Some of the material in the Department of Justice file was not reproduced. A letter from A.F. Gault, the president of the Montreal Cotton Company and a prominent Conservative, who had urged that the law be allowed to take its course, was not released after he wrote to Sir Hibbert saying: 'My letter to you was intended to be private and only for you. I hope you will see that it is not produced.' None of the correspondence between the Aberdeens and members of the cabinet was reproduced, apart from Lord Aberdeen's final communication commuting the sentence. Unhappily for Bergeron, his letters to the minister of justice were not included, which caused the local papers to speculate that they did not exist. The Shortis papers did not change anyone's mind. The *Progrès de Valleyfield* repeated its earlier position: 'there is nothing to prevent Shortis being placed on trial for the murder of Leboeuf, and our advice is, that the people of Valleyfield start a movement to petition Attorney-General Casgrain to have him again arraigned.'

The Liberals in Beauharnois felt they now had an issue to unseat Bergeron and the Conservatives in the coming election. Could they find a suitable candidate? With a petition containing seventeen hundred signatures, they approached Laurier's Quebec lieutenant, Israel Tarte. [26] He was at the time the sitting member of L'Islet and the party members there were not anxious for him to run elsewhere. As the *Herald* said: 'To have such a man as representative at Ottawa would confer distinction on any constituency in Canada.' Moreover, others were interested in running for the Liberals, including the manager of the Banque Jacques Cartier in Montreal, a relative of the murdered Maxime Leboeuf. Tarte was undecided, but Laurier wanted him to run in Beauharnois: the riding would symbolize Conservative incompetence and would therefore help the Liberals to win Quebec. [27]

Tarte was the son of a farmer 'habitant.' Now almost fifty, he had qualified as a notary, but then switched to a career as a journalist. For most of his life he was a Conservative and had been a member of the Quebec legislature. In 1891 he was elected to the House of Commons, publicly exposed the McGreevy-Langevin public works scandal involving the Conservatives, and then went over to Laurier and the opposition. He had been the key person shaping Laurier's Manitoba schools policy and he would be the leading strategist for the Liberals in Quebec in the next election. The Toronto *Week* described him as 'the mildest mannered man that ever scuttled a ship or cut a throat.' [28] He and Bergeron had worked together ten years earlier when they had gone to Ottawa to try to save the life of Louis Riel; [29] now, they were both arguing that Valentine Shortis should have been hanged.

On Saturday, 11 April, Laurier came from Ottawa to Tarte's nomination rally in Valleyfield. More than simply a nomination meeting, it was to be the opening of Laurier's election campaign. [30] Two thousand people, according to the *Herald* – one thousand said the Conservative *Star* – attended the afternoon rally at the decorated skating rink. Special half-price trains had brought Liberal supporters from Montreal. Large signs displayed the words 'Vive M. Laurier' and 'Down with the protectors of Shortis.' The meeting was presided over by Mayor Loy and County Warden Boyer, an English Protestant and a French Catholic, both of whom had formerly been staunch Conservatives. [31]

Laurier directed much of his speech to the Shortis case: [32] 'Valleyfield is well-known for its picturesque situation and the magnificence of its scenery; but it has been made known to the world by one of the most atrocious tragedies in the calendar of crime, and on that occasion was shown the insignificance, I must say the criminality of the Government. I do not want to arouse your prejudice, but I want justice.' The blame, he said, should be placed squarely on the government, not on the governor-general: 'We cannot blame [Mrs Shortis] for having tried to save her son, any mother would have done the same. But it is not the Governor General, who is responsible for having commuted the sentence; the reponsibility must fall upon the shoulders of the Cabinet Ministers.' He then referred to Riel: 'I am not a man to thirst for blood, but the law is the law, and justice must be equal for everybody. Riel was condemned to death, although his lawyers had pleaded insanity, and although the jury had recommended him for mercy, he was executed. I want equal justice for everybody, equal rights to everybody, to every race, and to every religion.'

Tarte's speech was equally hard-hitting, claiming that 'unfortunately everything is for sale in this country, even criminal justice.' He wanted Shortis to be retried: 'I want to know if you can say that there is equal justice for everybody in this country ... There is not a parallel in the history of the civilized world to the Shortis affair ... Shortis could stand another trial; for Maxime Leboeuf's horrible murder has not been avenged, but the father's $60,000 has poisoned all justice. I am an old Conservative and I love my country, but if you knew what I know, you would break the Government like a glass, for you have been robbed and betrayed at Ottawa.'

The rally, said the *Herald*, 'convinced everybody that Mr. Bergeron's political days are numbered.' Perhaps the only part of Laurier's speech that did not go down well in Valleyfield was his desire for a treaty of reciprocity with the United States. The Montreal Cotton Company and other industries in the area feared that an abandonment of protection through the 'National Policy' would harm their factories. The rally, which was fully reported in the Quebec papers, both French and English, clearly and deliberately introduced the Shortis case as a major issue in the election.[33]

13

The Election of 1896

IR CHARLES TUPPER, SR, was returned to the House of Commons in a Cape Breton by-election in early February, and arrived in Ottawa on Monday, 10 February 1896. Bowell refused to meet him at the train station and had so informed the governor-general.[1] The next day he took his seat and the minister of justice introduced the first reading of the 'Remedial Act of Manitoba,' drawn along the lines of the pre-1890 provincial legislation. A little over a month later, at 5:30 in the morning, after a continuous forty-hour sitting, the Bill received second reading.[2] Its progress was then delayed by direct, but unsuccessful, talks between Ottawa and Manitoba,[3] negotiations which had been promoted by Lord Aberdeen and Sir Donald Smith, an MP who had been one of the founders of the Canadian Pacific Railway, remembered today as the man who drove the last spike in 1885.

The Bill then moved into the committee of the whole for clause-by-clause analysis. Its passage was easily obstructed by the Liberals and the McCarthyite Conservatives, and there were no closure rules at the time to prevent filibustering: one member read an excerpt from Mark Twain, and another read parts of the Bible. At 2:30 in the morning of 16 April, after only 15 of the 112 clauses had passed, the Conservatives gave up attempting to get the Bill through the House and arranged for dissolution.[4]

It had been a remarkable session. The House had witnessed the desertion and reconciliation of the cabinet bolters and the spectacle of parliamentary obstruction. Further, a Canadian – and possibly a British Empire – record for the length of a continuous sitting had been established when the House sat for one week with only brief intermissions for meals.[5] In the middle of the session the Senate chamber had been the scene of the historical pageantry of the Aberdeens' fancy dress ball, which according to the Montreal *Star* 'was a brilliant affair – an unqualified success,'[6] better even than the grand ball given by the Dufferins twenty years earlier.

Thursday, 23 April, was the last day of the session and the governor-general was scheduled to dissolve Parliament at eight in the evening. To carry the government over until the new Parliament, the House passed the necessary Supply Bill, with the exception of an item of $7,600 for deepening the entrance to the channel of the Beauharnois Canal, which opposition members thought was politically motivated to help Bergeron. The Senate, meanwhile, passed a fast Atlantic service Act, which had been the alleged reason for Tupper's return to Canada in December. Fast travel, Bowell told his listeners, was 'the tendency of the age' – though one senator expressed the view that twenty knots was too fast for Canada.

At 7:30 in the evening the House met for the last formalities before adjourning to the Senate chamber. The guns on Nepean Point were booming to let the city know that the governor-general was on his way to the Parliament Buildings. Bergeron rose: 'Mr. Speaker, now that the work of the session is very nearly completed and that I may not be accused of obstruction, I desire, with your permission, to bring before the House a matter which I consider of sufficient importance to justify me in rising to speak about it at this time ... I mean the Shortis case.' Politicians, he said, 'have tried to make political capital out of this case, in the press and on the stump.' Extracts from a number of Quebec papers were cited by Bergeron. Israel Tarte's own paper, *Le Cultivateur*, had said: 'Shortis, the triple murderer of Valleyfield, is enjoying a splendid health at the St. Vincent de Paul penitentiary. With money, under the present Administration, criminals are pretty sure to be on the safe side. Before his departure for Europe, Shortis' father declared that his son's life had cost him $60,000. An investigation into the circumstances which accompanied the commutation of the murderer's sentence would bring to light extraordinary things.' The popular Montreal Liberal paper, *La Patrie*, declared that it would have to be explained 'why Shortis was not hung to pay for the crime of having butchered fathers of families, when Riel was executed for having loved his prairie lands and for having stood up for the sacred cause of liberty.' French and English papers throughout the province, including the independent press, Bergeron said, had given extensive coverage to Laurier's speech in Valleyfield: 'I am not a man to thirst for blood, but the law is the law, and justice must be equal for everybody.' The fight over Shortis, he said, was being fought across Quebec. Bergeron also read into the record letters he had earlier sent to the minister of justice asking that the sentence of death be carried out – letters the existence of which, as mentioned, the local Valleyfield press had doubted.

Laurier rose and defended the actions of the opposition: 'What is there wrong in my remarks upon that subject? ... I said at Valleyfield what I have said on the floor of this House, in this present session, and what I repeat again, that in the Riel case the Government laid down the proposition that when the defence of insanity had been entered on the part of a prisoner, and when the jury had passed upon that plea and had declared the prisoner guilty, it was not open to the Government to re-open the case and commute the sentence.' Had not Bergeron himself made the same point in his private letters to the minister of justice? 'I knew my political opponents would use that,' interjected Bergeron. The responsibility, said Laurier, rests on the government, not the governor-general.

The Aberdeens were not in the House to hear this debate. They were in the East Block, waiting to proceed to the Senate. Everyone was anxious to get a glimpse of Lady Aberdeen, who had miraculously recovered from a brush with death the day before, when her carriage had fallen into the Gatineau River: her head had gone under the icy water, but she had been saved by the fortunate presence of a quick-thinking Captain Sinclair. Now looking in perfect health, she was in a green velvet gown – she had worn blue for the opening – adorned with diamonds.[7] The Aberdeens had been asked to delay their entrance for twenty minutes because of the Shortis debate in the Commons.

The minister of justice, Arthur Dickey, added his complaint that Laurier was deliberately and improperly stirring up feelings on the issue: 'This was a crime which created great feeling in the district where it took place ... which shook the moral sense of the community ... The Hon. Leader of the Opposition went to that locality to begin his political campaign, and in that locality, where the feeling is of that character, a feeling which is deep down in the savage instinct that comes to us from the past, and which civilization ought to wipe out, he deliberately stirs up those feelings which lie against that criminal.' Then L.H. Davies, a former premier of Prince Edward Island who was to become chief justice of Canada (1918-24), began a speech attacking the government. After a few preliminary sentences, the Gentlemen

Usher of the Black Rod knocked three times at the door, summoning members to the Senate. Davies continued, resisting shouts of 'sit down,' but finally stopped in mid-sentence. 'There is no doubt about the responsibility of the government –' were his final words.

The Aberdeens arrived in the Senate accompanied by strains of *God Save the Queen*, played by the Governor-General's Foot Guards. His Excellency read the closing remarks prepared for him: 'I desire to express my regret that the mission which my Government recently despatched to confer with the local authorities of Manitoba has been unproductive of any immediate result, and that the question relating to schools in that province shall await settlement.'

Sir Charles Tupper assumed he would be called on by the governor-general to form a new ministry. 'By arrangement,' he wrote in his journal, 'I was to succeed Mackenzie Bowell as Prime Minister.'[8] It was not, however, an arrangement that Bowell accepted. He was prepared to recommend that Sir Donald Smith take over, but the future Lord Strathcona preferred to be high commissioner in London.[9]

Aberdeen had no choice, then, but to call on Sir Charles when Bowell resigned on 27 April. At Bowell's request, he did not ask for his advice on who should be his successor. In her diary Lady Aberdeen expressed distaste that her husband had to 'send for a man whose whole life has been devoted to scheming and who will spare no means of any sort which may be of use in securing the return of his party with himself as Premier,' and when Tupper accepted the task she remarked with mock pleasure that Sir Charles, 'wonderful to say, undertook the Commission to form a Ministry.'

Tupper was able to form a surprisingly strong cabinet. Caron and Ouimet were dropped and four French Canadians, men of 'unimpeachable character and integrity,'[10] were added. Desjardins remained; Angers returned; and J.J. Ross, a former Quebec premier, and L.-O. Taillon, the present premier, came in. At one point it even appeared as though the lieutenant-governor of Quebec, Chapleau – perhaps the most formidable French-Canadian Conservative – would join, but the scales were weighted against this possibility when Tarte promised him a second term as lieutenant-governor if the Liberals won.[11] Outside Quebec there was little change in the cabinet positions. Daly was replaced by Hugh Macdonald, Sir John A.'s son: he moved out west, eventually becoming a police magistrate in Winnipeg in 1907 and author of the once well-known Daly's *Canadian Criminal Procedure*.[12]

The Ontario representatives remained the same: they would have been stronger if Chief Justice Meredith had entered the government as many had predicted, and if the great Toronto lawyer, B.B. Osler, had joined, as he apparently would have except that he disagreed with the remedial legislation. Sir Hibbert Tupper became the solicitor-general, which was not then a cabinet position. Bowell declined to stay in the cabinet but he remained in the Senate where he continued as the Conservatives' House leader until 1906.

The election contest was not one-sided. At a large rally for Laurier in Montreal, the day after dissolution – twelve thousand attended and fifty thousand cheered the procession – Tarte predicted a Liberal majority in Quebec of twenty seats.[13] Privately, he was saying much the same, telling Willison, the editor of the *Globe*, that he was confident of 'a great success in Quebec.'[14] At the same time, Angers was telling Tupper in private that he could count on a Conservative majority of twenty in Quebec.[15] A week before the election on 23 June, Lady Aberdeen wrote in her diary: 'It is still impossible to forecast the result as both sides appear to be so confident.'

There were many issues in the election. The two crucial policy matters were the Manitoba schools question and tariff protection. The Shortis case, as we have seen, was also an important underlying issue, and in Beauharnois it was very important. Indeed, Bergeron said later that 'the election in my county was fought simply upon that case.'[16]

Bergeron held a large public meeting in Valleyfield at the end of April, attended by the new cabinet ministers, Desjardins and Taillon, and also by Donald Macmaster. Louis Simpson chaired the meeting – 'not a very enthusiastic gathering,' said the Huntingdon *Gleaner* – in front of the Windsor Hotel, the hotel where Shortis had stayed while in Valleyfield. Tarte listened to the speeches from a nearby window. Many who were angry over the Shortis case still supported the Conservatives. The *Gleaner* later published a letter complaining that some of the persons who 'tried to organize a lynching party ... are now working day and night for the party who were responsible for the commutation.' Simpson's answer to those who had switched to the Liberals was that 'in their seeking revenge they endanger the prosperity of a whole town'; he argued that the Liberal policy favouring reciprocity with the United States 'would take the bread out of the mouths of the citizens of this town.' The Montreal Cotton Company, like most major industries in Quebec, supported the Conservatives,[17] for they had erected the high tariff walls. Bergeron, to everyone's surprise, did not mention the Shortis case, but Macmaster did, saying that he would have acted differently if he had been the governor-general and asked the audience 'what had Mr. Bergeron done that he should be blamed for the reprieval of Shortis?'

A large public meeting for Tarte was held in Beauharnois shortly afterwards, again attended by Laurier, who pointed out that Tupper in French, 'tu perds,' meant 'you lose,' while Laurier meant 'laurel' or 'victory.' No mention was apparently made of Shortis.

Macmaster played an important part in the Conservative campaign throughout the country, having declined at least three offers to accept a nomination himself. A few days before the election he gave the closing speech in a rally for Tupper at Massey Hall in Toronto, 'the greatest political gathering that has ever taken place in the City of Toronto,' declared the Conservative Montreal *Star*. 'A decisive majority for the Government' was predicted by the Conservative press.

Wilfrid Laurier won the 1896 election. Lady Aberdeen, who had been watching the results as they were posted by means of a magic lantern, recorded in her diary: 'even before it was dark, the returns which were read out indicated that the unexpected had happened, and that the Province of Quebec, which was supposed to have been handed over to the Conservative Party at the bidding of the Bishops, had gone overwhelmingly for the Liberals.' The results outside of Quebec were more or less even: the parties tied in Ontario and Nova Scotia and the Conservatives won in New Brunswick and Manitoba. But in Quebec the Liberals won 49 seats and the Conservatives only 16. Angers, Desjardins, and Taillon were all defeated. So the victory in Quebec was even greater than Tarte had predicted. It was a surprising result, described by one writer as the 'weirdest upside-down episode in the Dominion's history. Laurier, the Quebec Catholic, supported the Manitoba Protestants against his own bishops. Yet he won Quebec and lost Manitoba.'[18]

There were so many issues involved in the 1896 election that it is impossible to say to what extent, or even whether, the Shortis case affected the result. But it is no exaggeration to say that the case played a significant role in the election campaign. Tarte and Laurier raised the issue publicly on a number of occasions and their speeches were widely reported in the press. Moreover, Tarte was selected by Laurier to run in Beauharnois and Laurier chose to open his campaign in Valleyfield, pressing the comparison between the Conservatives' treatment of Riel and Shortis. Further, the closing debate of the parliamentary session, one in which Laurier participated, and which was given prominence by the press, was specifically devoted to the Shortis case.

The Liberal victory in Quebec, which established their dominance of the province until the success of John Diefenbaker over sixty years later, was to a considerable extent owed to the tactical skills of Israel Tarte. 'Laurier owes his success in Quebec to Tarte more than to any other man, or a dozen men,' one observer wrote at the time.[19] There was no one in the Conservative camp who could match him after Caron was dropped.[20] Yet in Beauharnois itself Tarte lost to Bergeron, by forty-eight votes.[21] It was 'one of the regrettable features of the election,' said the Toronto *Globe*; 'Mr. Tarte should be in Parliament beside the leader, to whose success he has contributed so much.' Laurier easily found a seat for him in the Quebec riding of Iberville by elevating the incumbent Liberal to the Senate; the Conservatives did not oppose his election.

Tarte was bitter about his defeat, telling a Montreal *Herald* reporter the next day: 'I have been defeated by the cotton mills combine, which drove the workingmen to the polls like cattle. All the directors subscribed against me, and the manager Mr. Simpson, assisted by his personal friends, forced the two hundred voters who were in my favour in that manufactory to vote against me.' Tarte was probably expecting such action. In early June he had written privately to the editor of the *Globe* that the Montreal Cotton Company had hired 125 men in one day, committing them to the Conservative party. A further letter the day after the election charged that 100 men were locked up in the factory unable to vote, while 300 more were forced to vote against him. Two Montreal papers, *Le Soir* and *La Presse*, investigated and substantially confirmed the charges.[22] Witnesses told the papers that all the doors out of the mill were blocked, forcing the workmen to pass through Simpson's office; Conservatives were allowed to pass through freely, but Liberals were ordered back to their machines. Simpson denied the allegations, writing to the Huntingdon *Gleaner* that 'there is not one word of truth in the statement, that I prevented, during the last election or at any time, a single voter from going to the polls.'

A few years later Tarte, as minister of public works in Laurier's government, repeated his earlier charges against Simpson, stating that 'the men of Valleyfield were tyrannized in a way that no member of

Parliament would countenance.'[23] The subject came up when Bergeron's supporters complained that he had lost the 1900 election to the Liberal candidate, the former mayor, George Loy, because of improper conduct. The alleged impropriety was directed against the young deputy minister of labour W.L. Mackenzie King, who will later play a role in our story. King had gone down to Valleyfield just before the election to try to settle a major strike at the Montreal Cotton Company, a strike sufficiently serious that the troops had to be called in. It was alleged by Bergeron's supporters that King had introduced party politics by improperly calling on Liberal supporters.

King's Valleyfield experience, it should be noted, whatever the truth of the allegations, turned out to be important. He solved the strike and his success in that dispute – the first time the Conciliation Act of 1900 was used – led to the mediation technique being formalized in the 1907 Industrial Disputes Investigation Act, which he promoted.[24] In a letter to his family King described the strike: '[I] had a talk with some of the men, in order to get their point of view ... I drove them to the meeting and by putting leading questions to the meeting got the men to accept the plan of settlement I deemed wisest, and to make it appear to them as if it were their own proposal.'[25] As H.S. Ferns and B. Ostry wrote in their biography: 'Mackenzie King spent his years rewriting Valleyfield, elaborating, refining, embellishing and adapting to new media, but always adhering to the basic pattern.'[26]

Simpson, as it turned out, was no longer at the cotton mill when King arrived; he had been fired for mismanagement several months earlier, but returned to help Bergeron fight the election of 1900. He spent the next five years in Ottawa working on the electric smelting of iron ores, but returned to Valleyfield to manage the Montreal Cotton Company plant again in 1905, remaining there until 1909.

Ironically, the lawyer for the Conservative Montreal Cotton Company in the 1900 labour dispute was J.N. Greenshields, QC, who had defended Shortis and was a Liberal.

To add to these unpredictable events, in 1902 Tarte was fired from the cabinet by Laurier for talking publicly, without authorization, about a high protective tariff while the prime minister was out of the country; he remained a member of Parliament until 1904, without regaining a cabinet position, and died in 1907 at the age of fifty-nine. One of his accomplishments in the government was playing an instrumental role in bringing about a partial solution to the Manitoba schools crisis, the Laurier-Greenway settlement of November 1896, which permitted in certain cases separate religious instruction for Roman Catholics between 3:30 and 4:00 in the afternoon, provided for the hiring of Catholic teachers in particular circumstances, and allowed teaching in French when a specified number of parents requested it.[27] The settlement was denounced by a majority of the bishops and found defective by the Pope.

Tarte's opponent, Bergeron, continued to contest the Beauharnois riding, beating Loy in 1904, but losing again to another Liberal in 1908.

Sir Charles Tupper and his son, Sir Hibbert, were both elected in Nova Scotia, in spite of opposition from the Orange Lodge.[28] Sir Charles was of course the prime minister until Laurier assumed office and he sought to fill some of the government vacancies. The two available Senate seats from Quebec were, in a political sense, owed to Senators Desjardins and Angers, who had resigned to run for seats in the House, but had lost. Laurier, however, objected. He needed the Senate seats to bring into the cabinet people such as Oliver Mowat, from Ontario, who had not run in the election. And he needed a seat to pave the way for Tarte's election to the House. Lord Aberdeen refused to permit Tupper to make these important appointments and the colonial secretary later approved his actions.[29] Tupper was furious and the incident further soured relations between them: 'A weak and incapable Governor under the control of an ambitious and meddlesome woman,' Tupper later wrote privately to the editor of the London *Times*.[30]

The incident also caused a rupture in the relationship between Sir Hibbert and Lady Aberdeen.[31] They had continued a relatively close social involvement after Sir Hibbert had left the cabinet. In April she attended the christening of her godson, Victor Gordon – Victor because he was born on the day Sir Charles won the Cape Breton by-election and Gordon after the Aberdeens' clan.

Several months later the Aberdeens were out west and Lady Aberdeen requested that Sir Hibbert, who happened to be in Victoria at the time, come for luncheon: 'we agreed that no tiresome public affairs were ever to interfere with personal friendship, did we not?' That meeting did not, however, re-establish warm relations. In early 1897 Sir Hibbert rebuffed an invitation: 'the unconstitutional and unprecedented action of the Governor General towards the late Government, of which I was a member, makes it impossible for me to take advantage of the social relations your note suggests without compromising my self-respect and losing the confidence of the political party to which I belong.' Lady Aberdeen would not accept his position, arguing that it was not 'seemly that Ex-Ministers of the Crown should feel themselves in a position whereby they decline intercourse with the representative of the Queen.' She went on: ' ''The Crown can do no wrong.'' And subjects, especially when they happen .to be the Ex-Premier and his son, surely cannot feel themselves in the attitude of having a breach with the Sovereign's representative.' The Tuppers, she said, should at least attend the state dinners. Sir Hibbert replied that the Aberdeens had improperly identified themselves with the Liberal party of Canada.

Sir Hibbert moved out west permanently early in 1898 and, not surprisingly, became one of the leaders of the British Columbia bar.[32] In part, the move was for financial reasons: he now had four sons and three daughters. His father had told him privately in a letter several years earlier that 'he who does not provide for his own household is worse than an infidel.'[33] Another reason for the move was that Sir Hibbert was plagued with rheumatism and the medical opinion at the time was that the British Columbian climate would be good for his health.

He remained, however, a member of Parliament from Pictou, Nova Scotia, winning the 1900 election and a further election in 1904. He intended to contest the 1908 election as well, but decided not to do so when he was strongly attacked by the Orange Order, a prominent organ of which wrote that Orangemen can 'let Sir Hibbert and his supporters understand that they do not intend to be betrayed twice if they can prevent it.'

When the Aberdeens left Canada in 1898, Sir Hibbert went so far as to urge the Conservatives to oppose the traditional farewell address; however, this proposal was not supported by his colleagues.[34]

Lady Aberdeen returned to Canada on a number of occasions in connection with her charity work. The new governor-general, Lord Minto, was upset about one such visit and requested the colonial secretary, Joseph Chamberlain, to do what he could to stop 'this infernal woman prowling about.'[35]

Sir Charles Tupper, Sr, lost the 1900 election, as well as his seat, and dropped out of political life. Robert Borden, a former law partner of Sir Hibbert's from Halifax – with the active support of the Tuppers – took over the leadership of the Conservative party.[36] Lord Aberdeen had privately expressed to Willison of the *Globe* his great pleasure in Tupper's defeat by Laurier: 'we could not but feel that a victory for Sir Charles would mean disaster for Canada and very possibly to the Empire.'

Sir Charles died in 1915, in London, England – the last of the Fathers of Confederation to die. He was ninety-four, the same age as Mackenzie Bowell when he died two years later. Tupper's eldest son had died the previous year and the baronetcy therefore went to Sir Hibbert, who died in Vancouver in 1927 at the age of seventy-one. The fifth baronet, Sir Hibbert's grandson, also named Sir Charles Hibbert, and his heir, Charles Hibbert, now live in Vancouver.

In April 1896, Valentine Shortis' thumb had been almost wholly severed by careless use of a circular saw while working in the carpenter's shop in St Vincent de Paul Penitentiary. He had refused to have it amputated and it was clumsily attached. Gangrene set in, he became delirious, and his condition reportedly became critical. In July he was said to be still in the penitentiary hospital.[37] Thus, it seems possible that Shortis was unaware of the result of the election, an election in which he had unwittingly played a significant role.

St Vincent de Paul Penitentiary, c. 1890

14

On the Banks of the Rivière-des-Prairies

S T VINCENT DE PAUL PENITENTIARY, today known as the Laval Complex, is located on the north bank of the Rivière-des-Prairies, on a plateau overlooking the town of St Vincent de Paul, about ten miles from downtown Montreal. Formerly a Quebec reformatory for boys, the site had been purchased from Quebec by the Dominion government in 1872 and opened in 1873, when sixty convicts, mainly French Canadians who had been given special training in stonework, were brought by steamboat from Kingston Penitentiary, shackled with leg irons.[1]

The penitentiary at Kingston, constructed in the 1830s, had until 1873 been central Canada's only federal penal institution. The union of Upper and Lower Canada in 1841 had interrupted early plans for a penitentiary in Quebec. The British North America Act of 1867 had, in effect, given the central government exclusive authority over persons sentenced to two years or more and Kingston could no longer handle the growing numbers of prisoners, particularly the large numbers from the growing population in Quebec. Plans had been made shortly after Confederation to build another large penitentiary in the Kingston area – '5 wings rotating from a central rotunda' – but in the early 1870s it was decided it would be preferable to build new institutions in other provinces. In the 1870s and 1880s, therefore, new penitentiaries were created in Quebec, New Brunswick, Manitoba, and British Columbia. Kingston and St Vincent de Paul were by far the largest. When Shortis entered the penitentiary, there were about 400 inmates in St Vincent de Paul, 600 in Kingston, and only another 300 in the other three federal institutions. By the 1930s there would be over a thousand cells at St Vincent de Paul;[2] it was declared 'unfit for use' on a number of occasions, but was reopened in 1973 because of the large increase in Quebec prisoners.[3]

The St Vincent de Paul file on Shortis was destroyed in a fire in a storeroom at the penitentiary and so it is difficult to recreate through specific events what prison life was like for him. Still, from other sources, including a report by penitentiary commissioners on the institution in 1897,[4] the general pattern of prison life at the time can be portrayed.

It will be recalled that Shortis spent considerable time in the prison hospital during the election campaign in the spring of 1896 because of an accident in the carpenter's shop. He is mentioned in the surgeon's annual report that year as one of only two persons having had accidents in the penitentiary: 'March 17 – wound on thumb caused by circular saw – 27 days in hospital.'[5] It is not surprising that, whatever was done for him at the time, his condition became worse: there were constant complaints about the St Vincent de Paul hospital, which was simply an open ward on the second floor of the main building.[6] Moreover, sewage facilities were at the time inadequate: earlier in the year, as noted, typhoid fever had raged through the penitentiary causing at least one death. Diarrhoea was conceded by the officials to be chronic in the 1890s. Further, there were a large number of deaths from tuberculosis at the time, as there were in all penitentiaries throughout Canada. Shortis, it will be recalled, was believed by the doctors testifying at the trial to be consumptive.

The middle of the 1890s was a crucial period in the history of incarceration in the British Empire. The English Gladstone Commission[7] reported in 1895 that the old penal philosophy of deterrence had run its course; rehabilitation was to be the new philosophy. Many persons in Canada, particularly an influential group of prison reformers in Ontario, which included Dr C.K. Clarke, were urging the Dominion government to adopt the rehabilitation approach. The penitentiary system was in a state of transition, trapped by an investment in buildings constructed under an early regime of deterrence, with uncertainty over the future.

All the penitentiaries built in Canada in the nineteenth century followed the Kingston model, which in turn had been adopted from the New York, or Auburn, model, named after an institution at Auburn in the Finger Lakes district of central New York.[8] Such institutions were needed in Canada to deal with persons who in earlier years would have been deterred by the possibility of being hanged or banished or by being transported to Australia.

Repentance and deterrence were the objectives of the Canadian penitentiary system in the early periods. An 1831 report from Upper Canada put it this way:

A Penitentiary, as its name imports, should be a place to lead a man to repent of his sins and amend his life, and if it has that effect, so much the better, as the cause of religion gains by it, but it is quite enough for the purposes of the Public if the punishment is so terrible that the dread of a repetition of it deters him from crime, or his description of it, others. It should therefore be a place which by every means not cruel and not affecting the health of the offender shall be rendered so irksome and so terrible that during his after life he may dread nothing so much as a repetition of the punishment, and, if possible, that he should prefer death to such a contingency. This can all be done by hard labor and privations and not only without expense to the province, but possibly bringing it a revenue.[9]

Over the years, however, the reformative aspects for the most part ceased to be spoken of as one of the primary objectives. In 1871, the year before St Vincent de Paul was purchased, Sir John A. Macdonald, the prime minister, stated: 'the primary purpose of the penitentiary is punishment and the incidental one reformation.'[10]

The Auburn system was based on complete silence with solitary confinement at night and collective work during the day (the alternative system at the time, the Philadelphia system, required the inmate to sleep, eat, and work in his cell). The deputy keeper of Auburn, who was hired to help design and run Kingston, said as the plans were being made: 'the particularly excellent and distinguishing characteristic of the Auburn system is non-intercourse among the convicts, while at the same time, they are employed by day, in active useful labour. This is the grand foundation on which rests the whole fabric of Prison discipline.'[11]

The same foundation was in place when Shortis entered the penitentiary in 1896. The description given to Kingston in the 1840s by Susanna Moodie, well known for her *Roughing It in the Bush*, could equally be applied to Shortis' cell in St Vincent de Paul fifty years later: 'The cells are narrow, just wide enough to contain a small bed, a stool, and a wash-bowl, and the prisoners are divided from each other by thick stone walls. They are locked in every night at six o'clock, and their cell is so constructed, that one of the keepers can always look in upon the convict without his being aware of the scrutiny.'[12] Most of the St Vincent de Paul cells were only three feet wide, and some were only two and a half feet. Plumbing was not introduced into the penitentiaries until the turn of the century and so each prisoner would bring a night bucket into his cell along with his evening meal, a fact delicately not mentioned by Mrs Moodie.

Providing the inmates with useful work was not particularly difficult in the early days. Contracts could be entered into with entrepreneurs to use prison labour to make manufactured goods. 'This is exclusively an agricultural country,' was the reply to those who complained about unfair competition: 'it can be no objection with [the farmer] that by any means he gets all his manufactured goods at half price he at present pays.'[13] But Canada was a far different country in the latter part of the century, having developed an important industrial sector. The 'National Policy' of 1879 was designed to further industrialization by protecting Canadian industry from foreign competition. It was not long, therefore, before the manufacturers and unions wanted similar protection from cheap competition by prison labour. As a result, the Penitentiary Act of 1883 put a stop to contract labour,[14] and the last penitentiary contract ran out in 1887.

There was, therefore, very little useful work for inmates to do. One solution, widely used in the United States, was to manufacture goods for the government itself, referred to throughout North America as the 'state use' system.[15] The trouble was that other government departments were not entirely satisfied with the goods produced. The North West Mounted Police, for example, complained about the poor quality of the work done for them; some of the inmates may not have had their hearts in the task of producing comfortable boots and jackets for the very persons responsible for sending them to prison. Much of the work was therefore produced for a captive group, the penitentiaries themselves, including the construction and expansion of buildings, which might well account for some of the enthusiasm for prison construction during the latter part of the nineteenth century. A new wing was constructed at St Vincent de Paul in the 1880s, a perimeter wall in the 1890s, and a further wing at the turn of the century.[16] There was, however, not enough of this 'useful' work to go around. Many of the inmates were engaged in relatively unproductive labour. Penitentiaries did not start producing mail bags until the First World War. Breaking rocks was one of the commonest ways of keeping prisoners occupied.

We know that Shortis started out in the tailor's shop at St Vincent de Paul and then moved to the carpenter's shop. What specific tasks he worked on is not known, but it is likely that he was producing prison uniforms or clothing for the Department of Indian Affairs and then prison furniture.

Silence was still demanded in theory in 1896, although in practice it was not uniformly enforced. The penitentiary regulations of 1889 provided that 'No convict shall be permitted to speak to another convict upon any pretence whatever, nor to an officer, guard or any servant of the institution, except from necessity or with respect to the work at which he is employed and then only in the fewest words, and in a respectful manner ...'[17] Disciplinary punishments in the 1890s could include solitary confinement, flogging (the leather paddle replaced the lash in 1898), the water hose, or the Oregon boot, a weighted shoe appliance locked to the prisoner's foot.[18] In 1894 the new 'prison of isolation,' a special hundred-cell structure for solitary confinement, had been completed at Kingston and troublemakers from across Canada could be transferred there.

Another, less harsh technique had been developed, however, for enforcing prison discipline. Grafted on to the punitive, deterrent-based Auburn system, was a system of rewards drawn from the Irish Crofton system, named after the prison reformer in charge of Irish prisons, Sir Walter Crofton. Introduced in Canada just after Confederation, this system provided for partial remission of sentences for diligence and good behaviour. Even the prisoners' uniforms varied according to levels of behaviour, a technique abandoned around the time Shortis entered the penitentiary because of its expense.[19] Deprivation of chewing tobacco was also used as a technique of control, although the question of tobacco was always subject to controversy because its use led to illegal trafficking and corruption and was objected to by those who wanted prison life to be harsh, as well as by those who thought it to be an uncouth habit.[20] Specific rewards were given for good behaviour; in St Vincent de Paul, for example, lights were given to convicts to read by at night. Shortis was apparently a well-behaved inmate and so would probably have had these additional privileges.

Rehabilitation was subject to much discussion in the Canadian penitentiary system, but little headway was made in practice. Crime was thought by most to be like a disease which could be cured. Prison reform societies wanted the indeterminate sentence to be used, as had the Gladstone Commission in England. If crime is a disease to be cured, then the inmate should not be released until he is better. The new inspector of penitentiaries, Douglas Stewart, advocated indeterminate sentences for habitual criminals in his 1896 annual report, including a life sentence for a third offence.

Moreover, the 'disease' analogy called for the segregation of first offenders from hardened criminals to prevent 'contagion.' In 1895 money was appropriated for a so-called 'preferred class' penitentiary connected with St Vincent de Paul, but after two years' work on the building construction was stopped and the project abandoned. Such separate institutions were not constructed until the 1930s, when Collins Bay was built in the Kingston area and the Laval Building beside St Vincent de Paul.[21]

There were, therefore, around the turn of the century, three penal philosophies operating within Canadian society and the penitentiary service: deterrence through punishment, the encouragement of good conduct through rewards, and, to a lesser extent, rehabilitation. Not until after the Second World War would the rehabilitation philosophy become the dominant one, only to be replaced by the current philosophical uncertainty, an uncertainty not unlike that of a hundred years ago.

Mary Shortis returned to Canada to visit her son in late August 1896. Perhaps it was press reports of her visit that caused Joseph Bergeron to ask Laurier during question period whether the government was going to investigate Shortis' commutation, 'as promised by the Minister of Public Works [Tarte] during his campaign in Beauharnois.' 'This subject,' Laurier tersely replied, 'is now engaging the attention of the government.'[22] However, no investigation was subsequently made.

With special permission, she saw her son for three hours in the guards' room shortly after her arrival and was shocked at his condition: 'he is like a skeleton,' she wrote to Lady Aberdeen. In contrast, the warden, Télésphore Ouimet, an older brother of the former cabinet minister, Joseph Ouimet – who had been appointed a Quebec judge in the spring after he was excluded from Tupper's cabinet – told the press that Shortis was in perfect health and working as usual. It is likely his condition was a result of his medical problems in the spring. His mental condition appeared to be deteriorating, even in the eyes of his mother. 'I know to my great sorrow,' she wrote Lady Aberdeen, 'how unfit my poor boy is to be free from control; he has brought misery on too many and if I were offered to take him in my own charge today, much as I love him I would not dare to do so for he does not know right from wrong now.'

In the spring, Mrs Shortis had written to thank Lady Aberdeen and mentioned her planned trip to Canada: 'I wish I could prove my gratitude to you in some way. I hope to be able to go see our boy in the Autumn. I am sure you will allow me the pleasure of seeing you once more.' Lady Aberdeen informed her on her arrival in Montreal, however, that under the circumstances they could have no contact with each other, and even this reply should be destroyed. 'I destroyed your dear letter now although I'd love to keep it,' Mrs Shortis wrote: 'I only kept your signature. I intended writing to ask you if I might go up to Ottawa to see you once more, but I see now since I read your letter how injudicious it would have been.'

It is quite possible that Mary Shortis was unaware of her son's condition until she arrived in Canada. The royal commission investigating conditions in St Vincent de Paul the following year found hundreds of letters in the warden's office, unopened and undelivered; there was also evidence of hundreds of letters that had been burned. Many petitions to the governor-general and the minister of justice were never delivered.

The commission, set up by the new Liberal administration (a similar commission was established for Kingston Penitentiary), found gross mismanagement, blatant patronage, and corruption, and recommended that Warden Ouimet be fired and others removed from office.[23] The guards, with the warden's knowledge, sold tobacco, food, and liquor to the prisoners and allowed convicts to cook their own food outside the kitchen. There was political patronage: 'Much of the time of the officers of this prison has been devoted to advancing the interests of those political friends through whom they received their appointment.'

Warden Ouimet came in for exceptionally harsh treatment. One of twenty-one children and unable to read or write, he entered the prison in 1870 to work as a farmer when it was still a provincial reformatory. Although the report does not directly say so, it was clearly his politician brother, the youngest in the large family, who had advanced his career: 'There were strong influences behind him by which he attained to positions in the institution he had not the qualifications to fill.' The report documents how as deputy warden he had played a secret role in fomenting the prisoners' revolt in 1886 – the most serious prison riot in Canada in the late nineteenth century – in order to have the warden fired so he could replace him, which of course he did. There were many instances of corruption: Ouimet would routinely treat penitentiary property as his own; he would take coal from the prison without paying for it; he sold some of Judge Joseph Ouimet's broken-down horses to the penitentiary for exorbitant sums; he ordered unnecessary, expensive carriages, including harnesses with the warden's silver monogram, designed to match those of the lieutenant-governor; and he used prison labour at virtually no cost to construct and maintain Judge Ouimet's yacht. Warden Ouimet was of course removed from office; it is surprising that no attempt was made to dismiss Judge Ouimet as well.

There is some suggestion in Mrs Shortis' correspondence that Shortis, through his mother, was able to take advantage of this laxness. Her willingness to bribe public officials before the commutation and Warden Ouimet's obvious willingness to be corrupted certainly hint at the likelihood of special favours. On the other hand, he was not willing to bend the penitentiary rules by allowing Mrs Shortis to see her son again after the initial visit, which suggests there was no special relationship between them. Permission for daily visits was finally given by the Department of Justice after Greenshields sent a telegram to the minister of justice, Oliver Mowat, towards the end of the second week of her fortnight visit to Canada: 'Can you grant request asked by Mrs. Shortis limited to Saturday next for daily interview. She sails then for home.'

Visiting regulations were in theory strict. Only one visit was permitted every month and it had to be by a relative.[24] Even if Millie Anderson had wished to visit Shortis, the penitentiary regulations would have prevented it.

Mary Shortis returned to Canada again in the summer of 1897. This time she arranged for Greenshields to seek permission in advance for more frequent visits. He wrote to his friend and former co-counsel in the Riel case, Charles Fitzpatrick, now the solicitor-general: 'Last time she came out she was for a long time, owing to the red-tape-ism at Ottawa, unable to see Shortis, and it was only just as she was leaving again to go home that she received permission to visit him.' Greenshields requested daily visits, adding 'I wish you would do this for me if possible.' Fitzpatrick asked E.L. Newcombe, the deputy minister of justice, 'to meet Greenshields' wishes as far as you can.' Newcombe, in turn, authorized the acting warden – Warden Ouimet had at this point been suspended pending the outcome of the inquiry – to depart from the prison rules, if Mrs Shortis did not remain in Canada very long. 'There is generally great objection to allowing a convict to receive frequent visits,' Newcombe wrote Greenshields, 'as the practice is subversive to discipline and creates a troublesome precedent.'

Greenshields had been retained by Warden Ouimet to defend him against the various allegations of corruption and the commission of inquiry met throughout the summer at the convent of the Sisters of Providence in the town of St Vincent de Paul, the same place Mrs Shortis was staying. No doubt Greenshields had contact with her during her two-week visit, but there is no record of this.

There is a record, however, of a meeting between Mrs Shortis and Prime Minister Laurier,[25] perhaps suggested by Greenshields; Lady Laurier had arranged an interview with her husband after Mary Shortis had called on her at the Windsor Hotel in Montreal. What was discussed is not known. Possibly, Mrs Shortis requested that consideration be given to transferring her son to an asylum in Montreal. Dr Villeneuve, the medical director of the Longue Pointe asylum, examined Shortis at St Vincent de Paul during this period; however, because the file is no longer in existence it is difficult to fill in any details as to why the examination took place.

Later that fall the Montreal *Gazette* reported that Shortis was going to be returned to Ireland. Senator David Mills, the minister of justice (Mowat had become the lieutenant-governor of Ontario), was asked by the press if the rumour was true. If Shortis goes any place, he replied, it will be Kingston Penitentiary. The *Progrès de Valleyfield* told its readers that if Shortis started for Ireland he would be charged with the murder of Maxime Leboeuf.

The following spring of 1898, Mrs Shortis again returned to Canada, having first written to Laurier: 'excuse me if I ask you to give orders to whoever it is who can permit me to see my poor afflicted boy every day during the short visit I intend to make to Canada.' 'I see no reason why your demand should not be granted,' Laurier replied; 'When you arrive in Canada, please let me have your address, and your request, and I will endeavour to meet your wishes.'

She had also written to Douglas Stewart, the inspector of penitentiaries, whom she had met the previous year, and referred to the newly erected 'iron grating' she heard had been installed in the visitors' area: 'I implore you to have pity on me and allow me to meet my boy when I go see him shortly without having this barricade between us; it would break my heart not to be able to touch my child that I so tenderly reared and love so deeply.' She then added, gratuitously, 'I met Sir W.

Laurier the last time I was in Canada. He was so nice and kind to me.'

Stewart, who had been appointed in 1895, having formerly been Sir John Thompson's private secretary, gave the minister's permission for her to meet her son in the keeper's hall, but restricted the visits to one hour a day. The one-hour visiting limit was now to be strictly enforced for all inmates. Stewart instructed St Vincent de Paul's new warden that he should get her 'positive assurance' that she would not give her son anything. This was in line with a policy that tried to control contraband in the prison; a serious attempt was being made to eliminate the laxness of the Ouimet administration. It was also consistent with a serious attempt to centralize further the administration of penitentiaries in the late 1890s. Stewart would issue central directions on many subjects such as one limiting the expenditure each year on Christmas extras to twenty cents per convict. [26] He justified daily visits – a departure from the stated visiting rules – by reminding the warden of Shortis' good conduct and noting that 'it is quite possible that the advice of his mother has been beneficial in preventing him from giving trouble in the prison.' But he added: 'The fact of a special privilege being granted to her is liable to excite jealousies on the part of other convicts, and if she should in any way abuse the privilege you will be fully justified in refusing her further admission.'

Mrs Shortis wrote to Laurier shortly after her arrival in Canada, asking him to intervene. In the past, she said, 'I was allowed to spend part of the morning and all the afternoon with him, now I am only permitted to spend one hour a day with him. It is so dreary for me to sit in the Convent all the long day alone and be unable to be with my boy.' She noted that conditions in the prison had now become harsher for inmates: 'the time has been shortened for the visits paid to them' and 'things they used to be able to obtain from their friends were stopped,' which suggests, as mentioned earlier, that Shortis had been able to take advantage of the former laxness.

Laurier replied that he had 'called the attention of the Minister of Justice to your demand, and he has promised to give the matter his consideration and to do everything that can be done.' 'I take a deep interest in the sad misfortune which has befallen you,' Laurier wrote, 'but I can do very little other than to offer you my sympathy.'

David Mills, the minister of justice, was unwilling to extend the privilege. The department knew that the institution was a powder-keg, following the firing of many staff members and a tightening of the rules. The new warden, J.A. Duchesneau, took over the very month Mrs Shortis arrived and reported the 'lamentable feeling of acrimony and uneasiness among the officers of the institution, and also a dangerous and undefinable irritation among the convicts.' Inspector Stewart advised Mills that 'the privilege already granted is one which I have never known to be extended in any other case; and were it not that Mrs. Shortis has journeyed such a long distance to see her son and the conduct of the convict is generally satisfactory there would be no justification for the suspension of the rules in this case.' Mills in turn wrote Laurier: 'The privilege already granted Mrs. Shortis is unusual, and I feel very certain that the extension of the period of the interviews would have an injurious effect upon the discipline of the Institution, more especially as Shortis was convicted of so atrocious a crime.'

Mrs Shortis thanked Laurier for his unsuccessful intervention and asked him for his photograph, which she wanted to put with her pictures of Lord and Lady Aberdeen: 'if you would write your name on one of your photos and send it to me you would confer great pleasure to me.' Laurier did so and she again thanked him in a note from on board ship in early June: 'You have been very good to me, and I shall pray that every good gift shall be given to you.'

In May 1898, while Mrs Shortis was at St Vincent de Paul, Thomas Nulty, like Shortis an English-speaking Catholic who had pleaded insanity, was hanged by Radclive in Joliette, Quebec.[27] This was the first conviction of murder in Quebec since the Shortis case and the first person to be hanged in the province since 1890. Nulty had killed his brother and three sisters, but was supported throughout by his grieving parents. It almost appears as if his death was meant to re-establish a balance in Quebec society after the hanging of Riel and the commutation of Shortis. It must have had a powerful impact on the prisoners in St Vincent de Paul and it is not at all surprising that the warden later reported, as mentioned, that during this period there was 'a dangerous and undefinable irritation among the convicts.' What effect the hanging had on Shortis and his mother is not known.

Senator David Mills, the minister of justice at the time, took a hardline approach to the issue of commutation.[28] In another case in Quebec later the same year, for example, the accused was hanged, even though the jury had recommended mercy and had signed a petition for commutation. In the three-year period between 1898 and 1900, twenty-three persons in Canada were hanged, about two-thirds of the capital cases considered by the cabinet.

By contrast, Senator Oliver Mowat, Laurier's first minister of justice, had taken a somewhat more merciful approach during his sixteen months in office, before he resigned to become the lieutenant-governor of Ontario, recommending a commutation in half the cases he dealt with. His attitude to the insanity issue was far different from Sir Charles Hibbert Tupper's in the Chatelle and Shortis cases and from Sir John Thompson's in Riel's.[29]

The seventy-six-year-old Mowat, one of the Fathers of Confederation, had served as the premier of Ontario for twenty-four years before becoming the minister of justice. His public career spanned much of the nineteenth century. He knew and respected Daniel Clark, C.K. Clarke, and R.M. Bucke, the heads of the Toronto, Kingston, and London asylums, and, indeed, his administration had appointed them to their posts. He took pride in the fact that Ontario had a world-wide reputation in the field of mental health.

In the first case involving insanity to come before him, John Kearney, aged sixteen and nicknamed 'Jessie James,' was convicted of murder in Lindsay, Ontario, and was sentenced to be hanged in October 1896. Both Daniel Clark and C.K. Clarke had given evidence for the defence, similar to that they had given in the Shortis case, declaring that Kearney was a 'congenital imbecile' and did not know he was doing wrong in a moral sense. Augustus Power's memorandum to Mowat belittled their evidence: 'It is probably scarcely necessary to point out that both Doctors D. Clark and C.K. Clarke belong to the school of medical experts who consider the test of insanity and imbecility a moral rather than a mental one. It is, perhaps, a not unfair inference that their extreme opinions as to the prisoner's responsibility are due to their dissatisfaction with the legal test which they consider too severe. This was virtually admitted by Doctor C.K. Clarke in the Shortis case.'

Mowat was not satisfied. He wanted Newcombe, the deputy minister, to study the case and prepare a memorandum on the question that had been discussed by the cabinet in both the Riel and Shortis cases: 'Where the intellect is not low enough to justify a verdict of "not guilty," may it be sufficient to justify, or call for, the commutation of the death sentence? and if so, is the intellect of this man low enough to have this effect in the present case?' Newcombe did not favour a commutation: 'without denying that there may be cases of deficiency of intellect not justifying acquittal but properly appealing to the clemency of the Crown, I would consider the present case so far on the intellectual side of the boundary line as to exclude doubt with regard to the execution of the sentence.'

Again, Mowat was not satisfied. He sought the opinion of the Lindsay jail surgeon and the local county court judge who referred to the condemned as 'a morally crippled child.' Mowat's mind was finally made up to commute the sentence when he received an unsolicited letter from C.K. Clarke urging commutation, saying that he and Daniel Clark had been asked by the attorney-general of Ontario before the trial to examine the boy and each had independently come to the conclusion that 'the boy was an intellectual and moral imbecile and not a responsible being.' The same day the letter arrived, Mowat went to the cabinet and recommended that the sentence be commuted to life imprisonment in Kingston Penitentiary. Three years later Kearney died of tuberculosis in the penitentiary, just before his parents arrived to take him home to die.

There were two further murder cases in which Mowat took the same sympathetic approach. In the case of *Hansen*, he commuted the sentence after asking Daniel Clark to examine the man, the first time Clark had done so for the Department of Justice. In that of *Brennan*, later that year, Clark had given evidence for the defence of delusional insanity (that the accused's wife had been unfaithful), but the defendant was convicted. A letter from Montreal asking for mercy was obviously referring to Shortis: 'Think of the murderers more red-handed than Michael Brennan, who of late have escaped the gallows.' Mowat again recommended commutation.

The treatment of this issue by later ministers of justice has not been examined, but the McRuer report on insanity in 1956 clearly showed that the careful approach Mowat took was established practice in Ottawa in the period before capital punishment was abolished in Canada.[30]

Shortis remained in St Vincent de Paul for almost ten years. On 13 December 1905 he was transferred to the insane ward of Kingston Penitentiary. The press reported that he sang a 'favourite refrain' all the way from the train station to the penitentiary.

His life in St Vincent de Paul is almost a closed book. We know that his mother continued to visit him every year: his father, though, never did. Much of the rest is pure speculation. What was his reaction when Queen Victoria celebrated her Diamond Jubilee in 1897? When the persons who saved his life, the Aberdeens, left Canada in 1898? when the Boer War started in 1899? When the twentieth century arrived (and Laurier said that the twentieth century belonged to Canada)? When a prison break occurred in St Vincent de Paul in 1900? And when Queen Victoria died and Edward VII, the former high-living Prince of Wales, became King, resulting in the coronation clemency of a number of convicts from St Vincent de Paul, including John Hooper, with whom Shortis had worked for a time when he first arrived at the penitentiary?

In Valleyfield, the Shortis case continued to be discussed at every opportunity. When a French Canadian, David Dubé, was hanged in Quebec City in 1900, comparisons were inevitably made. Bergeron protested the execution – 'crocodile tears,' said the anti-Bergeron *Progrès de Valleyfield*; another recently established Valleyfield paper called for further prosecution of Shortis for the murder of Leboeuf.

In the 1900 election in Beauharnois, the Shortis affair played only a minor role. The *Progrès de Valleyfield* told its readers that Shortis was now comfortably housed in St Vincent de Paul, waiting for the Conservatives to get in again to regain his liberty. The Conservatives did not get in: Laurier won in 1900 and in every election until 1911. Tarte did not run again. George Loy, the former mayor and father of one of the mill victims, was the Liberal candidate, but Bergeron won again. A by-election took place in 1902, after the earlier election was contested as irregular, and this time Loy won. A subsequent libel suit by Loy against Bergeron, arising out of the election, was heard by the new local judge, Henri St Pierre, Shortis' former counsel, who had replaced Bélanger and sat in Beauharnois until 1909, when he was transferred to the Montreal district court, on which he served until his death in 1916.

Shortis was transferred to Kingston, it seems, in part because he was showing marked signs of paranoid insanity in St Vincent de Paul and in part because his life was in fact being threatened by other convicts. If the files still existed, the background to the move would no doubt be explained. And there is little in the files in Ottawa on the matter. The Kingston file, however, contains the following brief note accompanying the transfer, from Warden Oscar Beauchamp of St Vincent de Paul to Warden J.M. Platt of Kingston: 'Convict Shortis, the conduct of this convict has always been good. In different occasions he give signs of insanity, saying that some one attempt to his life on poisoning him.' [*sic*] Shortis later said that people were trying to poison him with prussic acid and by means of the steel laths of his bed.

In fact, people were trying to kill Shortis. He had been violently attacked at least twice by other inmates, he later told a psychiatrist, and he had the scars to back up his story. A convict by the name of Troy, who a few years earlier had had his capital sentence commuted to life imprisonment, had stabbed him a number of times in the cheek, abdomen, and back with a stiletto hammered out of an iron bar. Further, a man appropriately named Slaughter had tried to cut his throat. Shortis later described the incident to an examining psychiatrist, who noted on his file: 'Patient has another scar on the front of his neck, which was caused by a negro, named Slaughter, trying to cut his throat. He claims that Chartrand told this man that Shortis could hypnotize people, and Chartrand blamed Shortis for hypnotizing him and putting 2 frogs in his stomach. Shortis says that Chartrand used to go hopping around on his hands and feet to shake the frogs out of him. Chartrand told Slaughter that he would kill Shortis, if the latter did not do so first. Consequently, Slaughter slipped up behind Shortis, and cut him with a knife.'

The story is probably true. There were many insane convicts kept in St Vincent de Paul who should have been transferred to Kingston. But the insane ward there was overcrowded in the 1890s and early 1900s. The warden of St Vincent de Paul had complained in his 1898 annual report, for example, that during the tense months following the hanging of Nulty he wanted to transfer two troublesome insane inmates to Kingston, but there was no room for them. Built to accommodate twenty-eight persons, there were thirty-four in the Kingston ward in 1898 and forty-four in 1899. Further construction in 1905 permitted a greater number to be transferred, which may help explain why Shortis was sent that year. But Kingston was still not equipped to handle all of the insane because in 1906 the physician at St Vincent de Paul complained that the prison was still being forced to keep insane persons in the small punishment cells. Whether Greenshields or the new minister of justice, Charles Fitzpatrick, had anything to do with Shortis' move is not known. There is nothing in the existing files to indicate this was anything but a routine move because Shortis' presence at St Vincent de Paul was creating problems.

When Achille Bergevin, the provincial member who was born and had grown up in Valleyfield, heard about the move to Kingston as well as rumours in the press that Shortis might be released to Ireland, he wrote immediately to Charles Fitzpatrick:

> I beg to draw your attention to the fact that if Shortis gets out of penitentiary he would certainly be arrested again, for a trial on his second murder, that of Maxime Leboeuf.
>
> I hope that the statement made in the papers is only a false report, because

I would think it my duty to take action against the most dreadful murderer on record in the Province of Quebec, so as to have society sufficiently protected.

The minister of justice replied: 'I do not think you will be put to the inconvenience of taking proceedings against Shortis who has been removed to the Kingston Penitentiary for reasons best known to this Department.'

Kingston Penitentiary

15

On Portsmouth Bay

INGSTON PENITENTIARY, with its massive limestone walls, is located on Lake Ontario, on Portsmouth Bay just west of the city of Kingston. The site was chosen in part because there was good access by water and it was well protected by the army stationed nearby; but it was also chosen because, as an early report stated, 'the inexhaustible quarries of stone, which exist in every direction within the township of Kingston, will afford convicts that description of employment which has been found by actual experiment to be the most useful in Institutions such as your Committee recommend.' This was written in 1831.[1] When Valentine Shortis arrived in Kingston, breaking rocks was still the major activity, even though in 1905 there was no demand for the product. There were, however, few alternative activities. In 1915 the inspector of penitentiaries observed in his annual report: 'So far as Canadian Penitentiaries are concerned, the lack of suitable prison industries has been and still is the greatest handicap to successful management.'

Apart from a greater concentration on breaking rocks, the life of the general prison population did not differ substantially from that in St Vincent de Paul. For Shortis, however, life changed dramatically.

The three-storey stone and ironwork insane ward had been constructed in 1881 in the southwest grounds, within the high walls of the penitentiary. Built initially for twenty-eight persons, it had a dayroom on the third floor, cells that were two and a half feet wide on part of the two floors beneath, and a two-storey grist mill taking up the rest of the space. At first there was high praise for the building, 'lightsome, thoroughly ventilated, and solidly built,' said one government official; after the English psychiatrist Hack Tuke reported in 1884, however, that 'for criminals of the worst class this building is admirably suited, but it is astonishing that it should have been constructed for lunatics in recent times,' the institution was almost universally condemned.[2]

One major problem was the constant noise and vibration of the grist mill in the same building, 'eminently calculated to intensify their misery,' said James Moylan, the inspector of penitentiaries. Unlike the Ontario lunatic asylums, there were no open grounds. 'Stone walls in any direction they may look, unless they look upward to the sky,' complained the warden in 1900.[3]

Why was such an institution built? The construction of the insane ward in 1881 had been simply the latest solution to the problem of what to do with the criminally insane. When the penitentiary was first built the insane were held there, but later they were sent to the provincial lunatic asylum in Toronto. By the middle of the century, however, the asylum was reluctant to accept them any longer and once again they were housed in Kingston – in the basement of the dining hall. In 1856 land was purchased near the penitentiary and in 1865 Rockwood, today known as the Kingston Psychiatric Hospital, was officially opened for the criminally insane.[4] All the insane inmates were now in one place. Like the penitentiaries, Rockwood became a Dominion institution at Confederation. The solution did not last long, however, as the asylum began to be used for the non-criminally insane as well; the head of Rockwood, who was also the dean of medicine at Queen's University, declared in 1872 that 'it is, I think, the universal opinion of all persons having anything to do with the management of lunatic asylums, that the criminal and non-criminal classes ... should never be permitted to commingle, as one vicious criminal lunatic is sufficient to contaminate a whole ward full ... The criminal class of lunatics should never be permitted to go beyond the walls of the Penitentiary and they should be kept securely under locks and bars, so that their efforts to escape would be thoroughly guarded against.'[5] After many years of negotiation, Rockwood was sold to the province in 1877 and twenty-one insane convicts were taken the short distance back to Kingston Penitentiary and lodged in the lower ward of the prison hospital. Four years later, the insane ward in Kingston Penitentiary was completed and henceforth the very serious cases from across the country were sent there.

By 1886, Moylan, the inspector of penitentiaries, wanted the ward replaced, and he would continue to ask for this until his retirement in 1895. At one point it seemed certain that a new ward would be built. Sir John Thompson, the minister of justice, had money appropriated for the purpose in 1892 and the following year work was started on the project and then abandoned; apparently, the necessary prison labour was needed to construct the new 'prison of isolation.' Nothing further was done, however, even though, to use the words of a report to the Prisoners' Aid Society at the turn of the century, it was 'criminally insane' to keep the criminally insane in such conditions.[6] Some improvements were made, though: flush toilets were installed in the dayroom around 1900, and it appears that the grist mill was removed. But, basically, life in the insane ward in 1905 was not substantially different from what it had been in the earlier decades.

As late as 1913 the assistant superintendent of the nearby Rockwood asylum could describe the routine in the insane ward in Kingston as follows: 'Each patient is locked in his cell, without proper sanitary conveniences, from 4 p.m. to 7 a.m.; the door of each cell is simply a grating, and there is no provision for the isolation and care of noisy and filthy patients. There is no provision for the proper classification of patients, all of whom are gathered together in a large day room, the acute with the chronic, the old and helpless with the impulsive and violent, the lucid with the demented.'[7]

No psychiatric treatment was given. The Kingston warden conceded this in 1908: 'The medical superintendent, who is prison surgeon, makes a hurried call once a day, this constituting the whole care and treatment of the criminal insane.'[8] The prison surgeon, Dr Daniel Phelan, it should be noted, did not share these critical views, stating in one report that 'this hospital for insane criminals is a necessary adjunct to the prison' and in another that 'never have we been better equipped to care for them.'

Phelan's view was not accepted by the royal commission that investigated the penitentiary in 1913: 'Your Commissioners unreservedly condemn the provision made for the care and treatment of the insane at this institution, the only one in the country which is supposed to be specially equipped for such a class.' The insane ward 'is defective in structural arrangement, lacking in nursing and medical facilities and devoid of any means of providing occupation.' Moreover, they condemned the unofficial disciplinary techniques used in the ward, which included what was referred to as 'tubbing,' that is, holding a person in a bath of cold water and sometimes keeping his head under until he started to take in water. 'Many an unfortunate,' the commissioners said, 'must have been deprived of a fair chance of recovery by reason of the State's unpardonable neglect.'[9]

Another solution had to be found, and many were advanced. Dr

T.J.W. Burgess, for example, the head of the Verdun hospital in Montreal, argued in 1905 for a Dominion asylum, as promised by the government over ten years earlier. Dr W.M. English, the medical superintendent of the Hamilton asylum, wanted a federal institution in northern Ontario. C.K. Clarke, on the other hand, sought 'a small building, under the management of one of the Provincial Asylums' that could take convicts who were insane, as well as the insane then in regular provincial institutions who could not be tried or had been found not guilty by reason of insanity. J.P. Downey, one of the 1914 royal commissioners, hoped to use the newly constructed Whitby asylum, which would permit study by the medical school at the University of Toronto. [10]

Mrs Shortis was unaware of the move to Kingston until after it had taken place. She then wrote twice to the warden asking for permission to visit her son, who she had heard was in an asylum near Kingston, but got no reply. Once again she turned to Wilfrid Laurier: 'You were so kind to me the day I met you, you said if ever you could help at any time you'd do so ... It would be a terrible disappointment if I went to Portsmouth and could not see my only son, the only one who is alive of my children.' She told Laurier that she had visited Lord and Lady Aberdeen; he had recently returned to Ireland as lord lieutenant of Ireland under Campbell-Bannerman's new Liberal administration: 'I have your photo which you kindly sent me between my best friends Lord and Lady Aberdeens'. I went to see them not long ago since we are all or nearly all in Ireland. I'm glad to have Liberals once again in office in our Country. I heard it was Lord Aberdeen's casting vote the 31st of December which saved our poor mad son's life and caused the Liberals to get the ruling power in Canada.' The last speculation no doubt came from the Aberdeens.

The justice officials informed Laurier that 'there will be no difficulty in her being granted the privilege of visiting her son for half an hour every day for say 10 days.' They pointed out, though, that 'Young Shortis is developing insanity very rapidly, although his mother knows nothing about it.' Laurier did not mention the illness in his reply on 9 May 1906:

I have the honour to acknowledge the receipt of your favour. Your unfortunate son has been transferred to Kingston. As soon as you reach Ottawa, you will have to make application to the Minister of Justice to be allowed to see him and I can assure you that he will make it his duty to give you every opportunity to see him and to allow you the privilege of the extreme limit authorized by the by-laws in force.

With the sincere expression of my deepest sympathy,

Believe me, dear Mrs. Shortis,

Yours very sincerely,
Wilfrid Laurier

We do not know Mrs Shortis' reaction to her son's condition when she visited him.

The following year C.K. Clarke, who had left Rockwood just before Shortis arrived in Kingston and had become the superintendent of the Toronto asylum, held a half-hour interview with the prisoner. His notes show, not surprisingly, that his earlier judgment was confirmed: 'Today went through the insane ward of the Penitentiary with Dr. Phelan and while there saw Valentine Shortis ... Whatever impressions may have existed in some minds regarding his mental disease at the time of the trial, there can no longer be any doubt on the part of the most skeptical.'[11] There was now a proper label for his condition. 'The evidence in the Shortis case today, if published in full,' said Clarke, 'would rank as *the* classical description of paranoid dementia praecox.' Shortis was now clearly paranoid, believing that he was 'the victim of all sorts of machinations by unseen enemies. His food is poisoned every day and he persistently refuses everything brought to him; after the other criminals have finished their meals, he selects carefully what he wants from what is left. He cannot sleep on his bed because it is loaded with poison. He has found poisoned slivers and needles placed there, and his whole life is taken up fighting his persecutors.' His delusions, Clarke concluded, made him dangerous: 'Dr. Phelan informed me that Shortis becomes extremely violent when interfered with, and as the result of his delusions had a very lively scene with a dentist a few days ago ... Shortis would be a very dangerous man if left to his own devices, and at times has shown extreme violence.' Shortis told him, as he had many years earlier, that the first shot was 'a pure accident' and 'as soon as that shot was fired the thought struck him, now Simpson has me in his power and will persecute me to the bitter end and I will shoot right and left.' 'His animus against Simpson,' Clarke wrote, 'is as great as ever.'

Shortis had 'become stout, bald, and ... now resembles his father very much in appearance.' He asked Clarke 'to write at once to his mother as certain important letters he had written had been quietly suppressed for reasons he perfectly understood.'

That summer Clarke, along with Edward Ryan, the new superintendent of the Rockwood asylum, and another doctor, were appointed by the government of Ontario to study psychiatric facilities in Europe.[12] In addition to calls at such well-known places as Kraepelin's Munich clinic and Jung and Bleuler's Zurich asylum, two members of the commission – not Clarke, however – went to Ireland. In August 1907 they examined the district asylum at Waterford and the asylum at Clonmel. Whether they visited the Shortis home in Waterford is not known, although they may well have done so, if only to pay their respects to Francis Shortis. Mary Shortis had died on 2 June 1907, at the age of sixty-eight, after a three-month illness.

The local Irish papers described in detail the death and funeral of 'one of Waterford's prominent and most respected citizens.'[13] Her husband, one paper said, 'holds a premier place as a cattle exporter in this country, and his transactions must run to enormous sums.' The press noted her charitable work over the years with such groups as the Society for the Prevention of Cruelty to Children, the District and Jubilee Nurses organizations, the St Joseph's Clothing Society, the Maternity Society, and many more. 'A good and charitable lady has passed away and many a home will miss her charitable attentions.'

The bishop of Waterford presided at the service. 'Yesterday at noon the remains of the late Mrs. Shortis were removed from the Roman Catholic Cathedral, where they had been lying in state from the previous evening, for interment at the family burial ground, St. Mary's, Ballygunner. Not for a long time has there been such a large attendance of the general public, or one so representative, as on this occasion.' The newspapers contained long lists of mourners who attended. No mention was made of her only child.

She apparently left no will. This is somewhat surprising, as she was entitled to hold separate property,[14] and because of her independent nature would likely have had some. One would have thought, too, that she would have wanted to have made some provision for her son. Her death was not sudden and she had ample opportunity to prepare a will. If she did not have one, all her property would, under Irish law at the time, automatically go to her husband.[15] Shortis later believed that his mother's estate was somehow improperly kept from him.

Francis Shortis wrote his son later that month, telling him the sad news, the first letter, he claimed, he had ever received from his father. The news must have added depression to Shortis' paranoia. 'Ever since I received the news that broke my heart,' he would later write, 'life seemed not worth living without her.'

Very little is known about Shortis over the next four years, except that he remained in the insane ward in a continuing state of paranoia. His father visited him for the first time since 1896 in February 1908 and they corresponded several times a year, though none of the letters has been preserved. Mr Shortis remarried about 1910, but his son was apparently not told of this until much later. Shortis' uncle, his father's brother, a Catholic priest in New York, visited him in the summer of 1912, but Shortis refused to see him in the visitor's cage, convinced it was a trap. He later told a penitentiary inspector in a detailed four-page letter: 'Mother had good reason to warn me: those windows in the cage are charged with death *or worse* for me. I recollect after coming back they glowed with a ghastly flicker. God knows how the trap is set; all I know is uncle was the bait, you the unwilling, innocent, unknowing cats paw that would have sprung it. Probably if you will have them examined you'll find they're insulated from the earth and capable of being charged by wireless.'

That same summer Warden Platt, who had been at Kingston since Shortis arrived, retired. Under the new warden, the regulations with respect to mail were more vigorously enforced, and Shortis wrote to his father that it would be no use sending picture magazines any longer and that he would not be permitted to write for some time. The most recently enacted regulations did, in fact, prohibit the receiving of magazines and permitted only one letter to be sent every two months,[16] but to this point they had not been enforced against Shortis and others. A disturbance at the British Columbia Penitentiary apparently led to the new toughness.

Once again, Lady Aberdeen entered the story. Since 1906 her husband had been lord lieutenant in Ireland (a position he had occupied earlier in 1886) and he would remain in that position until after the Home Rule Bill was passed in 1914. In 1912 Francis Shortis called on Lady Aberdeen and told her of his concern for his son's welfare. She, in turn, wrote to William Lyon Mackenzie King, with whom she had developed a close relationship[17] over the years. They had first met in 1894 when, a University of Toronto student, he had acted as footman on the vice-regal visit to the campus. A friendship was later established and was renewed on King's periodic visits to England. Each used the other for confidential missions. During this period, for example, Lady Aberdeen undertook what she circumspectly described in one letter marked 'private and confidential' as 'the delicate mission you entrusted to me,' a mission that is never explained but was probably connected with his search for a wife which he had undertaken in earnest at the time. 'I know that if I can find the right one to share my life with, and can be freed from dependence on others,' he confided to his diary, 'I can be the Leader of the Liberal Party and ultimately Premier of Canada ...' [18]

On 14 November 1912, Lady Aberdeen sent a long letter in which she remarked: 'You are probably too young to remember the excitement over the trial of Valentine Shortis. I think it was about the year 1895.' In fact, King was completing his law degree in 1895-6, while working as a cub reporter for the Toronto *Globe*, and no doubt had heard of the case. He surely would have been reminded of it in 1900 when, as deputy minister of labour, he was in Valleyfield settling the strike at the Montreal Cotton Company. Elected to Parliament in 1908, he was minister of labour in Laurier's government from 1909 to 1911, losing his seat when the Conservatives again formed the government. At the time of Lady Aberdeen's letter, he was head of the Liberal Information Office and editor of the *Canadian Liberal Monthly*. [19]

Lady Aberdeen outlined in detail the history of the crime, the commutation of the death sentence ('the young man's parents were exceedingly grateful, probably because of the feeling that an execution in the family would be a slur which could never be wiped out'), and subsequent events:

> The father is now very anxious about his son's position, and is most anxious to know whether under the new regulations of the new Officials, he has got into trouble.
>
> His father is also intensely anxious that some arrangement should be come to before he dies whereby his son may be transferred to an asylum. He does not wish him to be set at freedom at all, firmly believing that he is not, and can never be responsible for his actions, but he is perfectly willing to pay for him in an Asylum, and as I understand, to set apart a sum of money which will enable this arrangement to be permanent ... Could you take the preliminary steps to find out what is the opinion of the officials regarding Valentine Shortis, and ascertain how and when the subject could be approached?

His Excellency was so vehemently attacked about the matter at the time that it would doubtless be better to keep his name out of it as much as possible, but we are most anxious to give relief to the poor father, and surely the ends of justice have been served.

Mackenzie King, the consummate politician, tackled the task through both civil servants and politicians. He asked M.R. Dawson, the inspector of penitentiaries, for 'particulars as to Shortis' behaviour and the attitude of the officials towards him.' He also spoke to a Liberal politician, Sidney Fisher, who had been in Laurier's last cabinet with King and was a friend of the present minister of justice. Then he wrote to Lady Aberdeen: 'I thought it well too to speak to Hon. Mr. Fisher who I knew would be familiar with all the circumstances. He knows well both Mr. Foster who was Shortis' counsel, and Judge Doherty, the present Minister of Justice, though they are both political opponents they are personal friends of Mr. Fisher, and he has promised to try to pave the way through them for a favourable consideration of any application that may be made.' Three days later, he met Dawson and wrote to Lady Aberdeen that the coast was now clear for an application: 'Oddly enough Mr. Dawson has just returned to the City and I have this moment concluded a talk with him. He tells me that Shortis' behaviour has been all that could be desired, that the officials have only the most sympathetic feelings towards him and that there is no intention whatever to impose any additional restriction upon him. As a matter of fact, he has been appointed a sort of orderly and appears to enjoy the authority given him in this connection. From the way Inspector Dawson speaks, I should judge that they have all found Shortis a good natured and satisfactory inmate ... He says there is no doubt about Shortis being partially out of his mind though he thinks that at the present time he is quite happy and contented.'

'The regular asylums of the Province have steadfastly refused to accept convicts,' said King, 'and Mr. Dawson says that he does not know of any case in Ontario where a convict has been transferred to other than the asylum ward of the Kingston Penitentiary.' The western provinces had made arrangements for the transfer to provincial asylums of federal prisoners, but not Ontario.[20] None the less, Dawson told King, the minister of justice might be able either to make some special arrangement with one of the Ontario asylums or have Shortis transferred to an asylum in another province. 'In view of what Mr. Dawson has said,' King advised, 'I do not see that any good purpose would be served by delaying an immediate application to the present Minister of Justice for a consideration of Shortis' case with a view to his transfer to an asylum.'

Lady Aberdeen did not receive King's letters before setting out on a quick trip to the United States. She also came briefly to Ottawa and saw King there, but oddly neither remembered to mention the Shortis case before King left on a family visit to Berlin (now Kitchener), Ontario. 'It was on the tip of my tongue to speak of Shortis several times,' King later wrote after he had received a telegram from her in Berlin specifically about Shortis. That she would send a special telegram to him suggests the importance of the matter to her, but the fact that they forgot to speak of it when they were together in Ottawa implies that their more personal intrigues, whatever they were, were foremost in their minds. King summarized what was in the letters waiting for her in Dublin, adding that Foster had spoken to Doherty, and concluding: 'I think it would be well for your Excellency to write, the way has been prepared and it is through Judge Doherty that the next step will have to be taken. He is a humane man, and his Inspector will further anything which may be referred to him.'

Lady Aberdeen wrote to the minister of justice, as King had suggested. Judge Charles Doherty, of course, knew about Shortis, for he had been a Queen's Bench judge in Montreal when he was tried and would certainly have followed the case carefully. Moreover, like Shortis, he was an Irish Catholic (both had gone to schools run by the Christian Brothers) and would therefore have had a special interest. A son of a judge and a gold medallist in law in 1876 from McGill (as was Greenshields the following year and Macmaster several years earlier), he later became a part-time professor of civil and international law at McGill.[21] At the time of the 1885 Riel Rebellion, he had been a captain in the 65th Regiment. In 1891 he replaced his father on the bench, resigning from the position in 1906. Judge Doherty, as he continued to be called, then entered Parliament in 1908 and became minister of justice in Robert Borden's cabinet when the Conservatives came to power in the 1911 election.

The election, it should be noted as an aside, brought Donald Macmaster and J.N. Greenshields together on the same political side. It was fought largely on the issue of reciprocity and the danger of American domination of Canada. Macmaster, who had gone to England in 1905 to concentrate his legal business on appeals to the Privy Council and was subsequently elected to the British House of Commons, returned to Canada to campaign for the Conservatives. Greenshields, who had slowly moved from law to business and finance, had now seen the light and the value of a high tariff wall and also supported the Conservatives. Reciprocity with the United States, said Macmaster, would mean 'the certain absorption of Canada by the United States' and 'the great betrayal of England.'[22] He was to die in England in 1922, extinguishing the baronetcy given him the previous year, his only son having died in the First World War. Like Macmaster and many of his generation, including Sir Charles Hibbert Tupper whose youngest son, Gordon, was killed at Vimy Ridge, Greenshields also lost a son in the war. Greenshields became seriously ill shortly after the war ended and retired from active legal business, but he did not die until 1937 at the age of eighty-five.

Judge Doherty asked for a report on Shortis and Dr Phelan replied: 'I desire to inform you that he is insane, and a very dangerous man.' As King later reported to Lady Aberdeen, the minister of justice 'was anxious to do something, but was afraid to make a move ... being an Irish Catholic himself, he was a little afraid of the race question being raised in consequence of any action he might take.' Doherty decided to visit Shortis and see for himself, and King reported the results to Lady Aberdeen; the visit had a profound effect on the minister of justice and influenced the future development of the treatment of insane convicts in Canada:

> Judge Doherty then told me that he had seen Shortis himself, had gone to the Prison and come away feeling satisfied that Shortis was insane ... Judge Doherty felt as a consequence of this visit, that some different provision should be made for insane criminals; he did not think it right as respects the insane prisoners nor fair to the prison authorities, that they should be kept there. This led him to say that he would confidentially direct the attention of the commission he has appointed to inquire into the conditions at the penitentiary to this subject, and possibly they would bring in recommendations in their report which would enable him to find a way of taking some action which would affect all alike, and be the means of securing Shortis' transfer to an asylum. I feel quite sure Judge Doherty would like to be the author of some such reform. I tried to impress upon him that it was a humane and desirable thing, and if effected apart from any individual would be pretty certain of meeting with popular approval.

Investigation of the insane ward was now part of the task of the royal commission on penitentiaries appointed in the summer of 1913,[23] and the assistant superintendent of the Rockwood Hospital for the Insane was asked to make a special report. Whether the subject would have been studied as carefully as it was if Doherty had not intervened is doubtful; in their report the commissioners naturally said nothing about Doherty's intervention, stating simply that in the course of their inquiry it became clear that 'a thorough investigation was needed.' The incident perhaps tells us something about the workings of royal commissions.

On 6 December 1913 Shortis testified before the commission.[24] He had very little to say, however, and one wonders why he was called, except perhaps to satisfy the curiosity of the commissioners. His entire evidence, which seems quite rational, is as follows:

VALENTINE F.C. SHORTIS, Sworn –
BY THE CHAIRMAN [G.M. Macdonnell, KC, of Kingston]
Q. Have you handled any money in the prison since you came here? A. No.
Q. None whatever? A. No.
Q. Has any been handled for you? A. No.
Q. Have you had the use of tobacco in the prison? A. None, except that which is given to me by the law, by the prison.
Q. Do you know that convicts get tobacco to a considerable extent? A. No, I never heard of it being done.
Q. Has any money been sent to any friends of yours for your use? A. Money has been sent to the office for my use and been disposed of as permitted outside.
Q. Have you used or disposed of any money except through the office? A. No. I have disposed of money outside: that is, I have told my uncle some time ago to have some masses and things said for me. I suppose that you understand. I have written home.
Q. We are not asking about that.
MR. DOWNEY. How long has he been in the insane ward?
DR. PHELAN. About eleven years [actually eight years].
MR. DOWNEY. Almost since he came here?
DR. PHELAN. Yes. He was transferred: he was very troublesome down below.

'Down below' must have been a way of referring to St Vincent de Paul. Having set the wheels in motion, Judge Doherty waited until the commission reported before taking any action.

The commissioners reported on 22 April 1914 and strongly condemned the insane ward and the treatment of its inmates. Referring to 'the

State's unpardonable neglect,' they 'unreservedly' condemned 'the provisions made for the care and treatment of the insane.' And they shared Judge Doherty's view that something must be done. Their recommendation that 'a separate institution for the criminal insane be established or that arrangements be made with the provincial government for taking over this class' received almost universal praise from prison officials, unlike most of their other recommendations. Inspector Stewart's reaction, conveyed to the deputy minister of justice, E.L. Newcombe, was typical: 'It is obvious that a penal institution is not a suitable place in which to care for men who have been deprived of reason.'[25] Stewart had held this position for years, and had said earlier that a penitentiary should not be used as a 'mad-house.' His successor, Inspector W.S. Hughes, who had been employed at Kingston before the war, later assessed the commission: 'About the only good thing ... is their report on the Insane Ward. From the day I first saw it ... it was a heartache to me.'[26]

The report strongly condemned other aspects of the penitentiary system as harsh and punitive and adopted the current rehabilitative approach: 'Undeniably, the trend of prison administration the world over is away from the purely punitive and toward the reformative.' The commissioners spoke of the 'scientific treatment of moral delinquents,' speculating that 'possibly some day there may be a prison in which each inmate will have his particular case analyzed by experts, with a view to special treatment, aiming at his readjustment.' A necessary part of the scientific rehabilitative approach was, of course, the 'indeterminate sentence' to 'cure' the accused, 'regarded by penologists as essential to the effective operation of any reformative system. It is at once a scientific and a common-sense proposal. It presupposes the necessity of the cure or reclamation of the man as well as his punishment ... Carried to its logical development the indeterminate sentence should have neither minimum or maximum limits.' This extreme version of the indeterminate sentence was not adopted into Canadian law – fortunately, as most have now come to believe. The view of the inspector of penitentiaries represented the general consensus in official and legal circles: 'At present the judge fixes a maximum and the convict himself determines the minimum by the amount of remission he may earn. I think the existing system preferable.'

Other recommendations were disliked by the prison authorities. Six of the seven penitentiary wardens criticized the notion that the close cropping of hair be eliminated because they saw it as a 'deterrent against escape and a means of identification after escape.' The proposal to elimate prison stripes was described by the inspector as 'puerile.' The wardens opposed the idea 'that hosing of convicts and confining them in a dark cell or dungeon and shackling with ball and chain be abolished'; as Stewart reported to Newcombe: 'The Wardens are unanimous in their disapproval of this recommendation as submitted, and I think they are in a better position to judge than men who are merely crying in the wilderness of inexperience. Kid glove penology, like some kinds of military boots, is too light for active service.'

This hard-line approach continued to be the philosophy of the penitentiary service until it again came under attack by the Archambault royal commission of 1938, which once again recommended the rehabilitation model.[27] On the issue of the removal of the insane ward, however, there was a clear mandate for the minister of justice to do something.

Coincidentally, another solution to Shortis' confinement in Kingston was emerging: deportation to Ireland. There had been considerable agitation for some years that too many mentally deficient persons were being admitted into Canada. The head of Montreal's Protestant Verdun asylum, where Anglin had worked, said, for example, in a 1905 address, that 'Canada is being made a "dumping ground" for the degenerates of Europe.'[28] C.K. Clarke took the same view, and raised the issue time and time again. In an article in 1904 he referred to the 'hordes of subsidized immigrants from Europe' and advocated sending them back if insanity was discovered even long after their arrival.[29] In 1907 his annual report as medical superintendent of the Toronto asylum pointed out that of the 262 people admitted in the past year, at least 77 were recent arrivals: 'the majority of these people,' he argued, 'should not have been allowed to enter Canada.'

It is not surprising, then, that an attempt was made in 1914 to have insane criminals, including Shortis, deported. The superintendent of immigration, W.D. Scott, had asked the warden at Kingston for a report of 'cases of insane prisoners of foreign birth,' and in August 1914, the very month the Great War broke out, Warden R.R. Creighton recommended that Shortis be deported.

Scott confirmed that Shortis was indeed subject to deportation. 'I beg to inform you,' he wrote the penitentiary branch in Ottawa, 'that this prisoner arrived at Quebec on the 2nd of September, 1893, and would, therefore, appear to be subject to deportation.' Before ascertaining whether the minister of justice would authorize his release, however, an investigation was made through the Canadian Immigration Office in London as to whether Francis Shortis would 'pay his son's transportation to Ireland and place him in an asylum for the insane in that country.' The immigration files were later destroyed, but enough is still to be found in the penitentiary files to make it clear that deportation to Ireland ceased to be an alternative. The assistant superintendent of immigration in London wrote to Scott in Ottawa explaining why deportation was now out of the question:

> We have made enquiry in Dublin respecting this case and found it is one in which His Excellency Lord Aberdeen, the Viceroy of Ireland, is interested. Mr. Francis Shortis, senior, is willing to pay for the transportation of his son to an Asylum at Longue Pointe, Montreal, of which apparently he has some knowledge and to pay for his keep there as long as it may be necessary to retain him as an inmate, but on no account would he authorize his return to Ireland.
>
> Lord Aberdeen has apparently expressed a desire that the request of Mr. Shortis in this particular should be met ...

The solution suggested by Francis Shortis and supported by Lord Aberdeen was pursued by Judge Doherty. He consulted the solicitor-general, Arthur Meighen (who would become prime minister in 1920), his memo concluding: 'If they will then accept him, I think he might be paroled on conditions he be admitted and kept there.' 'Yes,' Meighen noted on the memo, but then added: 'suppose though the Hospital discharges him. I presume we must rely on their undertaking to advise us of any such intention. The recommendation should be very carefully worked out.'

A report was then requested from Dr Phelan, who, in contrast to his report almost two years earlier that Shortis was 'insane, and a very dangerous man,' now declared 'he is insane, but a quiet, harmless man.' 'Shortis,' he concluded, 'is a person who can properly be looked after in an Asylum for the Insane without any danger to those who are willing to receive him and keep him in custody.' Either Shortis had changed or Phelan was giving the opinion he knew Doherty wanted to hear.

The proposal to accept Shortis was put to the Reverend Mother Superior at the Catholic Hospital for the Insane at Longue Pointe: 'Would you consent to receive this man under these conditions, the prisoner remaining under license, the primary condition of which would be that he should not leave the hospital before he is lawfully discharged from the obligations imposed by his sentence?' The sisters refused to do so, stating that the hospital was built along modern lines – it had been reopened in 1901 after a disastrous fire in 1890 in which eighty persons had died – without outside walls, to encourage the greatest possible freedom for their patients. They did not have a special place for insane criminals. Should they accept him, they would have to change their entire organization.

Shortis' fate now rested with the general question of the future of the insane ward. The Department of Justice had started negotiations in July 1914 with Ontario, Quebec, and the Maritime provinces for the reception into provincial asylums of the forty-seven inmates of the insane ward.[30] The government of Quebec quickly agreed to take the thirteen originally from Quebec into their privately run mental hospitals, if the hospitals would have them. As it turned out, the Longue Pointe asylum agreed to take most of the Quebec prisoners, but refused to take Shortis, the medical superintendent, Dr Villeneuve (who had been present but had not given evidence at the trial), stating: 'I think that Shortis should be returned to his native country. He is incurably insane.'[31]

Ontario at first refused to take even those from that province. Judge Doherty assured the provincial secretary, W.J. Hanna, that the arrangement was to be temporary until the Dominion government could establish a separate institution for all the criminally insane in Canada. Ontario was still reluctant, however, because of overcrowding in the institutions and because it was felt that it was unsound to mix the criminally insane with the general insane patients.[32] Doherty continued to press and wrote to Hanna in February 1915 of 'the very great importance' of finding a better way of dealing with the insane.[33]

A solution was eventually found: part of the provincial reformatory in Guelph, then under construction, would be set aside for the criminally insane. The inmates would be housed in three dormitories. Violent patients requiring detention in individual rooms were to go to the asylum in Hamilton. The province was even persuaded to take those who were not originally residents of Ontario, thus finally solving the problem of what to do with Shortis.

Why did Ontario change its mind? In part it was because W.J. Hanna and the Ontario officials had 'progressive' ideas and wanted to find a solution to the problem of the criminally insane. Perhaps more important, however, was the outbreak of war six months earlier, which had significantly depleted the potential prison population of the new and expensive Guelph Reformatory. The Dominion government was willing to pay $10.50 a week, or $42 a month, to house each insane federal inmate in the reformatory. As the Ontario prison population continued to dwindle, the offer must have seemed more and more attractive.

Mr Shortis continued to urge that his son be transferred to Longue Pointe, not knowing of the Guelph arrangement. He wrote to the mother superior, saying that he was 'prepared to pay liberally any institution which would look after his son.' But the answer was still 'no.'

In the spring of 1915 the finishing touches were being put on the new ward at Guelph. The transfer would not take place for several months. Somehow, in May of that year, Shortis was able to smuggle out a long, rambling six-page letter to Lady Aberdeen. He had earlier requested permission to write to her, but had been refused. 'This letter goes out sub rosa,' he noted; 'Any allusion to it whilst here would make a *big* lot of trouble for me.' Quite simply, he wanted her to help him get out to fight for his country: 'I am willing to go to certain death if accepted for active service ... I'll want a V.C. to lay on mother's tomb or death.' He even composed a poem he entitled 'The Voice of Duty,' the first verse of which reads:

The voice of Duty's telling me
Apply for leave to go
Fight for my dear King and Country
The Vandal Prussian foe.

For the most part the letter was composed of wild, impractical ideas. Lady Aberdeen was asked to persuade his father to arrange his deportation to Ireland so he could enlist: 'I know manual of arms fairly well – and as such acceptable (as a volunteer without pay) in Belgium army, if I fail to gain admittance in British one. Father should be told (and to be told tactfully by you ...) give me a fast motorcycle, to act as despatch bearer, motor or aeroplane motor cost from $250 to $500. A ''Mademoiselle'' model Biplane: Santos Dumont model: speed 58 miles per hour would cost under $1000. He is wealthy; let him give of his money and of his family as befits a patriotic Irishman.' Shortis wanted to enlist for Belgium because 'in Belgium army I believe men who wear glasses are accepted ... My eyes are myopic.' He asked Lady Aberdeen to send him a little Bible: 'You can mark a verse that will equal a reply to this. I'm quick to see a point.' We do not know if she responded.

On Wednesday, 14 July 1915, Shortis, along with forty other prisoners, was transferred from Kingston Penitentiary to the new provincial reformatory at Guelph. He was now forty years old.

Walter Nursey (front left) at Burwash, Ontario, 1918

16

On the Speed River

THE PROVINCIAL REFORMATORY at Guelph is located on the Speed River on almost a thousand acres of good farmland, just outside the city. Patterned after the reformatory in Elmira, New York, the institution was built primarily to provide useful work for the inmates.[1] Such an institution had been asked for by prison reformers for years. An 1890 Ontario commission had recommended that the Dominion government build a reformatory and Sir John Thompson, the prime minster, had purchased land for this purpose in 1894, but nothing was done with it.

Ontario's main prison, the Central Prison, built in 1873 in the west end of Toronto near the present Canadian National Exhibition grounds, housed all the inmates serving under two years who were not in local jails. There was little work for them to do, however, and shortly after the turn of the century, to a considerable extent because of union pressure, the last contract for outside work would run out. W.J. Hanna, the provincial secretary, wanted a new provincial institution, he told the legislature in 1907, within a reasonable distance from Toronto and easily accessible by railway.[2] A special committee was set up, which agreed that a new institution should be built:

> The first conclusion that has forced itself upon your committee is that the present property should be disposed of, a large tract of land purchased and a new institution erected thereon. This change would permit the inauguration of the farm system on a large scale. Wherever adopted the farm idea has been an unqualified success, even where the natural conditions were anything but favourable to successful agriculture. Here, in Ontario, with our splendidly productive soil, and the opportunities offered for the prosecution of intensive agriculture, there can be no question of the result from a monetary

standpoint. As to the effect upon the prisoners, the experience of all states and countries appears to be that the land is the greatest reformative agency available to prison management.

The produce from the farms and other industries would be used by other Ontario institutions. Moreover, the Central Prison in Toronto was now on prime commercial land. The city had expanded westward, placing the prison in 'the heart of a busy manufacturing section.' 'Year by year,' the committee noted, 'its unsuitability for prison purposes has become more apparent, while at a still greater ratio its value for commercial or industrial enterprise has advanced, until now it is said to be worth per foot what prison property should be worth per acre.' Nearby industrial plants wanted more land for expansion. As is often the case, progressive ideas seemed to match practical economics.

The main institution at Guelph, built of course with prison labour, was completed in 1915 and the Central Prison was subsequently demolished and the land sold to the Massey-Harris Company. The reformatory, which embodied many progressive new ideas, attracted interest throughout North America. There were no perimeter walls or fences, inmates no longer wore the usual striped prison suit, many of them were housed in dormitory wards, and – uniquely in Canada – the relatively large cells had doors without bars and windows that allowed sunlight to enter. All the existing federal institutions, partly for security and partly because they were built when punishment was the main object of confinement, had windowless cells with bars on the doors. Guelph appears today much as it was in 1915, except that security has been tightened and there is now a high perimeter fence around the institution.

In addition, the 1908 special committee strongly recommended the adoption of the indeterminate sentence and parole: 'The importance of the indefinite sentence and parole plans as features of a reformatory system can scarcely be over-estimated. New York, Massachusetts and Ohio have had a lengthy experience of these systems and that experience has been uniformly satisfactory. Indeed, the leading prison administrators in those States unite in declaring that without indeterminate sentence and parole, reformatory effort would be almost abortive.' As a result, the province established the Ontario Board of Parole in 1910 and convinced the central government to amend the law to permit Ontario judges to add a further two-year indeterminate sentence to a possible two-year fixed sentence for persons sent to the Guelph Reformatory.[3]

Some of these same ideas were repeated in the report of the 1914 Royal Commission on Penitentiaries, discussed in the previous chapter. This is not surprising, because the chairman of the Ontario report, Joseph Downey, was also a member of the later commission. As we saw, however, except for the recommendation respecting the criminally insane, the report was not adopted, being considered by the federal prison officials as 'kid glove penology.'

Forty-one insane convicts, without any mechanical restraint, left Kingston in a special CPR coach for Guelph on Wednesday, 14 July 1915. They arrived at the reformatory the same evening, accompanied by two federal guards and two provincial doctors. 'We will cure some of them,' Warden J.T. Gilmour stated; 'They think down in Kingston that these fellows are incurable, but we are going to help them all we can.'[4]

Some inmates from the Kingston insane ward had been deported and others had been sent to Quebec asylums, but most were sent to Guelph. The Valleyfield paper reported that Shortis had refused to go to the Longue Pointe asylum because he thought he would be poisoned there,[5] but, as we have seen, they had refused to take him. It was a strange assortment of individuals who went to Guelph. One murderer, the clinical notes state, 'thinks he is Jesus Christ and ... believes that he is to be crucified in the prison.' Another, Jessamine, whose insanity defence had failed when Mr Justice W.R. Riddell refused to leave 'uncontrollable impulse' to the jury,[6] 'bites hands and lacerates them frequently.' Two inmates, Chartrand and Troy, who had previously endangered Shortis' life, were also transferred. Joseph Chartrand was the one in St Vincent de Paul who was convinced that Shortis was responsible for putting frogs in his stomach; he continued to be paranoid and dangerous, the records from Kingston note: 'Has delusions of persecution the Deputy Warden and turnkeys put dope in his food and drink ... Is in a double guarded cell and Warden says he would escape through a rat-hole.' John Troy, it will be recalled, had attacked Shortis with a stiletto in St Vincent de Paul because he thought he was trying to hypnotize him; he continued to believe hypnosis was being used: 'Everything points to his being a dangerous paranoic and one who would require careful guarding.' Fortunately, these two men were placed in individual cells, but they still had contact with Shortis during the day. A further threatened attack by Troy shortly after they arrived in Guelph caused the prison physician to recommend that Shortis be given his own cell for protection, but this was not done at the time. Along with all but three of those transferred, he was kept in the dormitories in the west wing of the prison, next to the prison hospital.

In view of these earlier stabbings, it is not surprising that the doctor noted on the file shortly after his admission: 'He has a large scar across his throat, has a scar on the left cheek and left side of tongue where he was stabbed. Has several stab wounds on the body but these are all healed and are not giving any trouble.' It was also noted that he was 'very erect and active, with moustache and short beard, quite bald and complains of considerable myopia.' The Kingston officials must have allowed him to grow a beard and moustache before he left the penitentiary.

The admitting doctor's notes show that Shortis had not overcome the idea that people were trying to get him: 'Patient seems to have definite ideas that Simpson was persecuting him. He says that he has been much persecuted in the old country, and that they tried to poison him with prussic acid at St. Vincent de Paul. He then volunteered the statement "I guess it was some German secret agent who told one of the guards to put poison in my soup." '

Shortly after his arrival in Guelph he wrote to the warden of Kingston asking him to forward some items he had given to the chief keeper that were supposed to have been sent on to him: these included 'my prayerbook and an envelope containing a photo of my mother, a portrait of an old friend I'd taken out of a magazine sent to me from home, a lot of letters, book lists and poetry.' He added a few comments on his new life in Guelph: 'I was made orderly in dining room ... and have been working ever since. I attended a game of Baseball between Guelph and an industrial farm team on first monday of August. I get on very well with Dr. Gilmour and his staff ... and believe I'll get a chance to go on active service.'

Shortis proved to be a good worker and was given a job in the bakeshop, eventually becoming the head baker. On one occasion, however, he was temporarily removed from his position because he had strongly rebuked a German American who had lauded the Germans for sinking the liner, the *Lusitania*. During this period he was given a large measure of freedom, being permitted to walk about the grounds freely; indeed, he was at liberty to visit the town of Guelph unattended for the mere asking, and frequently did so. He was also given his own private cell.

His desire to join the army continued undiminished. Guelph made an extraordinary contribution to the war effort and this may have intensified his attempts to enlist. By the end of the war over five thousand men had been examined for service by the local recruiting office.[7] Guelph was, too, the home of Canada's famous poet-soldier, Lieutenant Colonel John McCrae, who had written 'In Flanders Fields' before being killed in the war; coincidentally, he had been the Sunday school teacher at the reformatory until the year before Shortis arrived. Another soldier from Guelph was George Drew, the future premier of Ontario, at the time a lieutenant in the army who, as it happens, knew Valentine Shortis.

Shortis pleaded his case before visiting members of Parliament and badgered government officials at every opportunity. Others in the insane ward were being released in order to enlist, including one person who was noted in the file to be 'a moron.' In January 1916 the inspector of Ontario prisons, under pressure from the Department of Justice in Ottawa, warned the superintendent of Guelph that 'steps had better be taken to relieve the insane ward of several of these patients who [the resident physician] claims eligible for enlistment.' One is left wondering about the quality of some of those enlisting in the army at this stage of the war. Shortis, however, remained in Guelph.

The prison population throughout Canada continued to decline, in part because potential criminals were enlisting and in part because prisoners were being released or not sentenced to imprisonment in order to enlist. 'The loyalty of our inmates,' Superintendent Gilmour wrote in his annual report, 'clearly demonstrates that it is only a step from prisoner to patriot.'[8] Whereas there had been 851 persons in Ontario prisons at the end of 1914, there were only 402 at the end of 1916. At the same time, there was an increasing need for hospital space for returning wounded soldiers. In 1917, therefore, Guelph Reformatory was turned over to the military to be used as an army hospital and vocational training camp. The prison population was transferred to Burwash, an industrial farm which had been established in northern Ontario near Sudbury in 1914. The insane convicts were sent to the Hamilton Mental Hospital, which had been redesigned with steel gates and window bars to accommodate them.

Shortis, however, was not transferred to Hamilton. Instead, at the request of the new warden of Guelph, C.F. Neelands, and with the concurrence of Judge Doherty, the minister of justice, he was permitted to go to Burwash to be in charge of the bakery there.

Burwash Industrial Farm consisted of a few wooden dormitory buildings on 35,000 acres of relatively inaccessible forest land about twenty miles south of Sudbury. It had been started by Neelands with a small group of inmates in 1914, a few months after he had graduated from the Ontario Agricultural College in Guelph. Brought back to be the superintendent of the reformatory when Dr Gilmour retired in late 1915, he welcomed the further move back to Burwash in 1917 because of his faith in the concept. 'For the first time, perhaps, in the history of the Province,' he wrote in his annual report for 1917, 'we have an Institution without bars or cells ... Instead of working in industries, the men, to a great extent, are employed in healthful outdoor work.' In spite of its isolation, Burwash unfortunately did not escape from the devastating influenza epidemic that swept through Canada in 1918: there were over a hundred cases and twenty deaths out of approximately three hundred inmates.[9]

Burwash was, it would seem, a successful institution. Ontario was able, by chance, Neelands later wrote, to take 'many steps forward, steps of advancement that in the natural course of events would probably have consumed many years.' 'The central idea' behind Burwash, he concluded, 'is that it is a paying investment to trust the people whether they are prisoners or free citizens.' Neelands' philosophy was certainly progressive in a progressive age.

Shortis stayed as chief baker at Burwash for only a few months, having developed a yeast infection in two of his fingers, which resulted in the amputation in the Sudbury hospital of part of one of them. He was then placed in charge of the issuing of tools, such as picks, shovels, and axes, to the prison gangs. Trusted by the prison officials, he was given freedom to go wherever he wished on the property and would often join the officials on hunting expeditions. Moreover, he was permitted to keep a large white sheepdog as a pet and took up photography. He became a close friend of the storekeeper, Walter Nursey, who was also the clerk of records, and enjoyed warm relations with Superintendent Neelands and his young wife, also a recent graduate of the Ontario Agricultural College. Life was therefore relatively pleasant for Shortis, who only a few years earlier in Kingston Penitentiary had been considered by Dr C.K. Clarke and others as 'incurably insane.' A picture of Shortis (in the back row on the right, labelled 8) and his dog, with Nursey and other officials, is reproduced at the beginning of this chapter.

A prisoner's council was set up and Shortis was chosen by his fellow prisoners as its chairman to represent their interests. 'He exerted a wholesome influence over the prisoners,' Neelands later wrote, 'and on more than one occasion prevented what undoubtedly would have been an extensive prison break.' Such a position, said Nursey, the storekeeper, requires 'firm, tactful, judicial and ... splendid control to satisfy the various elements that constitute the many hundred wayward thinkers who comprise the community.'

Shortis had earlier been unanimously chosen by the prisoners as their representative before a commission of inquiry appointed to look at conditions in Burwash. The commissioner, Judge E. Coatsworth, a former mayor of Toronto and later a county court judge in Toronto, gave Burwash and Neelands a clean bill of health. Shortis cross-examined some of the witnesses before the judge and gave lengthy testimony about conditions. 'This place is a happy home to a man that has spent twenty years in the Penitentiary,' he testified, and spoke highly of 'Square-deal Neelands,' who had told the inmates, 'Boys, I will give you all a square deal, but I want you to give me a square deal also.' In fact he no doubt painted too idyllic a picture:

Q. Did you ever see an official strike a man?
A. Oh no, my Lord, the Sergeant or Warden wouldn't stand for that; they would can him right away ...
Q. How about profanity?
A. I never heard an officer even use a discourteous word.
Q. I suppose there is some among the prisoners?
A. Not much, my Lord; the prisoners behave pretty well; a pretty good lot of poor fellows; a man will lose his temper sometimes and say a big d. but the average prisoner behaves very well ...
Q. How about recreation?
A. Well, my Lord, I am very fond of playing polo, if there is any attempt to start the game, but I understand we are sent here to work, not to idle.

At the conclusion of his testimony Shortis handed the judge a list of seventy-six names of inmates, including his own, who wished to enlist, asking him 'to use your good offices in our behalf. We desire to rehabilitate ourselves in the eyes of the world and to respond to the call of our King and country.'[10]

The Departments of Justice and Immigration again took up the question of deportation, even though Francis Shortis was not willing to have his son return to Ireland. In part this was because Shortis kept requesting such action and in part because deportation of the insane was government policy. C.K. Clarke continued to press for the exclusion of the insane. The eugenics movement, to protect society from the feeble-minded,[11] was at its height, and a manuscript by Clarke, 'The Amiable Morons,' loosely based on the Shortis case, was circulated to members of Borden's cabinet, which resulted in a further tightening of the Immigration Act by extending the list of prohibited persons.[12] 'The Amiable Morons' was never published: the Canadian office of J.M. Dent tactfully rejected it by saying that it should really be published in England, and the English office had no interest in the work.

Shortly after Shortis arrived in Burwash, the Department of Justice again raised the issue of deportation with the Department of Immigration: 'Will you be good enough to let me know for the information of the Minister of Justice if it would be possible to have this man deported to his home in Ireland? ... Apparently, the condition of the prisoner must have become recently better as ... the Provincial authorities transferred him to the Sudbury Industrial Farm at Burwash ... It is reported by the Inspector of the Penitentiaries that he is very anxious to be sent back to Ireland.' The superintendent of immigration saw no problems: 'If, therefore, Francis V. Shortis desires to be returned to Ireland and his release for deportation would be considered, I am of the opinion that he could now be returned to the Old Country, particularly in view of the fact that his mental condition has evidently improved and he could possibly be deported without an attendant.'

Nothing further was done, apparently, for eight months. The crisis following the passage of the Conscription Act[13] in the summer of 1917 may have fully occupied the attention of the Department of Justice. In any event, the new solicitor-general, Hugh Guthrie, took up the matter again in June 1918. There is nothing to indicate why he got involved except that, quite possibly, being from Guelph he had a personal interest in the case and might well have been one of the MPs asked by Shortis to look into the matter.

The superintendent of immigration replied to Guthrie's request for action by saying that deportation was now not possible 'for some considerable time ... owing to the fact that steamship sailings for civilians have been cancelled for the time being.' Had there been sailings for civilians at the time, it is likely that Shortis would have been deported.

Shortly after the end of the war, Mr Shortis changed his mind. He was now willing to look after his son in Ireland and arranged through the Irish inspector of lunatic asylums for Valentine to be admitted to a private asylum in Stillorgan, just outside Dublin.

No doubt to the surprise of the officials in Ottawa, the younger Shortis also changed his mind. Now forty-three, he decided he no longer wished to be deported; instead, he wanted release on 'ticket of leave' in Canada. At that time prisoners could be released on licence under the 1899 Ticket of Leave Act through the governor-general's executive prerogative on the recommendation of the minister of justice. Since 1913 the Act had been administered by the Remissions Branches in the Departments of Justice and the Secretary of State. Parole was not introduced into the federal system until after the Second World War, although in many respects the Ticket of Leave Act fulfilled the same objective.[14]

When the ticket-of-leave legislation was going through Parliament in 1899 there was an interesting exchange between Joseph Bergeron and Sir Wilfrid Laurier about whether the Act would apply to murderers. Bergeron obviously had Shortis in mind.[15]

MR. BERGERON: Is it to be for any kind of offence, or only for minor offences?

THE PRIME MINISTER: All kinds of offences.

MR. BERGERON: From murder down?

THE PRIME MINISTER: It would include manslaughter, but is not intended to apply to cases of murder, although there is no restriction.

MR. BERGERON: I understand that that is the intention, but that is not so expressed.

No such restriction was ever introduced and thus the Act could potentially be used in Shortis' case.

Walter Nursey spearheaded the campaign to have Shortis released, and claimed that 'Compulsory deportation would upset our hopes.' Over seventy years of age, Nursey had been the bursar of the Manitoba asylum, the deputy minister of agriculture, and later the chief auditor for Manitoba. His career had been varied and fascinating. Arriving in Canada from England in 1865, he served in the newly established Queen's Own Rifles, helping to repel the Fenian Raids in 1866. He worked for a time as a fur trader with the Hudson's Bay Company in the North-West, became a full-time magistrate, received a medal for his service at the Battle of Batoche in 1885, became involved in mining ventures in the United States, crossed Mexico and the Sierras with pack mules, and on and on. He was also a journalist and the author of some twenty books. How he ended up as storekeeper at Burwash is not known.

Nursey had a high regard for Shortis, and wrote to Newcombe, the deputy minister of justice, in early 1919 that he 'is an exceptional character. Instead of Prison life having dwarfed his naturally superior abilities, and killed his ambitions and self-respect, he has come through the ordeal, a strong personality. He has learned absolute self-control under most trying experiences. He has broadened a naturally fine intellect by extensive reading, and his mind and views and knowledge of men and affairs are wide and remarkably shrewd. He has lost none of his inherited refinement, but has retained fortunately that degree of self respect – a sheet anchor – and but for which, like most men during long imprisonment, he would doubtless have sunk below the level. He is mild and courteous both in disposition and speech – without one suspicion of homicidal tendency.'

Nursey, and apparently Valentine, distrusted Francis Shortis' motives: 'His father is trying to arrange for his deportation to Ireland. This is the very last place to which (if the fears of his friends are well grounded) in face of existing family circumstances, he should be, or wishes to be, consigned ... Shortis senior assured his son long ago that he would never marry again. We are informed, however, that he did marry about seven years ago, which fact he has carefully concealed from his son. This woman was a widow. (What I am saying in this respect must kindly be regarded as privileged and confidential.) It is said to be common talk in Waterford that she of course married Shortis for his money only. It is further stated she was (before her marriage to Shortis) and still is, a close intimate of a certain man in that city. This intimacy is such, that it is the belief of those who know the facts, that she is only awaiting the death of Shortis to marry her recognized lover and fall sole heir to her deceased husband's estate.' The object of deportation, therefore, Nursey went on to say, is 'not to restore to him his liberty and freedom, but to place him under disguised restraint': 'The motive is transparent, and if Val. Shortis insisted upon the restoration of his rights, it is not a stretch of the imagination to picture him, subject to the interested influence of this step-mother, ultimately labelled as one "labouring under delusions, – poor dear fellow"; and confined somewhere where he might forever protest in vain.' Nursey ended his long letter to Newcombe by stating that 'Shortis today, if the alternative was confinement in Burwash, or the doubtful liberty of a Dublin Institution, would prefer to remain here, where he is surrounded by friends, and given unrestricted freedom.'

Newcombe was impressed. He replied that Shortis seems to have 'such a degree of reasonable volition as would justify some regard for his own views upon a question as to whether he should remain where he is or be deported to Ireland.' He was not, however, optimistic about his release on ticket-of-leave: 'it must be remembered that he committed a most outrageous crime, and notwithstanding his present sanity, for which you are willing to vouch, I am very much afraid that the members of the community with whom he might come into contact if at large would feel that their safety was jeopardized. I am told that Shortis can be regarded as harmless only so long as he is not within the reach of firearms ... One must sympathize deeply with this unfortunate man, but I cannot help thinking it would be a very serious step to authorize his release.' Newcombe had been deputy minister of justice in 1895 and had been unsympathetic then to the commutation of the death sentence; he would remain as deputy minister until 1924, when, at the age of sixty-five, he was appointed to the Supreme Court of Canada.

Nursey's reply must have left the Justice officials wondering what type of an institution the province was running at Burwash: 'During the whole time of his imprisonment at Burwash he has had and still has daily and hourly access to firearms ... While assisting me as helper in the store-house, I allowed him purposely unrestricted access to any rifle or revolver, including my own which might be stored there.' He gave details of some of the many bear and deer hunting trips on which Shortis had gone with the staff.

Nursey then began to orchestrate pressure on the Department of Justice. In January 1919 Superintendent Neelands reported that in his opinion Shortis' 'conduct certainly entitles him to a Ticket of Leave': 'he has been tested time and time again, and has shown wonderful ability to control his temper, and to conduct himself properly as a good citizen should ... I believe that if granted Ticket of Leave, he will lead an honest life and conduct himself properly.' The resident physician at Burwash declared that 'his mental condition is exceedingly good.' A copy of this report had been sent to Hugh Guthrie, who forwarded it to the minister of justice, commenting that 'it would appear to be proper that Shortis should now be returned to the penitentiary' preparatory to his eventual release. Dr Walter English, the medical superintendent of the Hamilton asylum, visited Burwash, perhaps to find a new home in the far north for the criminally insane now in his asylum – a concept that he had earlier advocated – and he also declared Shortis to be sane. Moreover, the Salvation Army was willing to take care of Shortis if he was released, a senior officer stating that they were 'prepared to furnish him with employment in our Social Department, and to look after him in every sense of the word.' Brigadier Frazer of the Salvation Army, the head of the religious and training work of the Ontario Department of Prisons, and his wife, wanted Shortis, whom they and their daughter had known for years, to live in their home. Judge Coatsworth, the former mayor of Toronto who had conducted the investigation into Burwash in 1918, also supported his release. Further, Nursey reported to the department that 'several well known newspapers' were ready to 'openly espouse' Shortis' cause. He even tried to convince Francis Shortis to visit his son so he could see for himself that he was 'absolutely sane ... and worthy of your fatherly love,' and urged him to consider supporting his son in setting up a new life out west or possibly in Australia. 'The group of citizens who are taking a profound interest in poor Valentine Shortis' case is steadily growing in number and importance,' Nursey wrote to Newcombe.

'We are not asking Lady Aberdeen to co-operate,' he went on, but he did forward a handwritten copy of a letter she had sent to a 'Miss Hunt' in 1915 shortly after Shortis had arrived in Guelph. Nursey's point in sending on the letter was to prove that Shortis' father wished to have his son kept in confinement. Lady Aberdeen was visiting Canada at the time in connection with her work for the Council of Women and other interests, and she wrote from the elegant Queen's Hotel in Toronto (on the site of the present Royal York Hotel):

Oct. 21, 1915

Dear Miss Hunt

Your letter has been forwarded to me here and I write to say that I hope to make enquiries regarding your friend whilst in Canada. I have endeavoured to do what was possible to carry out the wishes of his father and have represented his case to those in authority ... His father does not wish him placed at liberty, but would much like him being transferred to a Catholic institution.

I shall do what I can in this matter. I can well understand your interest in your boyfriend of old days.

There is no record of any follow-up to this letter, but of course it may have occurred by telephone or even in person.

The letter is a curious one. No 'Miss Hunt' appeared in any previous document or newspaper story, either in Canada or in Ireland. It seems likely that she was actually Millie Anderson and that Nursey had changed her name in copying out the letter, probably because he did not want Newcombe and his colleagues to know that Miss Anderson and Shortis were still in touch. Lady Aberdeen's letter was probably sent by Millie to Shortis in Guelph. The name 'Hunt' may have been selected because she was probably then living in Huntingdon, Quebec, although her movements cannot be traced after Shortis entered St Vincent de Paul. As mentioned, though, they would certainly not have been permitted officially to correspond while he was in the penitentiaries.

Unfortunately for Shortis, not everyone supported his release. John Lowe, the paymaster at the Montreal Cotton Company in 1895 and now the general manager, objected strongly. In the spring of 1919 he wrote to Sir Thomas White, the minister of finance in Robert Borden's Union government and acting prime minister while Borden was in Europe for the Peace Conference. In the letter, which White forwarded to the Department of Justice, Lowe protested the degree of liberty Shortis already possessed in Burwash and he demanded assurances that the prime minister and the minister of justice were not in Great Britain helping to further Shortis' release. The chief of the Remissions Branch replied to White:

> This Department has no information that either Sir Robert Borden, or the Minister of Justice have been interesting themselves in any way with regard to the case of Shortis during their absence in Great Britain.
> I think that Mr. Lowe might be informed that his strong opposition to the release at any time of Shortis in Canada will not be overlooked when any application on behalf of the prisoner is made to the Department of Justice.

The case had again entered the political realm and the possibility of release under ticket of leave, or even deportation, was for the time being not on the cards. Doherty, the only Roman Catholic in the cabinet, could not be seen to favour Shortis, and powerful politicians such as Sir George Foster, who had been in Bowell's cabinet and opposed the commutation at the time, would see that nothing was done.

Guelph Reformatory was reopened under Superintendent C.F. Neelands' charge in January 1921 and shortly thereafter Shortis, along with many others, was brought back. He had been away almost four years. Burwash continued in operation, handling the more difficult cases, particularly inmates with drug problems; after the Second World War it accommodated over seven hundred people, mainly recidivists,[16] but it was closed down in 1976 and has not been reopened. In June 1921 the criminally insane – eighty in all – were moved from the Hamilton asylum back to Guelph; over the next few years more were added, and by 1925 there were over a hundred in the insane ward. Forty of them, reported Dr Norman Wallace, the psychiatrist in charge and also the prison physician, had 'one or more murders to their credit.'[17] Some, like Shortis, were transfers from the penitentiary, while others came from provincial institutions; still others had been found not guilty by reason of insanity or unfit to stand trial.

As before, Shortis had his own private cell, was in charge of the bakery, and was relatively free to come and go into the town as he pleased. He continued his hobby of photography and started to build radio sets. Hugh Guthrie, now the minister of militia in Arthur Meighen's Conservative government, continued to support his release, but only on condition he would consent to be deported to Ireland. As before, the prisoner was not interested. Contact with his father had ceased in 1919 when, in Shortis' own words, he 'declined to make any financial provisions for me to the Department of Justice, if freed, and called me down when I said that for £100,000 placed with the New Zealand Department of Agriculture for me to establish a ranch there, I'd sign off all claims on her [his mother's] estate.'

Shortis continued to impress all who met him. Once again, strong pressure was exerted to have him released on a ticket of leave. The mayor of Guelph, who had known him through a mutual interest in photography since he had first arrived, told him he could count on his support; in the summer of 1922 he wrote to Sir Lomer Gouin, the minister of justice in Mackenzie King's new Liberal administration, about 'Canada's most unfortunate prisoner, Mr. Valentine Shortis': 'I have at all times found him a cool, well-educated, kindly gentleman, one whom I feel convinced can be trusted to make good, whenever paroled.' Hamilton Cassels, head of the law firm of Cassels, Brock and Kelley and chairman of the Ontario Parole Board, was another who supported his release. A businessman in Guelph, formerly from Cape Breton Island, approached D.D. McKenzie, the solicitor-general, a fellow Cape Bretoner, about 'This man who is a splendid type of manhood ... a very intelligent type of man and quite capable of earning his livelihood in an executive position ... he is a loyal British subject and if given his liberty intends to settle in Northern Australia.'

This was a solution that strongly appealed to the Department of Justice: 'it would remove the man from this country and get some guarantee that there would not be a danger of his returning to the scene of his crime,' said the chief of the Remissions Branch. The department proceeded to obtain information on Shortis' mental state. Two respected psychiatrists, possibly the leading two in Canada at the time, provided exceptionally favourable reports. Dr W.M. English, head of the Hamilton asylum and later president of the American Psychiatric Association,[18] who had already seen him in Burwash, declared: 'I find that he has lost, or forgotten the persecutory ideas from which he suffered years ago ... I believe that he could be granted parole without any probability that he would molest or in any way interfere with the comfort or life of another.' Similarly, Dr Harvey Clare, superintendent of the Ontario Hospital in Toronto, who had taken over C.K. Clarke's position as professor of psychiatry (and has been described as the 'father of modern psychiatry in Ontario'),[19] had seen Shortis on a number of occasions over the past seven years:

> He shows no signs of dementia, and he spends his time reading good literature. He is neat, clean, tidy, and gentlemanly in his conversation. He shows no signs of delusions or hallucinations.
>
> I have no hesitation in recommending that Mr. Shortis be given his freedom, technically as well as practically. The man is not dangerous in any way, and has shown during the last seven years of work, that he can be trusted, in every way.

But Shortis was not interested in going to Australia. 'At the present time,' wrote Neelands, he 'has neither the intention nor the means with which to proceed to Australia ... He has talked recently of going West, to some town of the prairie provinces, and starting up either a bakery or a tea room business. At any rate, for some time, until he had collected some means, he cannot go far.' In the meantime, Neelands was willing to supervise him: 'If the prisoner is placed under my supervision, the department has agreed to give him a position in the bake shop of this institution, paying him a small salary to begin with so that he may have a little pocket money, and may gradually mingle with the people of the community, thus gradually working his way out of his long penal servitude. I feel positive that Shortis will make good.'

The department, however, was worried. The head of the Remissions Branch, perhaps prompted by Newcombe, pointed out to Neelands that perhaps he was not aware 'that at one time Shortis declared that if he obtained his liberty he would return to the district to get even with persons whom he imagined to be his enemies.' The superintendent replied that so far as he could see Shortis 'has no intention whatever of carrying out any threats, and he appears to me to be a man who is well contented to forget as far as possible what has passed, and to begin afresh.' Nothing further was done by the department for the next six months.

In early 1923 the Salvation Army again took an interest in the case. Staff Captain J.A. McElhiney of Toronto, an assistant parole officer with the Ontario Parole Board, pleaded in person (along with Brigadier Frazer) and by letter for Shortis' release: 'I know there are a great many conflicting elements in this case, but surely, surely if, under direct supervision of Mr. Neelands, and the assistance that the Salvation Army will give your department, and if needs be the stipulation that he does not go to the Province of Quebec, where they seem to be afraid of him, this man could be given a chance. Twenty-eight years is a long time to be behind the prison bars ... We beg you therefore to give us a chance with this man and give him a chance to make good.' Shortis was now forty-eight. In the spring, McElhiney sent another plea to the head of remissions – 'please do something for this man soon' – noting that he understood the department was simply 'awaiting some further information from one of the Ministers. I think you said Mr. Robb.'

The reader may recall that in 1895 James A. Robb was the foreman of the coroner's jury in the Shortis case and that following the commutation of the death sentence he was so incensed he switched from the Conservatives to the Liberals. From 1906 to 1910 he was the mayor of Valleyfield. Now the MP for Huntingdon, he was also the minister of trade and commerce in Mackenzie King's government. When Laurier had died in 1919, Robb was at his bedside. He was an important person, and his views would not go unnoticed.

Robb had been asked by the Department of Justice to make inquiries in Valleyfield, and his response was strongly against release. From his perspective, Shortis was simply a cold-blooded murderer: 'in an attempt to gain possession of the money,' Robb wrote, 'he shot down in cold blood, John Loy, one of the clerks.' He enclosed letters from two of the men who had been in the plant office the evening of the killings, John Lowe, then paymaster and now general manager, and Hugh Wilson, now the cashier of the company, who, Robb pointed out, 'bears to this day marks of splinters of lead in his cheek.' 'I cannot think for a moment,' Lowe had written, 'that any government would tolerate such a request ... I trust you will use your influence against any such movement.' Wilson was equally emphatic: 'As one of the principals in that tragedy, I hereby register through you my strong objection to any action which might lead to his release. In fact I consider that he is at present enjoying more liberty than he is entitled to, as he should never have been removed from the penitentiary.' He then added: 'If he should ever succeed in gaining his release I would have him rearrested and tried for the murder of Leboeuf.'

A few days later the governor-general, Baron Byng of Vimy, on the recommendation of Sir Lomer Gouin, the minister of justice, advised that the case 'is not one in which a further exercise of the Royal prerogative would now be warranted.'

Before the decision became known, several newspapers in Montreal, Toronto, and elsewhere reported on the application, news that brought further protests, including one from George Loy, father of the murdered John Loy, who referred to the 'gross miscarriage of justice' in commuting the sentence, adding: 'Let him bear his punishment to the end.' Meanwhile, the Salvation Army withdrew its support; as a senior officer said: 'we do not wish the name of the Salvation Army to be associated with this case ... we do not desire to come into any controversy.' On 23 May 1923 the assistant under-secretary of state wrote to Neelands: 'Will you be good enough to inform the prisoner, Valentine Shortis, that His Excellency the Governor General has given further consideration to his case, but is of opinion that it is not one in which further exercise of the Royal prerogative of mercy would be warranted.'

Shortis' life went on much as before. He continued to run the reformatory bakeshop, with the help of a number of assistants, and, generally, in the words of Superintendent Neelands, 'exerted the same useful and wholesome influence over the prisoners that he had at Burwash.' His behaviour was 'exemplary.' He continued his interest in radio transmitters and photography: a picture he took of Neelands and his family is reproduced at the beginning of the next chapter. The prison surgeon observed that he 'affords a great deal of pleasure to the inmates of the various wards by taking his gramaphone and giving concerts in the evenings in the wards.' He continued in his private cell, away from the insane ward, and his door was never locked at night. He went unaccompanied into Guelph every day to pick up the institutional mail, and on at least one occasion addressed a public meeting in the town.

The surviving records of his life in Guelph are sparse. We do not know, for example, whether any special arrangements were made to celebrate his fiftieth birthday, which took place on St Valentine's Day in 1925. Nor do we know what part he may have played in the Guelph centennial celebrations of 1927. Nor do we know much about his relationship with George Drew, who was the mayor of Guelph in 1925, and would in 1943 become the Conservative premier of the province. Drew later wrote Shortis that he had 'extremely pleasant recollections of the days when I used to see you at Guelph and of the chats we had on different occasions.'[20] During this period Shortis also met Hugh Guthrie, the local member of Parliament, who was minister of national defence and acting minister of justice in Meighen's short-lived Conservative government in 1926 and later minister of justice in R.B. Bennett's government from 1930 to 1935. Guthrie often visited the reformatory: he wanted the new, so-called 'preferred class' federal institutions (Collins Bay in Kingston and Laval at St Vincent de Paul) to follow 'as closely as possible the model of the reformatory at Guelph.' According to the report of the 1938 Archambault royal commission, Guthrie 'pointed to the reformatory at Guelph where there were neither stone walls nor fences and where men worked in the open, as the example to be followed.'[21]

Shortis' mental health remained good. On 9 March 1927 Dr Norman Wallace, the psychiatrist, noted on his medical record: 'Since returning here he has shown no signs of delusions, nor hallucinations, neither periods of excitement nor bad temper. He is always very courteous and dignified and carries himself like a gentleman ... He has good control of himself, and since his return has shown no evidence of any psychosis.'

In March 1927 Shortis' friend and champion, Walter Nursey, died in Toronto at the age of eighty, and Shortis was permitted to attend the funeral and burial in St James' Cemetery. In a long story covering the event, the Toronto *Telegram* described Shortis as 'the stranger, tall and distinguished looking, despite his shabby ill-fitting clothes ... the well-bred, educated gentleman, aristocratic in bearing, but kindliness and courtesy showing in his every act and speech.' 'I am the loneliest man in all the world,' he was heard to say in a soft-spoken voice. Many of those who had actively promoted his release, Walter Nursey, Hamilton Cassels, and Dr J.T. Gilmour, the former superintendent at Guelph, were now dead.

A Toronto businessman was touched by the story in the *Telegram* and sent it to Ernest Lapointe, the minister of justice and Mackenzie King's Quebec lieutenant: 'Can you conceive it possible this man has not yet expiated his crime?' Lapointe replied that Lucien Cannon, the solicitor-general, would be handling the matter; in the meantime, he asked the superintendent of penitentiaries to gather information on Shortis for him. Brigadier General W. St Pierre Hughes knew Shortis well: he had been the chief keeper at Kingston Penitentiary before the war, while Shortis was there, having first joined the penitentiary service as an accountant in 1893. He had risen rapidly in the military service during the First World War; many thought his older brother, Sir Sam Hughes, the minister of militia and defence, had helped his career.[22] Hughes returned to become the superintendent of penitentiaries in 1918. He was fond of Shortis and wrote a few years later: 'Shortis had all the instincts of a gentleman. The writer came in contact with Shortis daily for many years. He was a very good-looking, tall, Irishman ... He had a lovable disposition – in fact in many ways he was of great assistance to the officers of the Kingston institution, trustworthy, never breaking a promise and it was remarkable how clean he always kept his person and clothes. The writer, amongst most of the Kingston Penitentiary officers, had formed a strong affection for the man.' But he told Lapointe – devastatingly – that Shortis was 'insane' in one important respect: 'The writer found him perfectly sane while at Kingston on all subjects other than firearms and he assuredly was insane on that subject. Many times I would take him a magazine in which there would be one or more advertisements of firearms of one make or another. After having given him such a magazine and when next I would meet him it was not the literary contents he would discuss, but invariably he would refer to the advertisements of something new in connection with firearms.'

The Justice file also has a handwritten, but illegible, note with the word 'Robb' on it; J.A. Robb, of course, had strongly opposed release in 1923 and he no doubt objected again. Given these views, Lapointe was not interested in Shortis' release, and it may be the file was not even passed on to the solicitor-general for his advice. If it had been, Cannon, a former senior Crown prosecutor in Quebec, would surely have opposed the release.

The following year, 1928, A.L. Jolliffe, the commissioner of immigration, asked for the Shortis file and did not return it to the Justice Department for almost a year. All the relevant immigration files have since been destroyed and so it is not possible to say why the file was requested. Possibly Shortis' father was again interested in exploring the question of deportation. He was still alive, although the Department of Justice officials and Neelands at Guelph thought he was dead.

On 1 September 1931, C.F. Neelands became the deputy provincial secretary in Toronto. He was now in a better position to bring about a major change he had been advocating for years, namely, the removal of the criminally insane from the overcrowded Guelph Reformatory. The daily count there was sometimes over nine hundred. In his 1929 annual report, he had strongly recommended: 'In view of the fact that at the time of writing this report, the inmate population of the Ontario Reformatory is almost double that intended for the present accommodation, that other arrangements be made immediately for the housing of the criminal insane in the Ontario Hospital, Guelph, thus releasing space for the Ontario Reformatory.' With more space there could be more effective classification of the prisoners. Plans were made to remove the one hundred or so criminally insane inmates from Guelph to a new building then being constructed at the Ontario Hospital, Penetanguishene. The building was completed in late 1932 and the prisoners were to be transferred there in February of the following year. Shortis felt depressed, desolate, and abandoned.

TOP: Arthur Beall (far left), next to C.R. Brown, and friends, Fonthill, Ontario, 1931

BOTTOM: C.F. Neelands and family, in front of superintendent's residence, Guelph Reformatory, 1932

17

On Georgian Bay

THE PENETANGUISHENE MENTAL HOSPITAL (today officially called a mental health centre) had been established in 1904 on almost four hundred acres of land just outside the town of Penetanguishene, overlooking Georgian Bay. It had taken over property used by the boys' reformatory, begun in 1859 to get children out of Kingston Penitentiary, but no longer needed at the turn of the century because of declining numbers and the increasing importance of industrial schools. As so often happens, the availability of land and buildings dictated the choice of site for the new hospital. The reformatory had, in its turn, first used military barracks left over from the War of 1812. A new permanent reformatory building was not completed until the mid-1860s. [1]

The insane ward, built on a rise of land fifteen hundred feet from the main hospital building and designed to accommodate about a hundred and fifty persons, is still used today to house the criminally insane. U-shaped, with two-storey cell blocks on either side of an administrative section, and a high wire fence on the fourth side, the name of the building was quickly changed by administrators from the 'Criminal Insane Building' to the Indian name, 'Nepahwan,' meaning 'place of rest.' [2] Today, after further construction and with a capacity of about 250 persons, it is known as the 'Oak Ridge Division.' [3]

In November 1932 Shortis learned that he was to be transferred with the other insane inmates to Penetang. Indeed, he had already started to pack for the move. By chance, Neelands was visiting Guelph Reformatory at the time and Shortis sent him a note: 'Will you, please, spare me 5 minutes of your valuable time. The fact that you were unable to secure my retention here renders it essential that I see you today – probably the last time you and I will be here together ... I just want to ask you a question re deportation ... I feel desolate to contemplate the severing of the official ties between us.' Neelands was unable to see him, but wrote the next day to the new superintendent of Guelph, John Hunter: 'It appears from his letter that he believes he is to be moved to Penetang with the other inmates of the Ontario Hospital, Guelph. I have always been of the opinion that when the transfer was made he would be left in Guelph ... I told Mr. Robbins [the deputy minister of hospitals] that we would be glad to have him remain. Accordingly, as he is probably worrying about the matter tell him that there is no intention of transferring him but ask him to keep this information confidential as it might cause trouble with the other inmates.'

Shortis, Hunter later told Neelands, 'was relieved and grateful' when told he would remain in Guelph, having earlier been 'excited and talkative, but now the good news, I hope, will have a quieting and steadying effect.' A special order-in-council was passed by the Ontario government allowing him to remain where he was. When a new Mental Hospitals Act was passed in 1935, requiring that mental hospitals be named in the regulations, a further order-in-council was passed specifically designating 'K Cell No. 6' an Ontario mental hospital. Shortis' cell was therefore one of Ontario's twelve mental hospitals.

In early 1933 about a hundred insane convicts were transferred by train to Penetang. More came later that year directly from Kingston, following the penitentiary riots of 1932-3. [4]

Shortis, however, remained in Guelph. Neelands' son, James, then about eight years old, recollects visits he made with his father to Guelph when they would see Shortis, with his handle-bar moustache twirled and waxed at the ends. They would often be given freshly baked cookies.

By 1936 the character of Guelph Reformatory had changed; it was to be used solely for younger offenders and the sixty-year-old Shortis was now clearly out of place. Harry Nixon, the provincial secretary, later to become the last Liberal premier before some forty years of Conservative rule in Ontario, ordered him transferred to Penetang. Arrangements were made by Dr Kenneth Gray of the Department of Hospitals, who was both a psychiatrist and a lawyer and would later become the University of Toronto's first professor of forensic psychiatry.

Taking with him a camera, a radio and loudspeaker, two boxes of letters and postcards, and a large collection of other personal effects, Shortis made the trip, accompanied by a Kingston guard, from Guelph, through Toronto, to Penetanguishene. While waiting at Union Station in Toronto, he was permitted a measure of freedom and could marvel at the changes in the city since he had attended Nursey's funeral in 1927. The Royal York Hotel, then the largest hotel in the British Empire, had been completed several years earlier, as had the Canadian Bank of Commerce, the empire's tallest building.

Dr Charles Hanna examined him on his arrival and noted his 'long waxed moustache with Imperial beard' and 'distinguished appearance, well spoken, polite and cooperative in every way.' A later entry mentioned a large scar 'about the size of a goose egg over the left biceps which he states is the result of a gun shot wound received in the West ... on the side of the law and order.'

Whatever his initial reaction, in time Shortis saw some benefit in being sent to Penetanguishene. It was, he thought, a necessary step on the road to release. His plan was simple: he would officially be declared sane at Penetang and then be returned to Kingston Penitentiary, to be released from there. The head of the Remissions Branch in Ottawa had told his supporters that while he was 'an inmate of a mental hospital it is not possible to entertain clemency.' Dr Hanna commented that he was 'obsessed with the idea of being returned to Kingston Penitentiary where he apparently has hopes of being allowed out on parole or ticket-of-leave.'

His obsession was shared by an odd character, Arthur W. Beall, who, like Nursey many years earlier, had become his champion and promoter. Beall was in his late seventies and had met Shortis in 1933 while conducting 'spiritual interviews' with the inmates at Guelph. He later described their first bizarre meeting: 'After we became acquainted in that first interview – which lasted an hour – he opened his heart and revealed its throbbings. Suddenly, looking at his watch, he exclaimed, ''Mr. Beall, I have been in prison forty years'' – at which I was dumb-founded. Then he came over to me and before I knew what he was doing he kneeled down before me, saying, ''Mr. Beall, won't you give me your blessing?'' ' Shortis and Beall became close friends and kindred spirits.

A graduate of Queen's University in the late 1880s with a silver medal in 'moderns,' Beall taught English in the 1890s at the Imperial University in Tokyo, returning to Canada at the turn of the century because of failing eyesight. Since then he had been employed by the Department of Education in Ontario to travel around the province teaching what was called 'eugenics and personal hygiene.' He continued to do so, apparently without pay, after he retired. A great-nephew of his, C.R. Brown, with whom he lived after his wife died, attended the lectures when he was a young boy and remembers them as 'an appalling mass of junk, fable and misinformation,' as they undoubtedly were.[5] He distinctly recalls Beall telling the boys in class that if they practised 'self-abuse' they would be sent to an insane asylum, where their penises would be cut off. In 1933 Beall privately published a book, *The Living Temple*, containing his lectures, with a foreword by a former principal of the Royal Military College in Kingston, where he had also lectured. These lectures about the evil of 'bleeding away the precious LIFE FLUID' bear out his great nephew's recollections, except that in the published version the doctors 'came along and cut off the two LIFE GLANDS,' not the penis. Beall would instruct the students to 'repeat after me: "The more you use the penis muscle, the weaker it becomes; but the less you use the penis muscle, the stronger it becomes." '[6]

Beall greatly admired his new friend, Shortis, who was, he wrote the governor-general, Lord Tweedsmuir, in one of many letters to influential people asking for Shortis' release, 'A striking looking man who impressed me at once as having the air, manners, and language of a cultured English gentleman ... He was the soul of honour and a brilliant conversationalist, speaking French fluently, and having, under his mother's tutelage a working knowledge of Spanish ... His mother was of noble blood, a Fitzhenry, whose ancestors came over with the Conqueror.' Beall believed that Shortis' mother was a woman of great wealth and that he had spent considerable time with her at her castle in Spain. Moreover, he thought Shortis' conviction was a great miscarriage of justice because the killings had been done in self-defence. He had defended himself in a struggle that ensued after 'he was twitted by the men in the office with having had sexual relations with Miss Anderson owing to some liquid spilt on his trousers and was also called by them "A Royal Bastard." ' This did not come out at the trial, Beall told government officials, because if it had it would have revealed to the world, through the 'Royal Bastard' remark, what Lady Aberdeen and only a few others, but not his own counsel, knew, that Shortis' father was, in fact, the illegitimate son of Queen Victoria's husband, Albert. Like Beall's lectures, this was 'an appalling mass of junk, fable and misinformation.'

Neelands also remembered Beall's lectures when he was a boy growing up on a farm near Sarnia, but there is no record of his attitude to Beall's teaching. He must have been somewhat sympathetic, for he permitted him to visit Guelph and treated him with great respect in their frequent personal dealings. Every few months Beall would send him a letter asking for help to obtain Shortis' release. In late 1934, for example, while Shortis was still in Guelph, Beall wrote: 'Would you in the near future take the matter up with Mr. Guthrie [the minister of justice] and urge [parole] with a paid position at Guelph as head baker?' Neelands replied: 'At the first opportunity I shall discuss this matter with the Minister and advise you of the result.' A month later Beall sent another note: 'Keep his name on your desk so that whenever you can make an opportunity, do so.' Still later, while Shortis was in Penetang, he wrote: 'I, therefore, beg the Hon. Mr. Nixon and yourself to take up my appeal as a matter of supreme and of major importance.' Neelands had earlier warned Nixon that if Shortis were released he would find the world a strange and lonely place; he would have to be 'placed under the care of some reliable person who would give him rather constant attention and direction. He thinks that he is familiar with the outside world as it is to-day, but, obviously, he would be more or less a stranger in a strange land ...'

Beall also wrote to Governor-General Tweedsmuir: 'Personally I live in the hope that with your gracious help a reprieve may come – and how much it would mean if it were to synchronize with the accession to the throne of His Majesty, Edward VIII, next September!' In Beall, Shortis now had a dedicated and persistent advocate.

Shortis also now had money. In 1932 his father had died in Ireland, a fact that Shortis and the prison officials assumed had occurred many years earlier. The will provided his son with £50 a year (then about $200) while he was incarcerated, but left him £200 a year ($800) should he be released; he was to receive nothing, however, if he returned to live in Ireland, obviously an inducement for him to remain where he was. The will also provided that the Shortis family plot be 'cemented and covered ... it being my desire that after my interment therein the plot shall not be opened nor the remains of those interred there in any wise disturbed.' Apparently he did not want his son or his second wife to be buried with him. The estate, valued at over $150,000, provided a very modest annuity to his wife; after certain other specific bequests, the residue was left to his nieces and nephews.

Because Shortis was in the insane ward at Guelph, the public trustee handled the funds for him. Indeed, through a series of misunderstandings, he was not even told that money had been left to him until 1935, three years after his father's death. In the meantime, the government officials were trying to decide what the public trustee should do with the money. Obviously this was not a common occurrence. Should some of the money be set aside as a burial fund? Could the government charge for maintaining him? How much should he be allowed to use? In the end, they concluded that since it was Shortis' property 'it does not appear that it can be used for other than his personal purposes.' Some of it, however, Neelands instructed Superintendent Hunter, 'should be made available to him for proper purposes within the Institution.' By the time he left for Penetanguishene, he had about $600 accumulated to his credit in the hands of the public trustee.

The doctors in Penetang did not consider Shortis insane. Dr Hanna noted on the file: 'no psychotic manifestations. He appears to be one who in society would probably be considered eccentric.' Other psychiatrists, including those on the Provincial Board of Review, concurred, and the Hospitals Division of the Ontario Department of Health, which had jurisdiction over Penetang and was much concerned about overcrowding,[7] asked the Department of Justice in Ottawa to request that the penitentiary authorities take Shortis back: 'It is the opinion of two psychiatrists, who have recently examined this man, that he is not now insane and should be returned to the penitentiary.'

The Department of Justice was worried. W.S. Edwards, the deputy minister, prepared the necessary documents, but advised the acting minister, P.-J.-A. Cardin (the minister of public works) – Lapointe was in Europe at the time – that 'his retransfer to the penitentiary is likely to prove embarrassing from two points of view – (1) it will lead to renewed publicity in his case, and (2) he is likely to be a source of trouble to the penitentiary authorities. His present satisfactory condition of health is probably due to the kind of treatment he has received in the provincial institution, and I fear that if he is returned to the penitentiary, where he cannot receive similar treatment, his earlier tendencies may revive.' Cardin sensibly noted on the file: 'Hold until return of the Minister.' The inevitable delay was depressing to Shortis, who, as Beall wrote, had 'golden dreams of "Coronation Clemency." ' He was now convinced that it was too late and he would have to remain in Penetang for the rest of his life. But, as it turned out, there was no coronation of King Edward VIII in September 1936. In December the King would abdicate in order to marry Mrs Simpson; he had not wanted a coronation while the issue was still unresolved. 'For me to have gone through the Coronation ceremony harbouring in my heart the secret intention to marry contrary to the Church's tenets,' he later wrote, 'would have meant being crowned with a lie on my lips.'[8]

When Lapointe returned in October he signed the transfer, telling his deputy that he 'could not see how I could decline to sign the warrant.' The deputy returned it to the Ontario officials, but added that he was 'somewhat apprehensive that some change may take place in his condition and demeanour upon his return to the penitentiary. For that reason, although it is not strictly within my province, I am taking the liberty of suggesting that you give this aspect of the matter careful consideration before proceeding with the transfer. Is there a possibility that ... when he is transferred to the penitentiary and becomes subject to the ordinary rules of discipline and the manner of life which prevails there his mental health may be again adversely affected?'

Dr C.A. McClenahan, the superintendent of the Penetang hospital, was not concerned: 'in my opinion, a transfer of Valentine Shortis from Hospital care to the custodial care of the penitentiary will not tend to bring on a recurrence of his mental illness as he is now much older (60), and his moods, habits, thoughts, etc., have become more fully stabilized and settled.'

Shortis made plans for his return to Kingston Penitentiary. He donated his radio transmitter to a church-organized social group for young people, and sent his personal effects to a minister friend in Guelph. He tried to track down the suit he had owned in Burwash almost twenty years earlier, but no one seemed to know where it was. Neelands wrote to McClenahan: 'I have no doubt that if and when he is transferred to Kingston Penitentiary you will see that he is reasonably well outfitted with clothing.' On Monday, 3 November 1936, accompanied by a Kingston guard, a very distinguished looking Valentine Shortis, with his long, twirled, handle-bar moustache and imperial beard, wearing a new, three-piece tweed suit, returned to Kingston.

Warden R.M. Allan ordered that Shortis be admitted to the penitentiary hospital for observation. But first his beard and moustache were shaved off, his tweed suit replaced by the high-necked dark prison uniform with his old number 'E-190' sewn on it. Now, instead of looking like a distinguished English gentleman, he looked like a hardened thug. Inmates were deliberately made to look like prisoners in order to discourage attempts to escape. The penitentiary had become even more conscious of security since the escape of the infamous bank robber, 'Red' Ryan, in 1923. They now rigidly enforced the rule, for example, that bedding must not be pulled over one's head, so it would be more obvious if one had escaped. Another ingenious rule decreed that an inmate must shut his cell door himself because, as Superintendent Hughes remarked, 'a dummy cannot pull a door shut.'[9]

Kingston Penitentiary had not changed much in the twenty years Shortis had been away. Stone-breaking, though, was no longer an activity, having in part been replaced by the sewing of canvas mailbags, begun in 1918, which employed about a hundred persons. But there were still few useful activities for most of the inmates, who spent sixteen out of twenty-four hours in their poorly ventilated cells.[10] The 'rehabilitative' approach that had now been generally accepted throughout much of North America – and endorsed by the royal commission in 1914 – was still not much in evidence at Kingston, which continued to be run to a great extent on the philosophy of retribution and deterrence. This was to change slowly after the Archambault royal commission of 1938 brought in its devastating indictment of the penitentiary system and the twin philosophies of punishment and deterrence on which it was based. The commissioners stated: 'Now, however, it is admitted by all the foremost students of penology that the revengeful or retributive character of punishment should be completely eliminated, and that the deterrent effect of punishment alone ... is practically valueless in so far as it concerns those who have been before, or who are now, confined in prisons or penitentiaries ... the task of the prison should be ... the *transformation* of reformable criminals into law-abiding citizens.'[11]

The royal commission had been promised by the Liberals if returned to office. There had been a series of riots and fires at Kingston in recent years, particularly the serious uprising in 1932 to demonstrate sympathy for the Communist leader, Tim Buck, then an inmate. A book excerpted in the Toronto *Globe*, by a medical doctor who had been sent to Kingston for performing abortions, contributed to the pressure for an inquiry,[12] as did the First Canadian Penal Congress held in Montreal in 1935 (organized by the young activist, Professor Frank R. Scott), which called for a royal commission.[13] The Mackenzie King government was re-elected in October 1935 and the commission was established the following year, beginning to take evidence in Kingston the month before Shortis arrived. No doubt officials in the penitentiaries were on their best behaviour while the commission was in operation; nevertheless, the report provides a valuable picture of the state of affairs at the precise time Shortis returned.

Warden Allan had been appointed in 1934 to clear up conditions. 'His first action,' said the annual report, 'was to eliminate unauthorized deviations from the instructions, rules and regulations.' He was a no-nonsense administrator who had been in the penitentiary service since 1913, having started as a carpenter in the Saskatchewan Penitentiary. Although finding him 'conscientious and upright in the performance of his duties,' the Archambault commission concluded that 'he would perhaps be more fittingly employed in connection with penitentiary industry and construction work.' There were stronger words for the 'extreme dictatorial methods' and 'militaristic control' exercised by the superintendent of penitentiaries, General D.M. Ormond, who had replaced Brigadier General Hughes in 1932; they called for his dismissal and he left the following year. Allan, however, stayed on.

The hospital where Shortis spent his first week had not changed since he had left, even though it had been strongly condemned in the 1914 commission report. Indeed, it was much the same as it had been when constructed in the 1850s. The thirty-six locked cells were narrow and gloomy, without outside windows. Buckets were still used because there were only two toilets in the hospital. The conditions were 'so primitive and unsanitary,' concluded the Archambault commission, 'as almost to be beyond belief.'

Shortis was examined over a four-day period by Dr G. Platt, the hospital physician, and the son of the warden of Kingston when he had first arrived there in 1905. Platt reported 'no evidence of Psychosis. There is orientation as in a normal person; an absence of delusions and hallucinations. Conversation is logical and coherent. In the field of personality, I would state that the convict is abnormal.' His physical condition, however, was considered 'only fair ... he is short sighted; has Chronic Bronchitis and evidence of heart condition.' As a result, he was thought unfit for general prison labour and was given a position in the library. The prison rules now allowed inmates to borrow a novel every day and a magazine every other day; no newspapers were permitted, however, the royal commissioners observing that prisoners 'do not receive any newspapers and are therefore not aware of what is going on in the world.'

The rule of absolute silence, not rigidly followed in the recent past here or elsewhere in Canada, had been officially modified. General Ormond reported this 'experiment' to the First Canadian Penal Congress: 'As from January 1st, 1933, Wardens of penitentiaries have been permitted to allow convicts to converse before proceeding to work in the morning, during lunch hour and up to seven o'clock in the evening while confined in their cells. Up to the present time this experiment has not indicated that any greater dangers to the security of the institutions have developed than existed before abolition of the silence rule.'

Shortis was not entirely happy with the change. About a month after he arrived in Kingston, he appeared at what was called 'Noon-day Court' asking for a change of cell 'because of the excessive use of obscene language by convicts in the vicinity of his present location.' The warden approved a change and instructed his deputy to take steps 'to investigate this situation with a view to curbing the use of obscene language on the ranges to the utmost.'

Food was eaten in the cells and so Shortis may not have visited the kitchen or bakery, in which he would have had a special interest. Perhaps it is just as well he did not. The royal commissioners found evidence of cockroaches and mice, stating that 'the same water is used in cleaning 1,400 dishes ... both the kitchen and bakery are dirty ... the food poorly cooked, and rendered flavourless by steaming ... the entire situation in the kitchen is highly unsatisfactory.'

Shortis did, however, visit the former insane ward, which was now a shoe factory, employing about forty persons who made footwear for the inmates, guards, and the RCMP. The boots first given to him did not fit properly and on the recommendation of Dr Platt he was sent to the shop to be measured for custom-made boots. Since the ward had been closed in 1915, insane inmates were sent to provincial asylums, a process that would continue until 1948 when, because of overcrowding at Penetang, another insane ward was opened at Kingston Penitentiary. This time the old women's prison within the penitentiary walls, which had been closed down in 1934, was used. In 1959, because of growing numbers, the old 'prison of isolation' became the insane ward, and in 1982 the ward was officially designated as the Kingston Penitentiary Treatment Centre.[14] Psychotically insane convicts are sometimes still sent from Kingston to Penetang or to regional provincial psychiatric hospitals, but it seems that most prisoners suffering from mental illness (particularly of a psychopathic nature) are kept in Kingston. Most institutions over the years go 'full circle.' The treatment of the insane has gone 'full circle' twice: from Kingston to Rockwood asylum, then back to Kingston, then to Guelph and Penetang, and now, once again, back to Kingston. Plus ça change ...

Shortis' conduct, as noted in the files, was exemplary. He and his friend Beall were once again hoping for 'Coronation Clemency,' but it was now the coronation of George VI in May 1937 they were anticipating. Things looked hopeful, although there had been a general tightening up of release under ticket of leave after 'Red' Ryan had been shot dead in May 1936 while robbing a bank in Sarnia within a year of his leaving prison on ticket of leave, a release that had been supported by Prime Minister Bennett.[15]

Beall was able to visit Shortis in Kingston, the new penitentiary rules allowing a visit once a month (rather than every three months, as before) by a relative or by a 'respectable friend of the same sex.' Neelands had written Warden Allan in support of these visits. Conversation took place through the double close-wire mesh in the visitors' cage, the very cage Shortis had refused to enter out of fear when his uncle had come to see him many years earlier, and which was described the next year by the Archambault commission as one of the 'gruesome and humiliating relics of the past.'

With the assistance of his great-nephew, C.R. Brown, with whom he lived in the village of Fonthill in the Niagara Peninsula, Beall organized a further campaign to have Shortis released. Brown, who had a farm and greenhouse and a rapidly growing coal and wood business, offered Shortis a home and employment. 'If Shortis should come here,' he wrote the Department of Justice, 'I can assure you that he would be well taken care of, and treated with kindness and consideration.' Beall, along with ministers of different faiths, judges, farmers, businessmen, and others, wrote to the minister of justice and government officials asking for Shortis' release.

Another group made up of Dr William Sangster, Dr and Mrs E.S. Barker, and Colonel R.E. Halliday now enter the picture. Residents of Stouffville,[16] just north of Toronto, they had been friends of Walter Nursey, who had died almost ten years earlier. Dr Sangster, a medical doctor, had been the reeve of Stouffville and president of its board of trade. Dr Barker, a dentist, had been a member of the dramatic society and president of the Stouffville hockey team. Colonel Halliday had had a military career in China and now lived with the Barkers in a winterized cottage on Musselman's Lake, just outside the town. They had visited Shortis at Guelph and Penetanguishene and wanted to communicate with him in Kingston. The rules, however, would not permit it, and officials informed Gertrude Barker that Shortis could write only one letter to one person each month (when he was last in Kingston the rule was one letter every two months) and Beall had been selected as his correspondent. In any event, the friend selected had to be of the same sex. Other old friends, such as ministers Shortis knew at Guelph and Penetang, were also barred from writing him. Even letters from Colonel and Mrs George Drew, the leader of the opposition in Ontario, officially could not be shown to him, although in this case Warden Allan broke the rules. Shortis had sent the Drews a 'sandwich toaster' from Penetang. 'My wife and I were delighted with your present,' Drew replied, 'and will find it very useful.'

The Stouffville group had good political connections. Barker and Sangster both wrote the prime minister, Mackenzie King, the latter declaring that Shortis' 'many friends are fearful of the shock if he is not granted his freedom by the Coronation at latest ... Your kindly interest in his behalf will be greatly appreciated by me and his many friends among many classes of the country, including the Judiciary, the clergy of different churches, and others.' The prime minister's private secretary passed on these letters to Ernest Lapointe, the minister of justice, who later met the three men of the group in Ottawa. They wrote M.F. Gallagher, the chief of the Remissions Branch, after their return to Stouffville, outlining the steps they were prepared to take: 'At Musselman's lake Dr. Barker owns a fine cottage fully equipped for all the year round habitation, there Shortis would be welcome to live ... We will individually and collectively use our influence with Valentine Shortis not alone to guide him in whatever he may undertake financially but to the end your department shall never be subject to the least criticism if he be paroled.'

Not only did Shortis have friends with influence, but, as we have seen, he also had money. The public trustee had forwarded to the penitentiary over $800 which had been accumulated to his credit from his father's estate; he had deducted $40 for administrative costs, which Shortis objected to, asking Beall 'to ascertain if I can be mulcted for "services" by a public official who is paid to perform his duties by the Ontario government.' He also complained to Warden Allan about the fact that he had not been informed promptly of the money: 'Had the Public Trustee deigned inform me he had money belonging to me, in 1933, I would have promptly objected to his "guardianship," directed it turned over to me, evaded being billed for his unwanted services and purchased, with it, outright International Nickel shares then selling very cheap.'

The case was now again officially 'under study by the Department of Justice.' Shortis and Beall were optimistic. Beall wrote to Allan: 'I have faith that his record under you, Mr. Allan, will be so satisfactory that you will recommend to Mr. Lapointe that Mr. Shortis be given, not simply ''parole'' but pardon and freedom and liberty.'

On 9 January 1937, Shortis was summoned to the warden's office. 'I went in before you,' he later wrote, 'feeling for the first time since I came here good news was at hand.' But instead of presenting the anticipated ticket of leave, Warden Allan read a formal charge:

(1) Having an article in his possession other than such is permitted.

(2) Giving money to an officer with the alleged purpose of bribing said officer, in that he, on January 8th, 1937, did pass a two dollar bill to an officer, with the remark 'Don't say nothing, I know I can trust you.'

Shortis admitted giving guard McKenna the money, but denied having attempted to bribe him. He had admired the officer's tobacco pouch, he said, while they had been talking outside the chapel; it had been made in the mailbag shop and the guard said he would make one for him. He then gave him the money, 'animated,' he said, 'by a spirit of compassion for his poverty and warm gratitude for his assurances he'd make me a pouch.' The $2, along with another $5, which Shortis voluntarily gave to Allan, had been wrapped in rubber and concealed in Shortis' rectum when he entered Kingston. He had learned the technique, he said, in a book about Devil's Island.

On the spot, Allan found Shortis guilty of illegal possession but not guilty of bribery. There is 'no reason to believe that this money was given to Guard McKenna as a bribe,' he reported to Superintendent Ormond. The result was that he lost all his privileges for thirty days, with the exception of library privileges. He was lucky, for he could have been subjected to corporal punishment. The Archambault commission found fault with the summary justice meted out by Allan, without lawyers or the right to appeal, stating 'The majority of the complaints that were made against Warden Allan by inmates who appeared before the Commission may be traced to the difficulties and injustices of the present system of conducting warden's courts.'[17] Today, it should be noted, such a hearing would be conducted by an independent person not connected with the penitentiary service.[18] The guard was permitted to keep the $2, in accordance with the policy of encouraging officers to report the finding of contraband.

Shortis was devastated by what he called the first 'blob of ink on my spotless record.' He wrote a ten-page letter to Allan explaining how he 'went off side accidentally,' how the warden had altered the place: when he was here before, 'the guards were not afraid to bring in any thing a chap would pay for ... Now they are afraid and a poor chap can't get even a roll of "Life Savers." ' He was most concerned about the reactions of his friends to the news, for they had warned him to 'Do nothing you can be reported for. Keep your records spotless.' 'I earnestly trust,' he pleaded, 'you'll not tell Professor Beall when he comes or Mr. Neelands whenever you see him.' Nothing was apparently said to them, but the charge was reported to Ottawa at about the same time the Department of Justice officials were re-examining the case. Shortis' health started to deteriorate. He spent several weeks in the penitentiary hospital in March, expecting to die. He asked Warden Allan to send his $800 to Beall: 'I expect within a short time to be dead of appendicitis and want to secure the disposal of these cheques as I desire. I rely on ... you ... to personally attend to this, my last request ...'

Fortunately for Shortis, Lady Aberdeen again entered the picture. Beall had written her a long letter in January 1937, asking her to support Shortis' release. She passed it on to her old friend, Mackenzie King: 'After careful consideration, I think the best course for me to adopt will be for me to forward the said enclosures to the Prime Minister, Mr. Mackenzie King. I am sure he will decide rightly as to what advice to tender to His Excellency The Governor General.' King replied to Lady Aberdeen: 'On the receipt of your letter concerning Shortis I caused its representations to be made immediately known to the Department of Justice. I am glad to be able to tell you that in having the matter reviewed it was disclosed that officials of the Department had been discussing with Shortis' friends arrangements for his future which, at the time, were under study.' In less than a week the minister of justice, Ernest Lapointe, recommended to the governor-general, Lord Tweedsmuir, that Shortis be released on ticket of leave. The latter approved the recommendation on 25 March. In contrast to earlier attempts to release Shortis, no steps were taken to ascertain the attitudes of the people of Valleyfield.

Mackenzie King and Lady Aberdeen had maintained a close relationship over the years. They were both interested in spiritualism. Lord Aberdeen had died in March 1934 and King wrote to her about his experiences of communicating with the dead: 'I have come, dear Lady Aberdeen, to believe so absolutely in man's survival after death, and, in one way or another, have had so many evidences not only of the continued existence of those I love, but of their interest in and concern for me, and their constant touch with my life, guiding and guarding its every endeavour, that I cannot longer write of death as something which we should regret, save in what it may involve of momentary separation.'[19] Later that year, he was in London and Lady Aberdeen called him by telephone, as he noted in his diary: 'Lady Aberdeen rang me up from Scotland and we had a long and most interesting talk together, during which she told me of having had evidence of Lord Aberdeen's continued existence from automatic writing [at a seance table] and I told her of what I got from him by the table. We also talked of the position of the Liberal Party in Canada and here. She is as active as ever and I was amazed at the vigour of her voice and strength of her mentality. It was a quite remarkable experience.'[20] She then arranged a series of sessions for him with a medium in London.[21]

There is no record of what King may have said about Shortis to his friend and Quebec lieutenant, Ernest Lapointe. Perhaps the recommendation to the governor-general would have come when it did in any event. It seems reasonable to conclude, however, that King's intervention had some influence on the case.

The ticket of leave included the standard clause required by legislation that Shortis report to the police once a month. It also insisted he be released upon 'the express additional condition ... that he place himself under the supervision of Dr. W.A. Sangster, Dr. E.S. Barker, and R.E. Halliday, of Stouffville, Ontario.' On 1 April Shortis signed an undertaking 'to abide by the conditions' of the ticket of leave: 'I have been acquainted with the express additional conditions contained therein, that I place myself under the supervision of [the Stouffville group] ... and upon my release be governed by the dictates of the above mentioned gentlemen.' His friends were delighted and wired Allan: 'we look for further instructions and details relative to the date of his liberation.' Shortis would leave on Saturday, 3 April 1937.

The day before he was to be released, however, Shortis regretted what he had signed. He did not want to go to Stouffville, but wished instead to be under the supervision of his friend, Arthur Beall. He asked

Warden Allan to delay his departure: 'I have no intention to play around in any summer cottage by a pond out miles from Stouffville, enacting the role of a lounge lizzard when my duty and inclinations point to the task of procuring work, supporting myself from my earning pay – making good in every sense of the word.' To live in a cottage on Musselman's Lake – 'mosquitos and mists in summer: desolation in winter' – would, he said, be breaching one of the conditions of the ticket of leave by forcing him to lead 'an idle life.'

Shortis had written to Allan earlier urging him to 'block Stouffville guardianship': 'I won't go there for Gertrude to parade me as her Gigolo or be stared at as a social notoriety. I'm no damned Red Ryan notoriety monger thank God. Nor have I any desire to be Gertrude's lounge lizzard and spend my savings on outfit and good clothes.' 'I am A.W. Beall's adopted son,' he had written. He wanted to be under Beall's supervision, possibly with Reverend J.A. O'Reilly from Guelph as a co-guardian. He painted an idyllic picture of what life would then be like: 'I propose work for 3-4 years at anything no matter how humble – saving my annuity and anything I can out of my pay and then go West – Alberta foothills – buy a bit of land, put up a 4 room cottage, grow my vegetables, fruit, fowl, milk, cheese, butter, grain and hay for feed. I'll build a first class radio and small transmitter. Then I can pass the remaining years "the world forgetting, by the world forgot." ' Later he would go overseas: 'I'll buy a nice estate and settle down in Devon or Cornwall after AWB and I go on a long long (2-3 yr.) sea voyage ...'

Shortis realized, however, that he could not reject the Stouffville people outright: Gertrude Barker had warned Beall that to do so 'would very seriously jeopardize if not entirely prevent any chance of' release. What he wanted now was to have another clause added to the ticket of leave, permitting him to go to Toronto and look for a job. On 3 April such a clause was added and Shortis was free to leave the penitentiary.

Dressed in the tweed suit purchased in Penetanguishene, now baggy because of substantial loss of weight, he prepared to leave the penitentiary. Even with his ill-fitting clothing he was more fortunate than most who left with, in the words of the Archambault report, 'clothing made in the penitentiary, which is often all but labelled as such.'[22]

He was also given some money, an innovation implemented only in 1935, although authorized by the 1918 Penitentiary Act. Prisoners now got five cents a day for every day they worked from the time they entered the penitentiary.[23] This should have amounted to about $750, but because no payment was permitted while Shortis was considered insane and thus, in theory, unable to work, the sum was reduced to $223.63. He was given ten dollars in cash as he left the penitentiary, with the remainder to be sent along later.

Like most other prisoners leaving Kingston at the time, there was no one there to meet him. Beall had telegraphed that he had to remain in Windsor with his very sick brother-in-law. The Stouffville people were not there; rather, they were waiting for further instructions from Warden Allan about when Shortis would get out. At that time, no prisoners' aid association met a person leaving the penitentiary (without a specific request from the inmate), a point adversely commented on by the Archambault commission.[24] It was over a month later that the Montreal Prisoners' Aid and Welfare Association, by accident, saw a reference to Shortis in the press and wrote the warden asking 'whether he is returning to his former home and whether anyone undertook to assist him in readjustment of his broken life.' The executive secretary then added, almost as an afterthought: 'If at any time you have men coming our way who belong to this province we will be glad to receive them.' A telegram was sent by Allan to Dr Barker: 'Valentine Shortis leaving for Stouffville noon today, please arrange to meet him.'

That morning Shortis requested that he be permitted to testify before the Archambault royal commission, then investigating the penitentiary. It will be recalled that he had given evidence to the 1914 royal commission and the 1918 inquiry at Burwash. There is no official record of his testimony because all inmate testimony was taken in camera to encourage frankness. But a member of the royal commission, the late J.C. McRuer, remembered Shortis well. In a conversation in the spring of 1985, a few months before he died at the age of ninety-five, the distinguished former chief justice of the High Court of Ontario recounted how Warden Allan had informed the commissioners that a long-serving inmate wished to testify; it had to be immediately because he was being released that very day. McRuer remembered that he was so impressed with Shortis' distinguished bearing and manner that he visited him in his cell after he had given his evidence. Shortis told him about the crime and his life in various institutions. From what he had heard, McRuer could not understand why he was still in custody and when he returned to Toronto he, in his capacity as a commissioner, asked the Department of Justice to send him Shortis' file.

Almost fifty years later he could recall with amazing accuracy many of the details of the crime and the political events leading to commutation.

Shortly before noon on Saturday, 3 April 1937, after serving 15,071 days – over forty-two years – in continuous confinement, Valentine Shortis, now sixty-two, was a free man. He was – and the record may possibly still hold[25] – the longest serving prisoner in Canadian history. He would now be, as Neelands had remarked, 'a stranger in a strange land.'

18

A Stranger in a Strange Land

VALENTINE SHORTIS, now to be known under the assumed name of Francis V. Cuthbert, was met later that afternoon by Dr and Mrs Barker and others at the Stouffville train station. First taken to the local police station to report, as he was required to do under his ticket of leave, he then went to the Barkers' cottage on Musselman's Lake. There is no record of how his freedom was celebrated.

Early the next week he left for Toronto, taking a room in a house owned by friends of the Barkers at 46 Maitland Street, just off Yonge Street in downtown Toronto. One of his first acts was to call on C.F. Neelands at Queen's Park, who was taken completely by surprise: 'I had no knowledge of ... his impending release nor actual release until he called at my office about four days after he left Kingston Penitentiary.' The deputy provincial secretary kept in close touch with Shortis, inviting him occasionally for Sunday tea or dinner at his home at 417 Richview Avenue in Forest Hill village. Shortis of course also saw his friend, Arthur Beall, on a number of occasions, as well as old friends of Beall and of Walter Nursey.

A letter to Gertrude Barker in May 1937 showed him to be content: 'My life is full of quiet restfulness. Nothing worthwhile relating breaks the smooth regularity of the days and evenings.' His health was now improving, he said, using the excessive detail characteristic of all his letters: 'I am slowly but surely regaining my health; have added 8 pounds to weight. I drink 3 pints, sometimes 2 quarts of milk daily. Since I came to Toronto I drink fully a quart of water daily. That is something I never did before. In fact, I disliked and practically never took it. I walk 15 to 20 miles daily, have regained my colour and expect in another month or two to be back to my old times strength and

W.L. Mackenzie King, prime minister, in front of picture of his mother, Laurier House, Ottawa weight 189-195. I was only 161 when I reached Stouffville.' Shortis' days seemed to be full. He again took up his interest in photography, joined the YMCA, went to mass every Sunday, and spent considerable time in the public libraries, most likely the old reference library on College Street. He abstained from liquor. 'I was invited to have a Scotch ... on the train coming to Toronto and said no thanks,' he told Gertrude Barker, 'I never propose to drink. Don't care for it.' Shortis, or Cuthbert as he was known, became a familiar sight around Toronto, with his broad-brimmed hat, goatee, monocle, and cane. To help protect his identity, he did not regrow his handle-bar moustache.

The event that Shortis, and indeed virtually everyone, anticipated with great eagerness was the coronation of King George VI, to take place on Wednesday, 12 May 1937. He would also have been interested, in his first few weeks of freedom, in the issuing of a new constitution for Ireland; the bloody battle for control of Barcelona in the Spanish Civil War; the spectacular destruction of the giant German Zeppelin, *Hindenburg*, in New Jersey; the sentencing of rioters at Guelph Reformatory, the first riot in its history; and Toronto's largest ever May Day demonstration addressed by the former Kingston inmate, Tim Buck. But it was the coronation that held the centre ring for him.

Shortis had linked his release emotionally to the coronation, although, as it turned out, the events were not connected. There was to be no official 'Coronation Clemency,' as there had been at earlier coronations, a fact that so angered the inmates at Guelph that they threatened to stage a disturbance on 12 May. It should also not be forgotten that Shortis apparently believed that his father was the illegitimate son of Prince Albert. He was, therefore, part of royalty.

One hundred thousand people were at the Parliament Buildings at Queen's Park and along University Avenue for the celebrations, 'the greatest military display in Toronto since the days of the Great War,' claimed the *Globe*. Shortis, of course, was there, wishing he could have been a participant rather than a spectator. He witnessed the impressive parades, the unfurling of the royal standard, the twenty-one-gun salute, and the impressive volleys of rifle fire from the Queen's Own Rifles. 'Well, Coronation Day is over,' he wrote to Gertrude Barker, 'with its Pomp and Pageantry of Kings, its good wishes for their Majesties and the Empire and its sigh for poor Windsor ... The military parade was fine ...'

Shortly after the coronation Shortis' dream came true: he joined the

Queen's Own Rifles of Canada, named after Queen Victoria but with Queen Mary now the honorary head. The Toronto-based regiment, founded in 1860, had taken part in repelling the Fenian Raids in the 1860s (Shortis' friend Nursey had been a member at the time), the Riel Rebellion in 1885, the South African War, and the First World War, where over a thousand of its soldiers had died.[1] 'The drilling is doing me good and I like it,' he wrote Gertrude Barker, 'I find everyone from the Lieutenant-Colonel down that I have met very nice indeed.'

On 14 June 1937, using the name Francis V. Cuthbert and giving his age as forty (he was, in fact, sixty-two), he took the oath of allegiance to the sovereign and agreed to serve in the active militia force for a period of three years. The second in command of his unit at the time, Lieutenant Colonel W.T. Barnard, today in charge of the regimental museum in Casa Loma (Sir Henry Pellatt, who had built the castle, had been the commanding officer of the regiment), remembers him as 'somewhat eccentric.' 'Cuthbert stood out as the person who sang with the band whenever the National Anthem was played. He appeared to have plenty of money and offered rather expensive gifts, such as cigarette lighters to his peers and other members of the regiment.' He offered Barnard an expensive lighter, but he refused it.

Neither Barnard nor others in command of the regiment, it seems, knew of Shortis' background. Nor did they particularly care at the time. The regiment, which by 1937 had shrunk to one battalion, was desperate for volunteers – of almost any description. 'Recruits are scarce,' the regimental annual report stated: 'We are ... disheartened in the knowledge of Canada's need being left to be carried on the shoulders of the few.'[2]

In early May the Canadian Press reported from Ottawa that Shortis had been released from the penitentiary, though there was no reference to the fact that he was living in Toronto. Some papers, such as the *Globe* and the Toronto *Star*, carried only a short note, but others realized the importance of the story and gave more extensive coverage. The Toronto *Telegram*'s two-column headline was 'Murderer Whose Sentence Helped Wreck Government Is Released After 42 Years.' A Montreal *Gazette* editorial, under the heading 'A Famous Trial Recalled,' discussed the governor-general's commutation, declaring that 'it was generally considered that his action helped to defeat the Conservative Government in 1896.'[3]

'Well, I've had my baptism of newspaper fire and cannot complain,' Shortis wrote Gertrude, 'but how I would have enjoyed reading the howl I suppose the Quebec French press made.' A reporter from the Toronto *Star* found out from police sources where he was living and tried to induce him to sell his story: 'The Star still seeks copy – in vain. It made no definite offer – said they'd "pay well" 50 to $100 according to the copy I'd furnish, so I said no thanks. A Mr. Pascoe of that paper got my name and address from Police Headquarters – phoned and phoned and wrote 3 page letters seeking to induce me to meet and talk things over and offered if I provided notes to have a book written. If I so desired I could write my own biography but I don't care to do so. All I want is the peace and quietness, the obscurity I now enjoy.' Shortis changed his lodgings to another house on Maitland Street, anticipating an exposé in the *Star*, but no such story has been found. To its credit, the paper, it seems, did not share the information on his whereabouts with its readers.

The reports of Shortis' release in the Quebec press created considerable interest – and concern. On 14 May the MP from Beauharnois, Maxime Raymond, wrote to his fellow Liberal, P.J.A. Cardin, the acting minister of justice, as well as to M.F. Gallagher, the chief of the Remissions Branch, strongly condemning the release (Ernest Lapointe was with King in London to attend the coronation and the imperial conference). Raymond had received protests from many, including a letter from C. Ernest Loy of Montreal, the brother of the murdered John Loy, and from John Lowe, the man who had escaped into the vault with the money on the night of the tragedy. Forty-two years had gone by. Loy wrote that he 'was very much surprised to notice in the papers the release of Shortis and certainly disappointed that the Liberal Government would do so'; he demanded to know 'on what grounds and on whose recommendation he was released,' and ended with a threat that further action might be taken, possibly, although this was not explicitly stated, a further prosecution for the murder of Leboeuf.
   Lowe wrote to Raymond: 'I wish you would take up the question with the authorities at Ottawa why Shortis has been paroled and left to roam around Canada, a man who has committed a crime of such immensity and was condemned to die ...' He had been heard to say that 'if he ever got out he would shoot Lowe as I was the cause of his not cleaning the office out.' 'I am an interested party,' Lowe went on to say, 'and I would be pleased if you would take an interest in this matter and have him returned to fulfil his sentence.'
   Raymond, who had been twelve years old in 1895, was again in

touch with Cardin: 'It seems to me that under these circumstances, Shortis' Ticket of Leave ought to be cancelled and Shortis returned to the Kingston Penitentiary.' A meeting between the two men was arranged.

'The example of the notorious bandit, Red Ryan, ought to have taught you a lesson,' Raymond wrote to Gallagher. Moreover, he was annoyed that no inquiries had been made in the district where the crime was committed: 'I know from my own experience that for the slightest misdemeanour, for example, a person who steals because of hunger, he is not released from prison without first obtaining certificates from the priest, the mayor, aldermen, counsellors, the sentencing judge, etc., etc., etc. But in a case of a horrible murder like this one, the memory of which time cannot erase, nothing of this sort was done.'

Cardin instructed the deputy minister of justice to place all the papers before Lapointe immediately upon his return. There is nothing to indicate Lapointe's reaction. The files do show, however, that Raymond met him on his return and that Gallagher then contacted Dr Barker, who said Shortis was doing well and enclosed the long chatty letter to his wife to show his positive state of mind. Gallagher made an appointment to see Shortis in Toronto and on 22 June they met in Neelands' office in Queen's Park; he found Shortis 'to be quite happy and contented with his new life and surroundings.' The next day Neelands wrote to Gallagher: 'From my knowledge of him I do not think that there is the least likelihood of him engaging in any form of crime or going to Quebec or in any way violating the conditions or spirit of the Ticket-of-Leave.' He then accepted an arrangement that had been discussed at their meeting: 'In accordance with our conversation of yesterday I shall be glad to have some member of my staff contact him daily for the time being at least or until you are satisfied that such close supervision is no longer advisable. If such daily contact is broken I shall advise you immediately.'

Several months later Neelands reported to Gallagher that Shortis 'has carried on splendidly and shows every evidence of continuing as a really good citizen.' He had been reporting daily, 'late each afternoon so that we would be in a position to say that it was a physical impossibility for Shortis, if he were so inclined, to go to Western Quebec and return overnight and thus refute any possible argument or claim which might be put forward by those in Western Quebec who are hostile towards him.' Although inconvenient, they were prepared to continue the arrangement if Ottawa considered it advisable. Ottawa assured him that it was. Gallagher reported to Raymond all these circumstances, hoping he would agree they 'have exercised great care, and have taken all reasonable precautions.' Moreover, they had checked on possible threats to Lowe and had come to the conclusion that 'it was extremely doubtful that any such threats were made.' There is no further correspondence with Raymond in the files.

Shortis continued to enjoy 'the peace and quietness, the obscurity' he wanted. The available records contain little of note. He changed his lodgings on a number of occasions (Maitland to Gloucester to Isabella to Yorkville), remaining in much the same area of the city. None of these houses is still standing, except 119 Yorkville, which is now The Brass Bed shop. On one of these moves he mistakenly burned his ticket of leave, but the Department of Justice immediately sent a new one in an envelope to 'Francis Cuthbert.'

He continued to go every day to Neelands' office, but in early 1938, with Gallagher's permission, they started gradually 'easing off' from that requirement. A year later Neelands suggested that reporting was now no longer necessary: 'He certainly appears to have carried on properly as a good citizen since his release on Ticket-of-Leave and I respectfully suggest that it is not necessary for him to report further, other than is usually provided by law in Ticket-of-Leave cases.' Gallagher replied that 'the Right Honourable Mr. Lapointe has directed me to state ... that he has no objection to the conditions of his reporting to you being modified as you see fit. The Minister would prefer, however, that, in addition to living up to the ordinary conditions of his Licence, Shortis remain under your personal supervision, and that he keep in touch with you at certain intervals, which you yourself can best determine.'

Shortis now had to report only once a month. There is nothing to suggest he ever left the province. He was not permitted under the ticket of leave to go outside Canada, the Department of Justice had assured the lawyers for the Shortis estate, but Fergus Power, the Irish solicitor who handled the estate in the 1930s (and still does today) recollects that Shortis did, in fact, return to Ireland for a visit. Mr Power has refused to examine his records to assist me any further because of what he describes as 'the sensitive nature of the matter' and because of a solicitor's natural and understandable reluctance to disclose anything that might conceivably be considered a breach of a solicitor and client relationship.[4]

Shortis continued to serve with the Queen's Own Rifles, going on manoeuvres with them each year. In June 1938 he obtained Neelands' permission to 'go under canvas with the militia' and sent him the following letter from camp:

B Company

Niagara on the Lake Camp
Niagara on the Lake, Ont.

21/6/38

My dear Mr. Neelands

I left Toronto by boat and we sailed from warf of Canada Ship Lines (down at bottom of Bay I think) Sunday morn at 8 o'clock for this beautiful camp as a member of a 'special advance party.' I worked – hard as any 'bull gang' ever did up at Burwash in the Bush – with a grin on my face and a song in my heart until 10.20. Two officers and two N.C.O.'s also pulled their weight in the boat. Every one did his bit well. Took a shower, dressed and strolled down to town where I sought to drown my sorrows (a pair of sore hands) in drink. Oh yes, no good trying to conceal the fact: nor do I proudly profess I didn't. You'd have done the same. After sucking through a straw two glasses of cold cold milk I felt fine I thought. Then I bought a box of strawberries and another drink and felt fine. So I went home to 3rd tent in B lines to sleep the dreamless peaceful sleep of a simple soldier of the King, after saying – as usual – my prayers. And you and yours are always remembered in them ... Everyone is doing his bit, looking fit and acting as should the soldiers of the King. I'm treated so well. Was offered a Royal Military Police job yesterday afternoon. The night patrol in City. All O.K. No trouble. A few needed a bit of jollying and a cigarette to get them home. When my Company came up yesterday noon they gave me a cheer when they halted and came to 'stand easy' and saw

Your devoted and grateful friend
F.V. Cuthbert

It is hard to picture a happier Valentine Shortis, a royal military policeman, a 'soldier of the King,' cheered by his colleagues. Perhaps an even happier picture, though there is no record of it, would have been Shortis' participation in his regiment's march past when the King and Queen visited Toronto in 1939.

Shortis of course saw Beall, who continued to lecture around the province, whenever he was in Toronto. Beall wanted to complete his mission of obtaining a full pardon for his friend, and asked Neelands to take up the matter with Ottawa: 'I feel very strongly that after forty three years of punishment the time has fully come for him to be absolutely free.' Neelands disagreed, advising him that 'for the present we should leave well enough alone.'

But he did not accept the advice. He wrote again to Lady Aberdeen, urging her to ask Lapointe for a 'complete pardon.' He first described Shortis' present condition: 'He dresses as befitting his birth and station – an old country gentleman. He is a handsome looking man and everywhere attracts attention by his military bearing. He has thrown himself heartily into The Queen's Own Rifles where he has become a great favourite. He believes in the Empire and in its defence. With this in mind he is one of the best recruiting agents the Q.O.R. ever had. I keep in close touch with him. He is a welcome visitor at the homes of my friends. He is a brilliant conversationalist and never ceases to be a gentleman.' Beall then touched on the crime. He believed, it will be recalled, that Shortis had acted in self-defence when called 'A Royal Bastard,' a fact that was not disclosed to his counsel in order to protect Queen Victoria's honour but which Beall assumed Lady Aberdeen knew: 'No one in the world knows the history of his case better than you. He was never a criminal. He was grossly diabolically insulted and a tragedy ensued. You, dear Madam, by your intercession, saved his life ... I am sure you will gladly do your part to see that his few remaining years may be spent in freedom and service for Christ and Canada and others.'

Lady Aberdeen, now eighty-one, wrote to Lapointe:

> I have no right to trouble you in the matter beyond the fact of my acquaintance with the Shortis family in Ireland. They are a much respected family, but undoubtedly there has been a strain of mental trouble amongst them, which I suppose accounted for the tragedy.
>
> I know nothing of him personally, beyond what Mr. Beall writes, and I do not know Mr. Beall either. But I felt I could not refuse to hand on to you the plea made on his behalf.

She added that Shortis' late father 'was only anxious that the public should never hear of him again, and he did not want him to be free to return to Ireland,' a statement that, perhaps unintentionally, would act against the granting of a pardon.

On the same day, she wrote to Mackenzie King: 'The other letter of which I enclose a copy relates to that unfortunate man Valentine Shortis, whose release after 44 years in prison you helped to secure – two years ago. I hope there is nothing wrong in sending a copy of this letter to Mr. Lapointe, as requested. My only claim to a right to do this is my acquaintance with the Shortis family in Ireland.'

Lapointe replied immediately, to Lady Aberdeen and to Beall, that 'any variation of the Licence permitting Shortis to be at large, provisions of which require that he remain in Canada within the jurisdiction of the Canadian authorities, is not contemplated.'

About a month after receiving Lapointe's letter, Lady Aberdeen died. Arthur Beall died a few months later.

When war broke out in September 1939 the Queen's Own Rifles were secretly placed in a brigade held for possible hostilities on the Pacific coast.[5] Shortis continued to drill with the men. From 1 April to 31 May 1940, the regimental records show that he was paid for five days at $1.20 a day. On 5 June, however, the regiment was mobilized to go overseas as part of the 3rd Canadian Division. Shortis had tried to enlist for active service, but because of his age and his physical condition he was refused, and on 6 June he was honourably discharged from the regiment. Neelands' son recalls that he volunteered for the Finnish army, to help it in its struggle against the Soviet Union, but it was all over before he could go. The Finnish authorities, however, have not been able to confirm whether or not this was so.

In less than a year Shortis was dead. On 30 April 1941 he went into Mehr's drugstore on Bloor Street, complaining that he was feeling ill; the druggist gave him some medicine but he died within the hour.

His body was taken to the Coroner's Building on Lombard Street. It was then noticed that his wallet and watch were missing, suggesting to some that there had been foul play – perhaps, said the press, 'an act of vengeance.' A post-mortem was ordered 'to satisfy everybody concerned with his death.' The coroner confirmed he had had a heart attack.

As no one claimed the body – a wire to Waterford produced no response – the public trustee arranged the funeral in St Michael's Cathedral, with burial in the Catholic Mount Hope Cemetery in the north end of Toronto. Shortis' funds just about covered the cost.

Now for the first time the press disclosed his identity. 'Shortis was a familiar figure in Toronto,' said the *Telegram*; 'Distinguished by his goatee, monocle and cane, he was known to hundreds, but only a few had any inkling of his past.' The *Star* reported, wrongly, that he had been 'educated at Oxford ... the scion of an aristocratic Irish family.' And the *Telegram* added – again incorrectly – that he had 'the ability to speak at least half a dozen languages perfectly.'

About twenty-five people attended the requiem mass at St Michael's Cathedral, including Neelands and other government officials, Shortis' landlady, and friends from Toronto, Guelph, and Stouffville. The *Star* reported that Hugh Wilson's brother was also there: 'In the back of the Cathedral, sitting alone through the service, was a man whose life Shortis had closely touched. He was the brother of the one man of three shot by Shortis who had recovered.' A dozen friends accompanied the casket to the cemetery, where Shortis was buried in an unmarked grave.

The Toronto inspector of detectives officially informed the commissioner of the RCMP of Shortis' death, and Warden Allan at Kingston added the Toronto *Telegram* clipping to the voluminous Shortis file, noting that they were 'closing out a very interesting file so far as this Penitentiary was concerned.'

So ends a story that has cut a wide swath through Canadian history. At least five prime ministers were at one time or another actively involved in the case (Bowell, Tupper, Laurier, Meighen, and King), as were at least nine ministers of justice (Tupper, Dickey, Mowat, Mills, Fitzpatrick, Doherty, Gouin, Guthrie, and Lapointe), three governors-general (Aberdeen, Byng, and Tweedsmuir), and at least four justices of the Supreme Court of Canada (Davies, Mills, Fitzpatrick, and Newcombe). The people involved had public careers that stretched over a hundred and fifty years, from Mackenzie Bowell who entered public life in the 1830s, to J.C. McRuer who remained a public figure in the 1980s.

What conclusions can be drawn? As in my earlier study of the Lipski case in England,[6] I have tried to show the inherent frailty of the criminal process. The Shortis story again places a trial and its aftermath in the context of the social, political, and economic conditions of the time. In *The Trials of Israel Lipski* I wrote: 'Justice may in theory be blind, but in practice she has altogether too human a perspective.' The same is true here. The result of the trial, the commutation, the question of Shortis' release may in part have been influenced by the slip of a draughtsman's pen in preparing a criminal code, the improper failure to grant a change of venue, the extreme rivalry of counsel, the reaction of the press, the cry of popular opinion, the vulnerability of the government, a mother's tears, a father's wealth, the strong feelings of the family and friends of the victims, the continuing interest of Lady Aberdeen and her friendship with prominent politicians, and much more. Not only did these events affect the case, but the case influenced events, in particular the conduct and possibly the result of the 1896 election and the removal of the insane from Kingston Penitentiary in 1915.

The story also reveals the development of the law of insanity, although it shows we have not gone very far in resolving many of the inherently difficult issues. Basically, the same test is used today, with of course the legislative error (in using 'and' rather than 'or') corrected, and with a more liberal interpretation of the word 'appreciate.'[7] Nevertheless, if the Shortis case arose today, it is likely his plea of insanity would again fail. A new criminal code is now being prepared and the very issues debated in 1895 are still being discussed, in particular the extent to which irresistible impulse should be a valid defence to a crime.[8] Further, as in 1895, there is often a clash between counsel and psychiatrists on the issue of insanity. The handling of insane convicts continues to be debated: should they be held within a penitentiary or in a special institution outside? As we have seen, Canada has gone full circle twice on this issue and no doubt the wheel will continue to turn. We have also learned something of the inherent danger of predicting future conduct, and indeed this may be our most important conclusion. Shortis was declared 'incurably insane' in 1895 by the very best psychiatrists in Canada; he later became, in the eyes of many, a distinguished, Oxford-educated, cultured gentleman.

Further, the story touches in a selective manner on the history of corrections in Canada, from the punitive origins of Kingston Penitentiary through the period of rehabilitation to the present period of uncertainty. Our mammoth penal system, it can be seen, was not the outcome of sustained, logical growth. To a great extent it has been the result of accidents, economic factors, the desire to use existing structures, and the shifting demands of public opinion. What we have today was not inevitable.

Finally, the story itself. Was the crime premeditated? Was Shortis insane, as the psychiatrists said, or was he simulating insanity as Macmaster and the citizens of Valleyfield believed? Was he later pretending to be insane, as he once told Neelands, in order to be transferred from St Vincent de Paul to Kingston? These questions will be left to the reader.

Another question that I will leave to the reader is why Lady Aberdeen, over more than forty years, took such an interest in the case. Was it simply one mother's sympathy for another, or did she know something that never emerged at the trial? What did she tell Sir Charles Hibbert Tupper when she asked him to see her on 30 December 1895, and said: 'There is an aspect of the matter which I want to lay before you in a very few words and so as friends, I ask you to come and hear this.' We know that Shortis and Beall believed that his father was the illegitimate son of Prince Albert, but there is nothing in Queen Victoria's journals or correspondence to show any interest at all in the case. Moreover, none of the many biographies of Prince Albert even suggests the possibility that he fathered an illegitimate child, although many discuss the question of his own legitimacy and the known immorality of his parents. The most that can be said in favour of Shortis' belief is that Victoria and Albert visited southern Ireland around the time that his father was likely conceived,[9] though the exact date of his birth is not known.

A further possibility cannot be fully discounted. Neelands' son, James, claims that when his eighty-seven-year-old father was in the hospital in late 1974, dying of cancer of the liver, he told him for the first time the 'real story' of Valentine Shortis, a story that C.F. Neelands believed to be true. James Neelands has written this account at my request: 'When father was in the hospital in late 1974, a week or two before he died, he brought up Valentine's name and said to me, "Did I ever tell you the real story of Valentine?" He proceeded to tell me that Valentine was born as a "son of the church." I asked dad what he meant and he told me that Valentine's father was a cardinal.'[10] How Neelands acquired this 'information' is not known. Could it be true? Is it possible that Monsignor O'Bryen, who had married the parents, had been a priest in Ireland, had travelled to Valleyfield to attend the trial and died the following week in part from the emotional strain, was Valentine Shortis' father? Might this explain why Francis Shortis was anxious for his son to go to Canada and remain there. Except for a change of heart during a brief period at the end of the First World War, he never wanted him to return to Ireland.

The Irish solicitor, who undoubtedly still has records going back to the nineteenth century, might be able to shed light on these possibilities, but, as mentioned, he refuses to delve into the past.

One final question before we end the strange case of Valentine Shortis. What was the true relationship between Shortis and Millie Anderson? I have been unable to trace Millie Anderson's subsequent career. She apparently left the locality shortly after the trial. A story in the Huntingdon *Gleaner*, placed at my request, brought forward only one response. A farmer from the Eastern Townships used to see her in the early 1930s in the small town of Champlain, New York, where she spent her summers. She was, he said, 'very fancy and very rich. She drove a big Cadillac and had lots of jewellery.' He thinks she probably lived in Montreal. She would be well over a hundred, if still alive today.

There is one additional piece of information, contained in Neelands' Queen's Park file, which I have kept to the end. On 10 December 1937, seven months after Shortis' release from the penitentiary, the superintendent of the Guelph Reformatory, J.D. Heaslip, sent the following letter to Neelands in Toronto:

December 10, 1937

Dear Sir:

Re: Valentine Shortis

A Miss Anderson from Montreal called here asking for the address of the above-noted. She states that she was a girl of sixteen the night Shortis perpetrated his murders. Shortis was to have gone with members of her family on a sleigh riding expedition but it was too stormy. Instead he went to the factory with rather bad results. She states that she is a friend of his mother and father and that she gave evidence in court at his trial. Her mother, who has recently died, would never let her contact Shortis while he was in prison, although she states she always wanted to see him. She impresses me as being a respectable person.

I have taken the liberty of referring her to you. I told her that she would probably not be able to contact Shortis at all unless he wished to meet her. I also told her that you had Shortis' address and had contact with him, and if you saw fit you would probably give her the contact with Shortis that she wishes.

Shortis, it seems, was never told of this letter.

Notes

S PECIFIC REFERENCES to the principal government files on the Shortis case and the major newspapers examined have not been included in the endnotes. The following government files exclusively devoted to the case were extensively used: Department of Justice Capital Case File, Public Archives of Canada (PAC), RG13, C-1, vol. 1486-7; Privy Council Records, PAC, RG2, series 1, vol. 443; Ticket-of-Leave File, PAC, RG13, C-2, reel #M-1866; Kingston Penitentiary Records, PAC, Correctional Service Canada, file 83, Ott. Pri. Class. 0461; Beauharnois Court Records, Palais de Justice, Valleyfield, Quebec; Quebec Attorney-General's File, Archives Nationales du Québec; Ontario Provincial Secretary File, Ontario Archives, RG20, series D-1, file #M-4211; Colonial Office Records, CO42/837, #23024/95.

In addition, the relevant available papers of all the major participants in the case were examined, the following proving to be the most helpful: Lord and Lady Aberdeen, PAC and Haddo House, Scotland; Charles Hibbert Tupper, University of British Columbia Library; R.M. Bucke, University of Western Ontario Library; C.K. Clarke, Clarke Institute of Psychiatry, University of Toronto; W.L. Mackenzie King, PAC; and Wilfrid Laurier, PAC.

The following newspapers were examined: *Le Courrier du Canada*, *La Minerve*, *Le Monde*, *La Patrie*, *La Presse*, Montreal *Gazette*, Montreal *Daily Herald*, Montreal *Daily Star*, *Family Herald and Weekly Star*, Montreal *Weekly Witness*, Huntingdon *Gleaner*, Ottawa *Daily Free Press*, *Progrès de Valleyfield*, *True Witness and Catholic Chronicle*, Toronto *Globe*, Toronto *Mail and Empire*, Toronto *Star*, Toronto *World*, London *Times*, New York *Times*, plus a number of Irish papers: Clonmel *Chronicle*, Tipperary and Waterford *Advertiser*, *Irish Times*, Limerick *Leader*, Waterford *News*, and Waterford *Standard*.

No full transcript of the trial was discovered. The newspapers, however, contained extensive verbatim reports of the trial, and counsel's addresses to the jury and the judge's charges to the jury were published commercially at the time and are available.

CHAPTER 1: Tragedy at Valleyfield

1 For general descriptions of Valleyfield, see Abbé L.-A. Groulx, *Petite Histoire de Salaberry de Valleyfield* (Montreal: Libraire Beauchemin 1913); Mgr. J.-D. St-Aubin, *Salaberry de Valleyfield, 1842 à 1972* (Coteau-du-Lac 1972); C. Larivière, *Histoire des Travailleurs de Beauharnois et Valleyfield* (Albert St-Martin 1974).

2 An Act to Alter the Duties of Customs and Excise, Stat. Can. 1879, c. 15. See P.B. Waite, *Canada, 1874-1896: Arduous Destiny* (Toronto: McClelland and Stewart 1971) at pp 93 *et seq.*; see also R.C. Brown, *Canada's National Policy, 1883-1900: A Study in Canadian-American Relations* (Princeton University Press 1964). For a discussion of the cotton industry in Canada, see R.T. Naylor, *The History of Canadian Business, 1867-1914*, vol. 2 (Toronto: Lorimer 1975) at pp 168 *et seq.*; see also P.-A. Linteau, R. Durocher, J.-C. Robert, *Quebec: A History, 1867-1929* (Toronto: Lorimer 1983) at pp 116 *et seq.*

3 Toronto *Star*, 17 Aug. 1985

4 See Robert Sellar, *The History of Huntingdon* (Huntingdon *Gleaner* 1888, reprinted 1975).

5 See *La Presse*, 5 Oct. 1895.

6 For previous hangings see Capital Cases Register, 1884-1900, PAC, RG13, C-1, vol. 1397. United States comparisons can be found in Montreal *Gazette*, 4 Nov. 1895, and G.T. Denison, 'Canada and Her Relations to the Empire' (1895) 144 *Westminster Review* 248 at p 262. Today, the US murder rate is four times as high as the Canadian rate: see M.L. Friedland, 'Gun Control in Canada' in Friedland, *A Century of Criminal Justice: Perspectives on the Development of Canadian Law* (Toronto: Carswell 1984) at p 114, n11.

7 Obituaries, Montreal *Gazette* and *Daily Star*, 4 March 1922; *Who Was Who, 1916-1928*

8 See obituary, *Gazette*, 10 Jan. 1916; P.-G. Roy, *Les Juges de la Province de Quebec* (Quebec City 1933) at p 491; H.J. Morgan, *The Canadian Men and Women of the Time* (Toronto 1898) at p 902; G.M. Rose, *Canadian Biography* (Toronto 1888) at p 70.

9 *Brophy v. Attorney-General of Manitoba*, [1895] A.C. 202. See generally G. Bale, 'Law, Politics and the Manitoba School Question: Supreme

Court and Privy Council' (1985) 63 *Canadian Bar Review* 461; for Ewart quotation see the Toronto *Globe*, 5 March 1895.

10 See J.D. Borthwick, *History of the Montreal Prison from A.D. 1760 to A.D. 1907* (Montreal 1886).

11 See obituaries, Montreal *Daily Star*, 17 and 18 March 1937.

12 See P. Rutherford, *A Victorian Authority: The Daily Press in Late Nineteenth-Century Canada* (University of Toronto Press 1982) at p 236, a valuable source of information on many of the papers referred to in this manuscript.

CHAPTER 2: Pre-Trial Manoeuvres

1 The Criminal Code, Stat. Can. 1892, c. 29, s. 651

2 *Rex* v. *Harris* (1762), 3 Burr. 1330 at p 1333, 97 E.R. 858 at p 859

3 See R.E. Salhany, *Canadian Criminal Procedure*, 4th ed. (Aurora: Canada Law Book 1984) at pp 36 *et seq.*

CHAPTER 3: The Crown's Case

1 See obituary, Montreal *Gazette*, 31 July 1916; P.-G. Roy, *Les Juges de la Province de Quebec* (Quebec City 1933) at p 353.

2 See D.G. Browne and E.V. Tullett, *Bernard Spilsbury* (London: Harrap 1951) at p 61.

3 Criminal Law Amendment Act, 1985, Stat. Can. 1985, c. 20, s. 120; Administration of Justice (Miscellaneous Provisions) Act 1933, s. 1 (U.K.)

4 Criminal Code, s. 555; see generally R.E. Salhany, *Canadian Criminal Procedure*, 4th ed. (Aurora: Canada Law Book 1984) at p 274

5 *The Queen* v. *Yancey* (1899), 2 C.C.C. 320 at p 322 (Quebec Q.B.). Mixed juries came in, following Lord Durham's report, more to help prosecutors get convictions, particularly in political cases, than to help the accused: see G.M. Craig, ed., *Lord Durham's Report* (Carleton Library 1963) at p 41.

6 See P.B. Waite, *Canada, 1874-1896: Arduous Destiny* (Toronto: McClelland and Stewart 1971) at pp 161-2. Cf. T. Flanagan, *Riel and the 1885 Rebellion Reconsidered* (Saskatoon: Western Producer Prairie Books 1983) at p 119. S. 556 of the Criminal Code relating to mixed juries in Manitoba was repealed by Stat. Can. 1977-8, c. 36, s. 3.

7 See M.L. Friedland, *A Century of Criminal Justice: Perspectives on the Development of Canadian Law* (Toronto: Carswell 1984) at pp 233 *et seq.*

8 See *Smythe* v. *The King*, [1941] S.C.R. 17. The reverse onus provision of s. 16 has so far withstood attack using the Canadian Charter of Rights and Freedoms: see *Regina* v. *Godfrey* (1984), 11 C.C.C. (3d) 233 (Man. C.A.); *Regina* v. *Fisher* (Ont. C.A.), 7 June 1984, unreported.

9 See *Regina* v. *Cooper* (1980), 51 C.C.C. (2d) 129, and at p 145; *Regina* v. *Barnier* (1980), 51 C.C.C. (2d) 193. Cf. *Kjeldsen* v. *The Queen* (1981), 64 C.C.C. (2d) 161; *Regina* v. *Abbey* (1982), 68 C.C.C. (2d) 394.

10 (1843), 10 Cl. & Fin. 200, 8 E.R. 718 (H.L.). See generally R. Moran, *Knowing Right from Wrong: The Insanity Defence of Daniel McNaughtan* (New York: The Free Press 1981).

11 *Can. H. of C. Debates*, 17 May 1892, at p 2707

12 See, for example, *Rex* v. *True* (1922), 127 Law Times 561 at p 563 (C.C.A.) ('The word is not "and" but "or." '); *Rex* v. *Dillon* (1939), 27 Cr. App. R. 149 at p 152 ('the word is "or," not "and" ').

13 See *Can. H. of C. Debates*, 17 May 1892, at p 2708, Sir John Thompson stating: 'The words are the same as those of the English Act.' See Stephen's Criminal Code (Indictable Offences) Bill, Bill 178, 1878; *Report of the Royal Commission appointed to consider the law Relating to Indictable Offences*, 1879, C. 2345 (Lord Blackburn, chairman); Bill 47, Bill to establish a Criminal Code, 1880. See generally M.L. Friedland, 'R.S. Wright's Model Criminal Code: A Forgotten Chapter in the History of the Criminal Law' (1981), 1 *Oxford Journal of Legal Studies* 307, reprinted in Friedland, *A Century of Criminal Justice*.

14 Montreal *Herald*, 10 Sept. 1895

15 See *The Queen v Louis Riel*, introduction by D. Morton (University of Toronto Press 1974) at p 348.

16 (1931), 56 C.C.C. 190 at p 193 (Ont. C.A.)

17 See PAC, Capital Cases Files, RG13, C-1.

18 *Minutes of Proceedings of the Sixteenth Annual Meeting of the Canadian Bar Association, 1931* (Toronto: Carswell 1932) at pp 60-4

19 *Rex* v. *Jeanotte*, [1932] 2 W.W.R. 283 (Sask. C.A.)

20 Stat. Can. 1953-4, c. 51, s. 16

21 See, for example, *Rex* v. *Harrop*, [1940] 3 W.W.R. 77 (Man. C.A.).

22 Capital Cases, RG13, C-1, vol. 1832

23 Capital Cases, RG13, C-1, vol. 1432

24 Criminal Code, s. 573(2)

CHAPTER 4: The Defence

1 See generally H.B. Neatby and J.T. Saywell, 'Chapleau and the Conservative Party in Quebec' (1956), 37 *Canadian Historical Review* 1.

2 See generally O.D. Skelton, *Life and Letters of Sir Wilfrid Laurier*, vol. 1 (Oxford University Press 1922) at pp 463-5; P. Crunican, *Priests and Politicians: Manitoba Schools and the Election of 1896* (University of Toronto Press 1974) at p 122; L.C. Clark, *The Manitoba School Question: Majority Rule or Minority Rights* (Toronto: Copp Clark 1968).

CHAPTER 5: The Psychiatrists

1 See generally C. Greenland, 'L'Affaire Shortis and the Valleyfield Murders' (1962) 7 *Canadian Psychological Association Journal* 261; Greenland, 'Dangerousness, Mental Disorder, and Politics' in C.D. Webster, M.H. Ben-Aron, and S.J. Hucker, eds., *Dangerousness: Probability and Prediction, Psychiatry and Public Policy* (Cambridge University Press 1985) at pp 25 *et seq.*
2 See H.J. Morgan, *The Canadian Men and Women of the Time* (Toronto 1912). Between 1866 and 1892 the medical school was not, in fact, officially part of Queen's University, although Queen's conferred the degrees and graduates 'thought of themselves as Queen's men': See D.D. Calvin, *Queen's University at Kingston* (Kingston: Queen's University 1941) at p 197.
3 See generally C.H. Cahn, *Douglas Hospital: 100 Years of History and Progress* (Montreal 1981).
4 *M'Naghten's Case* (1843), 10 Cl. & Fin. 200 at p 211, 8 E.R. 718 at p 723 (H.L.)
5 See *Bleta* v. *The Queen*, [1965] 1 C.C.C. 1 (S.C.C.).
6 See the fine study by C.E. Rosenberg, *The Trial of the Assassin Guiteau: Psychiatry and Law in the Gilded Age* (University of Chicago Press 1968). See now H.I. Kaplan and B.J. Sadock, eds., *Comprehensive Textbook of Psychiatry*, 4th ed. (Baltimore: Williams and Wilkins 1985) at pp 635 *et seq.*
7 See obituaries, Montreal *Gazette* and Toronto *Daily Star*, 21 Jan. 1924; (1924) 55 *Canadian Journal of Medicine and Surgery* 135; [1924] *Ontario Journal of Neuro-Psychiatry*; [1924] *University of Toronto Monthly* 223; C. Greenland, 'C.K. Clarke: A Founder of Canadian Psychiatry' (1966), 95 *Canadian Medical Association Journal* 155; Greenland, *Charles Kirk Clarke: A Pioneer of Canadian Psychiatry* (Clarke Institute of Psychiatry 1966); Greenland, 'A Revealing Portrait of Dr. C.K. Clarke,' [1980] *Ontario Medical Review* 581; R. Baehre, 'The Ill-Regulated Mind: A Study in the Making of Psychiatry in Ontario, 1830-1921,' unpublished Ph.D. thesis, York University, 1985.
8 See G.A. Tucker, *Lunacy in Many Lands* (Sydney 1887) at p 595.

9 (London 1874) at p 171

10 See D. Hack Tuke, *A Dictionary of Psychological Medicine*, vol. 1 (Philadelphia 1892) at p 813; Tuke, *Prichard and Symonds* (London 1891) pp 68 and 101; Pitt-Lewis, *Smith and Hawke* (London 1895) at p 223. See also C.K. Clarke, 'Canadian Law in Regard to Responsibility,' [1898] *Queen's Quarterly* 273.

11 *Guiteau's Case* (1882), 10 Federal Reporter 161 (D.C.). See Rosenberg, *The Trial of the Assassin Guiteau*.

12 See Kaplan and Sadock, *Comprehensive Textbook of Psychiatry* at pp 631 *et seq.*

13 See 'The Case of F.V.C. Shortis,' an undated, unpublished document in the C.K. Clarke Papers at the Clarke Institute of Psychiatry, Toronto, and chap. 9, p 4, of 'The Amiable Morons.' This condition is described today in DSM-III in category 295.3x, schizophrenic disorder, paranoid type: see American Psychiatric Association, *Diagnostic Statistical Manual of Mental Disorders*, 3rd ed. (1980 APA) at p 191. The present head of the Clarke Institute of Psychiatry, Dr Vivian Rakoff, would, however, place Shortis in category 301.70 of DSM-III (pp 317 *et seq.*), antisocial personality disorders.

14 See J. Malcolm, *In the Freud Archives* (New York: Knopf 1984) at p 44.

15 G.M. Rose, *Cyclopaedia of Canadian Biography* (Toronto 1886); Morgan, *Canadian Men and Women* (1898); W.S. Wallace, *Dictionary of Canadian Biography* (Toronto 1926); see also T.E. Brown, 'Living with God's Afflicted: A History of the Provincial Lunatic Asylum at Toronto, 1830-1911,' unpublished Ph.D. thesis, Queen's University, 1980

16 Tucker, *Lunacy in Many Lands* at p 591; T.J.W. Burgess, 'A Historical Sketch of Our Canadian Institutions for the Insane,' [1898] *Transactions of the Royal Society of Canada* 3 at p 26. I am grateful to Dr J.D. Griffin for his help with the history of the Toronto asylum.

17 See D. Clark, 'A Psycho-Medical History of Louis Riel' (1887), 44 *American Journal of Insanity* 33; Clark, 'A Few Canadian Cases in Criminal Courts in which the Plea of Insanity was Presented' (1895), 2 *Transactions of the American Medico-Psychological Association* 171 at pp 173, 182 *et seq.*; *Mental Diseases: A Synopsis of Twelve Lectures* (Toronto 1895).

18 See obituaries, Toronto *Globe* and Montreal *Gazette*, 21 Feb. 1902; C.K. Clarke, 'Richard Maurice Bucke,' [1902] *American Journal of Insanity* 1; J.H. Coyne, 'Richard Maurice Bucke – A Sketch,' [1906] *Royal Society of Canada* at pp 159 *et seq.*; G.H. Stevenson, 'The Life and Work of Richard Maurice Bucke' (1937), 93 *American Journal of*

Psychiatry 1127; E. Seaborn, *The March of Medicine in Western Ontario* (Toronto: Ryerson Press 1944) at pp 290 *et seq.*; A. Lozynsky, *Richard Maurice Bucke: Medical Mystic* (Wayne State University Press 1977); Baehre, 'The Ill-Regulated Mind'; A Lozynsky and J.R. Reed, *A Whitman Disciple Visits Tennyson* (Lincoln, Neb.: Tennyson Research Centre 1977); R. Cook, *The Regenerators: Social Criticism in Late Victorian English Canada* (University of Toronto Press 1985); J.R. Colombo, 'A Doctor of Mysticism: Richard Maurice Bucke' (1961), 41 *Canadian Theosophist* 133; plus a number of helpful articles by C. Greenland in the following journals: (1963), 11 *Canada's Mental Health* 1; (1964), 91 *Canadian Medical Association Journal* 385; (1966), 11 *Canadian Psychiatric Association Journal* 146; (1967), 200 *Journal of the American Medical Association* 833; (1972), 17 *Canadian Psychiatric Association Journal* 71. The Bucke Papers are in the University of Western Ontario Library: see M.A. Jameson, ed., *Richard Maurice Bucke: A Catalogue Based upon the Collections of the University of Western Ontario Libraries* (University of Western Ontario 1978). I am grateful to Beth Miller, the Rare Books and Special Collections Librarian at Western, for her kind assistance.

19 Tucker, *Lunacy in Many Lands* at p 592. Bucke cited in Stevenson, 'The Life and Work of Richard Maurice Bucke' at p 1133
20 Ontario Legislative Assembly, *Sessional Papers* (no. 11), 1896, at p 40
21 T.J.W. Burgess, 'Richard Maurice Bucke' (1902), 9 *Transactions of the American Medico-Psychological Association* 301 at p 302
22 See W. White, ed., *The Collected Writings of Walt Whitman: Daybooks and Notebooks*, vol. 3 (New York University Press 1978) at pp 642-3.
23 'Cosmic Consciousness' (1894), 1 *Transactions of the American Medico-Psychological Association* 316
24 J. Kaplan, *Walt Whitman: A Life* (New York: Simon and Schuster 1980) at p 37
25 See obituary, Montreal *Star*, 25 Oct. 1895; *True Witness and Catholic Chronicle*, 23, 30 Oct. 1895. I am grateful to Father John Finlayson, Liverpool, for supplying additional biographical material.

CHAPTER 6: Rebuttal

1 *Canadian Who's Who* (Toronto 1910)
2 See M.L. Friedland, *A Century of Criminal Justice* (Toronto: Carswell 1984) at p 126.
3 *Ibid.* at p 240

4 *Guiteau's Case* (1882), 10 Federal Reporter 161 (D.C.). See generally C.E. Rosenberg, *The Trial of the Assassin Guiteau: Psychiatry and Law in the Gilded Age* (University of Chicago Press 1968).

5 See Taylor, *Evidence*, 8th ed. (Philadelphia 1887); Roscoe, *Evidence in Criminal Cases*, 11th ed. (London 1890); Archbold, *Pleading and Evidence in Criminal Cases*, 20th ed. (London 1886).

6 Montreal *Gazette*, 24 Oct. 1895

7 Criminal Code, 1892, s. 661

CHAPTER 7: Towards the Verdict

1 *Regina v. Burton* (1863), 3 F. & F. 772 at p 780, 176 E.R. 354 at p 357

2 See '*The Queen v. F.V.C. Shortis*: English Addresses of Counsel and the Charge of the Hon. Mr. Justice Mathieu to the Jury' (Montreal: Drysdale and Co. 1895), from the notes taken by Lomax and Urquhart, the official court stenographers.

3 *Affaire Shortis* (Montreal: Beauchemin 1896), the address of St Pierre and the judge's charge to the jury

4 First enacted by Stat. Can. 1948, c. 39, s. 39; now s. 573 of the Criminal Code. It would be highly unlikely that even with this power a court today would not adjourn in these circumstances.

5 I am grateful to Tim McCourt and Richard Owens for assisting with the translation of this and other passages.

6 See M.L. Friedland, 'Criminal Justice and the Constitutional Division of Power in Canada' in Friedland, *A Century of Criminal Justice* (Toronto: Carswell 1984) at pp 49 *et seq.*

7 *The Queen v. Oxford* (1840), Wallis State Trials 497

8 *Taylor on Evidence*, 8th ed. (Philadelphia 1887) at p 79

9 *Tracy Peerage* (1843), 10 Cl. & Fin. 154 at p 191, 8 E.R. 700 at p 715

CHAPTER 8: After the Trial

1 S. 744. The necessity for the consent of the attorney-general was abolished in 1900: see M.L. Friedland, *Double Jeopardy* (Oxford University Press 1969) at p 229.

2 See generally the excellent MA thesis, Carleton University, 1971, by M.K. Evans, 'The Prerogative of Pardon in Canada: Its Development 1864-1894.'

3 See W.P.M. Kennedy, *Documents of the Canadian Constitution, 1759-1915* (Oxford University Press 1918) at pp 698-9; see also A. Todd,

Parliamentary Government in the British Colonies (London: Longmans, Green 1894) at pp 365-6.

4 From the Capital Cases Register

5 See P.B. Waite, *The Man from Halifax: Sir John Thompson, Prime Minister* (University of Toronto Press 1985) at p 145; see generally R.A.J. Phillips, *The East Block* (Ottawa 1967).

6 See Waite, *ibid.* at pp 171 and 187-8.

7 See *Can. H. of C. Debates*, 23 April 1896, pp 7176-7.

8 See obituary, Montreal *Gazette*, 31 March 1927; F.H. Patterson, 'Some Incidents in the Life of Sir Charles Hibbert Tupper,' [1966] *Proceedings of the Nova Scotia Historical Society* 127; a biographical sketch by G.H. Cowan found in the Borden Papers, PAC, MG26H, vol. 268, pt. 2, p 150207. The extensive Charles Hibbert Tupper Papers are at the University of British Columbia Library; I am greatly indebted to librarian George Brandak for his courteous assistance.

9 See, for example, Patterson, *ibid.*

10 D. Macmaster, *The Seal Arbitration 1893* (apparently privately printed)

11 See L.C. Clark, 'A History of the Conservative Administrations: 1891 to 1896,' unpublished Ph.D. thesis, University of Toronto, 1968, at p 164.

12 See the excellent introductory essay by John Tupper Saywell, editor of the Champlain Society's edition of *The Canadian Journal of Lady Aberdeen, 1893-1898* (Toronto: The Champlain Society 1960). See also *Dictionary of National Biography*, 1931-40; and Lady Aberdeen's books, *The Musings of a Scottish Granny* (London: Heath Cranton 1936), and *'We Twa': Reminiscences of Lord and Lady Aberdeen*, 2 vols. (London: Collins 1925).

13 See J. Schull, *Laurier* (Toronto: Macmillan 1966) at p 294.

14 See the Gladstone Papers, British Library, add. 44090, Lady Aberdeen to Gladstone, 28 March 1895. I am indebted to Peter Waite of Dalhousie University for providing me with copies of his notes of this material.

15 S. Gwyn, *The Private Capital: Ambition and Love in the Age of Macdonald and Laurier* (Toronto: McClelland and Stewart 1984) at p 276

16 Saywell, *Journal of Lady Aberdeen* at p 166

CHAPTER 9: December 1895

1 See *Can. H. of C. Debates*, 23 April 1896, pp 7177-8.

2 See generally P.B. Waite, *The Man from Halifax: Sir John Thompson, Prime Minister* (University of Toronto Press 1985) at pp 198-9.

3 See Waite, *ibid.*; H. Charlesworth, *Candid Chronicles* (Toronto: Macmillan 1925) at pp 216-17; F.W. Anderson, *Hanging in Canada* (Calgary: Frontier Publishing 1973) at pp 39-48; Ottawa *Free Press*, 17 June 1895. For information on *Birchall* (Radclive's fourth hanging) see the Toronto *Globe*, 14 Nov. 1890; C. Kingston, *A Gallery of Rogues* (London: Stanley Paul 1924) at pp 204-10.
4 Many of these documents are reproduced in the printed volume, *Papers in the case of Valentine F.C. Shortis* (Ottawa 1896).

CHAPTER 10: Cabinet Meetings

1 See the obituary, Montreal *Gazette*, 11 Dec. 1917; G. Donaldson, *Sixteen Men: The Prime Ministers of Canada* (Toronto: Doubleday 1980) at p 52; Gladstone Papers, British Library, add. 44090, 26 July 1895; P.B. Waite, *The Man from Halifax: Sir John Thompson, Prime Minister* (University of Toronto Press 1985) at p 349.
2 Waite, *ibid.* at p 346; J. T. Saywell, *The Canadian Journal of Lady Aberdeen, 1893-1898* (Toronto: The Champlain Society 1960) at p 163; and see K. Hughes, *Father Lacombe* (New York: Moffat, Yard 1914) at p 359.
3 See M. Pope, *Public Servant: The Memoirs of Sir Joseph Pope* (Toronto: Oxford University Press 1960) at pp 104-6.
4 The case, with a complete transcript, can be found in PAC, Capital Cases Files, RG13, C-1, vol. 752, file 1832.
5 A. Bridle, *Sons of Canada: Short Studies of Characteristic Canadians* (Toronto: Dent 1916) at p 222
6 *The Queen* v. *Kehoe*, Capital Cases Files
7 See Pope, *Public Servant* at pp 105-6.
8 Waite, *The Man from Halifax* at p 302
9 Attendance at cabinet meetings is noted in PAC, Privy Council records RG2, series 1, vol. 441-3; series 3, vol. 112.
10 See generally P. Crunican, *Priests and Politicians: Manitoba Schools and the Election of 1896* (University of Toronto Press 1974); Hughes, *Father Lacombe.*
11 Montreal *Star*, 21 Dec. 1895
12 Saywell, *Journal of Lady Aberdeen* at p lvii
13 Public Record Office, London, C.O. 42/837, no. 21207
14 Rules respecting executions, Order-in-Council, 6 Jan. 1870, an extract of which is contained in the Nulty file, PAC, RG13, C-1

CHAPTER 11: Repercussions

1 J. Crankshaw, *Criminal Code*, ed. G.P. Rodriques, 8th ed. (Toronto: Carswell 1979). See generally M.L. Friedland, *Double Jeopardy* (Oxford University Press 1969).

CHAPTER 12: Political Turmoil

1 See J.T. Saywell, *The Canadian Journal of Lady Aberdeen, 1893-1898* (Toronto: The Champlain Society 1960) pp lvi *et seq.* and pp 298 *et seq.* See also an undated memorandum by George Foster: PAC, MG27, DII, D7, vol. 31, file 11. The C.H. Tupper and Aberdeen Papers provide many of the details of the crisis. See generally P.B. Waite, *Canada, 1874-1896: Arduous Destiny* (Toronto: McClelland and Stewart 1971) at pp 252 *et seq.*; P. Crunican, *Priests and Politicians: Manitoba Schools and the Election of 1896* (University of Toronto Press 1974) at pp 137 *et seq.*; L.C. Clark, 'A History of the Conservative Administrations: 1891 to 1896,' unpublished Ph.D. thesis, University of Toronto, 1968, at pp 323 *et seq.*; K.M. McLaughlin, 'Race, Religion and Politics: The Election of 1896 in Canada,' unpublished Ph.D. thesis, University of Toronto, 1974.
2 PAC, MG26F, vol. 24, file 30 May 1893-1 Jan. 1897
3 See letter from Tupper to Van Horne, 6 Jan. 1896, Tupper Papers, PAC, MG26F, vol. 10, 1895.
4 Undated memorandum by Costigan found in the Laurier Papers, PAC, MG27,ID5, vol. 2
5 Bowell Papers, PAC, MG27, IB5, vol. 1, pp 143-4
6 *Can. H. of C. Debates*, 7 Jan. 1896, pp 6-13
7 *Can. Senate Debates*, 1 March 1905, at pp 72 *et seq.*
8 Montreal *Star*, 14 Jan. 1896
9 *Can. H. of C. Debates*, 15 Jan. 1896, at p 75
10 Contained in Lady Aberdeen's Journal, PAC, MG27, IB5, vol. 10, 13 Jan. 1896
11 J. Willison, *Reminiscences: Political and Personal* (Toronto: McClelland and Stewart 1919) at p 124; F.H. Patterson, 'Some Incidents in the Life of Sir Charles Hibbert Tupper,' [1966] *Proceedings of the Nova Scotia Historical Society* 127 at p 160
12 Montreal *Herald*, 6 Jan. 1896
13 Foster memo at p 3
14 Archives of the New Brunswick Museum, Leonard Tilley Papers, box 9, pkt. 5, #2, Foster to Tilley, 23 Jan. 1896

15 See Crunican, *Priests and Politicians* at p 152. I am grateful to Father Crunican for this translation. The French original is as follows: 'Et puis commier Shortis, ce qui exaspère nos gens! C'est une fatalité contre nous.'

16 Tupper Papers, pp 1634-5

17 Tupper to Father Burke, 3 Feb. 1896, at p 1649

18 At p 159

19 *Can. H. of C. Debates*, 29 Jan. 1896, at p 827

20 30 Jan. 1896

21 *Can. H. of C. Debates*, 23 April 1896, at pp 7175-6

22 *Ibid.*, 29 Jan. 1896, at pp 834-5

23 *Ibid.*, 21 Jan. 1896, at p 364

24 See D.J.A. McMurchy, 'David Mills: Nineteenth Century Canadian Liberal,' unpublished Ph.D. thesis, University of Rochester, 1969.

25 W.E. O'Brien, 'The Prerogative of Mercy and the Shortis Case' (1896), 32 *Canadian Law Journal* 53 at p 58

26 See generally obituary, Montreal *Gazette*, 19 Dec. 1907; *Dictionary of National Biography*, 1901-11; L. Lapierre, 'Politics, Race and Religion in French Canada: Joseph Israel Tarte,' unpublished Ph.D. thesis, University of Toronto, 1962; R. Rumilly, *Histoire de la Province de Québec*, vol. 10, *Tarte* (Montreal: Bernard Valiquette 1943).

27 See Montreal *Herald*, 6, 31 March, 1, 4, 8 April 1896; Montreal *Star*, 6, 8 March 1896.

28 *Week*, 8 May 1891, cited in Waite, *Canada, 1874-1896* at p 227

29 Rumilly, *Histoire de la Province de Québec*, vol. 5, *Louis Riel* at pp 102-3

30 See Dickey in *Can. H. of C. Debates*, 23 April 1896, at p 7183.

31 See the Montreal *Star*, 13 April; *Herald*, 13 April; Huntingdon *Gleaner*, 16 April 1896.

32 The quotations are from the *Herald*, 13 April 1896.

33 See generally *Can. H. of C. Debates*, 23 April 1896, at pp 7171-85.

CHAPTER 13: The Election of 1896

1 P.B. Waite, *Canada, 1874-1896: Arduous Destiny* (Toronto: McClelland and Stewart 1971) at p 264

2 J.T. Saywell, *The Canadian Journal of Lady Aberdeen, 1893-1898* (Toronto; The Champlain Society 1960) at p lxvii

3 L. Lapierre, 'Politics, Race and Religion in French Canada: Joseph Israel Tarte, ' unpublished Ph.D. thesis, University of Toronto, 1962, at p 282

4 See generally P. Crunican, *Priests and Politicians: Manitoba Schools and the Election of 1896* (University of Toronto Press 1974) at p 232; L.C. Clark, 'A History of the Conservative Administrations: 1891 to 1896,' unpublished Ph.D. thesis, University of Toronto, 1968, at p 476; O.D. Skelton, *Life and Letters of Sir Wilfrid Laurier*, vol. 1 (Oxford University Press 1922) at p 479.

5 Crunican, *ibid.* at p 231

6 Montreal *Star*, 24 Feb. 1896; see also S. Gwyn, *The Private Capital: Ambition and Love in the Age of Macdonald and Laurier* (Toronto: McClelland and Steward 1984) at pp 287 *et seq.*

7 *Star*, 24 April 1896; see also Gwyn, *ibid.* at p 289

8 C. Tupper, *Recollections of Sixty Years in Canada* (London: Cassel 1914) at p 309

9 See Clark, 'History of the Conservative Administrations' at p 485.

10 Clark, *ibid.* at p 489

11 *Ibid.* at p 491. Moreover, Chapleau continued to be suspicious of the government's sincerity on the school question: see Crunican, *Priests and Politicians* at p 242.

12 (Toronto: Carswell 1911)

13 Montreal *Herald*, 25 April 1896

14 Tarte to Willison, 29 May 1896, cited in Lapierre, 'Politics, Race and Religion' at p 306

15 Waite, *Canada, 1874-1896* at p 277

16 *Can. H. of C. Debates*, 30 Sept. 1896, at p 2279. On Manitoba schools question, see generally Crunican, *Priests and Politicians*; Waite, *Canada, 1874-1896* at pp 274 *et seq.*; Lapierre, 'Politics, Race and Religion'; Saywell, *Journal of Lady Aberdeen*; Skelton, *Sir Wilfrid Laurier*.

17 R. Rumilly, *Histoire de la Province de Québec*, vol. 8, *Laurier* (Montreal 1942) at p 50

18 G. Donaldson, *Sixteen Men: The Prime Ministers of Canada* (Toronto: Doubleday 1980) at p 57. See generally Waite, *Canada, 1874-1896* at p 276; Crunican, *Priests and Politicians* at pp 274 *et seq.*; Saywell, *Journal of Lady Aberdeen* at pp lxiv *et seq.*; Lapierre, 'Politics, Race and Religion' at pp 304 *et seq.*

19 J.C. Patterson to Pope, 29 June 1896, PAC, Pope Papers, vol. 1, cited in Waite, *Canada, 1874-1896* at pp 277 and 317

20 See R. Cartwright, *Reminiscences* (Toronto: Briggs 1912) at p 354.

21 See generally Lapierre, 'Politics, Race and Religion' at pp 308 *et seq.* for the following material on Tarte.

22 See the Montreal *Herald*, 29 and 30 June 1896.

23 *Can. H. of C. Debates,* 7 May 1901, at p 4561
24 Stat. Can. 1907, c. 20. See P. Craven, *'An Impartial Umpire': Industrial Relations and the Canadian State, 1900-1911* (University of Toronto Press 1980) at pp 230 *et seq.*
25 King cited in J.E. Esberey, *Knight of the Holy Spirit: A Study of William Lyon Mackenzie King* (University of Toronto Press 1980) at p 198
26 Ferns and Ostry, *The Age of Mackenzie King: The Rise of the Leader* (London: Heinemann 1955) at pp 55-6
27 See Lapierre, 'Politics, Race and Religion' at pp 318 *et seq.; Can. H. of C. Debates,* 11 May 1898, at pp 5335 *et seq.*
28 F.H. Patterson, 'Some Incidents in the Life of Sir Charles Hibbert Tupper,' [1966] *Proceedings of the Nova Scotia Historical Society* 127 at p 147
29 See Saywell, *Journal of Lady Aberdeen* at pp lxxvii-viii, 349-50.
30 Clark, 'History of the Conservative Administrations' at p 325
31 See generally Saywell, *Journal of Lady Aberdeen* lxxx, lxxxi, the Aberdeen Papers, and the Sir Hibbert Tupper Papers.
32 See generally Patterson, 'Life of Sir Charles Hibbert Tupper.'
33 Cited in P.B. Waite, *The Man from Halifax: Sir John Thompson, Prime Minister* (University of Toronto Press 1985) at p 404
34 Saywell, *Journal of Lady Aberdeen* at p 456
35 See C. Miller, *The Canadian Career of the Fourth Earl of Minto* (Wilfrid Laurier University Press 1980) at p 56.
36 See R.C. Brown, *Robert Laird Borden: A Biography,* vol. 1 (Toronto: Macmillan 1975) at pp 46 *et seq.* See also Borden's later views of Sir Hibbert: Borden Papers, PAC, MG26, vol. 268, pt. 2, pp 150217-20; I am grateful to R.J. Sharpe for bringing this document to my attention.
37 See the Montreal *Star,* 23 April 1896; Huntingdon *Gleaner,* 16 July 1896.

CHAPTER 14: On the Banks of the Rivière-des-Prairies

1 See generally the important work by W.A. Calder, 'The Federal Penitentiary System in Canada, 1867-1899: A Social and Institutional History,' unpublished Ph.D. thesis, University of Toronto, 1979, and a short article drawn from the thesis, 'Convict Life in Canadian Federal Penitentiaries, 1867-1900' in L.A. Knafla, *Crime and Criminal Justice in Europe and Canada* (Wilfrid Laurier University Press 1981) at p 297. See also R.B. Splane, *Social Welfare in Ontario, 1791-1893: A Study of Public Welfare Administration* (University of Toronto Press 1965) at pp 128 *et seq.;* J.W. Ekstedt and C.T. Griffiths, *Corrections in Canada: Policy and Practice* (Toronto: Butterworths 1983); M. Jackson, *Prisoners of*

Isolation: Solitary Confinement in Canada (University of Toronto Press 1983); K. Joliffe, *Penitentiary Medical Services, 1835-1983* (Ottawa: Ministry of the Solicitor-General 1984); M.S. Cross, 'Imprisonment in Canada: A Historical Perspective,' John Howard Society of Ontario, Community Education Series 1, no. 6, no date; J.A. Edmison, 'Some Aspects of Nineteenth-Century Canadian Prisons' in W.T. McGrath, *Crime and Its Treatment in Canada*, 2nd ed. (Toronto: Macmillan 1976) at p 347. The *Annual Reports* of the minister of justice on penitentiaries, containing individual reports from the wardens, surgeons, and others, is a valuable source of information.

2 *Reports of the Royal Commission to Investigate the Penal System of Canada* (Ottawa 1938) (the Archambault Report) at p 13

3 See Jackson, *Prisoners of Isolation* at p 147; see also the *Report to Parliament by the Sub-Committee on the Penitentiary System in Canada* (Ottawa 1976) (M. MacGuigan, chairman) at p 29.

4 PAC, RG73, vol. 43, file 3-20-10

5 *Report of the Minister of Justice as to Penitentiaries in Canada for the year ended 30th June, 1896* (Ottawa 1897) at p 44

6 See generally the fine study by Joliffe, *Penitentiary Medical Services, passim.*

7 *Report from the Departmental Committee on Prisons*, C. 7702, 1895

8 See generally J.M. Beattie, *Attitudes towards Crime and Punishment in Upper Canada, 1830-1850: A Documentary Study* (Centre of Criminology, University of Toronto 1977); see also D. Curtis, A. Graham, L. Kelly, A. Patterson, *Kingston Penitentiary: The First Hundred and Fifty Years, 1835-1985* (Ottawa: Supply and Services 1985). See also, for a discussion of the origins of penitentiaries, M. Ignatieff, *A Just Measure of Pain: The Penitentiary in the Industrial Revolution, 1750-1850* (New York: Pantheon 1978).

9 *Report of a Select Committee on the Expediency of Erecting a Penitentiary, Journal of the House of Assembly*, 1831, appendix, at pp 211-12, cited in Beattie, *ibid.* at p 82

10 Cited in Edmison, 'Nineteenth-Century Canadian Prisons' at p 367

11 Cited in Beattie, *Attitudes towards Crime* at p 93

12 Moodie, *Life in the Clearings versus the Bush* (London: Richard Bentley 1853) at p 209

13 *Select Committee Report*, 1831, at pp 211-12, cited in Beattie, *Attitudes towards Crime* at p 84

14 See generally Calder, 'Federal Penitentiary System' at pp 296 *et seq.* and Stat. Can. 1883, c. 37, s. 50.

15 See generally Calder, *ibid.* at pp 309 *et seq.*

16 See *ibid.* at pp 74, 75, and 128.
17 Penitentiary Regulations, Consolidated Orders in Council of Canada, 1889, c. 60, s. 309
18 See generally Calder, 'Federal Penitentiary System' at pp 259 *et seq.*
19 See generally Calder, *ibid.* at pp 196 *et seq.* and at p 324; Cross, 'Imprisonment in Canada,' *passim.* Peter Oliver's forthcoming study of corrections in Ontario will show that a system of merit badges was introduced in the early 1860s.
20 See *Can. H. of C. Debates*, 21 June 1895, at p 3142.
21 Archambault Report, at pp 283-5, 302-11
22 *Can. H. of C. Debates*, 31 Aug. 1896, at p 407
23 See generally the approximately 200-page *Report on Investigation by the Penitentiary Commissioners held at the St. Vincent de Paul Penitentiary, Jan. 27, 1898*, PAC, RG73, vol. 43, file 3-20-10.
24 Penitentiary Regulations, Consolidated Orders in Council of Canada, 1889, c. 60, s. 326
25 See Laurier Papers, PAC, MG26G, vol. 791K, pp 224770-2, 224842-6, 224889-94.
26 Calder, 'Federal Penitentiary System' at pp 118 *et seq.*
27 The cases discussed in this section can be found in the PAC, Capital Cases Files, and in the Capital Cases Register, RG13, C-1, vol. 1397.
28 Cf. D.J.A. McMurchy, 'Davis Mills: Nineteenth Century Canadian Liberal,' unpublished Ph.D. thesis, University of Rochester, 1969, at pp 532-4
29 Thompson was not the minister of justice when the decision not to commute was initially made, but he was the minister at the later stages of the controversy: see P.B. Waite, *The Man from Halifax: Sir John Thompson, Prime Minister* (University of Toronto Press 1985) at p 149.
30 *Report of the Royal Commission on the Law of Insanity as a Defence in Criminal Cases* (Ottawa 1956) at pp 1-3

CHAPTER 15: On Portsmouth Bay

1 *Report of a Select Committee on the Expediency of Erecting a Penitentiary*, 1831, cited in J.M. Beattie, *Attitudes towards Crime and Punishment in Upper Canada, 1830-1850: A Documentary Study* (Centre of Criminology, University of Toronto 1977) at pp 85-6; and see generally D. Curtis *et al., Kingston Penitentiary: The First Hundred and Fifty Years, 1835-1985* (Ottawa: Supply and Services 1985); and references cited in n1, Chapter 14.

2 For discussions of the insane ward, see in particular W.A. Calder, 'The Federal Penitentiary System in Canada, 1867-1899: A Social and Institutional History,' unpublished Ph.D. thesis, University of Toronto, 1979, at pp 348 *et seq.*; and K. Joliffe, *Penitentiary Medical Services, 1835-1983* (Ottawa: Ministry of the Solicitor-General 1984) at pp 113 *et seq.*; D. Hack Tuke, *The Insane in the United States and Canada* (London: H.K. Lewis 1885) at pp 237-8.

3 Moylan cited in Calder, *ibid.* at p 349; *Warden's Annual Report*, 1900

4 See generally G. Laverty, *125 Years Keeping People Healthy: Kingston Psychiatric Hospital* (Kingston 1981); J.S. Pratten, 'The History of the Rockwood Hospital,' a paper presented to the Kingston Historical Society, 22 May 1968. See also the *Second Report of the Brown Commission investigating Kingston Penitentiary, Journal of the Legislative Assembly* (1849), Appendix B.B.B.B.B.

5 *Report of the Medical Superintendent of Rockwood Lunatic Asylum, Kingston, 1872,* in the *Fifth Annual Report of the Inspectors of Asylums,* 1873, cited in J.D. Griffin and C. Greenland's valuable unpublished collection of materials, 'Treating Mental Illness in Ontario: A Documentary History of the Development of Mental Health Services in Ontario from 1867 to 1914,' Toronto 1979, at p 169

6 Remark by A.E. Lavell to the annual meeting of the Prisoners' Aid Association in 1901, cited in Calder, 'Federal Penitentiary System' at p 350

7 Report by Dr E.H. Young, set out in the *Report of the Royal Commission on Penitentiaries* (Ottawa 1914) at p 10

8 *Warden's Report* for 1908, cited in J.P. Downey, 'The Separate Care of the Criminal Insane' (1915), 8 *Bulletin of the Ontario Hospitals for the Insane* 51 at p 53

9 See generally the *Report of the Royal Commission on Penitentiaries* (1914) at pp 9-13 (G.M. Macdonnell, KC, chairman).

10 See T.J.W. Burgess, 'The Insane in Canada,' Presidential Address to the American Medico-Psychological Association, 1905, 87 at p 115; W.M. English, 'Special Hospital for the Care of the Criminal Insane and Insane Criminals' (1914), 8 *Bulletin of the Ontario Hospitals for the Insane* 3 at p 5; C.K. Clarke, *Report of the Lunatic and Idiot Asylums, Ontario, 1899,* at p 103; and Downey, 'Separate Care' at p 56.

11 See the C.K. Clarke Papers, Clarke Institute of Psychiatry, Toronto.

12 See C.K. Clarke, 'The Psychiatric Clinics of Germany' (1908), 1 *Bulletin of the Toronto Hospital for the Insane* 3; and E. Ryan, 'Remarks on French and Irish Asylums,' *ibid.* at pp 37-40.

13 See the Clonmel *Chronicle*, Tipperary *Advertiser*, and the *Mail*, 5 June 1907.

14 See generally L. Holcombe, *Wives and Property: Reform of the Married Women's Property Law in Nineteenth-Century England* (University of Toronto Press 1983).

15 See 17 *Halsbury's Laws of England*, 4th ed. (London: Butterworths 1976) at p 739.

16 See the *Report to Advise upon the Revision of the Penitentiary Regulations and the Amendment of the Penitentiary Act, 1921* at p 9.

17 The letters in this section are contained in the King Papers and the Aberdeen Papers.

18 Mackenzie King Diary, Jan. 1912: see C.P. Stacey, *A Very Double Life: The Private World of Mackenzie King* (Toronto: Macmillan 1976) at p 110.

19 See generally R.M. Dawson, *William Lyon Mackenzie King: A Political Biography*, vol. 1, *1874-1923* (University of Toronto Press 1958); H.S. Ferns and B. Ostry, *The Age of Mackenzie King: The Rise of the Leader* (London: Heinemann 1955); Stacey, *A Very Double Life*; J.E. Esberey, *Knight of the Holy Spirit: A Study of William Lyon Mackenzie King* (University of Toronto Press 1980); B. Saint-Aubin, *King et son époque* (Montreal: La Presse 1982).

20 See An Act further to Amend the Penitentiary Act, Stat. Can. 1895, c. 41, s. 3; see also Stat. Can. 1899, c. 48, s. 7.

21 See generally the obituary, Montreal *Gazette*, 29 July 1931; P.-G. Roy, *Les Juges de la Province de Québec* (Quebec City 1933) at p 171. See also R.C. Brown and R. Cook, *Canada, 1896-1921: A Nation Transformed* (Toronto: McClelland and Stewart 1974) at p 191.

22 Some documents relating to Macmaster can be found in the Hanna Papers, box 17, Ontario Archives. For a discussion of Greenshields' involvement in 1903 in the affair of *La Presse*, see R.C. Brown, *Robert Laird Borden: A Biography*, vol. 1 (Toronto: Macmillan 1975) at pp 77 *et seq*.

23 *Report of the Royal Commission on Penitentiaries* (1914) (Sessional Paper no. 252). For an illustration of Judge Doherty's interference with the administration of justice, see J.G. Snell and F. Vaughan, *The Supreme Court of Canada: History of the Institution* (Toronto: Osgoode Society 1985) at p 138, and D.R. Williams, *Duff: A Life in the Law* (University of British Columbia Press 1984) at p 130.

24 The evidence can be found in PAC, RG73, vol. 40, file 1-20-10, vol. 2.

25 Reactions to the commission report can be found in *ibid.*, vol. 41, file 1-20-10, vol. 6.

26 See generally Joliffe, *Penitentiary Medical Services* at pp 149 *et seq.*
27 See the *Report of the Royal Commission to Investigate the Penal System of Canada* (Ottawa 1938); see also the *Report to Advise upon the Revision of the Penitentiary Regulations and the Amendment of the Penitentiary Act, 1921.*
28 Burgess, 'The Insane in Canada,' at p 107
29 See C.K. Clarke, 'The Care and Treatment of the Criminal' (1904), 15 *Canadian Journal of Medicine and Surgery* 1 at p 9; Clarke's 1907 *Annual Report as Medical Superintendent of the Hospital for the Insane, Toronto,* cited in J.D. Griffin and C. Greenland, 'Treating Mental Illness in Ontario' at p 79. See generally the fine study by H.G. Simmons, *From Asylum to Welfare* (Toronto: National Institute on Mental Retardation 1982).
30 See generally the valuable discussion by Joliffe, *Penitentiary Medical Services* at pp 121 *et seq.*
31 PAC, RG73, vol. 95, file 3-1-6
32 *Ibid.,* vol. 104, file 4-1-6
33 Ontario Archives, McPherson Papers, box 44, Doherty file

CHAPTER 16: On the Speed River

1 See the *Report of the Special Committee to Investigate the Question of Prison Labor, 1908.* See generally J. Kidman, *The Canadian Prison: The Story of a Tragedy* (Toronto: Ryerson 1947); C.W. Topping, *Canadian Penal Institutions* (Toronto: Ryerson 1929); C.F. Neelands, 'History of Provincial Institutions' in the *Annual Report on Prisons and Reformatories for 1934* (1935) at pp 5 *et seq.*
2 26 Feb. 1907. See Kidman, *ibid.* at pp 68-9.
3 See the Prisons and Reformatories Amendment Act, Stat. Can. 1913, c. 39, s. 1.
4 *Globe,* 15 July 1915
5 *Progrès de Valleyfield,* 22 July 1915
6 *R. v. Jessamine* (1912), 19 C.C.C. 214 (Ont. C.A.)
7 Information on Guelph has been obtained from L.A. Johnson, *History of Guelph, 1827-1977* (Guelph Historical Society 1977).
8 *Annual Report,* 1916, at p 46. For a discussion of recruitment in Ontario, see B.M. Wilson, *Ontario and the First World War, 1914-1918* (Toronto: The Champlain Society 1977). I am grateful to Barbara Wilson and Craig Brown for their guidance on the question of recruitment. How many convicts were released and whether they went overseas is not clear without further research.

9 *Report from the Provincial Medical Inspector of Health, Nov. 11, 1918,* in Ontario Archives, McPherson Papers, box 32, Burwash file

10 *Report of His Honour Judge E. Coatsworth re Industrial Farm Investigation, Burwash, Feb. 2, 1918, along with the evidence taken,* Ontario Archives

11 See generally H.G. Simmons, *From Asylum to Welfare* (Toronto: National Institute on Mental Retardation 1982).

12 See C. Greenland, *Charles Kirk Clarke: A Pioneer of Canadian Psychiatry* (Clarke Institute of Psychiatry 1966) at p 21. See the Immigration Amendment Act, Stat. Can. 1919, c. 25, s. 3.

13 Military Service Act, 1917, Stat. Can. 1917, c. 19

14 The Conditional Liberation of Penitentiary Convicts Act, Stat. Can. 1899, c. 49. See generally the *Report of the Royal Commission to Investigate the Penal System of Canada* (Ottawa 1938) (the Archambault Report) at pp 236 *et seq.; Report of a Committee Appointed to Inquire into the Principles and Procedures Followed in the Remission Service of the Department of Justice of Canada* (Ottawa 1956) (the Fauteux Report); P. Landreville and P. Carrière, 'Release Measures in Canada' in *Studies on Imprisonment* (Law Reform Commission of Canada 1976) 79 at pp 107 *et seq.*

15 *Can. H. of C. Debates,* 7 Aug. 1899, at p 9728

16 Fauteux Report, at p 43

17 N.C. Wallace, 'The Criminally Insane at Guelph' [1925] *Ontario Journal of Neuro-Psychiatry* 72 at p 74

18 See J.D. Griffin and C. Greenland, 'Treating Mental Illness in Ontario,' an unpublished documentary history, 1979, at pp 522 *et seq.*

19 *Ibid.* at pp 508 *et seq.*

20 Kingston Penitentiary Records, PAC, Correctional Service Canada, file 83, Ott. Pri. Class. 0461

21 Archambault Report, at p 284

22 See D. Morton, *A Peculiar Kind of Politics: Canada's Overseas Ministry in the First World War* (University of Toronto Press 1982) at p 119.

CHAPTER 17: On Georgian Bay

1 See A. Jones, ' "Closing Penetanguishene Reformatory": An attempt to Deinstitutionalize Treatment of Juvenile Offenders in Early Twentieth Century Ontario' (1978) 70 *Ontario History* 227; C.K. McKnight, J.W. Mohr, and B.B. Swadron, 'The Mentally Ill Offender in the Oak Ridge

Hospital Unit' (1962) 5 *Criminal Law Quarterly* 248; J.D. Griffin and C. Greenland, 'Treating Mental Illness in Ontario,' an unpublished documentary history, 1979, at pp 220 *et seq.*; R.B. Splane, *Social Welfare in Ontario, 1791-1893* (University of Toronto Press 1965) at pp 148-51.

2 *Annual Report on the Ontario Hospitals for the Mentally Ill, Mentally Subnormal and Epileptic for 1933* at pp 26 *et seq.*

3 See the recent report to the Ministry of Health on the institution: *Oak Ridge: A Review and an Alternative* (S.J. Hucker, chairman) (1985). The 'recommended alternative' is to 'close Oak Ridge and rebuild two smaller units, one at Penetanguishene and the other near a large urban centre' (p 121).

4 See *Annual Report on the Prisons and Reformatories of Ontario for 1933* at pp 35 *et seq.*; D.O. Lynch, 'Some Observations on the Criminally Insane with Special Reference to those Charged with Murder' (1937) 12 *Ontario Journal of Neuro-Psychiatry* 39.

5 From an unpublished document entitled 'Arthur Wellesley Beall, M.A.' by C.R. Brown of Fonthill, to whom I am indebted for his kind assistance in providing documents and personal recollections.

6 A.W. Beall, *The Living Temple* (Whitby: Penhale Publishing 1933) at pp 65 and 67. See generally M. Bliss, ' "Pure Books on Avoided Subjects": Pre-Freudian Sexual Ideas in Canada,' *Canadian Historical Association Papers* 1970, at p 89 *et seq.*

7 Letter from the Deputy Minister of Health, Ontario, 29 June 1936, to the Superintendent of Penitentiaries, PAC, RG73, vol. 104, file 4-1-6

8 Cited in F. Donaldson, *Edward VIII* (London: Weidenfeld and Nicolson 1974) at p 251

9 See PAC, RG73, vol. 79, file 1-21-37. For details of 'Red' Ryan, see D. Curtis *et al.*, *Kingston Penitentiary: The First Hundred and Fifty Years, 1835-1985* (Ottawa: Supply and Services 1985) at pp 113-15.

10 *Report of the Royal Commission to Investigate the Penal System of Canada* (Ottawa 1938) (the Archambault Report) at p 109

11 *Ibid.* at p 9

12 O.C.J. Withrow, *Shackling the Transgressor: An Indictment of the Canadian Penal System* (Toronto: Thomas Nelson 1933)

13 See the unpublished 'Summary of Proceedings of the First Canadian Penal Congress, June 13 and 14, 1935, Montreal.' I am grateful to the Solicitor-General's Library, Ottawa, for supplying this document.

14 See K. Joliffe, *Penitentiary Medical Services, 1835-1983* (Ottawa: Ministry of the Solicitor-General 1984) at pp 173 and 202.

15 Curtis *et al.*, *Kingston Penitentiary* at p 115

16 See generally the fine centennial book, J. Barkey, *Stouffville, 1877-1977* (Stouffville 1977).

17 At p 290

18 Penitentiary Service Regulations, s. 38, passed under the Penitentiary Act, R.S.C. 1970, c. P-6

19 King to Lady Aberdeen, 8 April 1934, Aberdeen Papers, Haddo House, Box 8/3

20 Mackenzie King Diary, 12 Oct. 1934

21 See C.P. Stacey, *A Very Double Life: The Private World of Mackenzie King* (Toronto: Macmillan 1976) at pp 180 and 243.

22 Archambault Report, at p 250

23 *Ibid.* at pp 139 *et seq.*

24 *Ibid.* at pp 249 *et seq.*

25 Mr Murray Millar, director of the National Correctional Staff College, Kingston, who has done a considerable amount of research on penitentiary records, knows of no one who has served a longer period. I am grateful for his assistance on this point.

CHAPTER 18: A Stranger in a Strange Land

1 See W.T. Barnard, *A Short History of the Queen's Own Rifles of Canada* (Toronto: MacKinnon and Atkins 1954). I am greatly indebted to Lt.-Col. Barnard for his assistance.

2 The Queen's Own Rifles of Canada Association, *1937 Year Book*, at p 8

3 *Telegram*, 4 May 1937; *Gazette*, 5 May 1937 (see also 4 May 1937)

4 Telephone conversation with Mr Fergus Power, June 1985

5 Barnard, *Queen's Own Rifles* at p 13

6 M.L. Friedland, *The Trials of Israel Lipski* (London: Macmillan 1984)

7 See *Regina* v. *Cooper* (1980), 51 C.C.C. (2d) 129 (S.C.C.); *Regina* v. *Barnier* (1980), 51 C.C.C. (2d) 193 (S.C.C.). The definition of wrong is still very narrowly construed: see *Schwartz* v. *Regina* (1976), 29 C.C.C. (2d) 1 (S.C.C.).

8 Law Reform Commission of Canada, *Working Paper* 29, 'The General Part: Liability and Defences' (1982) at pp 41 *et seq.*

9 See, for example, R.R. James, *Albert, Prince Consort* (London: Hamish Hamilton 1983) at pp 21-2; D. Bennett, *King without a Crown* (London: Heinemann 1977) at pp 8-9, 166-7; T. Martin, *The Prince Consort*, 5th ed., vol. 2 (London: Smith, Elder 1880) at pp 205 *et seq.*

10 Document prepared by J.M. Neelands, June 1985

Index